THE STUDY

OF

SOCIOLOGY.

BY

HERBERT SPENCER,

AUTHOR OF

"A SYSTEM OF PHILOSOPHY," "DESCRIPTIVE SOCIOLOGY," ETC., ETC.

NEW YORK:

D. APPLETON & COMPANY,

549 & 551 BROADWAY.

1874.

PREFACE TO THE AMERICAN EDITION.

IT is desirable that the present volume, the origin of which is explained in the author's preface, should be accompanied by a brief statement in relation to Mr. Spencer's other works upon sociological science. The "Principles of Sociology" was projected by Mr. Spencer as a part of his philosophical system, the publication of which was commenced in 1860. Five volumes of that system have appeared, viz.: "First Principles," in one volume; the "Principles of Biology," in two volumes; and the "Principles of Psychology," in two volumes. "First Principles" develops the general method of the philosophy to be carried out in the subsequent works. In the two succeeding parts that method is applied to the interpretation of the phenomena of Life and Mind, the whole course of exposition being preparatory to the "Principles of Sociology," in three volumes, which are next in order. Upon this work Mr. Spencer has now entered, and it will be published in quarterly parts, by subscription, in the same form that was adopted with the previous divisions of the work.

Several years since Mr. Spencer foresaw a difficulty that

would arise in working out the principles of social science from a lack of the data or facts necessary as a basis of reasoning upon the subject; and he saw that, before the philosophy could be elaborated, these facts must be systematically and exhaustively collected. How early and how clearly Mr. Spencer perceived the nature, diversity, and extent of the facts upon which a true social science must rest is well shown in the following passage from a review article published in 1859,[1] before he had commenced his great undertaking:

"That which constitutes history, properly so called, is in great part omitted from works on this subject. Only of late years have historians commenced giving us, in any considerable quantity, the truly valuable information. As in past ages the king was every thing and the people nothing, so, in past histories, the doings of the king fill the entire picture, to which the national life forms but an obscure background. While only now, when the welfare of nations rather than of rulers is becoming the dominant idea, are historians beginning to occupy themselves with the phenomena of social progress. The thing it really concerns us to know is, the natural history of society. We want all facts which help us to understand how a nation has grown and organized itself. Among these, let us of course have an account of its government; with as little as may be of gossip about the men who officered it, and as much as possible about the structure, principles, methods, prejudices, corruptions, etc., which it exhibited; and let this account include not only the nature and actions of the central government, but also those of local governments, down to their minutest ramifications. Let us of course also have a parallel description of the ecclesiastical government—its organization, its conduct, its power, its relations to the state; and, accompanying this, the ceremonial, creed, and religious ideas —not only those nominally believed, but those really believed and acted upon. Let us at the same time be informed of the control exercised by

[1] "What Knowledge is of most Worth?"—(*Westminster Review.*)

class over class, as displayed in social observances—in titles, salutations, and forms of address.   Let us know, too, what were all the other customs which regulated the popular life out-of-doors and in-doors, including those concerning the relations of the sexes, and the relations of parents to children. The superstitions, also, from the more important myths down to the charms in common use, should be indicated. Next should come a delineation of the industrial system: showing to what extent the division of labor was carried; how trades were regulated, whether by caste, guilds, or otherwise; what was the connection between employers and employed; what were the agencies for distributing commodities; what were the means of communication; what was the circulating medium. Accompanying all which should be given an account of the industrial arts technically considered: stating the processes in use, and the quality of the products. Further, the intellectual condition of the nation in its various grades should be depicted; not only with respect to the kind and amount of education, but with respect to the progress made in science, and the prevailing manner of thinking. The degree of æsthetic culture, as displayed in architecture, sculpture, painting, dress, music, poetry, and fiction, should be described. Nor should there be omitted a sketch of the daily lives of the people—their food, their homes, and their amusements. And, lastly, to connect the whole, should be exhibited the morals, theoretical and practical, of all classes, as indicated in their laws, habits, proverbs, deeds. These facts, given with as much brevity as consists with clearness and accuracy, should be so grouped and arranged that they may be comprehended in their *ensemble*, and contemplated as mutually-dependent parts of one great whole. The aim should be so to present them that men may readily trace the *consensus* subsisting among them, with the view of learning what social phenomena coexist with what others, And then the corresponding delineations of succeeding ages should be so managed as to show how each belief, institution, custom, and arrangement, was modified, and how the *consensus* of preceding structures and functions was developed into the *consensus* of succeeding ones. Such alone is the kind of information, respecting past times, which can be of service to the citizen for the regulation of his conduct. The only history that is of practical value is, what may be called Descriptive Sociology. And the highest office which the historian can discharge is that of so narrating the lives of nations as to furnish materials for a Comparative Sociology, and for the subsequent determination of the ultimate laws to which social phenomena conform."

Such were the character and scope of the facts which required to be collected concerning all forms and grades of human societies before any thing like a valid social science could be constructed. A descriptive Sociology, furnishing comprehensive data, must precede the establishment of principles, and so Mr. Spencer began the collection of his materials five years ago. He first devised a system of tables suited to present all orders of social facts displayed by any community—facts of structure, function, and development, in such a manner that they can be compared with each other at a glance—each table being a kind of chart of the social condition of the community to which it is devoted. His object was at first solely to facilitate his own work, but it soon appeared that the results would be of great general importance, and Mr. Spencer decided to execute the undertaking with a view to publication. The communities of mankind were divided into three great groups: 1. Uncivilized Societies; 2. Civilized Societies, Extinct or Decayed; 3. Civilized Societies, Recent or still Flourishing. Having arranged his plan, Mr. Spencer engaged three educated gentlemen to devote themselves to the systematic collection of the various orders of facts pertaining to these three groups of societies. In each case, the tables are filled in with the facts under their appropriate heads, while extracts are separately given from the authorities consulted. The description of the Uncivilized Societies, by Prof. David Duncan, embracing seventy tables, is substantially completed. Of the second division, in charge of Dr. Richard Scheppig, the first installment, including the four ancient American civilizations, is nearly finished. The third division, dealing with civilized societies, under charge of Mr. James Collier, of St. Andrew's and Edinburgh Universities, is well advanced, and the first part, treating of the English civilization, or the Sociological History of England, is now published. It covers seven consecutive tables, and the verifying extracts occupy seventy pages folio.

This series of works, which will be published as they are completed, will form a regular Cyclopædia of Descriptive Sociology, and, as the facts are given independently of theory, they will have value for all students of social phenomena. Of the execution and influence of this work, the *British Quarterly Review* well observes : "No words are needed to indicate the immense labor here bestowed, or the great sociological benefit which such a mass of tabulated matter done under such competent direction will confer. The work will constitute an epoch in the science of comparative sociology."

It will be understood that these works do not form a part of Mr. Spencer's Philosophical System, but a separate preparation for the third division of it. Mr. Spencer will use his extensive materials in establishing the inductions of the science which will be presented in the successive parts of the "Principles of Sociology."

E. L. Y.

PREFACE.

THIS little work has been written at the instigation of my American friend, Professor Youmans. When, some two years ago, he was in England making arrangements for that *International Scientific Series* which he originated and succeeded in organizing, he urged me to contribute to it a volume on the Study of Sociology. Feeling that the general undertaking in which I am engaged, is extensive enough to demand all my energies, I continued for a long time to resist; and I finally yielded only to the modified proposal that I should furnish the ideas and materials, and leave the embodiment of them to some fit *collaborateur*. As might have been expected, it was difficult to find one in all respects suitable; and, eventually, I undertook the task myself.

After thus committing myself, it occurred to me as desirable that, instead of writing the volume simply for the

International Scientific Series, I should prepare it for previous issue in a serial form, both here and in the United States. In pursuance of this idea, arrangements were made with the *Contemporary Review* to publish the successive chapters; and in America they have been simultaneously published in the *Popular Science Monthly.* Beginning in May, 1872, this publication by instalments has, with two brief intervals, since continued, and will be completed on the 1st October next : the issue of this volume being delayed until after that date.

Since commencing the work, I have not regretted that I was led to undertake it. Various considerations which seemed needful by way of introduction to the *Principles of Sociology,* presently to be written, and which yet could not be conveniently included in it, have found, in this preliminary volume, a fit place. Much illustrative material also, partly accumulated during past years and lying unused, I have thus gained an occasion for turning to account. Further, the opportunity has been afforded me of commenting on special topics which the *Principles of Sociology* could not properly recognize; and of commenting on them in a style inadmissible in a purely-philosophical treatise—a style adapted, however, as I hope, to create such interest in the subject as may excite to serious pursuit of it.

In preparing the successive chapters for final publication, I have, besides carefully revising them, here and there enforced the argument by a further illustration. Not much, however, has been done in this way: the only additions of moment being contained in the Appendix. One of these, pursuing in another direction the argument concerning academic discipline, will be found among the notes to Chapter IX.; and another, illustrative of the irrelation between intellectual culture and moral feeling, will be found in the notes to Chapter XV.

LONDON, *July*, 1873.

CONTENTS.

—♦—

CHAPTER I.

PAGE

CHAPTER II.

CHAPTER III.

CHAPTER IV.

CHAPTER V.

CHAPTER VI.

CHAPTER VII.

THE

STUDY OF SOCIOLOGY.

CHAPTER I.

OUR NEED OF IT.

OVER his pipe in the village ale-house, the labourer says very positively what Parliament should do about the "foot and mouth disease." At the farmer's market-table, his master makes the glasses jingle as, with his fist, he emphasizes the assertion that he did not get half enough compensation for his slaughtered beasts during the cattle-plague. These are not hesitating opinions. On a matter affecting the agricultural interest, statements are still as dogmatic as they were during the Anti-Corn-Law agitation, when, in every rural circle, you heard that the nation would be ruined if the lightly-taxed foreigner was allowed to compete in our markets with the heavily-taxed Englishman: a proposition held to be so self-evident that dissent from it implied either stupidity or knavery.

Now, as then, may be daily heard among other classes, opinions just as decided and just as unwarranted. By men called educated, the old plea for extravagant expenditure, that "it is good for trade," is still continually urged with full belief in its sufficiency. Scarcely any decrease is observable in the fallacy that whatever gives employment is beneficial: no regard being had to the value for ulterior purposes of that which the labour produces;

no question being asked what would have resulted had the capital which paid for the labour taken some other channel and paid for some other labour. Neither criticism nor explanation appreciably modifies these beliefs. When there is again an opening for them they are expressed with undiminished confidence. Along with delusions of this kind go whole families of others. 'People who think that the relations between expenditure and production are so simple, naturally assume simplicity in other relations among social phenomena. Is there distress somewhere? They suppose nothing more is required than to subscribe money for relieving it.' On the one hand, they never trace the reactive effects which charitable donations work on bank accounts, on the surplus-capital bankers have to lend, on the productive activity which the capital now abstracted would have set up, on the number of labourers who would have received wages and who now go without wages—they do not perceive that certain necessaries of life have been withheld from one man who would have exchanged useful work for them, and given to another who perhaps persistently evades working. Nor, on the other hand, do they look beyond the immediate mitigation of misery. 'They deliberately shut their eyes to the fact that as fast as they increase the provision for those who live without labour, so fast do they increase the number of those who live without labour; and that with an ever-increasing distribution of alms, there comes an ever-increasing outcry for more alms. Similarly throughout all their political thinking. Proximate causes and proximate results are alone contemplated. There is scarcely any consciousness that the original causes are often numerous and widely different from the apparent cause; and that beyond each immediate result there will be multitudinous remote results, most of them quite incalculable.

Minds in which the conceptions of social actions are thus rudimentary, are also minds ready to harbour wild hopes of benefits to be achieved by administrative agencies. In each such mind there seems to be the unexpressed postulate that every evil in a society admits of cure; and that the cure lies within the reach of law. ' "Why is not there a better inspection of the mercantile marine?" asked a córrespondent of the *Times* the other day: apparently forgetting that within the preceding twelve months the power he invoked had lost two of its own vessels, and barely saved a third. "Ugly buildings are eyesores, and should not be allowed," urges one who is anxious for æsthetic culture. Meanwhile, from the agent which is to foster good taste, there have come monuments and public buildings of which the less said the better; and its chosen design for the Law-Courts meets with almost universal condemnation. "Why did those in authority allow such defective sanitary arrangements?" was everywhere asked, after the fevers at Lord Londesborough's; and this question you heard repeated, regardless of the fact that sanitary arrangements having such results in this and other cases, were themselves the outcome of appointed sanitary administrations—regardless of the fact that the authorized system had itself been the means of introducing foul gases into houses.[1] "The State should purchase the railways," is confidently asserted by those who, every morning, read of chaos at the Admiralty, or cross-purposes in the dockyards, or wretched army-organization, or diplomatic bungling that endangers peace, or frustration of justice by technicalities and costs and delays,—all without having their confidence in officialism shaken. "Building Acts should insure better ventilation in small houses," says one who either never knew or has forgotten that, after Messrs. Reid and Barry had spent £200,000 in failing to ventilate the Houses of Parliament, the First Commissioner of Works proposed that, "the House should get some competent engineer, above suspicion of partiality, to let them see what ought to be done."[2] And similarly there are continually cropping out in the press, and at meetings, and in conversations, such notions as that the State might provide "cheap capital" by some financial sleight of hand; that "there ought to be bread-overseers appointed by Government:"[3] that

" it is the duty of Government to provide a suitable national asylum for the reception of all illegitimate children."[4]   And here it is doubtless thought by some, as it is in France by M. de Lagevenais, that Government, by supplying good music, should exclude the bad, such as that of Offenbach.[5]   We smile on reading of that French princess, celebrated for her innocent wonder that people should starve when there was so simple a remedy.   But why should we smile ?   A great part of the current political thought evinces notions of practicability not much more rational.

That connexions among social phenomena should be so little understood, need not surprise us if we note the ideas which prevail respecting the connexions among much simpler phenomena.   Minds left ignorant of physical causation, are unlikely to appreciate clearly, if at all, that causation so much more subtle and complex, which runs through the actions of incorporated men.   In almost every house, servants and those who employ them, alike believe that a poker leaned up in front of the bars, or across them, makes the fire burn ; and you will be told, very positively, that experience proves the efficacy of the device—the experience being that the poker has been repeatedly so placed and the fire has repeatedly burned ; and no comparisons having been made with cases in which the poker was absent, and all other conditions as before.   In the same circles the old prejudice against sitting down thirteen to dinner still survives : there actually exists among ladies who have been at finishing schools of the highest character, and among some gentlemen who pass as intelligent, the conviction that adding or subtracting one from a number of people who eat together, will affect the fates of some among them.   And this state of mind is again displayed at the card-table, by the opinion that So-and-so is always lucky or unlucky—that influences are at work which, on the average, determine more good cards to one person than to another.   Clearly, those in whom the consciousness of causation in these simple cases is so vague, may be expected to have the wildest notions of social causation. Whoever even entertains the supposition that a poker put across the fire can make it burn, proves himself to have neither a qualitative nor a quantitative idea of physical causation; and if, during his life, his experiences of material objects and actions have failed to give him an idea so accessible and so simple, it is not likely that they have given him ideas of the qualitative and quantitative relations of cause and effect holding throughout society. Hence, there is nothing to exclude irrational interpretations and disproportioned hopes. Where other superstitions flourish, political superstitions will take root. A consciousness in which there lives the idea that spilling salt will be followed by some evil, obviously allied as it is to the consciousness of the savage, filled with beliefs in omens and charms, gives a home to other beliefs like those of the savage. It may not have faith in the potency of medicine-bags and idols, and may even wonder how any being can reverence a thing shaped with his own hands; and yet it readily entertains subtler forms of the same feelings. For, in those whose modes of thought we have been contemplating, there is a tacit supposition that a government moulded by themselves, has some efficiency beyond that naturally possessed by a certain group of citizens subsidized by the rest of the citizens. True, if you ask them, they may not deliberately assert that a legislative and administrative apparatus can exert power, either mental or material, beyond the power proceeding from the nation itself. They are compelled to admit, when cross-examined, that the energies moving a governmental machine are energies which would cease were citizens to cease working and furnishing the supplies. But, nevertheless, their projects imply an unexpressed belief in some store of force that is not measured by taxes. When there arises the question—Why does not Government do this for us? there is not the accompanying thought—Why does not Government put its hands in our pockets, and, with the proceeds, pay officials to do this, instead of leaving us to do

it ourselves; but the accompanying thought is—Why does not
Government, out of its inexhaustible resources, yield us this
benefit?

Such modes of political thinking, then, naturally go along
with such conceptions of physical phenomena as are current.
Just as the perpetual-motion schemer hopes, by a cunning
arrangement of parts, to get from one end of his machine more
energy than he puts in at the other; so the ordinary political
schemer is convinced that out of a legislative apparatus, properly
devised and worked with due dexterity, may be had beneficial
State-action without any detrimental reaction. He expects to
get out of a stupid people the effects of intelligence, and to
evolve from inferior citizens superior conduct.

But while the prevalence of crude political opinions among
those whose conceptions about simple matters are so crude, might
be anticipated, it is surprising that the class disciplined by
scientific culture should bring to the interpretation of social
phenomena, methods but little in advance of those used by
others. Now that the transformation and equivalence of forces
is seen by men of science to hold not only throughout all inorganic actions, but throughout all organic actions; now that
even mental changes are recognized as the correlatives of cerebral changes, which also conform to this principle; and now,
that there must be admitted the corollary, that all actions
going on in a society are measured by certain antecedent
energies, which disappear in effecting them, while they themselves become actual or potential energies from which subsequent actions arise; it is strange that there should not have
arisen the consciousness that these highest phenomena are to
be studied as lower phenomena have been studied—not, of
course, after the same physical methods, but in conformity
with the same principles. And yet scientific men rarely display such a consciousness.

A mathematician who had agreed or disagreed with the view

of Professor Tait respecting the value of Quaternions for pursuing researches in Physics, would listen with raised eyebrows were one without mathematical culture to express a decided opinion on the matter. Or, if the subject discussed was the doctrine of Helmholtz, that hypothetical beings occupying space of two dimensions, might be so conditioned that the axioms of our geometry would prove untrue, the mathematician would marvel if an affirmation or a negation came from a man who knew no more of the properties of space than is to be gained by daily converse with things around, and no more of the principles of reasoning than the course of business taught him. And yet, were we to take members of the Mathematical Society, who, having severally devoted themselves to the laws of quantitative relations, know that, simple as these are intrinsically, a life's study is required for the full comprehension of them—were we to ask each of these his opinion on some point of social policy, the readiness with which he answered would seem to imply that in these cases, where the factors of the phenomena are so numerous and so much involved, a general survey of men and things gives data for trustworthy judgments.

Or, to contrast more fully the mode of reaching a conclusion which the man of science uses in his own department, with that which he regards as satisfactory in the department of politics, let us take a case from a concrete science : say, the question— What are the solar spots, and what constitution of the Sun is implied by them?   Of tentative answers to this question there is first Wilson's, adopted by Sir William Herschel, that the visible surface of the Sun is a luminous envelope, within which there are cloudy envelopes covering a dark central body; and that when, by some disturbance, the luminous envelope is broken through, portions of the cloudy envelope and of the dark central body, become visible as the penumbra and umbra respectively. This hypothesis, at one time received with favour mainly because it seemed to permit that teleological interpretation which required that the Sun should be habitable, accounted tolerably

well for.certain of the appearances—more especially the appearance of concavity which the spots have when near the limb of
the Sun. But though Sir John Herschel supported his father's
hypothesis, pointing out that cyclonic action would account for
local dispersions of the photosphere, there has of late years
become more and more manifest the fatal objection that the
genesis of light and heat remained unexplained, and that no supposition of auroral discharges did more than remove the difficulty
a step back ; since, unless light and heat could be perpetually
generated out of nothing, there must be a store of force perpetually being expended in producing them. A counter-hypo-
thesis, following naturally from the hypothesis of nebular origin,
is that the mass of the Sun must be incandescent ; that its in-
candescence has been produced, and is maintained, by progressing aggregation of its once widely-diffused matter ; and that
surrounding its molten surface there is an atmosphere of metallic
gases continually rising, condensing to form the visible photosphere, and thence precipitating. What, in this case, are the
solar spots ? Kirchhoff, proceeding upon the hypothesis just
indicated, which had been set forth before he made his discoveries
by the aid of the spectroscope, contended that the solar spots are
simply clouds, formed of these condensed metallic gases, so large
as to be relatively opaque ; and he endeavoured to account for
their changing forms as the Sun's rotation carries them away, in
correspondence with this view. But the appearances as known
to astronomers, are quite irreconcilable with the belief that the
spots are simply drifting clouds. Do these appearances, then,
conform to the supposition of M. Faye, that the photosphere
encloses matter which is wholly gaseous and non-luminous ; and
that the spots are produced when occasional up-rushes from the
interior burst through the photosphere ? This supposition, while
it may be held to account for certain traits of the spots, and to
be justified by the observed fact that there *are* up-rushes of gas,
presents difficulties not readily disposed of. It does not explain
the manifest rotation of many spots ; nor, indeed, does it seem

really to account for that darkness which constitutes them spots; since a non-luminous gaseous nucleus would be permeable by light from the remoter side of the photosphere, and hence holes through the near side of the photosphere would not look dark. There is, however, another hypothesis which more nearly reconciles the facts. Assuming the incandescent molten surface, the ascending metallic gases, and the formation of a photosphere at that outer limit where the gases condense; accepting the suggestion of Sir John Herschel, so amply supported by evidence, that zones north and south of the Sun's equator are subject to violent cyclones; this hypothesis is, that if a cyclone occurs within the atmosphere of metallic gases between the molten surface and the photosphere, its vortex will become a region of rarefaction, of refrigeration, and therefore of precipitation. There will be formed in it a dense cloud extending far down towards the body of the Sun, and obstructing the greater part of the light radiating from below. Here we have an adequate cause for the formation of an opaque vaporous mass—a cause which also accounts for the frequently observed vortical motion; for the greater blackness of the central part of the umbra; for the formation of a penumbra by the drawing-in of the adjacent photosphere; for the elongation of the luminous masses forming the photosphere, and the turning of their longer axes towards the centre of the spot; and for the occasional drifting of them over the spot towards its centre. Still, there is the difficulty that vortical motion is by no means always observable; and it remains to be considered whether its non-visibility in many cases is reconcilable with the hypothesis. At present none of the interpretations can be regarded as established.   See, then, the rigour of the inquiry. Here are sundry suppositions which the man of science severally tests by observations and necessary inferences. In this, as in other cases, he rejects such as unquestionably disagree with unquestionable truths. Continually excluding untenable hypotheses, he waits to decide among the more tenable ones until further evidence discloses further congruities or incongruities. Checking every statement of fact and every conclusion drawn, he keeps his judgment suspended until no anomaly remains unexplained. Not only is he thus careful to shut out all possible error from inadequacy in the number and variety of data, but he is careful to shut out all possible error caused by idiosyncrasy in himself. Though not perhaps in astronomical observations such as those above implied, yet in all astronomical observations where the element of time is important, he makes allowance for the intervals occupied by his nervous actions. To fix the exact moment at which a certain change occurred, his perception of it has to be corrected for the "personal equation." As the speed of the nervous discharge varies, according to the constitution, from thirty to ninety metres per second, and is somewhat greater in summer than in winter; and as between seeing a change and registering it with the finger, there is an interval which is thus appreciably different in different persons; the particular amount of this error in the particular observer has to be taken into account.

Suppose now that to a man of science, thus careful in testing all possible hypotheses and excluding all possible sources of error, we put a sociological question—say, whether some proposed institution will be beneficial. An answer, and often a very decided one, is forthcoming at once. It is not thought needful, proceeding by deliberate induction, to ascertain what has happened in each nation where an identical institution, or an institution of allied kind, has been established. It is not thought needful to look back in our own history to see whether kindred agencies have done what they were expected to do. It is not thought needful to ask the more general question—how far institutions at large, among all nations and in all times, have justified the theories of those who set them up. Nor is it thought needful to infer from analogous cases, what is likely to happen if the proposed appliance is not set up—to ascertain, inductively, whether in its absence some equivalent appliance will arise. And still less is it thought needful to inquire what

will be the inidrect actions and reactions of the proposed organization—how far it will retard other social agencies, and how far
it will prevent the spontaneous growth of agencies having like
ends. I do not mean that none of these questions are recognized
as questions to be asked ; but I mean that no attempts are made
after a scientific manner to get together materials for answering
them. True, some data have been gathered from newspapers,
periodicals, foreign correspondence, books of travel ; and there
have been read sundry histories, which, besides copious accounts
of royal misdemeanours, contain minute details of every military
campaign, and careful disentanglings of diplomatic trickeries.
And on information thus acquired a confident opinion is based.
Most remarkable of all, however, is the fact that no allowance is
made for the personal equation. In political observations and
judgments, the qualities of the individual, natural and acquired,
are by far the most important factors. The bias of education,
the bias of class-relationships, the bias of nationality, the political bias, the theological bias—these, added to the constitutional
sympathies and antipathies, have much more influence in determining beliefs on social questions than has the small amount of
evidence collected. Yet, though in his search after a physical
truth, the man of science allows for minute errors of perception
due to his own nature, he makes no allowance for the enormous
errors which his own nature variously modified and distorted by
his conditions of life, is sure to introduce into his perceptions of
political truth. Here, where correction for the personal equation is all-essential, it does not occur to him that there is any
personal equation to be allowed for.

This immense incongruity between the attitude in which the
most disciplined minds approach other orders of natural phenomena, and the attitude in which they approach the phenomena
presented by societies, will be best illustrated by a series of
antitheses thus :—

The material media through which we see things, always more

2

or less falsify the facts : making, for example, the apparent direction of a star slightly different from its real direction, and sometimes, as when a fish is seen in the water, the apparent place is so far from the real place, that great misconception results unless large allowance is made for refraction ; but sociological observations are not thus falsified : through the daily press light comes without any bending of its rays, and in studying past ages it is easy to make allowance for the refraction due to the historic medium.   The motions of gases, though they conform to mechanical laws which are well understood, are nevertheless so involved, that the art of controlling currents of air in a house is not yet mastered ; but the waves and currents of feeling running through a society, and the consequent directions and amounts of social activities, may be readily known beforehand.   Though molecules of inorganic substances are very simple, yet prolonged study is required to understand their modes of behaviour to one another, and even the most instructed frequently meet with interactions of them producing consequences they never anticipated ; but where the interacting bodies are not molecules but living beings of highly-complex natures, it is easy to foresee all results which will arise.   Physical phenomena are so connected that between seeming probability and actual truth, there is apt to be a wide difference, even where but two bodies are acting : instance the natural supposition that during our northern summer the Earth is nearer to the Sun than during the winter, which is just the reverse of the fact; but among sociological phenomena, where the bodies are so multitudinous, and the forces by which they act on one another so many, and so multiform, and so variable, the probability and the actuality will of course correspond.   Matter often behaves paradoxically, as when two cold liquids added together become boiling hot, or as when the mixing of two clear liquids produces an opaque mud, or as when water immersed in sulphurous acid freezes on a hot iron plate ; but what we distinguish as Mind, especially when massed together in the way which causes social action, evolves no paradoxical results—always such results come from it as seem likely to come.

The acceptance of contradictions like these, tacitly implied in the beliefs of the scientifically cultivated, is the more remarkable when we consider how abundant are the proofs that human nature is difficult to manipulate; that methods apparently the most rational disappoint expectation; and that the best results frequently arise from courses which common sense thinks unpractical. Even individual human nature shows us these startling anomalies. A man of leisure is the man naturally fixed upon if something has to be done; but your man of leisure cannot find time, and the man most likely to do what is wanted, is the man who is already busy. That the boy who studies longest will learn most, and that a man will become wise in proportion as he reads much, are propositions which look true but are quite untrue; as teachers are now-a-days finding out in the one case, and as Hobbes long ago found out in the other. How obvious it appears that when minds go deranged, there is no remedy but replacing the weak internal control by a strong external control. Yet the "non-restraint system" has had far more success than the system of strait-waistcoats. Dr. Batty Tuke, a physician of much experience in treating the insane, has lately testified that the desire to escape is great when locks and keys are used, but almost disappears when they are disused : the policy of unlocked doors has had 95 per cent. of success and 5 per cent. of failure.[6] And in further evidence of the mischief often done by measures supposed to be curative, here is Dr. Maudsley, also an authority on such questions, speaking of "asylum-made lunatics." Again, is it not clear that the repression of crime will be effectual in proportion as the punishment is severe ? Yet the great amelioration in our penal code, initiated by Romilly, has not been followed by increased criminality but by decreased criminality; and the testimonies of those who have had most experience—Maconochie in Norfolk Island, Dickson in Western Australia,

Obermier in Germany, Montesinos in Spain—unite to show that in proportion as the criminal is left to suffer no other penalty than that of maintaining himself under such restraints only as are needful for social safety, the reformation is great : exceeding, indeed, all anticipation. French schoolmasters, never questioning the belief that boys can be made to behave well only by rigid discipline and spies to aid in carrying it out, are astonished on visiting England to find how much better boys behave when they are less governed : nay more—among English boys themselves, Dr. Arnold has shown that more trust is followed by improved conduct. Similarly with the anomalies of incorporated human nature. We habitually assume that only by legal restraints are men to be kept from aggressing on their neighbours ; and yet there are facts which should lead us to qualify our assumption. So-called debts of honour, for the non-payment of which there is no legal penalty, are held more sacred than debts that can be legally enforced ; and on the Stock-Exchange, where only pencil memoranda in the respective note-books of two brokers guarantee the sale and purchase of many thousands, contracts are safer than those which, in the outside world, are formally registered in signed and sealed parchments.

Multitudes of cases might be accumulated showing how, in other directions, men's thoughts and feelings produce kinds of conduct which, à priori, would be judged very improbable. And if, going beyond our own society and our own time, we observe what has happened among other races, and among the earlier generations of our own race, we meet, at every step, workings-out of human nature utterly unlike those which we assume when making political forecasts. Who, generalizing the experiences of his daily life, would suppose that men, to please their gods, would swing for hours from hooks drawn through the muscles of their backs, or let their nails grow through the palms of their clenched hands, or roll over and over hundreds of miles to visit a shrine ? Who would have thought it possible that a public sentiment and a private feeling might be as in China,

where a criminal can buy a substitute to be executed in his
stead : the substitute's family having the money ?   Or, to take
historical cases more nearly concerning ourselves—Who foresaw
that the beliefs in purgatory and priestly intercession would
cause one-half of England to lapse into the hands of the Church ?
or who foresaw that a defect in the law of mortmain would lead to
bequests of large estates consecrated as graveyards ? Who could
have imagined that robber-kings and bandit-barons, with vassals
to match, would, generation after generation, have traversed all
Europe through hardships and dangers to risk their lives in getting
possession of the reputed burial place of one whose injunction
was to turn the left cheek when the right was smitten ?   Or who,
again, would have anticipated that when, in Jerusalem, this same
teacher disclaimed political aims, and repudiated political instrumentalities, the professed successors of his disciples would by
and by become rulers dominating over all the kings of Europe ?
Such a result could be as little foreseen as it could be foreseen
that an instrument of torture used by the Jews would give the
ground-plans to Christian temples throughout Europe ; and as
little as it could be foreseen that the process of this torture, recounted in Christian narratives, might come to be mistaken for
a Christian institution, as it was by the Malay chief who, being
expostulated with for crucifying some rebels, replied that he was
following " the English practice," which he read in " their sacred
books." [7]
Look where we will at the genesis of social phenomena, we
shall similarly find that while the particular ends contemplated
and arranged for have commonly not been more than temporarily
attained if attained at all, the changes actually brought about
have arisen from causes of which the very existence was unknown.

How, indeed, can any man, and how more especially can any
man of scientific culture, think that special results of special
political acts can be calculated, when he contemplates the incalculable complexity of the influences under which each individual,

and *à fortiori* each society, develops, lives, and decays? The multiplicity of the factors is illustrated even in the material composition of a man's body. Every one who watches closely the course of things, must have observed that at a single meal he may take in bread made from Russian wheat, beef from Scotland, potatoes from the midland counties, sugar from the Mauritius, salt from Cheshire, pepper from Jamaica, curry-powder from India, wine from France or Germany, currants from Greece, oranges from Spain, as well as various spices and condiments from other places ; and if he considers whence came the draught of water he swallows, tracing it back from the reservoir through the stream and the brook and the rill, to the separate rain-drops which fell wide apart, and these again to the eddying vapours which had been mingling and parting in endless ways as they drifted over the Atlantic, he sees that this single mouthful of water contains molecules which, a little time ago, were dispersed over hundreds of square miles of ocean swell. Similarly tracing back the history of each solid he has eaten, he finds that his body is made up of elements which have lately come from all parts of the Earth's surface.

And what thus holds of the substance of the body, holds no less of the influences, physical and moral, which modify its actions. You break your tooth with a small pebble among the currants, because the industrial organization in Zante is so imperfect. A derangement of your digestion goes back for its cause to the bungling management in a vineyard on the Rhine several years ago; or to the dishonesty of the merchants at Cette, where imitation wines are produced. Because there happened a squabble between a consul and a king in Abyssinia, an increased income-tax obliges you to abridge your autumn holiday ; or because slave-owners in North America try to extend the " peculiar institution " further west, there results here a party dissension which perhaps entails on you loss of friends. If from these remote causes you turn to causes at home, you find that your doings are controlled by a *plexus* of influences too

involved to be traced beyond its first meshes. Your hours of
business are pre-determined by the general habits of the community, which have been slowly established no one knows how.
Your meals have to be taken at intervals which do not suit your
health; but under existing social arrangements you must submit. Such intercourse with friends as you can get, is at hours
and under regulations which everybody adopts, but for which
nobody is responsible; and you have to yield to a ceremonial
which substitutes trouble for pleasure. Your opinions, political
and religious, are ready moulded for you; and unless your
individuality is very decided, your social surroundings will prove
too strong for it. Nay, even such an insignificant event as the
coming-of-age of grouse affects your goings and comings throughout life. For has not the dissolution of Parliament direct reference to the 12th of August? and does not the dissolution end
the London season? and does not the London season determine
the times for business and relaxation, and so affect the making
of arrangements throughout the year? If from co-existing
influences we turn to influences that have been working through
past time, the same general truth becomes still more conspicuous.
Ask how it happens that men in England do not work every
seventh day, and you have to seek through thousands of past
years to find the initial cause. Ask why in England, and still
more in Scotland, there is not only a cessation from work, which
the creed interdicts, but also a cessation from amusement, which
it does not interdict; and for an explanation you must go back
to successive waves of ascetic fanaticism in generations long
dead. And what thus holds of religious ideas and usages, holds
of all others, political and social. Even the industrial activities
are often permanently turned out of their normal directions by
social states that passed away many ages ago: witness what has
happened throughout the East, or in Italy, where towns and
villages are still perched on hills and eminences chosen for
defensive purposes in turbulent times, and where the lives of the
inhabitants are now made laborious by having daily to carry

themselves and all the necessaries of life from a low level to a high level.

The extreme complexity of social actions, and the transcendent difficulty which hence arises of counting on special results, will be still better seen if we enumerate the factors which determine one simple phenomenon, as the price of a commodity,—say, cotton. A manufacturer of calicoes has to decide whether he will increase his stock of raw material at its current price. Before doing this, he must ascertain, as well as he can, the following data:—Whether the stocks of calico in the hands of manufacturers and wholesalers at home, are large or small; whether by recent prices retailers have been led to lay in stocks or not; whether the colonial and foreign markets are glutted or otherwise; and what is now, and is likely to be, the production of calico by foreign manufacturers. Having formed some idea of the probable demand for calico, he has to ask what other manufacturers have done, and are doing, as buyers of cotton— whether they have been waiting for the price to fall, or have been buying in anticipation of a rise. From cotton-brokers' circulars he has to judge what is the state of speculation at Liverpool—whether the stocks there are large or small, and whether many or few cargoes are on their way. The stocks and prices at New Orleans, and at other cotton-ports through- out the world, have also to be taken note of; and then there come questions respecting forthcoming crops in the Southern States, in India, in Egypt, and elsewhere. Here are sufficiently- numerous factors, but these are by no means all. The consumption of calico, and therefore the consumption of cotton, and therefore the price of cotton, depends in part on the supplies and prices of other textile fabrics. If, as happened during the American Civil War, calico rises in price because its raw material becomes scarce, linen comes into more general use, and so a further rise in price is checked. Woollen fabrics, also, may to some extent compete. And, besides the competition caused by relative prices, there is the competition caused by fashion, which may or may not presently change. Surely the factors are now all enumerated? By no means. There is the estimation of mercantile opinion. The views of buyers and sellers respecting future prices, never more than approximations to the truth, often diverge from it very widely. Waves of opinion, now in excess now in defect of the fact, rise and fall daily, and larger ones weekly and monthly, tending, every now and then, to run into mania or panic; for it is among men of business as among other men, that they stand hesitating until some one sets the example, and then rush all one way, like a flock of sheep after a leader. These characteristics in human nature, leading to these perturbations, the farseeing buyer takes into account—-judging how far existing influences have made opinion deviate from the truth, and how far impending influences are likely to do it. Nor has he got to the end of the matter even when he has considered all these things. He has still to ask what are the general mercantile conditions of the country, and what the immediate future of the money market will be; since the course of speculation in every commodity must be affected by the rate of discount. See, then, the enormous complication of causes which determine so simple a thing as the rise or fall of a farthing per pound in cotton some months hence!

If the genesis of social phenomena is so involved in cases like this, where the effect produced has no concrete persistence but very soon dissipates, judge what it must be where there is produced something which continues thereafter to be an increasing agency, capable of self-propagation. Not only has a society as a whole a power of growth and development, but each institution set up in it has the like—draws to itself units of the society and nutriment for them, and tends ever to multiply and ramify. Indeed, the instinct of self-preservation in each institution soon becomes dominant over everything else; and maintains it when it performs some quite other function than that intended, or no function at all. See, for instance, what has come of the "Society of Jesus," Loyola set up; or see what grew out of the company of traders who got a footing on the coast of Hindostan.

To such considerations as these, set down to show the inconsistency of those who think that prevision of social phenomena is possible without much study, though much study is needed for prevision of other phenomena, it will doubtless be replied that time does not allow of systematic inquiry. From the scientific, as from the unscientific, there will come the plea that, in his capacity of citizen, each man has to act—must vote, and must decide before he votes—must conclude to the best of his ability on such information as he has.

In this plea there is some truth, mingled with a good deal more that looks like truth. It is a product of that "must-do-something" impulse which is the origin of much mischief, individual and social. An amiable anxiety to undo or neutralize an evil, often prompts to rash courses, as you may see in the hurry with which one who has fallen is snatched up by those at hand; just as though there were danger in letting him lie, which there is not, and no danger in incautiously raising him, which there is. Always you find among people in proportion as they are ignorant, a belief in specifics, and a great confidence in pressing the adoption of them. Has some one a pain in the side, or in the chest, or in the bowels? Then, before any careful inquiry as to its probable cause, there comes an urgent recommendation of a never-failing remedy, joined probably with the remark that if it does no good it can do no harm. There still prevails in the average mind a large amount of the fetishistic conception clearly shown by a butler to some friends of mine, who, having been found to drain the half-emptied medicine-bottles, explained that he thought it a pity good physic should be wasted, and that what benefited his master would benefit him. But as fast as crude conceptions of diseases and remedial measures grow up into Pathology and Therapeutics, we find increasing caution, along with increasing proof that evil is often done instead of good. This contrast is traceable not only as we pass from popular ignorance to professional knowledge, but as we pass from the smaller professional knowledge of early times to the greater professional knowledge of our own. The question with the modern physician is not as with the ancient—shall the treatment be blood-letting? shall cathartics, or shall diaphoretics be given? or shall mercurials be administered? But there rises the previous question—shall there be any treatment beyond a wholesome regimen? And even among existing physicians it happens that in proportion as the judgment is most cultivated, there is the least yielding to the "must-do-something" impulse.

Is it not possible, then—is it not even probable, that this supposed necessity for immediate action, which is put in as an excuse for drawing quick conclusions from few data, is the concomitant of deficient knowledge? Is it not probable that as in Biology so in Sociology, the accumulation of more facts, the more critical comparison of them, and the drawing of conclusions on scientific methods, will be accompanied by increasing doubt about the benefits to be secured, and increasing fear of the mischiefs which may be worked? Is it not probable that what in the individual organism is improperly, though conveniently, called the *vis medicatrix naturæ*, may be found to have its analogue in the social organism? and will there not very likely come along with the recognition of this, the consciousness that in both cases the one thing needful is to maintain the conditions under which the natural actions have fair play? Such a consciousness, to be anticipated from increased knowledge, will diminish the force of this plea for prompt decision after little inquiry; since it will check this tendency to think of a remedial measure as one that may do good and cannot do harm. Nay more, the study of Sociology, scientifically carried on by tracing back proximate causes to remote ones, and tracing down primary effects to secondary and tertiary effects which multiply as they diffuse, will dissipate the current illusion that social evils admit of radical cures. Given an average defect of nature among the units of a society, and no skilful manipulation of them will prevent that defect from producing its equivalent of bad results. It is possible to change the form of these bad results; it is possible to change the places at which they are manifested; but it is not possible to get rid of them. The belief that faulty character can so organize itself socially, as to get out of itself a conduct which is not proportionately faulty, is an utterly-baseless belief. You may alter the incidence of the mischief, but the amount of it must inevitably be borne some-where. Very generally it is simply thrust out of one form into another; as when, in Austria, improvident marriages being pre-vented, there come more numerous illegitimate children; or as when, to mitigate the misery of foundlings, hospitals are provided for them, and there is an increase in the number of infants abandoned; or as when, to insure the stability of houses, a Building Act prescribes a structure which, making small houses unremunerative, prevents due multiplication of them, and so causes overcrowding; or as when a Lodging-House Act forbids this overcrowding, and vagrants have to sleep under the Adelphi-arches, or in the Parks, or even, for warmth's sake, on the dung-heaps in mews. Where the evil does not, as in cases like these, reappear in another place or form, it is necessarily felt in the shape of a diffused privation. For suppose that by some official instrumentality you actually suppress an evil, instead of thrusting it from one spot into another—suppose you thus successfully deal with a number of such evils by a number of such instru-mentalities; do you think these evils have disappeared absolutely? To see that they have not, you have but to ask—Whence comes the official apparatus? What defrays the cost of working it? Who supplies the necessaries of life to its members through all their gradations of rank? There is no other source but the labour of peasants and artizans. When, as in France, the ad-ministrative agencies occupy some 600,000 men, who are taken from industrial pursuits, and, with their families, supported in more than average comfort, it becomes clear enough that heavy extra work is entailed on the producing classes. The already-tired labourer has to toil an additional hour; his wife has to help in the fields as well as to suckle her infant; his children are still more scantily fed than they would otherwise be; and beyond a decreased share of returns from increased labour, there is a diminished time and energy for such small enjoyments as the life, pitiable at the best, permits. How, then, can it be supposed that the evils have been extinguished or escaped? The repressive action has had its corresponding reaction; and instead of intenser miseries here and there, or now and then, you have got a misery that is constant and universal.

When it is thus seen that the evils are not removed, but at best only re-distributed, and that the question in any case is whether re-distribution, even if practicable, is desirable; it will be seen that the "must-do-something" plea is quite insufficient. There is ample reason to believe that in proportion as scientific men carry into this most-involved class of phenomena, the methods they have successfully adopted with other classes, they will perceive that, even less in this class than in other classes, are conclusions to be drawn and action to be taken without pro-longed and critical investigation.

Still there will recur the same plea under other forms "Political conduct must be matter of compromise." "We must adapt our measures to immediate exigencies, and cannot be deterred by remote considerations." "The data for forming scientific judgments are not to be had: most of them are un-recorded, and those which are recorded are difficult to find as well as doubtful when found." "Life is too short, and the demands upon our energies too great, to permit any such elabo-rate study as seems required. We must, therefore, guide our-selves by common sense as best we may."

And then, behind the more scientifically-minded who give this answer, there are those who hold, tacitly or overtly, that guidance of the kind indicated is not possible, even after any amount of inquiry.   They do not believe in any ascertainable order among social phenomena—there is no such thing as a social science.   This proposition we will discuss in the next chapter.

CHAPTER II.

IS THERE A SOCIAL SCIENCE?

ALMOST every autumn may be heard the remark that a hard winter is coming, for that the hips and haws are abundant : the implied belief being that God, intending to send much frost and snow, has provided a large store of food for the birds. Interpretations of this kind, tacit or avowed, prevail widely. Not many weeks since, one who had received the usual amount of culture said in my hearing, that the swarm of lady-birds which overspread the country some summers ago, had been providentially designed to save the crop of hops from the destroying aphides. Of course this theory of the divine government, here applied to occurrences bearing but indirectly, if at all, on human welfare, is applied with still greater confidence to occurrences that directly affect us, individually and socially. It is a theory carried out with logical consistency by the Methodist who, before going on a journey or removing to another house, opens his Bible, and in the first passage his eye rests upon, finds an intimation of approval or disapproval from heaven. And in its political applications it yields such appropriate beliefs as that the welfare of England in comparison with Continental States, has been a reward for better observance of the Sunday, or that an invasion of cholera was consequent on the omission of *Dei gratia* from an issue of coins.

The interpretation of historical events in general after this same method, accompanies such interpretations of ordinary passing events; and, indeed, outlives them. Those to whom the natural genesis of simpler phenomena has been made manifest by increasing knowledge, still believe in the supernatural genesis of phenomena that are very much involved, and cannot have their causes readily traced. The form of mind which, in an official despatch, prompts the statement that " it has pleased Almighty God to vouchsafe to the British arms the most successful issue to the extensive combinations rendered necessary for the purpose of effecting the passage of the Chenaub," [1] is a form of mind which, in the records of the past, everywhere sees interpositions of the Deity to bring about results that appear to the interpreter the most desirable. Thus, for example, Mr. Schomberg writes :—

" It seemed good to the All-beneficent Disposer of human events, to overrule every obstacle ; and through His instrument, William of Normandy, to expurgate the evils of the land ; and to resuscitate its dying powers." [2]

And elsewhere:—

" The time had now arrived when the Almighty Governor, after having severely punished the whole nation, was intending to raise its drooping head—to give a more rapid impulse to its prosperity, and to cause it to stand forth more prominently as an EXEMPLAR STATE. For this end, He raised up an individual eminently fitted for the intended work " [Henry VII.].[3]

And again :—

" As if to mark this epoch of history with greater distinctness, it was closed by the death of George III., the GREAT and the GOOD, who had been raised up as the grand instrument of its accomplishment." [4]

The late catastrophes on the Continent are similarly explained by a French writer who, like the English writer just quoted, professes to have looked behind the veil of things ; and who tells us what have been the intentions of God in chastising his chosen people, the French. For it is to be observed in passing that, just as the evangelicals among ourselves think we are divinely blessed because we have preserved the purity of the faith, so it is obvious to the author of *La Main de l'Homme et le Doigt de Dieu*, as to other Frenchmen, that France is hereafter still to be, as it has hitherto been, the leader of the world. This writer, in chapters entitled " Causes providentielles de nos malheurs," " Les Prussiens et les fléaux de Dieu," and " Justification de la Providence," carries out his interpretations in ways we need not here follow, and then closes his " Epilogue " with these sentences :—

" La Révolution modérée, habile, sagace, machiavélique, diaboliquement sage, a été vaincue et confondue par la justice divine dans la personne et dans le gouvernement de Napoléon III.

" La Révolution exaltée, bouillonnante, étourdie, a été vaincue et confondue par la justice divine dans les personnes et dans les gouvernements successifs de Gambetta et de Félix Pyat et compagnie.

" La sagesse humaine, applaudie et triomphante, personnifiée dans M. Thiers, ne tardera pas à être vaincue et confondue par cette même Révolution deux fois humiliée, mais toujours renaissante et agressive."

" Ce n'est pas une prophétie : c'est la prévision de la philosophie et de la foi chrétiennes.

" Alors ce sera vraiment le tour du Très-Haut ; car il faut que Dieu et son Fils règnent par son Évangile et par son Église.˙

" Ames françaises et chrétiennes, priez, travaillez, souffrez et ayez confiance ! nous sommes près de la fin. C'est quand tout semblera perdu que tout sera vraiment sauvé.

" Si la France avait su profiter des désastres subis, Dieu lui eût rendu ses premières faveurs. Elle s'obstine dans l'erreur et le vice. Croyons que Dieu la sauvera malgré elle, en la régénérant toutefois par l'eau et par feu. C'est quand l'impuissance humaine apparait qu'éclate la sagess:˙ divine. Mais quelles tribulations ! quelles angoisses ! Heureux ceux qui survivront et jouiront du triomphe de Dieu et de son Église sainte, catholique, apostolique et romaine." ⁵

Conceptions of this kind are not limited to historians whose names have dropped out of remembrance, and to men who, while the drama of contemporary revolution is going on, play the part of a Greek chorus, telling the world of spectators what has been the divine purpose and what are the divine intentions; but we have lately had a Professor of ·History setting forth conceptions essentially identical in nature. Here are his words :—

" And now, gentlemen, was this vast campaign [of Teutons against Romans] fought without a general ? If Trafalgar could not be won without the mind of a Nelson, or Waterloo without the mind of a Wellington, was there no one mind to lead those innumerable armies on whose success depended the future of the whole human race ? Did no one marshal them in that impregnable convex front, from the Euxine to the North Sea ? No one guide them to the two great strategic centres of the Black Forest and Trieste ? No one cause them, blind barbarians without maps or science, to follow those rules of war without which victory in a protracted struggle is impossible ; and by the pressure of the Huns behind, force on their flagging myriads to an enterprise which their simplicity fancied at first beyond the powers of mortal men ? Believe it who will : but I cannot. I may be told that they gravitated into their places, as stones and mud do. Be it so. They obeyed natural laws of course, as all things do on earth, when they obeyed the laws of war : those, too, are natural·laws, explicable on simple mathematical principles. But while I believe that not a stone or a handful of mud gravitates into its place without the will of God ; that it was ordained, ages since, into what particular spot each grain of gold should be washed down from an Australian quartz reef, that a certain man might find it at a certain moment and crisis of his life ;—if I be superstitious enough (as, thank God, I am) to hold that creed, shall I not believe that, though this great war had no general upon earth, it may have had a general in heaven ? and that, in spite of all their sins, the hosts of our forefathers were the hosts of God." [6]

It does not concern us here to seek a reconciliation of the incongruous ideas bracketed together in this paragraph— to ask how the results of gravitation, which acts with such uniformity that under given conditions its effect is calculable with certainty, can at the same time be regarded as the results of will, which we class apart because, as known by our experience, it is comparatively irregular ;·or to ask how, if the course of human affairs is divinely pre-determined just as material changes are, any distinction is to be drawn between that prevision of material changes which constitutes physical science and historical prevision: the reader may be left to evolve the obvious conclusion that either the current idea of physical causation has to be abandoned, or the current idea of will has to be abandoned. All which I need call attention to as indicating the general character of such interpretations, is the remarkable title of the chapter containing this passage—" The Strategy of Providence."

In common with some others, I have often wondered how the Universe looks to those who use such names for its Cause as " The Master Builder," or " The Great Artificer; " and who seem to think that the Cause of the Universe is made more marvellous by comparing its operations to those of a skilled mechanic. But really the expression, " Strategy of Providence," reveals a conception of this Cause which is in some respects more puzzling. Such a title as " The Great Artificer," while suggesting simply the process of shaping a pre-existing material, and leaving the question whence this material came untouched, may at any rate be said not to negative the assumption that the material is created by "The Great Artificer" who shapes it. The phrase, " Strategy of Providence," however, necessarily implies difficulties to be overcome. The Divine Strategist must have a skilful antagonist to make strategy possible. So that we are inevitably introduced to the conception of a Cause of the Universe continually impeded by some independent cause which has to be out-generalled. It is not every one who would thank God for a belief, the implication of which is that God is obliged to overcome opposition by subtle devices.

The disguises which piety puts on are, indeed, not unfrequently suggestive of that which some would describe by a quite opposite name. To study the Universe as it is manifested to us; to ascertain by patient observation the order of the manifestations; to discover that the manifestations are connected with one another after a regular way in Time and Space ; and, after repeated failures, to give up as futile the attempt to understand the Power manifested ; is condemned as irreligious. And meanwhile the character of religious is claimed by those who figure to themselves a Creator moved by motives like their own; who conceive themselves as discovering his designs; and who even speak of him as though he laid plans to outwit the Devil!

This, however, by the way. The foregoing extracts and comments are intended to indicate the mental attitude of those for whom there can be no such thing as Sociology, properly so called. That mode of conceiving human affairs which is implied alike by the " D.V." of a missionary-meeting placard and by the phrases of Emperor William's late despatches, where thanks to God come next to enumerations of the thousands slain, is one to which the idea of a Social Science is entirely alien, and indeed repugnant.

An allied class, equally unprepared to interpret sociological phenomena scientifically, is the class which sees in the course of civilization little else than a record of remarkable persons and their doings. One who is conspicuous as the exponent of this view writes :—" As I take it, universal history, the history of what man has accomplished in this world, is at bottom the history of the great men who have worked here." And this, not perhaps distinctly formulated, but everywhere implied, is the belief in which nearly all are brought up. Let us glance at the genesis of it.

Round their camp-fire assembled savages tell the events of the day's chase; and he among them who has done some feat of skill or agility is duly lauded. On a return from the war-path, the sagacity of the chief and the strength or courage of this or that warrior, are the all-absorbing themes. When the day, or the immediate past, affords no remarkable deed, the topic is the achievement of some noted leader lately dead, or some traditional founder of the tribe : accompanied, it may be, with a dance dramatically representing those victories which the chant recites. Such narratives, concerning, as they do, the prosperity and indeed the very existence of the tribe, are of the intensest interest; and in them we have the common root of music, of the drama, of poetry, of biography, of history, and of literature in general. Savage life furnishes little else worthy of note; and the chronicles of tribes contain scarcely anything more to be remembered. Early historic races show us the same thing. The Egyptian frescoes and the wall-sculptures of the Assyrians, represent the deeds of leading men; and inscriptions such as that on the Moabite stone, tell of nothing more than royal achievements: only by implication do these records, pictorial, hieroglyphic, or written, convey anything else. And similarly from the Greek epics, though we gather incidentally that there were towns, and war-vessels, and war-chariots, and sailors, and soldiers to be led and slain, yet the direct intention is to set forth the triumphs of Achilles, the prowess of Ajax, the wisdom of Ulysses, and the like. The lessons given to every civilized child tacitly imply, like the traditions of the uncivilized and semi-civilized, that throughout the past of the human race, the doings of conspicuous persons have been the only things worthy of remembrance. How Abraham girded up his loins and gat him to this place or that; how Samuel conveyed divine injunctions which Saul disobeyed; how David recounted his adventures as a shepherd, and was reproached for his misdeeds as a king—these, and personalities akin to these, are the facts about which the juvenile reader of the Bible is interested and respecting which he is catechized: such indications of Jewish institutions as have unavoidably got into the narrative, being regarded neither by him nor by his teacher as of moment. So too, when, with hands behind him, he stands to say his lesson out of *Pinnock*, we see that the things set down for him to learn, are—when and by whom England was invaded, what rulers opposed the invasions and how they were killed, what Alfred did and what Canute said, who fought at Agincourt and who conquered at Flodden, which king abdicated and which usurped, &c.; and if by some chance it comes out that there were serfs in those days, that barons were local rulers, some vassals of others, that subordination of them to a central power took place gradually, these are facts treated as relatively unimportant.   Nay, the like happens when the boy passes into the hands of his classical master, at home or elsewhere. "Arms and the man" form the end of the story as they form its beginning. After the mythology, which of course is all-essential, come the achievements of rulers and soldiers from Agamemnon down to Cæsar : what knowledge is gained of social organization, manners, ideas, morals, being little more than the biographical statements involve. And the value of the knowledge is so ranked that while it would be a disgrace to be wrong about the amours. of Zeus, and while inability to name the commander at Marathon would be discreditable, it is excusable to know nothing of the social condition that preceded Lycurgus or of the origin and functions of the Areopagus.

Thus the great-man-theory of History finds everywhere a ready-prepared conception—is, indeed, but the definite expression of that which is latent in the thoughts of the savage, tacitly asserted in all early traditions, and taught to every child by multitudinous illustrations.   The glad acceptance it meets with has sundry more special causes.   There is, first, this universal love of personalities, which, active in the aboriginal man, dominates still—a love seen in the urchin who asks you to tell him a story, meaning, thereby, somebody's adventures ; a love gratified in adults by police-reports, court-news, divorce-cases, accounts of accidents, and lists of births, marriages, and deaths ; a love displayed even by conversations in the streets, where fragments of dialogue, heard in passing, show that mostly between men, and always between women, the personal pronouns recur every instant. If you want roughly to estimate any one's mental calibre, you cannot do it better than by observing the ratio of generalities to personalities in his talk—how far simple truths about individuals are replaced by truths abstracted from numerous experiences of men and things. And when you have thus measured many, you find but a scattered few likely to take anything more than a biographical view of human affairs.   In the second place, this great-man-theory commends itself as promising instruction along with amusement. Being already fond of hearing about people's sayings and doings, it is pleasant news that, to understand the course of civilization, you have only to read diligently the lives of distinguished men. What can be a more acceptable doctrine than that while you are satisfying an instinct not very remotely allied to that of the village gossip—while you are receiving through print instead of orally, remarkable facts concerning notable persons, you are gaining that knowledge which will make clear to you why things have happened thus or thus in the world, and will prepare you for forming a right opinion on each question coming before you as a citizen.   And then, in the third place, the interpretation of things thus given is so beautifully simple—seems so easy to comprehend.   Providing you are content with conceptions that are out of focus, as most people's conceptions are, the solutions it yields appear quite satisfactory.   Just as that theory of the Solar System which supposes the planets to have been launched into their orbits by the hand of the Almighty, looks feasible so long as you do not insist on knowing exactly what is meant by the hand of the Almighty; and just as the special creation of plants and animals seems a tenable hypothesis until you try and picture to yourself definitely the process by which one of them is brought into existence ; so the genesis of societies by the actions of great men, may be comfortably believed so long as, resting in general notions, you do not ask for particulars.

But now, if, dissatisfied with vagueness, we demand that our ideas shall be brought into focus and exactly defined, we discover the hypothesis to be utterly incoherent.   If, not stopping at the explanation of social progress as due to the great man, we go back a step and ask whence comes the great man, we find that the theory breaks down completely.   The question has two conceivable answers : his origin is supernatural, or it is natural. Is his origin supernatural ? Then he is a deputy-god, and we have Theocracy once removed—or, rather, not removed at all; for we must then agree with Mr. Schomberg, quoted above, that "the determination of Cæsar to invade Britain" was divinely inspired, and that from him, down to "George III. the GREAT and the GOOD," the successive rulers were appointed to carry out successive designs. Is this an unacceptable solution? Then the origin of the great man is natural; and immediately this is recognized he must be classed with all other phenomena in the society that gave him birth, as a product of its antecedents. Along with the whole generation of which he forms a minute part—along with its institutions, language, knowledge, manners, and its multitudinous arts and appliances, he is a resultant of an enormous aggregate of forces that have been co-operating for ages. True, if you please to ignore all that common observation, verified by physiology, teaches—if you assume that two European parents may produce a Negro child, or that from woolly-haired prognathous Papuans may come a fair, straight-haired infant of Caucasian type—you may assume that the advent of the great man can occur anywhere and under any conditions. If, disregarding those accumulated results of experience which current proverbs and the generalizations of psychologists alike express, you suppose that a Newton might be born in a Hottentot family, that a Milton might spring up among the Andamanese, that a Howard or a Clarkson might have Fiji parents, then you may proceed with facility to explain social progress as caused by the actions of the great man. But if all biological science, enforcing all popular belief, convinces you that by no possibility will an Aristotle come from a father and mother with facial angles of fifty degrees, and that out of a tribe of cannibals, whose chorus in preparation for a feast of human flesh is a kind of rhythmical roaring, there is not the remotest chance of a Beethoven arising; then you must admit that the genesis of the great man depends on the long series of complex influences which has produced the race in which he appears, and the social state into which that race has slowly grown. If it be a fact that the great man may modify his nation in its structure and actions, it is also a fact that there must have been those antecedent modifications constituting national progress before he could be evolved. Before he can re-make his society, his society must make him. So that all those changes of which he is the proximate initiator have their chief causes in the generations he descended from. If there is to be anything like a real explanation of these changes, it must be sought in that aggregate of conditions out of which both he and they have arisen.

Even were we to grant the absurd supposition that the genesis of the great man does not depend on the antecedents furnished by the society he is born in, there would still be the quite-sufficient facts that he is powerless in the absence of the material and mental accumulations which his society inherits from the past, and that he is powerless in the absence of the co-existing population, character, intelligence, and social arrangements. Given a Shakspeare, and what dramas could he have written without the multitudinous traditions of civilized life—without the various experiences which, descending to him from the past, gave wealth to his thought, and without the language which a hundred generations had developed and enriched by use ? Suppose a Watt, with all his inventive power, living in a tribe ignorant of iron, or in a tribe that could get only as much iron as a fire blown by hand-bellows will smelt ; or suppose him born among ourselves before lathes existed ; what chance would there have been of the steam-engine ? Imagine a Laplace unaided by that slowly-developed system of Mathematics which we trace back to its beginnings among the Egyptians ; how far would he have got with the *Mécanique Céleste ?* Nay, the like questions may be put and have like answers, even if we limit ourselves to those classes of great men on whose doings hero-worshippers more particularly dwell—the rulers and generals. Xenophon could not have achieved his celebrated feat had his Ten Thou-

3

sand been feeble, or cowardly, or insubordinate. Cæsar would
never have made his conquests without disciplined troops, inheriting their *prestige* and tactics and organization from the
Romans who lived before them. And, to take a recent instance,
the strategical genius of Moltke would have triumphed in no great
campaigns had there not been a nation of some forty millions to
supply soldiers, and had not those soldiers been men of strong
bodies, sturdy characters, obedient natures, and capable of carrying out orders intelligently.

Were any one to marvel over the potency of a grain of detonating powder, which explodes a cannon, propels the shell, and
sinks a vessel hit—were he to enlarge on the transcendent virtues
of this detonating powder, not mentioning the ignited charge,
the shell, the cannon, and all that enormous aggregate of appliances by which these have severally been produced, detonating
powder included; we should not regard his interpretation as
very rational. But it would fairly compare in rationality with
this interpretation of social phenomena which, dwelling on the
important changes the great man works, ignores that vast pre-
existing supply of latent power he unlocks, and that immeasurable accumulation of antecedents to which both he and this power
are due.

Recognizing what truth there is in the great-man-theory, we
may say that, if limited to early societies, the histories of which
are histories of little else than endeavours to destroy or subjugate one another, it approximately expresses the fact in representing the capable leader as all-important; though even here
it leaves out of sight too much the number and the quality of
his followers. But its immense error lies in the assumption that
what was once true is true for ever; and that a relation of ruler
and ruled which was possible and good at one time is possible
and good for all time. Just as fast as this predatory activity of
early tribes diminishes, just as fast as larger aggregates are
formed by conquest or otherwise, just as fast as war ceases to
be the business of the whole male population, so fast do societies

begin to develop, to show traces of structures and functions not before possible, to acquire increasing complexity along with increasing size, to give origin to new institutions, new activities, new ideas, sentiments, and habits: all of which unobtrusively make their appearance without the thought of any king or legislator. And if you wish to understand these phenomena of social evolution, you will not do it though you should read yourself blind over the biographies of all the great rulers on record, down to Frederick the Greedy and Napoleon the Treacherous.

In addition to that passive denial of a Social Science implied by these two allied doctrines, one or other of which is held by nine men out of ten, there comes from some an active denial of it—either entire or partial. Reasons are given for the belief that no such thing is possible. The invalidity of these reasons can be shown only after the essential nature of Social Science, overlooked by those who give them, has been pointed out; and to point this out here would be to forestal the argument. Some minor criticisms may, however, fitly precede the major criticism. Let us consider first the positions taken up by Mr. Froude :—

" When natural causes are liable to be set aside and neutralized by what is called volition, the word Science is out of place. If it is free to a man to choose what he will do or not do, there is no adequate science of him. If there is a science of him, there is no free choice, and the praise or blame with which we regard one another are impertinent and out of place." [7]

" It is in this marvellous power in men to do wrong . . . that the impossibility stands of forming scientific calculations of what men will do before the fact, or scientific explanations of what they have done after the fact." [8]

" Mr. Buckle would deliver himself from the eccentricities of this and that individual by a doctrine of averages. . . . Unfortunately the average of one generation need not be the average of the next : . . . no two generations are alike." [9]

" There [in history] the phenomena never repeat themselves. There we are dependent wholly on the record of things said to have happened once, but which never happen or can happen a second time. There no experiment is possible ; we can watch for no recurring fact to test the worth of our conjectures." [10]

Here Mr. Froude changes the venue, and joins issue on the old battle-ground of free will *versus* necessity : declaring a Social Science to be incompatible with free will. The first extract implies, not simply that individual volition is incalculable—that " there is no adequate science of " man (no Science of Psychology) ; but it also asserts, by implication, that there are no causal relations among his states of mind : the volition by which " natural causes are liable to be set aside," being put in antithesis to natural, must be supernatural. Hence we are, in fact, carried back to that primitive form of interpretation contemplated at the outset.   A further comment is, that because volitions of some kinds cannot be foreseen, Mr. Froude argues as though no volitions can be foreseen: ignoring the fact that the simple volitions determining ordinary conduct, are so regular that prevision having a high degree of probability is easy. If, in crossing a street, a man sees a carriage coming upon him, you may safely assert that, in nine hundred and ninety-nine cases out of a thousand, he will try to get out of the way. If, being pressed to catch a train, he knows that by one route it is a mile to the station and by another two miles, you may conclude with considerable confidence that he will take the one-mile route ; and should he be aware that losing the train will lose him a fortune, it is pretty certain that, if he has but ten minutes to do the mile in, he will either run or call a cab. If he can buy next door a commodity of daily consumption better and cheaper than at the other end of the town, we may affirm that, if he does not buy next door, some special relation between him and the remoter shop-keeper furnishes a strong reason for taking a worse commodity at greater cost of money and trouble. And though, if he has an estate to dispose of, it is within the limits of possibility that he will sell it to A for £1,000, though B has offered

£2,000 for it; yet the unusual motives leading to such an act need scarcely be taken into account as qualifying the generaliza- . tion that a man will sell to the highest bidder. Now, since the predominant activities of citizens are determined by motives of this degree of regularity, there must be resulting social pheno-mena that have corresponding degrees of regularity—greater degrees, indeed, since in them the effects of exceptional motives become lost in the effects of the aggregate of ordinary mo-tives. Another comment may be added. Mr. Froude exagge-rates the antithesis he draws by using a conception of science which is too narrow: he speaks as though there were no science but exact science. Scientific previsions, both qualitative and quantitative, have various degrees of definiteness; and because among certain classes of phenomena the previsions are approximate only, it is not, therefore, to be said that there is no science of those phe-nomena: if there is *some* prevision, there is *some* science. Take, for example, Meteorology. The Derby has been run in a snow-storm, and you may occasionally want a fire in July; but such anomalies do not prevent us from being perfectly certain that the coming summer will be warmer than the past winter. Our south-westerly gales in the autumn may come early or may come late, may be violent or moderate, at one time or at inter-vals; but that there will be an excess of wind from the south-west at that part of the year we may be sure. The like holds with the relations of rain and dry weather to the quantity of water in the air and the weight of the atmospheric column: though exactly-true predictions cannot be made, approximately-true ones can. So that, even were there not among social phenomena more definite relations than these (and the all-im-portant ones are far more definite), there would still be a Social Science. Once more, Mr. Froude contends that the facts presented in history do not furnish subject-matter for science, because they "never repeat themselves,"—because "we can watch for no recurring fact to test the worth of our conjectures." I will not meet this assertion by the counter-assertion often made, that historic phenomena *do* repeat themselves; but, admitting that Mr. Froude here touches on one of the great difficulties of the Social Science (that social phenomena are in so considerable a degree different in each case from what they were in preceding cases), I still find a sufficient reply. For in no concrete science is there absolute repetition; and in some concrete sciences the repetition is no more specific than in Sociology. Even in the most exact of them, Astronomy, the combinations are never the same twice over: the repetitions are but approximate. And on turning to Geology, we find that, though the processes of denudation, deposition, upheaval, subsidence, have been ever going on in conformity with laws more or less clearly generalized, the effects have been always new in their proportions and arrangements; though not so completely new as to forbid comparisons, consequent deductions, and approximate previsions based on them.

Were there no such replies as these to Mr. Froude's reasons, there would still be the reply furnished by his own interpretations of history; which make it clear that his denial must be understood as but a qualified one. Against his professed theory may be set his actual practice, which, as it seems to me, tacitly asserts that explanations of some social phenomena in terms of cause and effect are possible, if not explanations of all social phenomena. Thus, respecting the Vagrancy Act of 1547, which made a slave of a confirmed vagrant, Mr. Froude says:—" In the condition of things which was now commencing . . . . neither this nor any other penal act against idleness could be practically enforced." [11]   That is to say, the operation of an agency brought into play was neutralized by the operation of natural causes coexisting. Again, respecting the enclosure of commons and amalgamation of farms, &c., Mr. Froude writes: —" Under the late reign these tendencies had, with great difficulty, been held partially in check, but on the death of Henry they acquired new force and activity." [12]   Or, in other words, certain social forces previously antagonized by certain other forces, produced their natural effects when the antagonism ceased. Yet again, Mr. Froude explains that, "unhappily, two causes [debased currency and an alteration of the farming system] were operating to produce the rise of prices." [13] And throughout Mr. Froude's *History of England* there are, I need scarcely say, other cases in which he ascribes social changes to causes rooted in human nature. Moreover, in his lecture on *The Science of History*, there is a distinct enunciation of " one lesson of History ; " namely, that " the moral law is written on the tablets of eternity. . . . . Justice and truth alone endure and live. Injustice and falsehood may be long-lived, but dooms-day comes at last to them, in French revolutions and other terrible ways." And elsewhere he says that " the miseries and horrors which are now destroying the Chinese Empire are the direct and organic results of the moral profligacy of its inhabi-tants." [14] Each of these statements tacitly asserts that certain social relations, and actions of certain kinds, are inevitably bene-ficial, and others inevitably detrimental—an historic induction furnishing a basis for positive deduction. So that we must not interpret Mr. Froude too literally when he alleges the " impossi-bility of forming scientific calculations of what men will do before the fact, or scientific explanations of what they have done after the fact."

Another writer who denies the possibility of a Social Science, or who, at any rate, admits it only as a science which has its relations of phenomena so traversed by providential influences that it does not come within the proper definition of a science, is Canon Kingsley. In his address on *The Limits of Exact Science as applied to History*, he says :—

" You say that as the laws of matter are inevitable, so probably are the laws of human life ? Be it so : but in what sense are the laws of matter inevitable ? Potentially or actually ? Even in the seemingly most uniform and universal law, where do we find the inevitable or the irresistible ? Is there not in nature a perpetual competition of law against law, force against force, producing the most endless and unexpected variety of results? Cannot each law be interfered with at any moment by some other law, so that the first law, though it may struggle for the mastery, shall be for an indefinite time utterly defeated? The law of gravity is immutable enough : but do all stones veritably fall to the ground? Certainly not, if I choose to catch one, and keep it in my hand. It remains there by laws ; and the law of gravity is there, too, making it feel heavy in my hand : but it has not fallen to the ground, and will not, till I let it. So much for the inevitable action of the laws of gravity, as of others. Potentially, it is immutable ; but actually, it can be conquered by other laws." [15]

This passage, severely criticized, if I remember rightly, when the address was originally published, it would be scarcely fair to quote were it not that Canon Kingsley has repeated it at a later date in his work, *The Roman and the Teuton.* The very unusual renderings of scientific ideas which it contains, need here be only enumerated. Mr. Kingsley differs profoundly from philosophers and men of science, in regarding a law as itself a power or force, and so in thinking of one law as " conquered by other laws; " whereas the accepted conception of law is that of an established *order,* to which the manifestations of a power or force conform. He enunciates, too, a quite-exceptional view of gravitation. As conceived by astronomers and physicists, gravitation is a universal and ever-acting *force,* which portions of matter exercise on one another when at sensible distances ; and the *law* of this force is that it varies directly as the mass and inversely as the square of the distance. Mr. Kingsley's view, is that the law of gravitation is " defeated " if a stone is prevented from falling to the ground —that the law " struggles " (not the force), and that because it no longer produces motion, the " inevitable action of the laws of gravity " (not of gravity) is suspended : the truth being that neither the force nor its law is in the slightest degree modified. Further, the theory of natural processes which Mr. Kingsley has arrived at, seems to be that when two or more forces (or laws, if he prefers it) come into play, there is a partial or complete suspension of one by another. Whereas the doctrine held by men of science is, that the forces are all in full operation, and the effect is their *resultant;* so that, for example, when a shot is fired horizontally from a cannon, the force impressed on it produces in a given time just the same amount of horizontal motion as though gravity were absent, while gravity produces in that same time a fall just equal to that which it would have produced had the shot been dropped from the mouth of the cannon. Of course, holding these peculiar views of causation as displayed among simple physical phenomena, Canon Kingsley is consistent in denying historical sequence ; and in saying that " as long as man has the mysterious power of breaking the laws of his own being, such a sequence not only cannot be discovered, but it cannot exist." [16] At the same time it is manifest that until he comes to some agreement with men of science respecting conceptions of forces, of their laws, and of the modes in which phenomena produced by compositions of forces are interpretable in terms of compound laws, no discussion of the question at issue can be carried on with profit.

Without waiting for such an agreement, however, which is probably somewhat remote, Canon Kingsley's argument may be met by putting side by side with it some of his own conclusions set forth elsewhere. In an edition of *Alton Locke* published since the delivery of the address above quoted from, there is a new preface containing, among others, the following passages:—

" The progress towards institutions more and more popular may be slow, but it is sure. Whenever any class has conceived the hope of being fairly represented, it is certain to fulfil its own hopes, unless it employs, or provokes, violence impossible in England. The thing will be.[17] . . . " If any young gentlemen look forward. . . . . to a Conservative reaction of any other kind than this . . . . to even the least stoppage of what the world calls progress—which I should define as the putting in practice the results of inductive science ;—then do they, like King Picrochole in *Rabelais,* look for a kingdom which shall be restored to them at the coming of the Cocqcigrues." [18]

And in a preface addressed to working men, contained in an earlier edition, he says :—

" If you are better off than you were in 1848, you owe it principally to those laws of political economy (as they are called), which I call the brute natural accidents of supply and demand," &c.[19]

Which passages offer explanations of changes now gone by as having been wrought out by natural forces in conformity with natural laws, and also predictions of changes which natural forces at present in action will work out. That is to say, by the help of generalized experiences there is an interpretation of past phenomena and a prevision of future phenomena. There is an implicit recognition of that Social Science which is explicitly denied.

A reply to these criticisms may be imagined. In looking for whatever reconciliation is possible between these positions which seem so incongruous, we must suppose the intended assertion to be, that only general interpretations and previsions can be made, not those which are special. Bearing in mind Mr. Froude's occasional explanations of historical phenomena as naturally caused, we must conclude that he believes certain classes of sociological facts (as the politico-economical) to be scientifically explicable, while other classes are not: though, if this be his view, it is not clear how, if the results of men's wills, separate or aggregated, are incalculable, politico-economical actions can be dealt with scientifically; since, equally with other social actions, they are determined by aggregated wills. Similarly, Canon Kingsley, recognizing no less distinctly economical laws, and enunciating also certain laws of progress—nay, even warning his hearers against the belief that he denies the applicability of the inductive method to social phenomena,—must be assumed to think that the applicability of the inductive method is here but partial. Citing the title of his address and some of its sentences, he may say they imply simply that there are limits to the explanation of social facts in precise ways; though this position does not seem really reconcilable with the doctrine that social laws are liable to be at any time overruled, providentially or otherwise. But, merely hinting these collateral criticisms, this reply is to be met by the demurrer that it is beside the question. If the sole thing meant is that sociological previsions can be approximate only—if the thing denied is the possibility of reducing Sociology to the form of an exact science; then the rejoinder is that the thing denied is a thing which no one has affirmed. Only a moiety of science is exact science—only phenomena of certain orders have had their relations expressed quantitatively as well as qualitatively. Of the remaining orders there are some produced by factors so numerous and so hard to measure, that to develop our knowledge of their relations into the quantitative form will be extremely difficult, if not impossible. But these orders of phenomena are not therefore excluded from the conception of Science. In Geology, in Biology, in Psychology, most of the previsions are qualitative only; and where they are quantitative their quantitativeness, never quite definite, is mostly very indefinite. Nevertheless we unhesitatingly class these previsions as scientific. It is thus with Sociology. The phenomena it presents, involved in a higher degree than all others, are less than all other, capable of precise treatment: such of them as can be generalized, can be generalized only within wide limits of variation as to time and amount; and there remains much that cannot be generalized. But so far as there can be generalization, and so far as there can be interpretation based on it, so far there can be science. Whoever expresses political opinions—whoever asserts that such or such public arrangements will be beneficial or detrimental, tacitly expresses belief in a Social Science; for he asserts, by implication, that there is a natural sequence among social actions, and that as the sequence is natural results may be foreseen.

Reduced to a more concrete form, the case may be put thus:— Mr. Froude and Canon Kingsley both believe to a considerable extent in the efficiency of legislation—probably to a greater extent than it is believed in by some of those who assert the existence of a Social Science. To believe in the efficiency of legislation is to believe that certain prospective penalties or rewards will act as deterrents or incentives—will modify individual conduct, and therefore modify social action. Though it may be impossible to say that a given law will produce a foreseen effect on a particular person, yet no doubt is felt that it will produce a foreseen effect on the mass of persons. Though Mr. Froude, when arguing against Mr. Buckle, says that he "would deliver himself from the eccentricities of this and that individual by a doctrine of averages," but that "unfortunately, the average of one generation need not be the average of the next;" yet Mr. Froude himself so far believes in the doctrine of averages as to hold that legislative interdicts, with threats of death or imprisonment behind them, will restrain the great majority of men in ways which can be predicted. While he contends that the results of individual will are incalculable, yet, by approving certain laws and condemning others, he tacitly affirms that the results of the aggregate of wills are calculable. And if this be asserted of the aggregate of wills as affected by legislation, it must be asserted of the aggregate of wills as affected by social influences at large. If it be held that the desire to avoid punishment will so act on the average of men as to produce an average foreseen result; then it must also be held that on the average of men, the desire to get the greatest return for labour, the desire to rise into a higher rank of life, the desire to gain applause, and so forth, will each of them produce a certain average result. And to hold this is to hold that there can be prevision of social phenomena, and therefore Social Science.

In brief, then, the alternative positions are these. On the one hand, if there is no natural causation throughout the actions of incorporated humanity, government and legislation are absurd. Acts of Parliament may, as well as not, be made to depend on the drawing of lots or the tossing of a coin; or, rather, there may as well be none at all : social sequences having no ascertainable order, no effect can be counted upon—everything is chaotic. On the other hand, if there is natural causation, then the combination of forces by which every combination of effects is produced, produces that combination of effects in conformity with the laws of the forces. And if so, it behoves us to use all diligence in ascertaining what the forces are, what are their laws, and what are the ways in which they co-operate.

Such further elucidation as is possible will be gained by discussing the question to which we now address ourselves—the Nature of the Social Science. Along with a definite idea of this, will come a perception that the denial of a Social Science has arisen from the confusing of two essentially-different classes of phenomena which societies present—the one class, almost ignored by historians, constituting the subject-matter of Social Science, and the other class, almost exclusively occupying them, admitting of scientific co-ordination in a very small degree, if at all.

CHAPTER III.

OUT of bricks, well burnt, hard, and sharp-angled, lying in heaps by his side, the bricklayer builds, even without mortar, a wall of some height that has considerable stability. With bricks made of bad materials, irregularly burnt, warped, cracked, and many of them broken, he cannot build a dry wall of the same height and stability. The dockyard-labourer, piling cannon-shot, is totally unable to make these spherical masses stand at all as the bricks stand. There are, indeed, certain definite shapes into which they may be piled—that of a tetrahedron, or that of a pyramid having a square base, or that of an elongated wedge allied to the pyramid. In any of these forms they may be put together symmetrically and stably ; but not in forms with vertical sides or highly-inclined sides. Once more, if, instead of equal spherical shot, the masses to be piled are boulders, partially but irregularly rounded, and of various sizes, no definite stable form is possible. A loose heap, indefinite in its surface and angles, is all the labourer can make of them. Putting which several facts together, and asking what is the most general truth they imply, we see it to be this—that the character of the aggregate is determined by the characters of the units.

If we pass from units of these visible, tangible kinds, to the units contemplated by chemists and physicists as making up masses of matter, the same truth meets us. Each so-called element, each combination of elements, each re-combination of the compounds, has a form of crystallization. Though its crystals differ in their sizes, and are liable to be modified by truncations of angles and apices, as well as by partial mergings into one another, yet the type of structure, as shown by cleavage, is constant: particular kinds of molecules severally have particular shapes into which they settle themselves as they aggregate. And though in some cases it happens that a substance, simple or compound, has two or even more forms of aggregation, yet the recognized interpretation is, that these different forms are the forms assumed by molecules made different in their structures by allotropic or isomeric changes. So constant is the relation between the nature of any molecules and their mode of crystallizing, that, given two kinds of molecules which are known, from their chemical actions, to be closely allied in their natures, and it is inferred with certainty that their crystals will be closely allied. In brief, it may be unhesitatingly affirmed, as an outcome of physics and chemistry, that throughout all phenomena presented by dead matter, the natures of the units necessitate certain traits in the aggregates.

This truth is again exemplified by aggregates of living matter. In the substance of each species of plant or animal, there is a proclivity towards the structure which that plant or animal presents—a proclivity conclusively proved in cases where the conditions to the maintenance of life are sufficiently simple, and where the tissue has not assumed a structure too finished to permit re-arrangement. The perpetually-cited case of the polype, each part of which, when it is cut into several, presently puts on the polype-shape, and gains structures and powers like those of the original whole, illustrates this truth among animals. Among plants it is well exemplified by the Begonias. Here a complete plant grows from a fragment of a leaf stuck in the ground ; and, in *Begonia phyllomaniaca*, complete plants grow even out of scales that fall from the leaves and the stem—a fact showing, like the fact which the polype furnishes, that the units everywhere present, have for their type of aggregation the type of the organism they belong to; and reminding us of the universal fact that the units composing every germ, animal or vegetal, have a proclivity towards the parental type of aggregation.

Thus, given the natures of the units, and the nature of the aggregate they form is pre-determined. I say the *nature*, meaning, of course, the essential traits, and not including the incidental. By the characters of the units are necessitated certain limits within which the characters of the aggregate must fall. The circumstances attending aggregation greatly modify the results; but the truth here to be recognized is, that these circumstances, in some cases perhaps preventing aggregation altogether, in other cases impeding it, in other cases facilitating it more or less, can never give to the aggregate, characters that do not consist with the characters of the units. No favouring conditions will give the labourer power to pile cannon-shot into a vertical wall; no favouring conditions will make it possible for common salt, which crystallizes on the regular system, to crystallize, like sulphate of soda, on the oblique prismatic system; no favouring conditions will enable the fragment of a polype to take on the structure of a mollusk.

Among such social aggregates as inferior creatures fall into, more or less definitely, the same truth holds. Whether they live in a mere assemblage, or whether they live in something like an organized union with division of labour among its members, as happens in many cases, is unquestionably determined by the properties of the units. Given the structures and consequent instincts of the individuals as we find them, and the community they form will inevitably present certain traits; and no community having such traits can be formed out of individuals having other structures and instincts.

Those who have been brought up in the belief that there is one law for the rest of the Universe and another law for mankind, will doubtless be astonished by the proposal to include aggregates of men in this generalization. And yet that the properties of the units determine the properties of the whole they make up, evidently holds of societies as of other things. A general survey of tribes and nations, past and present, shows clearly enough that it is so; and a brief consideration of the conditions shows, with no less clearness, that it must be so.

Ignoring for the moment the special traits of races and individuals, observe the traits common to members of the species at large; and consider how these must affect their relations when associated.

They have all needs for food, and have corresponding desires. To all of them exertion is a physiological expense; must bring a certain return in nutriment, if it is not to be detrimental; and is accompanied by repugnance when pushed to excess, or even before reaching it. They are all of them liable to bodily injury, with accompanying pain, from various extreme physical actions; and they are liable to emotional pains, of positive and negative kinds, from one another's actions. As says Shylock, insisting on that human nature which Jews have in common with Christians—

"Hath not a Jew eyes? hath not a Jew hands, organs, dimensions, senses, affections, passions? fed with the same food, hurt with the same weapons, subject to the same diseases, healed by the same means, warmed and cooled by the same winter and summer, as a Christian is? If you prick us, do we not bleed? if you tickle us, do we not laugh? if you poison us, do we not die? and if you wrong us, shall we not revenge? If we are like you in the rest, we will resemble you in that."

Conspicuous, however, as is this possession of certain fundamental qualities by all individuals, there is no adequate recognition of the truth that from these individual qualities must result certain qualities in an assemblage of individuals; that in proportion as the individuals forming one assemblage are like in their qualities to the individuals forming another assemblage, the two assemblages will have likenesses; and that the assem-

blages will differ in their characters in proportion as the component individuals of the one differ from those of the other. Yet
when this, which is almost a truism, has been admitted, it cannot be denied that in every community there is a group of
phenomena growing naturally out of the phenomena presented
by its members—a set of properties in the aggregate determined
by the sets of properties in the units; and that the relations of
the two sets form the subject-matter of a science. It needs but
to ask what would happen if men avoided one another, as various
inferior creatures do, to see that the very possibility of a society
depends on a certain emotional property in the individual. It
needs but to ask what would happen if each man liked best the
men who gave him most pain, to perceive that social relations,
supposing them to be possible, would be utterly unlike the social
relations resulting from the greater liking which men individually have for others who give them pleasure. It needs but to
ask what would happen if, instead of ordinarily preferring the
easiest ways of achieving their ends, men preferred to achieve
their ends in the most troublesome ways, to infer that then, a
society, if one could exist, would be a widely-different society
from any we know. And if, as these extreme cases show us,
cardinal traits in societies are determined by cardinal traits in
men, it cannot be questioned that less-marked traits in societies
are determined by less-marked traits in men; and that there
must everywhere be a *consensus* between the special structures
and actions of the one and the special structures and actions of
the other.

Setting out, then, with this general principle, that the properties of the units determine the properties of the aggregate,
we conclude that there must be a Social Science expressing the
relations between the two, with as much definiteness as the
natures of the phenomena permit. Beginning with types of men
who form but small and incoherent social aggregates, such a
science has to show in what ways the individual qualities, intellectual and emotional, negative further aggregation. It has to

explain how slight modifications of individual nature, arising under modified conditions of life, make somewhat larger aggregates possible. It has to trace out, in aggregates of some size, the genesis of the social relations, regulative and operative, into which the members fall. It has to exhibit the stronger and more prolonged social influences which, by further modifying the characters of the units, facilitate further aggregation with consequent further complexity of social structure. Among societies of all orders and sizes, from the smallest and rudest up to the largest and most civilized, it has to ascertain what traits there are in common, determined by the common traits of human beings; what less-general traits, distinguishing certain groups of societies, result from traits distinguishing certain races of men; and what peculiarities in each society are traceable to the peculiarities of its members. "In every case it has for its subject-matter the growth, development, structure, and functions of the social aggregate, as brought about by the mutual actions of individuals whose natures are partly like those of all men, partly like those of kindred races, partly distinctive.

These phenomena of social evolution have, of course, to be explained with due reference to the conditions each society is exposed to—the conditions furnished by its locality and by its relations to neighbouring societies. Noting this merely to prevent possible misapprehensions, the fact which here concerns us, is, not that the Social Science exhibits these or those special truths, but that, given men having certain properties, and an aggregate of such men must have certain derivative properties which form the subject-matter of a science. "

"But were we not told some pages back, that in societies, causes and effects are related in ways so involved that prevision is often impossible? Were we not warned against rashly taking measures for achieving this or that desideratum, regardless of the proofs, so abundantly supplied by the past, that agencies set in action habitually work out results never foreseen? And were not instances given of all-important changes that were due to influences from which no one would have anticipated them ? If so, how can there be a Social Science ? If Louis Napoleon could not have expected that the war he began to prevent the consolidation of Germany, would be the very means of consolidating it ; if to M. Thiers, five-and-twenty years ago, it would have seemed a dream exceeding all ordinary dreams in absurdity, that he would be fired at from his own fortifications; how in the name of wonder is it possible to formulate social phenomena in anything approaching scientific order ?"

The difficulty thus put in as strong a form as I can find for it, is that which, clearly or vaguely, rises in the minds of most to whom Sociology is proposed as a subject to be studied after scientific methods, with the expectation of reaching results having scientific certainty. Before giving to the question its special answer, let me give it a general answer.

The science of Mechanics has reached a development higher than has been reached by any but the purely-abstract sciences. Though we may not call it perfect, yet the great accuracy of the predictions which its ascertained principles enable astronomers to make, shows how near to perfection it has come ; and the achievements of the skilful artillery-officer prove that in their applications to terrestrial motions these principles yield previsions of considerable exactness. But now, taking Mechanics as the type of a highly-developed science, let us note what it enables us to predict, and what it does not enable us to predict, respecting some concrete phenomenon. Say that there is a mine to be exploded. Ask what will happen to the fragments of matter sent into the air. Then observe how much we can infer from established dynamical laws. By that common observation which precedes the more exact observations of science, we are taught that all the fragments, having risen to heights more or less various, will fall; that they will reach the ground at scattered places within a circumscribed area, and at somewhat different times. Science enables us to say more than this. From those same principles whence are inferable the path of a planet or a projectile, it deduces the truth that each fragment will describe a curve ; that all the curves, though individually different, will be specifically alike ; that (ignoring deviations caused by atmospheric resistance) they will severally be portions of ellipses so eccentric as to be indistinguishable from parabolas—such parts of them, at least, as are described after the rush of gases ceases further to accelerate the fragments. But while the principles of Mechanics help us to these certainties, we cannot learn from them anything more definite respecting the courses that will be taken by particular fragments. Whether, of the mass overlying the powder to be exploded, the part on the left will be propelled upwards in one fragment or several ? whether this piece will be shot higher than that ? whether any, and if so, which, of the projected masses will be stopped in their courses by adjacent objects they strike ?—are questions it cannot answer. *Not that there will be any want of conformity to law in these results ;* but that the data on which predictions of them are to be based, cannot be obtained.

Observe, then, that respecting a concrete phenomenon of some complexity, the most exact science enables us to make predictions that are mainly general, or only partially special. Seeing that this is so, even where the causes and effects are not greatly involved, and where the science of them is well developed, much more may we expect it to be so among the most involved causes and effects, the science of which is but rudimentary. This contrast between the generalities that admit of prevision and the specialities that do not admit of prevision, will be still more clearly seen on passing from this preliminary illustration to an illustration in which the analogy is closer.

What can we say about the future of this newly-born child ? Will it die of some disorder during infancy ? Will it survive awhile, and be carried off by scarlet fever or whooping-cough ? Will it have measles or small-pox, and succumb to one or the

other? None of these questions can be answered. Will it some
day fall down-stairs, or be run over, or set fire to its clothes;
and be killed or maimed by one or other of these accidents?
These questions also have no answers. None can tell whether in
boyhood there may come epilepsy, or St. Vitus's dance, or other
formidable affection. Looking at the child now in the nurse's
arms, none can foresee with certainty that it will be stupid or
intelligent, tractable or perverse. Equally beyond possibility of
prediction are those events which, if it survives, will occur to it
in maturity—partly caused by its own nature, and partly by
surrounding conditions. Whether there will come the success
due to skill and perseverance; whether the circumstances will
be such as to give these scope or not; whether accidents will
thwart or favour efforts; are wholly-unanswerable inquiries.
That is to say, the facts we ordinarily class as biographical, do
not admit of prevision.

If from quite special facts we turn to facts somewhat less
special which the life of this infant will present, we find, among
those that are *quasi*-biographical, a certain degree of prevision
possible. Though the unfolding of the faculties is variable
within limits, going on here precociously and there with unusual
slowness, yet there is such order in the unfolding as enables us
to say that the child will not be a mathematician or a dramatist
at three years old, will not be a psychologist by the time he is
ten, will not reach extended political conceptions while his voice
is still unbroken. Moreover, of the emotional nature we may
make certain predictions of a kindred order. Whether he will
marry or not, no one can say; but it is possible to say, if not
with certainty still with much probability, that after a certain
age an inclination to marry will arise; and though none can tell
whether he will have children, yet that, if he has, some amount
of the paternal feeling will be manifested, may be concluded as
very likely.

But now if, looking at the entire assemblage of facts that will
be presented during the life of this infant as it becomes mature,

decays, and dies, we pass over the biographical and *quasi*-biographical, as admitting of either no prevision or but imperfect prevision; we find remaining classes of facts that may be asserted beforehand: some with a high degree of probability, and some with certainty—some with great definiteness and some within moderate limits of variation. I refer to the facts of growth, development, structure, and function.

Along with that love of personalities which exalts everything inconstant in human life into a matter of interest, there goes the habit of regarding whatever is constant in human life as a matter of no interest; and so, when contemplating the future of the infant, there is a tacit ignoring of all the vital phenomena it will exhibit—phenomena that are alike knowable and important to be known. The anatomy and physiology of Man, comprehend- ing under these names not only the structures and functions of the adult, but the progressive establishment of these structures and functions during individual evolution, form the subject-matter of what every one recognizes as a science. Though there is imperfect exactness in the generalized coexistences and sequences making up this science; though general truths respect- ing structures are met by occasional exceptions in the way of malformations; though anomalies of function also occur to nega- tive absolute prediction; though there are considerable variations of the limits within which growth and structure may range, and considerable differences between the rates of functions and between the times at which functions are established; yet no one doubts that the biological phenomena presented by the human body, may be organized into a knowledge having the definiteness which constitutes it scientific, in the understood sense of that word.

If, now, any one, insisting on the incalculableness of a child's future, biographically considered, asserted that the child, there-fore, presented no subject-matter for science, ignoring altogether what we will for the moment call its anthropology (though the meaning now given to the word scarcely permits this use of it), he would fall into a conspicuous error—an error in this case made conspicuous because we are able daily to observe the difference between an account of the living body, and an account of its conduct and the events that occur to it.

The reader doubtless anticipates the analogy. What Biography is to Anthropology, History is to Sociology—History, I mean, as commonly conceived. The kind of relation which the sayings and doings that make up the ordinary account of a man's life, bear to an account of his bodily and mental evolution, structural and functional, is like the kind of relation borne by that narrative of a nation's actions and fortunes its historian gives us, to a description of its institutions, regulative and operative, and the ways in which their structures and functions have gradually established themselves. And if it is an error to say that there is no Science of Man, because the events of a man's life cannot be foreseen, it is equally an error to say that there is no Science of Society, because there can be no prevision of the occurrences which make up ordinary history.

Of course, I do not say that the parallel between an individual organism and a social organism is so close, that the distinction to be clearly drawn in the one case may be drawn with like clearness in the other. The structures and functions of the social organism are obviously far less specific, far more modifiable, far more dependent on conditions that are variable and never twice alike. All I mean is that, as in the one case so in the other, there lie underneath the phenomena of conduct, not forming subject-matter for science, certain vital phenomena, which do form subject-matter for science. Just as in the man there are structures and functions which make possible the doings his biographer tells of, so in the nation there are structures and functions which make possible the doings its historian tells of ; and in both cases it is with these structures and functions, in their origin, development, and decline, that science is concerned.

To make better the parallel, and further to explain the nature of the Social Science, we must say that the morphology and physiology of Society, instead of corresponding to the morphology and physiology of Man, correspond rather to morphology and physiology in general. Social organisms, like individual organisms, are to be arranged into classes and sub-classes—not, indeed, into classes and sub-classes having anything like the same definiteness or the same constancy, but nevertheless having likenesses and differences which justify the putting of them into major groups most-markedly contrasted, and, within these, arranging them in minor groups less-markedly contrasted. And just as Biology discovers certain general traits of development, structure, and function, holding throughout all organisms, others holding throughout certain great groups, others throughout certain sub-groups these contain ; so Sociology has to recognize truths of social development, structure, and function, that are some of them universal, some of them general, some of them special.

For, recalling the conclusion previously reached, it is manifest that in so far as human beings, considered as social units, have properties in common, the social aggregates they form will have properties in common ; that likenesses of nature holding throughout certain of the human races, will originate likenesses of nature in the nations arising out of them ; and that such peculiar traits as are possessed by the highest varieties of men, must result in distinctive characters possessed in common by the communities into which they organize themselves.

So that whether we look at the matter in the abstract or in the concrete, we reach the same conclusion. We need but to glance, on the one hand, at the varieties of uncivilized men and the structures of their tribes, and, on the other hand, at the varieties of civilized men and the structures of their nations, to see inference verified by fact. And thus recognizing, both à priori and à posteriori, these relations between the phenomena of individual human nature and the phenomena of incorporated

4

human nature, we cannot fail to see that the phenomena of incorporated human nature form the subject-matter of a science.

And now to make more definite the conception of a Social Science thus shadowed forth in a general way, let me set down a few truths of the kind indicated. Some that I propose to name are very familiar; and others I add, not because of their interest or importance, but because they are easy of exposition. The aim is simply to convey a clear idea of the nature of socio-logical truths.

Take, first, the general fact that along with social aggregation there always goes some kind of organization. In the very lowest stages, where the assemblages are very small and very incoherent, there is no established subordination—no centre of control. Chieftainships of settled kinds come only along with larger and more coherent aggregates. The evolution of a govern-mental structure having some strength and permanence, is the condition under which alone any considerable growth of a society can take place. A differentiation of the originally-homogeneous mass of units into a co-ordinating part and a co-ordinated part, is the indispensable initial step.

Along with evolution of societies in size there goes evolution of their co-ordinating centres; which, having become permanent, presently become more or less complex. In small tribes, chief-tainship, generally wanting in stability, is quite simple; but as tribes become larger by growth, or by reduction of other tribes to subjection, the co-ordinating apparatus begins to develop by the addition of subordinate governing agencies.

Simple and familiar as are these facts, we are not, therefore, to overlook their significance. That men rise into the state of social aggregation only on condition that they lapse into rela-tions of inequality in respect of power, and are made to co-operate as a whole only by the agency of a structure securing obedience, is none the less a fact in science because it is a trite fact. This is a primary common trait in social aggregates derived from a

common trait in their units. It is a truth in Sociology, com-
parable to the biological truth that the first step in the production of any living organism, high or low, is a certain differentiation
whereby a peripheral portion becomes distinguished from a
central portion. And such exceptions to this biological truth as
we find in those minute non-nucleated portions of protoplasm
that are the very lowest living things, are paralleled by those
exceptions to the sociological truth, seen in the small incoherent
assemblages formed by the very lowest types of men.

The differentiation of the regulating part and the regulated
part, is, in small primitive societies, not only imperfectly established but vague. The chief does not at first become unlike
his fellow-savages in his functions, otherwise than by exercising
greater sway. He hunts, makes his weapons, works, and manages
his private affairs, in just the same ways as the rest; while in
war he differs from other warriors only by his predominant
influence, not by ceasing to be a private soldier. And along
with this slight separation from the rest of the tribe in military
functions and industrial functions, there is only a slight separation politically : judicial action is but very feebly represented
by exercise of his personal authority in keeping order.

At a higher stage, the power of the chief being well established,
he no longer supports himself. Still he remains undistinguished
industrially from other members of the dominant class, which
has grown up while chieftainship has been getting settled ; for
he simply gets productive work done by deputy, as they do.
Nor is a further extension of his power accompanied by complete separation of the political from the industrial functions ;
for he habitually remains a regulator of production, and in many
cases a regulator of trade, presiding over acts of exchange. Of
his several controlling activities, this last is, however, the one
which he first ceases personally to carry on. Industry early
shows a tendency towards self-control, apart from the control
which the chief exercises more and more as political and military
head. The primary social differentiation which we have noted

between the regulative part and the operative part, is presently
followed by a distinction, which eventually becomes very marked,
between the internal arrangements of the two parts : the operative part slowly developing within itself agencies by which processes of production, distribution, and exchange are co-ordinated,
while co-ordination of the non-operative part continues on its
original footing.

Along with a development which renders conspicuous the
separation of the operative and regulative structures, there goes
a development within the regulative structures themselves. The
chief, at first uniting the characters of king, judge, captain, and
often priest, has his functions more and more specialized as the
evolution of the society in size and complexity advances. Though
remaining supreme judge, he does most of his judging by deputy ;
though remaining nominally head of his army, the actual leading
of it falls more and more into the hands of subordinate officers ;
though still retaining ecclesiastical supremacy, his priestly functions practically almost cease ; though in theory the maker and
administrator of the law, the actual making and administration
lapse more and more into other hands.   So that, stating the facts
broadly, out of the original co-ordinating agent having undivided
functions, there eventually develop several co-ordinating agencies
which divide these functions among them.

Each of these agencies, too, follows the same law.   Originally
simple, it step by step subdivides into many parts, and becomes
an organization, administrative, judicial, ecclesiastical, or military, having graduated classes within itself, and a more or less
distinct form of government within itself.

I will not complicate this statement by doing more than recognizing the variations that occur in cases where supreme power
does not lapse into the hands of one man (which, however, in
early stages of social evolution is an unstable modification).
And I must explain that the above general statements are to be
taken with the qualification that differences of detail are passed
over to gain brevity and clearness.   Add to which that it is

beside the purpose of the argument to carry the description beyond these first stages. But duly bearing in mind that without
here elaborating a Science of Sociology, nothing more than a
rude outline of cardinal facts can be given, enough has been said
to show that in the development of social structures, there may
be recognized certain most-general facts, certain less-general
facts, and certain facts successively more special; just as there
may be recognized general and special facts of evolution in individual organisms.

To extend, as well as to make clearer, this conception of the
Social Science, let me here set down a question which comes
within its sphere. What is the relation in a society between
structure and growth? Up to what point is structure necessary
to growth? after what point does it retard growth? at what
point does it arrest growth?

There exists in the individual organism a duplex relation
between growth and structure which it is difficult adequately to
express. Excluding the cases of a few low organisms living
under special conditions, we may properly say that great growth
is not possible without high structure. The whole animal
kingdom, throughout its invertebrate and vertebrate types, may
be cited in evidence. On the other hand, among the superior
organisms, and especially among those leading active lives,
there is a marked tendency for completion of structure to go
along with arrest of growth. While an animal of elevated type
is growing rapidly, its organs continue imperfectly developed—
the bones remain partially cartilaginous, the muscles are soft,
the brain lacks definiteness; and the details of structure throughout all parts are finished only after growth has ceased. Why
these relations are as we find them, it is not difficult to see.
That a young animal may grow, it must digest, circulate blood,
breathe, excrete waste products, and so forth; to do which it
must have tolerably-complete viscera, vascular system, &c.
That it may eventually become able to get its own food, it has
to develop gradually the needful appliances and aptitudes; to

which end it must begin with limbs, and senses, and nervous
system, that have considerable degrees of efficiency. But along
with every increment of growth achieved by the help of these
partially-developed structures, there has to go an alteration of
the structures themselves. If they were rightly adjusted to the
preceding smaller size, they are wrongly adjusted to the succeeding greater size. Hence they must be re-moulded—un-built
and re-built. Manifestly, therefore, in proportion as the previous
building has been complete, there arises a great obstacle in the
shape of un-building and re-building. The bones show
us how this difficulty is met. In the thigh-bone of a boy,
for instance, there exists between the head and the cylindrical
part of the bone, a place where the original cartilaginous state
continues; and where, by the addition of new cartilage in which
new osseous matter is deposited, the shaft of the bone is
lengthened: the like going on in an answering place at the
other end of the shaft. Complete ossification at these two
places occurs only when ‧ the bone has ceased to increase in
length; and, on considering what would have happened had the
bone been ossified from end to end before its lengthening was
complete, it will be seen how great an obstacle to growth is thus
escaped. What holds here, holds throughout the organism:
though structure up to a certain point is requisite for growth,
structure beyond that point impedes growth. How necessary is this relation we shall equally perceive in a more
complex case—say, the growth of an entire limb. There is a
certain size and proportion of parts, which a limb ordinarily has
in relation to the rest of the body. Throw upon that limb extra
function, and within moderate limits it will increase in strength
and bulk. If the extra function begins early in life, the limb
may be raised considerably above its usual size; but if the extra
function begins after maturity, the deviation is less: in neither
case, however, being great. If we consider how increase of the
limb is effected, we shall see why this is so. More active
function brings a greater local supply of blood; and, for a time,

new tissue is formed in excess of waste. But the local supply of blood is limited by the sizes of the arteries which bring it; and though, up to a certain point, increase of flow is gained by temporary dilatation of them, yet beyond that point increase can be gained only by un-building and re-building the arteries. Such alterations of arteries slowly take place—less slowly with the smaller peripheral ones, more slowly with the larger ones out of which these branch; since these have to be altered all the way back to their points of divergence from the great central blood vessels. In like manner, the channels for carrying off waste products must be re-modelled, both locally and centrally. The nerve-trunks, too, and also the centres from which they come, must be adjusted to the greater demands upon them. Nay, more; with a given visceral system, a large extra quantity of blood cannot be permanently given to one part of the body, without decreasing the quantities given to other parts; and, therefore, structural changes have to be made by which the drafting-off of blood to these other parts is diminished. Hence the great resistance to increase in the size of a limb beyond a certain moderate limit. Such increase cannot be effected without un-building and re-building not only the parts that directly minister to the limb, but, eventually, all the remoter parts. So that the bringing of structures into perfect fitness for certain requirements, immensely hinders the adaptation of them to other requirements—re-adjustments become difficult in proportion as adjustments are made complete.

How far does this law hold in the social organism? To what extent does it happen here, too, that the multiplying and elaborating of institutions, and the perfecting of arrangements for gaining immediate ends, raise impediments to the development of better institutions and to the future gaining of higher ends? Socially, as well as individually, organization is indispensable to growth: beyond a certain point there cannot be further growth without further organization. Yet there is not a little reason for suspecting that beyond this point organization is indirectly repressive—increases the obstacles to those re-adjustments required for larger growth and more perfect structure. Doubtless the aggregate we call a society is much more plastic than an individual living aggregate to which it is here compared—its type is far less fixed. Nevertheless, there is evidence that its type tends continually to become fixed, and that each addition to its structures is a step towards the fixation. A few instances will show how this is true alike of the material structures a society develops and of its institutions, political or other.

Cases, insignificant, perhaps, but quite to the point, are furnished by our appliances for locomotion. Not to dwell on the minor ones within cities, which, however, show us that existing arrangements are impediments to better arrangements, let us pass to railways. Observe how the inconveniently-narrow gauge (which, taken from that of stage-coach wheels, was itself inherited from an antecedent system of locomotion), has become an insuperable obstacle to a better gauge. Observe, also, how the type of carriage, which was derived from the body of a stage-coach (some of the early first-class carriages bearing the words "*tria juncta in uno*"), having become established, it is immensely difficult now to introduce the more convenient type later established in America; where they profited by our experience, but were not hampered by our adopted plans. The enormous capital invested in our stock of carriages cannot be sacrificed. Gradually to introduce carriages of the American type, by running them along with those of our own type, would be very difficult, because of our many partings and joinings of trains. And thus we are obliged to go on with a type that is inferior.

Take, again, our system of drainage. Urged on as it was some thirty years ago as a panacea for sundry sanitary evils, and spread as it has been by force of law through all our great towns, this system cannot now be replaced by a better system without extreme difficulty. Though, by necessitating decomposition where oxygen cannot get, and so generating chemical compounds that are unstable and poisonous, it has in many cases produced the very diseases it was to have prevented; though, by delivering the morbid products from fever-patients, &c., into a branching tube which, communicating with all houses, effectually conveys to them infecting gases that are kept out only so long as stink-traps are in good order; yet it has become almost out of the question now to adopt those methods by which the *excreta* of towns may be got rid of at once innocuously and usefully. Nay, worse—one part of our sanitary administration having insisted on a sewage-system by which Oxford, Reading, Maidenhead, Windsor, &c., pollute the water London has to drink, another part of our sanitary administration makes loud protests against the impurity of the water, which it charges with causing disease (not remarking, however, that law-enforced arrangements have produced the impurity). And now there must be a re-organization that will be immensely impeded by the existing premature organization, before we can have either pure air or pure water.

Our mercantile arrangements, again, furnish abundant illustrations teaching the same lesson. In each trade there is an established course of business; and however obvious may be some better course, the difficulties of altering the settled routine are, if not insurmountable, still very considerable. Take, for instance, the commerce of literature. In days when a letter cost a shilling and no book-post existed, there grew up an organization of wholesalers and retailers to convey books from publishers to readers: a profit being reaped by each distributing agent, primary and secondary. Now that a book may be ordered for a half-penny and sent for a few pence, the old system of distribution might be replaced by one that would diminish the cost of transfer, and lower the prices of books. But the interests of distributors practically negative the change. An advertised proposal to supply a book direct by post at a reduced rate, offends the trade; and by ignoring the book they check its sale more than its sale is otherwise furthered. And so an old organization, once very serviceable, now stands in the way of a better organization.   The commerce of literature furnishes another illustration. At a time when the reading public was small and books were dear, there grew up circulating libraries, enabling people to read books without buying them. At first few, local, and unorganized, these circulating libraries have greatly multiplied, and have become organized throughout the kingdom : the result being that the demand for library-circulation is in many cases the chief demand. This arrangement being one which makes few copies supply many readers, the price per copy must be high, to obtain an adequate return on the edition. And now reading people in general, having been brought up to the habit of getting books through libraries, usually do not think of buying the books themselves—would still get most of them through libraries even were they considerably cheapened. We are, therefore, except with works of very popular authors, prevented by the existing system of book-distribution in England from adopting the American system—a system which, not adjusting itself to few libraries but to many private purchasers, issues large editions at low prices.

Instances of another class are supplied by our educational institutions. Richly endowed, strengthened by their *prestige*, and by the bias given to those they have brought up, our colleges, public schools, and other kindred schools early founded, useful as they once were, have long been enormous impediments to a higher education. By subsidizing the old, they have starved the new. Even now they are retarding a culture better in matter and manner ; both by occupying the field, and by partially incapacitating those who pass through them for seeing what a better culture is.   Evidence of a kindred kind is offered by the educational organization developed for dealing with the masses. The struggle going on between Secularism and Denominationalism in teaching, might alone show to any one who looks for the wider meanings of facts, that a structure which has ramified throughout a society, acquired an army of salaried officials looking for personal welfare and promotion, backed by classes, ecclesiastical and political, whose ideas and interests they further, is a structure which, if not unalterable, is difficult to alter in proportion as it is highly developed.

These few examples, which might be supported by others from the military organization, the ecclesiastical organization, the legal organization, will make comprehensible the analogy I have indicated; while they make clearer the nature of the Social Science, by bringing into view one of its questions. That with social organisms, as with individual organisms, structure up to a certain point is needful for growth is obvious. That in the one case, as in the other, continued growth implies un-building and re-building of structure, which therefore becomes in so far an impediment, seems also obvious. Whether it is true in the one case, as in the other, that completion of structure involves arrest of growth, and fixes the society to the type it has then reached, is a question to be considered. Without saying anything more by way of answer, it is, I think, manifest enough that this is one belonging to an order of questions entirely overlooked by those who contemplate societies from the ordinary historical point of view; and one pertaining to that Social Science which they say does not exist.

Are there any who utter the *cui bono* criticism? Probably not a few. I think I hear from some whose mental attitude is familiar to me, the doubt whether it is worth while to ask what happens among savage tribes; in what way chiefs and medicine-men arise; how the industrial functions become separated from the political; what are the original relations of the regulative classes to one another; how far the social structure is determined by the emotional natures of individuals, how far by their ideas, how far by their environment. Busied as men of this stamp are with what they call " practical legislation " (by which they seemingly mean legislation that recognises proximate causes and effects while ignoring remote ones), they doubt whether conclusions of the kind Social Science proposes to draw, are good for much when drawn.

Something may, however, be said in defence of this study which they thus estimate. Of course, it is not to be put on the same level with those historical studies so deeply interesting to them. The supreme value of knowledge respecting the genealogies of kings, and the fates of dynasties, and the quarrels of courts, is beyond question. Whether or not the plot for the murder of Amy Robsart was contrived by Leicester himself, with Queen Elizabeth as an accomplice; and whether or not the account of the Gowrie Conspiracy, as given by King James, was true; are obviously doubts to be decided before there can be formed any rational conclusions respecting the development of our political institutions. That Friedrich I. of Prussia quarrelled with his stepmother, suspected her of trying to poison him, fled to his aunt, and when he succeeded to the Electorate, intrigued and bribed to obtain his kingship; that half-an-hour after his death his son Friedrich Wilhelm gave his courtiers notice to quit, commenced forthwith to economize his revenues, made it his great object to recruit and drill his army, and presently began to hate and bully his son—these, and facts like these about all royal families in all ages, are facts without which civilization would obviously be incomprehensible. Nor can one dispense with full knowledge of events like those of Napoleon's wars—his Italian conquests and exactions, and perfidious treatment of Venice; his expedition to Egypt, successes and massacres there, failure at Acre, and eventual retreat; his various campaigns in Germany, Spain, Russia, &c., including accounts of his strategy, tactics, victories, defeats, slaughters; for how, in the absence of such information, is it possible to judge what institutions should be advocated, and what legislative changes should be opposed ?

Still, after due attention has been paid to these indispensable matters, a little time might, perhaps, with advantage be devoted to the natural history of societies. Some guidance for political conduct would possibly be reached by asking—What is the normal course of social evolution, and how will it be affected by this or that policy? It may turn out that legislative action of no kind can be taken that is not either in agreement with, or at variance with, the processes of national growth and development as naturally going on; and that its desirableness is to be judged by this ultimate standard rather than by proximate standards. Without claiming too much, we may at any rate expect that, if there does exist an order among those structural and functional changes which societies pass through, knowledge of that order can scarcely fail to affect our judgments as to what is progressive and what retrograde—what is desirable, what is practicable, what is Utopian.

To those who think such an inquiry worthy to be pursued, will be addressed the chapters that are to follow. There are sundry considerations important to be dwelt upon, before commencing Sociology. To a clear idea of the nature of the science have to be added clear ideas of the conditions to successful study of it. These will henceforth occupy us.

CHAPTER IV.

FROM the intrinsic natures of its facts, from our own natures as observers of its facts, and from the peculiar relation in which we stand towards the facts to be observed, there arise impediments in the way of Sociology greater than those in the way of any other science.

The phenomena to be generalized are not of a directly-perceptible kind—cannot be noted by telescope and clock, like those of Astronomy; cannot be measured by dynamometer and thermometer, like those of Physics; cannot be elucidated by scales and test-papers, like those of Chemistry; are not to be got at by scalpel and microscope, like the less obvious biological phenomena; nor are to be recognized by introspection, like the phenomena Psychology deals with. They have severally to be established by putting together many details, no one of which is simple, and which are dispersed, both in Space and Time, in ways that make them difficult of access. Hence the reason why even cardinal truths in Sociology, such as the division of labour, remain long unrecognized. That in advanced societies men follow different occupations, was indeed a generalization easy to make; but that this form of social arrangement had neither been specially created, nor enacted by a king, but had grown up without forethought of any one, was a conclusion which could be reached only after many transactions of many kinds between men had been noted, remembered, and accounted for,

and only after comparisons had been made between these transactions and those taking place between men in simpler societies
and in earlier times. And when it is remembered that the data
for the inference that labour becomes specialized, are far more
accessible than the data for most other sociological inferences,
it will be seen how greatly the advance of Sociology is hindered
by the nature of its subject-matter.

The characters of men as observers, add to this first difficulty
a second that is perhaps equally great. Necessarily men take
with them into sociological inquiries, the modes of observation
and reasoning which they have been accustomed to in other
inquiries—those of them, at least, who make any inquiries worthy
to be so called. Passing over the great majority of the educated,
and limiting ourselves to the very few who consciously collect
data, compare them, and deliberately draw conclusions ; we may
see that even these have to struggle with the difficulty that the
habits of thought generated by converse with relatively-simple
phenomena, partially unfit them for converse with these highly-
complex phenomena. Faculty of every kind tends always to
adjust itself to its work. Special adjustment to one kind of work
involves more or less non-adjustment to other kinds. And hence,
intellects disciplined in dealing with less-involved classes of facts,
cannot successfully deal with this most-involved class of facts
without partially unlearning the methods they have learnt.
From the emotional nature, too, there arise great obstacles.
Scarcely any one can contemplate social arrangements and
actions with the unconcern felt when contemplating arrangements and actions of other kinds. For correct observation and
correct drawing of inferences, there needs the calmness that is
ready to recognize or to infer one truth as readily as another.
But it is next to impossible thus to deal with the truths of
Sociology. In the search for them, each is moved by feelings, more or less strong, which make him eager to find this
evidence, oblivious of that which is at variance with it, reluctant
to draw any conclusion but that already drawn. And though

perhaps one in ten among those who think, is conscious that his judgment is being warped by prejudice, yet even in him the warp is not adequately allowed for. Doubtless in nearly every field of inquiry emotion is a perturbing intruder: mostly there is some preconception, and some *amour propre* that resists disproof of it. But a peculiarity of Sociology is, that the emotions with which its facts and conclusions are regarded, have unusual strength. The personal interests are directly affected; or there is gratification or offence to sentiments that have grown out of them; or else other sentiments which have relation to the existing form of society, are excited, agreeably or disagreeably.

And here we are introduced to the third kind of difficulty—that caused by the position occupied, in respect to the phenomena to be generalized. In no other case has the inquirer to investigate the properties of an aggregate in which he is himself included. His relation towards the facts he here studies, we may figure to ourselves by comparing it to the relation between a single cell forming part of a living body, and the facts which that living body presents as a whole. Speaking generally, the citizen's life is made possible only by due performance of his function in the place he fills; and he cannot wholly free himself from the beliefs and sentiments generated by the vital connexions hence arising between himself and his society. Here, then, is a difficulty to which no other science presents anything analogous. To cut himself off in thought from all his relationships of race, and country, and citizenship—to get rid of all those interests, prejudices, likings, superstitions, generated in him by the life of his own society and his own time—to look on all the changes societies have undergone and are undergoing, without reference to nationality, or creed, or personal welfare; is what the average man cannot do at all, and what the exceptional man can do very imperfectly.

The difficulties of the Social Science, thus indicated in vague outline, have now to be described and illustrated in detail.

CHAPTER V.

OBJECTIVE DIFFICULTIES.

ALONG with much that has of late years been done towards changing primitive history into myth, and along with much that has been done towards changing once-unquestioned estimates of persons living in past ages, much has been said about the untrustworthiness of historical evidence. Hence there will be ready acceptance of the statement that one of the impediments to sociological generalization, is the uncertainty of our data. We find this uncertainty not alone in early stories, such as those about the Amazons, their practices, the particular battles with them, &c.; which are recorded and sculptured as circumstantially as they might be were the persons and events historic. We find it even in accounts of a well-known people like the New-Zealanders, who "by some . . . are said to be intelligent, cruel, and brave; by others weak, kindly, and cowardly."[1] And on remembering that between these extremes we have to deal with an enormous accumulation of conflicting statements, we cannot but feel that the task of selecting valid evidence is in this case a more arduous one than in any other case. Passing over remote illustrations, let us take an immediate one.

Last year advertisements announced the "Two-headed Nightingale," and the walls of London were placarded with a figure in which one pair of shoulders was shown to bear two heads looking the same way (I do not refer to the later placards, which partially differed from the earlier). To some, this descriptive name and answering diagram seemed sufficiently exact; for in my hearing a lady, who had been to see this compound being, referred to the placards and handbills as giving a good representation. If we suppose this lady to have repeated in a letter that which I heard her say, and if we ask what would appear the character of the evidence to one who, some fifty years hence, had before him the advertisement, the representation, and the letter, we shall see that the alleged fact would be thought by him incontestable. Only if, after weary search through all the papers and periodicals of the time, he happened to come upon a certain number of the *Lancet*, would he discover that this combination was not that of two heads on one body, but that of two individuals united back to back, with heads facing opposite ways, and severally complete in all respects, except where the parts were so fused as to form a double pelvis, containing certain pelvic viscera common to the two. Seeing, then, that about facts so simple and so easily verifiable, where no obvious motive for misrepresentations exists, we cannot count on true representations, how shall we count on true representations of social facts, which, being so diffused and so complex, are so difficult to observe, and in respect to which the perceptions are so much perverted by interests, and prepossessions, and party-feelings?

In exemplifying this difficulty, I will limit myself to cases supplied by the life of our own time : leaving it to be inferred that if, in a comparatively calm and critical age, sociological evidence is vitiated by various influences, much more must there have been vitiation of such evidence in the past, when passions ran higher and credulity was greater.

Those who have lately become conscious of certain facts are apt to suppose those facts have lately arisen. After a changed state of mind has made us observant of occurrences we were before indifferent to, there often results the belief that such occurrences are more common than they were. It happens so even with accidents and diseases. Having lamed himself, a man is surprised to find how many lame people there are ; and, becoming dyspeptic, he discovers that dyspepsia is much more frequent than he supposed when he was young. For a kindred reason he is prone to think that servants do not behave nearly so well as they did during his boyhood : not remembering that in Shakespeare's day the service obtainable was similarly reprobated in comparison with "the constant service of the antique world." In like manner, now that he has sons to establish in life, he fancies that the difficulty of getting places is much greater than it used to be.

As witnesses to social phenomena, men thus impressed by facts which did not before impress them, become perverters of evidence. Things they have suddenly recognized, they mistake for things that have suddenly come into existence ; and so are led to regard as a growing evil or good, that which is very likely a diminishing evil or good. Take an example or two.

In generations not long passed away, sobriety was the exception rather than the rule : a man who had never been drunk was a rarity. Condiments were used to create thirst; glasses were so shaped that they would not stand, but must be held till emptied ; and a man's worth was in part measured by the number of bottles he could take in. After a reaction had already diminished the evil among the upper and middle ranks, there came an open recognition of the evil ; resulting in Temperance Societies, which did their share towards further diminishing it. Then came the Teetotal Societies, more thorough-going in their views and more energetic in their acts, which have been making the evil still less. Such has been the effect of these causes, that for a long time past among the upper classes, the drinking which was once creditable has been thought a disgrace ; while among the lower classes it has greatly decreased, and come to be generally reprobated. Those, however, who, carrying on the agitations against it, have had their eyes more and more widely opened to the vice, assert or imply in their speeches and petitions that the vice is not only great but growing. Having in the course of a generation much mitigated it by their voluntary efforts, they now make themselves believe, and make others believe, that it is too gigantic to be dealt with otherwise than by repressive enactments—Maine-Laws and Permissive-Prohibitory Bills.   And, if we are to be guided by a Select Committee which has just reported, fines and imprisonments for drunkenness must be made far more severe than now, and reformatories must be established in which inebriates shall be dealt with much as criminals are dealt with.

Take, again, the case of education.   Go back far enough, and you find nobles not only incapable of reading and writing, but treating these accomplishments with contempt.   Go back not quite so far, and you find, along with a slight encouragement by authority of such learning as referred to Theology, a positive discouragement of all other learning;[2] joined with the belief that only for the clergy is learning of any kind proper.   Go back a much smaller distance, and you find in the highest classes inability to spell tolerably, joined with more or less of the feeling that good spelling was a pedantry improper for ladies—a feeling akin to that named by Shakespeare as shown by those who counted it " a meanness to write fair."   Down even to quite modern times, well-to-do farmers and others of their rank were by no means all of them able to read and write.   Education, spreading thus slowly during so many centuries, has during the last century spread with comparative rapidity.   Since Raikes commenced Sunday-schools in 1771; since Lancaster, the Quaker, in 1796 set up the first of the schools that afterwards went by his name ; since 1811, when the Church had to cease its opposition and become a competitor in educating poor children ; the strides have been enormous.   A degree of ignorance which had continued the rule during so many centuries, was made, in the course of half a century, the exception.   And then in 1834, after this unobtrusive but speedy diffusion of knowledge, there came, along with a growing consciousness of the still-remaining deficiency, the system of State-subsidies ; which, beginning with

£20,000, grew, in less than thirty years, to more than a million. Yet now, after this vast progress at an ever-increasing rate, there has come the outcry that the nation is perishing for lack of knowledge. Any one not knowing the past, and judging from the statements of those who have been urging on educational organizations, would suppose that strenuous efforts are imperative to save the people from some gulf of demoralization and crime into which ignorance is sweeping them.

How testimonies respecting objective facts are thus perverted by the subjective states of the witnesses, and how we have to be ever on our guard against this cause of vitiation in sociological evidence, may indeed be inferred from the illusions that daily mislead men in their comparisons of past with present. Returning after many years to the place of his boyhood, and finding how insignificant are the buildings he remembered as so imposing, every one discovers that in this case it was not that the past was so grand, but that his impressibility was so great and his power of criticism so small. He does not perceive, however, that the like holds generally ; and that the apparent decline in various things is really due to the widening of his experiences and the growth of a judgment no longer so easily satisfied. Hence the mass of witnesses may be under the impression that there is going on a change just the reverse of that which is really going on ; as we see, for example, in the notion current in every age, that the size and strength of .the race have been decreasing, when, as proved by bones, by mummies, by armour, and by the experiences of travellers in contact with aboriginal races, they have been on the average increasing.

Most testimony, then, on which we have to form ideas of sociological states, past and present, has to be discounted to meet this cause of error ; and the rate of discount has to be varied according to the epoch, and the subject, and the witness.

Beyond this vitiation of sociological evidence by general subjective states of the witnesses, there are vitiations due to more special subjective states. Of these, the first to be noted are of the class which foregone conclusions produce.

Extreme cases are furnished by fanatical agitators, such as members of the Anti-Tobacco Society; in the account of whose late meeting we read that "statistics of heart-disease, of insanity, of paralysis, and the diminished bulk and stature of the population of both sexes proved, according to the Report, that these diseases were attributable to the use of tobacco." But without making much of instances so glaring as this, we may find abundant proof that evidence is in most cases unconsciously distorted by the pet theories of those who give it.

Early in the history of our sanitary legislation, a leading officer of health, wishing to show the need for those measures he advocated, drew a comparison between the rate of mortality in some salubrious village (in Cumberland, I think it was) and the rate of mortality in London; and then, pointing out the marked difference, alleged that this difference was due to "preventible causes"—to causes, that is, which good sanitary administration would exclude. Ignoring the fact that the carbonic acid exhaled by nearly three millions of people and by their fires, caused in the one case a vitiation of the air which in the other case did not exist—ignoring the fact that most city-occupations are of necessity indoor, and many of them sedentary, while the occupations of village life are out-of-door and active—ignoring the fact that in many of the Londoners the activities are cerebral in a degree beyond that to which the constitution of the race is adapted, while in the villagers the activities are bodily, in a degree appropriate to the constitution of the race; he set down the whole difference in the death-rate to causes of the kind which laws and officials might get rid of.

A still more marked example of this effect of a cherished hypothesis in vitiating evidence, was once unconsciously yielded to me by another enthusiast for sanitary regulation. Producing his papers, he pointed out the great contrast between the number of deaths *per annum* in the small town near London where he lived, and the number of deaths *per annum* in a low district of London—Bermondsey, or Lambeth, or some region on the Surrey side. On this great contrast he triumphantly dilated, as proving how much could be done by good drainage, ventilation, &c. On the one hand, he passed over the fact that his suburban place was, in large measure, inhabited by a picked population— people of means, well fed and clothed, able to secure all appliances for comfort, leading regular lives, free from over-work and anxiety. On the other hand, he passed over the fact that this low region of London was, by virtue of its lowness, one out of which all citizens pecuniarily able to take care of themselves escaped if they could, and into which were thrust great numbers whose poverty excluded them from better regions—the ill-fed, the drunken, the dissolute, and others on the highway to death. Though, in the first case, the healthiness of the locality obviously drew to it an excess of persons otherwise likely to live long ; and though, in the second case, the unhealthiness of the locality made it one in which an excess of those not likely to live long were left to dwell, or hid themselves to die ; yet the whole differ- ence was put down to direct effects of pure air and impure air respectively.

Statements proceeding from witnesses whose judgments are thus warped—statements republished by careless sub-editors, and readily accepted by the uncritical who believe all they see in print, diffuse erroneous prepossessions ; which, again, tend to justify themselves by drawing the attention to confirmatory facts and away from facts that are adverse. Throughout all past time vitiations of evidence by influences of this nature have been going on in degrees varying with each people and each age ; and hence arises an additional obstacle to the obtainment of fit data.

Yet another, and perhaps stronger, distorting influence exist- ing in the medium through which facts reach us, results from the self-seeking, pecuniary or other, of those who testify. We require constantly to bear in mind that personal interests affect most of the statements on which sociological conclusions are based, and on which legislation proceeds.

Everyone knows this to be so where the evidence concerns mercantile affairs. That railway-enterprise, at first prompted by pressing needs for communication, presently came to be prompted by speculators, professional and financial; and that the estimates of cost, of traffic, of profits, &c., set forth in prospectuses were grossly misleading; many readers have been taught by bitter experience. That the gains secured by schemers who float companies have fostered an organized system which has made falsification of data a business, and which, in the case of bubble Insurance Companies, has been worked so methodically that it has become the function of a journal to expose the frauds continually repeated, are also familiar facts: reminding us how, in these directions, it is needful to look very sceptically on the allegations put before us. But there is not so distinct a consciousness that in other than business-enterprises, self-seeking is an active cause of misrepresentation.

Like the getting-up of companies, the getting-up of agitations and of societies is, to a considerable extent, a means of advancement. As in the United States politics has become a profession, into which a man enters to get an income, so here there has grown up, though happily to a smaller extent, a professional philanthropy, pursued with a view to position, or to profit, or to both. Much as the young clergyman in want of a benefice, feeling deeply the spiritual destitution of a suburb that has grown beyond churches, busies himself in raising funds to build a church, and probably does not, during his canvass, understate the evils to be remedied; so every here and there an educated man with plenty of leisure and small income, greatly impressed with some social evil to be remedied or benefit to be achieved, makes himself the nucleus to an institution, or the spur to a movement. And since his success depends mainly on the strength of the case he makes out, it is not to be expected that the evils to be dealt with will be faintly pictured, or that he will insist very strongly upon facts adverse to his plan. As I can personally testify, there are those who, having been active in getting up schemes for alleged beneficial public ends, consider themselves aggrieved when not afterwards appointed salaried officials. The recent exposure of the " Free Dormitory Association," which, as stated at a meeting of the Charity-Organization Society, was but one of a class, shows what this process may end in. And the vitiation of evidence is an inevitable concomitant. One whom I have known during his thirty years' experience of Leagues, Alliances, Unions, &c., for various purposes, writes :—" Like religious bodies, they [Associations] form creeds, and every adherent is expected to cry up the shibboleth of his party. . . . All facts are distorted to the aid of their own views, and such as cannot be distorted are suppressed." " In every association with which I have had any connection, this fraud has been practised."

The like holds in political agitations. Unfortunately, agencies established to get remedies for crying evils, are liable to become agencies maintained and worked in a considerable degree, and sometimes chiefly, for the benefit of those who reap incomes from them. An amusing instance of this was furnished, not many years ago, to a Member of Parliament who took an active part in advocating a certain radical measure which had for some years been making way, and which then seemed not unlikely to be carried. Being a member of the Association that had pushed forward this measure, he happened to step into its offices just before a debate which was expected to end in a majority for the bill, and he found the secretary and his subs in a state of consternation at the prospect of their success : feeling, as they obviously did, that their occupation was in danger.

Clearly, then, where personal interests come into play, there must be, even in men intending to be truthful, a great readiness to see the facts which it is convenient to see, and such reluctance to see opposite facts as will prevent much activity in seeking for

5

them. Hence, a large discount has mostly to be made from the evidence furnished by institutions and societies in justification of the policies they pursue or advocate. And since much of the evidence respecting both past and present social phenomena comes to us through agencies calculated thus to pervert it, there is here a further impediment to clear vision of facts.

That the reader may fully appreciate the difficulties which* these distorting influences, when combined, put in the way of getting good materials for generalization, let him contemplate a case.

All who are acquainted with such matters know that up to some ten years since, it was habitually asserted by lecturers when addressing students, and by writers in medical journals, that in our day, syphilis is a far less serious evil than it was in days gone by. Until quite recently this was a commonplace statement, called in question by no one in the profession. But just as, while a decrease of drunkenness has been going on, Temperance-fanatics have raised an increasing outcry for strenuous measures to put down drunkenness ; so, while venereal disease has been diminishing in frequency and severity, certain instrumentalities and agencies have created a belief that rigorous measures are required to check its progress. This incongruity would by itself be a sufficient proof of the extent to which, on the one side or the other, evidence must have been vitiated. What, then, shall we say of the incongruity on finding that the first of these statements has recently been repeated by many of the highest medical authorities, as one verified by their experience ? Here are some of their testimonies.

The Chairman of the late Government Commission for inquiring into the treatment and prevention of syphilis, Mr. Skey, Consulting Surgeon to St. Bartholomew's Hospital, gave evidence before a House of Lords' Committee. Referring to an article expressing the views of the Association for promoting the extension of the Contagious Diseases Acts, he said it was—

"largely overcharged," and "coloured too highly." "The disease is by no means so common or universal, I may say, as is represented in that article, . . . and I have had an opportunity since I had the summons to appear here to-day of communicating with several leading members in the profession at the College of Surgeons, and we are all of the same opinion, that the evil is not so large by any means as it is represented by the association."

Mr. John Simon, F.R.S., for thirty-five years a hospital surgeon, and now Medical Officer to the Privy Council, writes in his official capacity—

"I have not the least disposition to deny that venereal affections constitute a real and great evil for the community ; though I suspect that very exaggerated opinions are current as to their diffusion and malignity."

By the late Prof. Syme it was asserted that—

"It is now fully ascertained that the poison of the present day (true syphilis) does not give rise to the dreadful consequences which have been mentioned, when treated without mercury. . . . None of the serious effects that used to be so much dreaded ever appear, and even the trivial ones just noticed comparatively seldom present themselves. We must, therefore, conclude either that the virulence of the poison is worn out, or that the effects formerly attributed to it depended on treatment." [3]

The *British and Foreign Medico-Chirurgical Review,* which stands far higher than any other medical journal, and is friendly to the Acts as applied to military and naval stations, writes thus :—

"The majority of those who have undergone the disease, thus far [including secondary manifestations] live as long as they could otherwise have expected to live, and die of diseases with which syphilis has no more to do than the man in the moon." [4] . . . "Surely 455 persons suffering from true syphilis in one form or another, in a poor population of a million and a half [less than 1 in 3000] . . . cannot be held to be a proportion so large as to call for exceptional action on the part of any Government." [5]

Mr. Holmes Coote, F.R.C.S., Surgeon and Lecturer on Surgery at St. Bartholomew's Hospital, says—

" It is a lamentable truth that the troubles which respectable hardworking married women of the working class undergo are more trying to the health, and detrimental to the looks, than any of the irregularities of the harlot's career."

Again, it is stated by Mr. Byrne, Surgeon to the Dublin Lock Hospital, that " there is not nearly so much syphilis as there used to be ; " and, after describing some of the serious results that were once common, he adds :—" You will not see such a case for years—a fact that no medical man can have failed to remark." Mr. W. Burns Thompson, F.R.C.S., for ten years head of the Edinburgh Dispensary, testifies as follows :—

" I have had good opportunities of knowing the prevailing diseases, and I can only say that the representations given by the advocates of these Acts are to me perfectly unintelligible ; they seem to me to be gross exaggerations."

Mr. Surgeon-Major Wyatt, of the Coldstream Guards, when examined by the Lords' Committee, stated that he quite concurred with Mr. Skey. Answering question 700, he said :—

" The class of syphilitic diseases which we see are of a very mild character ; and, in fact, none of the ravages which used formerly to be committed on the appearance and aspect of the men are now to be seen. . . . It is an undoubted fact that in this country and in France the character of the disease is much diminished in intensity.—*Question* 708 : I understand you to say, that in your opinion the venereal disease has generally, independent of the Act, become more mitigated, and of a milder type ? *Answer:* Yes ; that is the experience of all surgeons, both civil and military."

Dr. Dr, uittPresident of the Association of the Medical Officers of Health for London, affirmed at one of its meetings—

" that, speaking from thirty-nine years' experience, he was in a position to say that cases of syphilis in London were rare among the middle and better classes, and soon got over."

Even Mr. Acton, a specialist to whom more than to any

other man the Acts are due, admitted before the Lords' Committee that "the disease is milder than it was formerly."

And then, most important of all, is the testimony of Mr. Jonathan Hutchinson, who is recognized as the highest authority on inherited syphilis, and to whose discoveries, indeed, the identifications of syphilitic taint are mainly due. Though thus under a natural bias rather to over-estimate than under-estimate the amount of inherited syphilis, Mr. Hutchinson, while editor of the *British Medical Journal,* wrote:—

"Although there is an impression to the contrary, yet recent discoveries and more accurate investigations, so far from extending the domain of syphilis as a cause of chronic disease, have decidedly tended to limit it . . . . although we have admitted as positively syphilitic certain maladies of a definite kind not formerly recognized, we have · excluded a far larger number which were once under suspicion. . . . . We can identify now the subject of severe hereditary taint by his teeth and physiognomy ; but those who believe most firmly in the value of these signs, believe also *that they are not displayed by one in five thousand of our population.* [6]

Like testimony is given by continental surgeons, among whom it was long ago said by Ambrose Paré, that the disease "is evidently becoming milder every day ;" and by Auzias Turenne, that "it is on the wane all over Europe." Astruc and Diday concur in this statement. And the latest authority on syphilis, Lancereaux, whose work is so highly valued that it has been translated by the Sydenham Society, asserts that:—

"In these cases, which are far from being rare, syphilis is but an abortive disease ; slight and benignant, it does not leave behind any troublesome trace of its passage. It is impossible to lay too much stress upon this point. At the present day especially, when syphilis still inspires exaggerated fears, it should be known that this disease becomes dissipated completely in a great number of cases after the cessation of the cutaneous eruptions, and perhaps sometimes even with the primary lesion." [7]

It will, perhaps, be remarked that these testimonies of medical men who, by their generally high position, or their lengthened experience, or their special experience, are so well qualified to judge, are selected testimonies; and against them will be set the testimonies of Sir James Paget, Sir W. Jenner, and Mr. Prescott Hewett, who regard the evil as a very grave one. Possibly there will be quoted in reply an authoritative State-document, which, referring to the views of the three gentle-men just named as having "the emphatic concurrence of numerous practitioners," says that they "are hardly answered by a few isolated opinions that the evil has been exaggerated"—a somewhat inadequate description of the above-quoted testi-monies, considering not only the general weight of the names, but also the weight of sundry of them as those of specialists. To gather accurately the *consensus* of medical opinion would be impracticable without polling the whole body of physicians and surgeons; but we have a means of judging which view most truly meets with "the emphatic concurrence of numerous prac-titioners": that, namely, of taking a local group of medical men. Out of fifty-eight physicians and surgeons residing in Nottingham and its suburbs, fifty-four have put their signatures to a public statement that syphilis is "very much diminished in frequency, and so much milder in form that we can scarcely recognize it as the disease described by our forefathers." And among these are the medical men occupying nearly all the official medical positions in the town—Senior Physician to the General Hospital, Honorary Surgeon ditto, Surgeons to the Jail, to the, General Dispensary, to the Free Hospital, to the Union Hospital, to the Lock Hospital (four in number), Medical Officers to the Board of Health, to the Union, to the County Asylum, &c., &c. Even while I write there comes to me kindred evidence in the shape of a letter published in the *British Medical Journal* for 20th July, 1872, by Dr. Carter, Honorary Physician to the Liverpool Southern Hospital, who states that, after several debates at the Liverpool Medical Institution, "a form of petition strongly condemnatory of the Acts was written out by myself, and . . . . in a few days one hundred and eight signatures [of medical men] were obtained." Meanwhile, he adds, "earnest efforts were being made by a number of gentlemen to procure medical signatures to the petition in favour of the Acts known as the 'London Memorial,'—efforts which resulted in twenty-nine signatures only."

Yet notwithstanding this testimony, great in quantity and much of it of the highest quality, it has been possible so to present the evidence as to produce in the public mind, and in the Legislature, the impression that peremptory measures for dealing with a spreading pest are indispensable. As lately writes a Member of Parliament,—"We were assured, on what appeared unexceptionable testimony, that a terrible constitutional disease was undermining the health and vigour of the nation, and especially destroying innocent women and children."

And then note the startling circumstance that while so erroneous a conception of the facts may be spread abroad, there may, by the consequent alarm, be produced a blindness to facts of the most unquestionable kind, established by the ever-accumulating experiences of successive generations. Until quite recently, our forms of judicial procedure embodied the principle that some overt injury must be committed before legal instrumentalities can be brought into play; and conformity to this principle was in past times gradually brought about by efforts to avoid the terrific evils that otherwise arose. As a Professor of Jurisprudence reminds us, "the object of the whole complicated system of checks and guards provided by English law, and secured by a long train of constitutional conflicts, has been to prevent an innocent man being even momentarily treated as a thief, a murderer, or other criminal, on the mere alleged or real suspicion of a policeman." Yet now, in the state of groundless fright that has been got up, "the concern hitherto exhibited by the Legislature for the personal liberty of the meanest citizen has been needlessly and recklessly lost sight of."[8] It is an à priori inference from human nature that irresponsible power is sure, on the average of cases, to be grossly abused. The histories of all nations, through all times, teem with proofs that irresponsible power has been grossly abused. The growth of representative governments is the growth of arrangements made to prevent the gross abuse of irresponsible power. Each of our political struggles, ending in a further development of free institutions, has been made to put an end to some particular gross abuse of irresponsible power. Yet the facts thrust upon us by our daily experiences of men, verifying the experiences of the whole human race throughout the past, are now tacitly denied; and it is tacitly asserted that irresponsible power will not be grossly abused. And all because of a manufactured panic about a decreasing disease, which kills not one-fifteenth of the number killed by scarlet fever, and which takes ten years to destroy as many as diarrhœa destroys in one year.

See, then, what we have to guard against in collecting socio-logical data—even data concerning the present, and, still more, data concerning the past. For testimonies that come down to us respecting bygone social states, political, religious, judicial, physical, moral, &c., and respecting the actions of particular causes on those social states, have been liable to perversions not simply as great, but greater; since while the regard for truth was less, there was more readiness to accept unproved statements.

Even where deliberate measures are taken to obtain valid evidence on any political or social question raised, by summon-ing witnesses of all classes and interests, there is difficulty in getting at the truth; because the circumstances of the inquiry tend of themselves to bring into sight some kinds of evidence, and to keep out of sight other kinds. In illustration may be quoted the following statement of Lord Lincoln on making his motion concerning the enclosures of commons:—

" This I know, that in nineteen cases out of twenty, committees sitting in this House on private bills neglected the rights of the poor. I do not say that they wilfully neglected those rights—far from it;

but this I affirm, that they were neglected in consequence of the committees being permitted to remain in ignorance of the rights of the poor man, because by reason of his very poverty he is unable to come up to London to fee counsel, to procure witnesses, and to urge his claims before a committee of this House."—*Hansard,* 1 May, 1845.[9]

Many influences of a different order, but similarly tending to exclude particular classes of facts pertinent to an inquiry, come into play. Given a question at issue, and it will very probably happen that witnesses on the one side may, by evidence of a certain nature, endanger a system on which they depend for the whole or for part of their livelihood; and by evidence of an opposite nature may preserve it. By one kind of testimony they may offend their superiors and risk their promotion: doing the reverse by another kind. Moreover, witnesses not thus directly interested are liable to be indirectly swayed by the thought that to name certain facts they know will bring on them the ill-will of important persons in their locality—a serious consideration in a provincial town. And while such influences strongly tend to bring out evidence, say in support of some established organization, there may very possibly, and, indeed, very probably, be no organized adverse interest with abundant resources which busies itself to bring out a contrary class of facts—no occupation in danger, no promotion to be had, no applause to be gained, no odium to be escaped. The reverse may happen: there may be positive sacrifices serious in amount to be made before such contrary class of facts can be brought to light. And thus it may result that, perfectly open and fair as the inquiry seems, the circumstances will insure a one-sided representation.

A familiar optical illusion well illustrates the nature of these illusions which often deceive sociological inquirers. When standing by a lake-side in the moonlight, you see stretching over the rippled surface towards the moon, a bar of light which, as shown by its nearer part, consists of flashes from the sides of

separate wavelets. You walk, and the bar of light seems to go
with you. There are, even among the educated classes, many
who suppose that this bar of light has an objective existence,
and who believe that it really moves as the observer moves—
occasionally, indeed, as I can testify, expressing surprise at the
fact. But, apart from the observer there exists no such bar of
light; nor when the observer moves is there any movement of
this line of glittering wavelets. All over the dark part of the
surface the undulations are just as bright with moonlight as
those he sees; but the light reflected from them does not reach
his eyes. Thus, though there seems to be a lighting of some
wavelets and not of the rest, and though, as the observer moves,
other wavelets seem to become lighted that were not lighted
before, yet both these are utterly false seemings. The simple
fact is, that his position in relation to certain wavelets brings
into view their reflections of the moon's light, while it keeps out
of view the like reflections from all other wavelets.

Sociological evidence is largely vitiated by illusions thus
caused. Habitually the relations of observers to the facts are
such as make visible the special, and exceptional, and sensational,
and leave invisible the common-place and uninteresting, which
form the great body of the facts. And this, which is a general
cause of deceptive appearances, is variously aided by those more
special causes above indicated; which conspire to make the
media through which the facts are seen, transparent in respect
of some and opaque in respect of others.

Again, very serious perversions of evidence result from the
unconscious confounding of observation with inference. Everywhere, a fertile source of error is the putting down as something
perceived what is really a conclusion drawn from something perceived; and this is a more than usually fertile source of error in
Sociology. Here is an instance.

A few years ago Dr. Stark published the results of comparisons he had made between the rates of mortality among the

married and among the celibate: showing, as it seemed, the greater healthfulness of married life. Some criticisms made on his argument did not seriously shake it; and he has been since referred to as having conclusively proved the alleged relation. More recently I have seen quoted from the *Medical Press and Circular*, the following summary of results supposed to tell the same tale :—

"M. Bertillon has made a communication on this subject ('The Influence of Marriage') to the Brussels Academy of Medicine, which has been published in the *Revue Scientifique*. From 25 to 30 years of age the mortality per 1000 in France amounts to 6·2 in married men, 10·2 in bachelors, and 21·8 in widows. In Brussels the mortality of married women is 9 per 1000, girls the same, and widows as high as 16·9. In Belgium from 7 per 1000 among married men, the number rises to 8·5 in bachelors, and 24·6 in widows. The proportion is the same in Holland. From 8·2 in married men, it rises to 11·7 in bachelors, and 16·9 in widowers, or 12·8 among married women, 8·5 in spinsters, and 13·8 in widows. The result of all the calculations is that from 25 to 30 years of age the mortality per 1000 is 4 in married men, 10·4 in bachelors, and 22 in widows. This beneficial influence of marriage is manifested at all ages, being always more strongly marked in men than in women."

will not dwell on the fallacy of the above conclusions as referring to the relative mortality of widows—a fallacy sufficiently obvious to any one who thinks awhile. I will confine myself to the less-conspicuous fallacy in the comparison between the mortalities of married and celibate, fallen into by M. Bertillon as well as by Dr. Stark. Clearly as their figures seem to furnish proof of some direct causal relation between marriage and longevity, they really furnish no proof whatever. There may be such a relation; but the evidence assigned forms no warrant for inferring it.

We have but to consider the circumstances which in many cases determine marriage, and those which in other cases prevent marriage, to see that the connexion which the figures apparently imply is not the real connexion. Where attachments exist what most frequently decides the question for or against marriage? The possession of adequate means. Though some improvidently marry without means, yet it is undeniable that in many instances marriage is delayed by the man, or forbidden by the parents, or not assented to by the woman, until there is reasonable evidence of ability to meet the responsibilities. Now of men whose marriages depend on getting the needful incomes, which are the most likely to get the needful incomes? The best, physically and mentally—the strong, the intellectually capable, the morally well-balanced. Often bodily vigour achieves a success, and therefore a revenue, which bodily weakness, unable to bear the stress of competition, cannot achieve. Often superior intelligence brings promotion and increase of salary, while stupidity lags behind in ill-paid posts. Often caution, self-control, and a far-seeing sacrifice of present to future, secure remunerative offices that are never given to the impulsive or the reckless. But what are the effects of bodily vigour, of intelligence, of prudence, on longevity; when compared with the effects of feebleness, of stupidity, of deficient self-control? Obviously, the first further the maintenance of life, and the second tend towards premature death. That is, the qualities which, on the average of cases, give a man an advantage in gaining the means of marrying, are the qualities which make him likely to be a long-liver; and conversely.

There is even a more direct relation of the same general nature. In all creatures of high type, it is only when individual growth and development are nearly complete, that the production of new individuals becomes possible; and the power of producing and bringing up new individuals, is measured by the amount of vital power in excess of that needful for self-maintenance. The reproductive instincts, and all their accompanying emotions, become dominant when the demands for individual evolution are diminishing, and there is arising a surplus of energy which makes possible the rearing of offspring as well as the preservation of self; and, speaking generally, these instincts and emotions are strong in proportion as this surplus vital energy is great. But to have a large surplus of vital energy implies a good organization—an organization likely to last long. So that, in fact, the superiority of *physique* which is accompanied by strength of the instincts and emotions causing marriage, is a superiority of *physique* also conducive to longevity.

One further influence tells in the same direction. Marriage is not altogether determined by the desires of men; it is determined in part by the preferences of women. Other things equal, women are attracted towards men of power—physical, emotional, intellectual; and obviously their freedom of choice leads them in many cases to refuse inferior samples of men: especially the malformed, the diseased, and those who are ill-developed, physically and mentally. So that, in so far as marriage is determined by female selection, the average result on men is that while the best easily get wives, a certain proportion of the worst are left without wives. This influence, therefore, joins in bringing into the ranks of married men those most likely to be long-lived, and keeping in bachelorhood those least likely to be long-lived.

In three ways, then, does that superiority of organization which conduces to long life, also conduce to marriage. It is normally accompanied by a predominance of the instincts and emotions prompting marriage; there goes along with it that power which can secure the means of making marriage practicable; and it increases the probability of success in courtship. The figures given afford no proof that marriage and longevity are cause and consequence; but they simply verify the inference which might be drawn à *priori*, that marriage and longevity are concomitant results of the same cause.

This striking instance of the way in which inference may be mistaken for fact, will serve as a warning against another of the dangers that await us in dealing with sociological data. Statistics having shown that married men live longer than single men, it seems an irresistible implication that married life is healthier than single life. And yet we see that the implication is not at all irresistible: though such a connexion may exist, it is not demonstrated by the evidence assigned. Judge, then, how difficult it must be, among social phenomena that have more entangled dependencies, to distinguish between the seeming relations and the real relations.

Once more, we are liable to be led away by superficial, trivial facts, from the deep-seated and really-important facts they indicate. Always the details of social life, the interesting events, the curious things which serve for gossip, will, if we allow them, hide from us the vital connexions and the vital actions underneath. Every social phenomenon results from an immense aggregate of general and special causes; and we may either take the phenomenon itself as intrinsically momentous, or may take it along with other phenomena, as indicating some inconspicuous truth of real significance. Let us contrast the two courses.

Some months ago a correspondent of the *Times*, writing from Calcutta, said:—

" The Calcutta University examinations of any year would supply curious material for reflection on the value of our educational systems. The prose test in the entrance examination this year includes *Ivanhoe*. Here are a few of the answers which I have picked up. The spelling is bad, but that I have not cared to give :—

" Question :—' Dapper man ? ' (Answer 1.) ' Man of superfluous knowledge.' (A. 2.) ' Mad.' (Q.) ' Democrat ? ' (A. 1.) ' Petticoat Government.' (A. 2.) ' Witchcraft.' (A. 3.) ' Half turning of the horse.' (Q.) ' Babylonish jargon ? ' (A. 1.) ' A vessel made at Babylon.' (A. 2.) ' A kind of drink made at Jerusalem.' (A. 3.) ' A kind of coat worn by Babylonians.' (Q.) ' Lay brother ? ' (A. 1.) ' A bishop.' (A. 2.) ' A step-brother.' (A. 3.) ' A scholar of the same godfather.' (Q.) ' Sumpter mule ? ' (A.) ' A stubborn Jew.' (Q.) ' Bilious-looking fellow ? ' (A. 1.) ' A man of strict character.' (A. 2.) ' A person having a nose like the bill of an eagle.' (Q.) ' Cloister ? ' (A.) ' A kind of shell.' (Q.) ' Tavern politicians ? ' (A. 1.) ' Politicians in charge of the alehouse.' (A. 2.) ' Mere vulgars.'

(A. 3.) 'Managers of the priestly church.' (Q.) 'A pair of cast-off galli-
gaskins?' (A.) 'Two gallons of wine.'

The fact here drawn attention to as significant, is, that these
Hindu youths, during their matriculation examination, betrayed
so much ignorance of the meaning of words and expressions
contained in an English work they had read. And the intended
implication appears to be that they were proved unfit to begin
their college careers. If, now, instead of accepting that which
is presented to us, we look a little below it, that which may
strike us is the amazing folly of an examiner who proposes to
test the fitness of youths for commencing their higher education,
by seeing how much they know of the technical terms, cant-
phrases, slang, and even extinct slang, talked by the people of
another nation. Instead of the unfitness of the boys, which is
pointed out to us, we may see rather the unfitness of those concerned in educating them.

If, again, not dwelling on the particular fact underlying the
one offered to our notice, we consider it along with others of the
same class, our attention is arrested by the general fact that
examiners, and especially those appointed under recent systems
of administration, habitually put questions of which a large proportion are utterly inappropriate. As I learn from his son, one
of our judges not long since found himself unable to answer an
examination-paper that had been laid before law-students. A
well-known Greek scholar, editor of a Greek play, who was appointed examiner, found that the examination-paper set by his
predecessor was too difficult for him. Mr. Froude, in his in-
augural address at St. Andrews, describing a paper set by an
examiner in English history, said, "I could myself have answered
two questions out of a dozen." And I learn from Mr. G. H. Lewes
that he could not give replies to the questions on English literature which the Civil Service examiners had put to his son.
Joining which testimonies with kindred ones coming from
students and professors on all sides, we find the really-noteworthy

thing to be that examiners, instead of setting questions fit for students, set questions which make manifest their own extensive learning. Especially if they are young, and have reputations to make or to justify, they seize the occasion for displaying their erudition, regardless of the interests of those they examine.

If we look through this more significant and general fact for the still deeper fact it grows out of, there arises before us the question—Who examines the examiners? How happens it that men competent in their special knowledge, but so incompetent in their general judgment, should occupy the places they do? This prevailing faultiness of the examiners shows conclusively that the administration is faulty at its centre. Somewhere or other, the power of ultimate decision is exercised by those who are unfit to exercise it. If the examiners of the examiners were set to fill up an examination-paper which had for its subject the right conduct of examinations, and the proper qualifications for examiners, there would come out very unsatisfactory answers.

Having seen through the small details and the wider facts down to these deeper facts, we may, on contemplating them, perceive that these, too, are not the deepest or most significant. It becomes clear that those having supreme authority suppose, as men in general do, that the sole essential thing for a teacher or examiner is complete knowledge of that which he has to teach, or respecting which he has to examine. Whereas a co-essential thing is a knowledge of Psychology; and especially that part of Psychology which deals with the evolution of the faculties. Unless, either by special study or by daily observation and quick insight, he has gained an approximately-true conception of how minds perceive, and reflect, and generalize, and by what processes their ideas grow from concrete to abstract, and from simple to complex, no one is competent to give lessons that will effectually teach, or to ask questions which will effectually measure the efficiency of teaching. Further, it becomes manifest that, in common with the public, those in authority assume that the goodness of education is to be tested by the quantity of knowledge acquired. Whereas it is to be much more truly tested by the capacity for using knowledge—by the extent to which the knowledge gained has been turned into faculty, so as to be available both for the purposes of life and for the purposes of independent investigation. Though there is a growing consciousness that a mass of unorganized information is, after all, of little value, and that there is more value in less information well-organized, yet the significant truth is that this consciousness has not got itself officially embodied ; and that our educational administration is working, and will long continue to work, in pursuance of a crude and out-worn belief.

As here, then, so in other cases meeting us in the present and all through the past, we have to contend with the difficulty that the greater part of the evidence supplied to us as of chief interest and importance, is of value only for what it indicates. We have to resist the temptation to dwell on those trivialities which make up nine-tenths of our records and histories; and which are worthy of attention solely because of the things they indirectly imply or the things tacitly asserted along with them.

Beyond those vitiations of evidence due to random observations, to the subjective states of the observers, to their enthusiasms, or prepossessions, or self-interests—beyond those arising from the general tendency to set down as a fact observed what is really an inference from an observation, and also those arising from the general tendency to omit the dissection by which small surface results are traced to large interior causes ; there come those vitiations of evidence consequent on its distribution in Space. Of whatever class, political, moral, religious, commercial, &c., may be the phenomena we have to consider, a society presents them in so diffused and multitudinous a way, and under such various relations to us, that the conceptions we can frame are at best extremely inadequate.

Consider how impossible it is truly to conceive so relatively-simple a thing as the territory which a society covers. Even by the aid of maps, geographical and geological, slowly elaborated by multitudes of surveyors—even by the aid of descriptions of towns, counties, mountainous and rural districts—even by the aid of such personal examinations as we have made here and there in journeys during life; we can reach nothing approaching to a true idea of the actual surface—arable, grass-covered, wooded; flat, undulating, rocky; drained by rills, brooks, and slow rivers; sprinkled with cottages, farms, villas, cities. Imagination simply rambles hither and thither, and fails utterly to frame an adequate thought of the whole. How then shall we frame an adequate thought of a diffused moral feeling, of an intellectual state, of a commercial activity, pervading this territory; unaided by maps, and aided only by the careless statements of careless observers? Respecting most of the phenomena, as displayed by a nation at large, only dim apprehensions are possible; and how untrustworthy they are, is shown by every parliamentary debate, by every day's newspapers, and by every evening's conversations; which severally disclose quite conflicting estimates.

See how various are the statements made respecting any nation in its character and actions by each traveller visiting it. There is a story, apt if not true, of a Frenchman who, having been three weeks here, proposed to write a book on England; who, after three months, found that he was not quite ready; and who, after three years, concluded that he knew nothing about it. And every one who looks back and compares his early impressions respecting states of things in his own society with the impressions he now has, will see how erroneous were the beliefs once so decided, and how probable it is that even his revised beliefs are but partially true. On remembering how wrong he was in his pre-conceptions of the people and the life in some un-visited part of the kingdom—on remembering how different from those he had imagined, were the characters he actually found in certain alien classes and along with certain alien creeds;

he will see how greatly this wide diffusion of social facts impedes true appreciation of them.

Moreover, there are illusions consequent on what we may call moral perspective, which we do not habitually correct in thought, as we correct in perception the illusions of physical perspective. A small object close to, occupies a larger visual area than a mountain afar off; but here our well-organized experiences enable us instantly to rectify a false inference suggested by the subtended angles. No such prompt rectification for the perspective is made in sociological observations. A small event next door, producing a larger impression than a great event in another country, is over-estimated. Conclusions prematurely drawn from social experiences daily occurring around us, are difficult to displace by clear proofs that elsewhere wider social experiences point to opposite conclusions.

A further great difficulty to which we are thus introduced is, that the comparisons by which alone we can finally establish relations of cause and effect among social phenomena, can rarely be made between cases in all respects fit for comparison. Every society differs specifically, if not generically, from every other. Hence it is a peculiarity of the Social Science that parallels drawn between different societies, do not afford grounds for decided conclusions—will not, for instance, show us with certainty, what is an essential phenomenon in a given society and what is a non-essential one. Biology deals with numerous individuals of a species, and with many species of a genus, and by comparing them can see what traits are specifically constant and what generically constant; and the like holds more or less with the other concrete sciences. But comparisons between societies, among which we may almost say that each individual is a species by itself, yield much less definite results : the necessary characters are not thus readily distinguishable from the accidental characters.

So that even supposing we have perfectly-valid data for our sociological generalizations, there still lies before us the difficulty that these data are, in many cases, so multitudinous and diffused that we cannot adequately consolidate them into true conceptions; the additional difficulty that the moral perspective under which they are presented, can scarcely ever be so allowed for as to secure true ideas of proportions; and the further difficulty that comparisons of our vague and incorrect conceptions concerning one society with our kindred conceptions concerning another society, have always to be taken with the qualification that the comparisons are only partially justifiable, because the compared things are only partially alike in their other traits.

An objective difficulty, even greater still, which the Social Science presents, arises from the distribution of its facts in Time. Those who look on a society as either supernaturally created or created by Acts of Parliament, and who consequently consider successive stages of its existence as having no necessary dependence on one another, will not be deterred from drawing political conclusions from passing facts, by a consciousness of the slow genesis of social phenomena. But those who have risen to the belief that societies are evolved in structure and function, as in growth, will be made to hesitate on contemplating the long unfolding through which early causes work out late results.

Even true appreciation of the successive facts which an individual life presents, is generally hindered by inability to grasp the gradual processes by which ultimate effects are produced; as we may see in the foolish mother who, yielding to her perverse child, gains the immediate benefit of peace, and cannot foresee the evil of chronic dissension which her policy will hereafter bring about. And in the life of a nation, which, if of high type, lasts at least a hundred individual lives, correct estimation of results is still more hindered by this immense duration of the actions through which antecedents bring their consequents. In judging of political good and evil, the average legislator thinks much after the manner of the mother dealing with the spoiled child : if a course is productive of immediate benefit, that is considered sufficient justification. Quite recently an inquiry has been made into the results of an administration which had been in action some five years only, with the tacit assumption that supposing the results were proved good, the administration would be justified.

And yet to those who look into the records of the past not to revel in narratives of battles or to gloat over court-scandals, but to find how institutions and laws have arisen and how they have worked, there is no truth more obvious than that generation after generation must pass before the outcome of an action that has been set up can be seen. Take the example furnished us by our Poor Laws. When villeinage had passed away and serfs were no longer maintained by their owners—when, in the absence of any one to control and take care of serfs, there arose an increasing class of mendicants and " sturdy rogues, preferring robbery to labour "—when, in Richard the Second's time, authority over such was given to justices and sheriffs, out of which there presently grew the binding of servants, labourers, and beggars, to their respective localities—when, to meet the case of beggars, " impotent to serve," the people of the districts in which they were found, were made in some measure responsible for them (so re-introducing in a more general form the feudal arrangement of attachment to the soil, and reciprocal claim on the soil) ; it was not suspected that the foundations were laid for a system which would, in after times, bring about a demoralization threatening general ruin. When, in subsequent centuries, to meet the evils of again-increasing vagrancy which punishment failed to repress, these measures, re-enacted with modifications, ended in making the people of each parish chargeable with the maintenance of their poor, while it re-established the severest penalties on vagabondage, even to death without benefit of clergy, no one ever anticipated that while the penal elements of this legislation would by and by become so mollified as to have little practical effect in checking idleness, the accompanying arrangements would eventually take such forms as immensely to encourage idleness. Neither legislators nor others foresaw that in 230 years the poor's-rate, having grown to seven millions, would become a public spoil of which we read that—

" The ignorant believed it an inexhaustible fund which belonged to them. To obtain their share the brutal bullied the administrators, the profligate exhibited their bastards which must be fed, the idle folded their arms and waited till they got it ; ignorant boys and girls married upon it ; poachers, thieves, and prostitutes, extorted it by intimidation ; country justices lavished it for popularity, and guardians for convenience. . . . Better men sank down among the worse : the rate-paying cottager, after a vain struggle, went to the pay-table to seek relief ; the modest girl might starve while her bolder neighbour received 1s. 6d. per week for every illegitimate child."

As sequences of the law of Elizabeth, no one imagined that, in rural districts, farmers, becoming chief administrators, would pay part of their men's wages out of the rates (so taxing the rest of the ratepayers for the cultivation of their fields); and that this abnormal relation of master and man would entail bad cultivation. No one imagined that, to escape poor's-rates, landlords would avoid building cottages, and would even clear cottages away : so causing over-crowding, with consequent evils, bodily and mental. No one imagined that workhouses, so called, would become places for idling in; and places where married couples would display their " elective affinities " time after time.[10] Yet these, and detrimental results which it would take pages to enumerate, culminating in that general result most detrimental of all—helping the worthless to multiply at the expense of the worthy—finally came out of measures taken ages ago merely to mitigate certain immediate evils.

Is it not obvious, then, that only in the course of those long periods required to mould national characters and habits and sentiments, will the truly-important results of a public policy show themselves ? Let us consider the question a little further.

In a society living, growing, changing, every new factor becomes a permanent force ; modifying more or less the direction
of movement determined by the aggregate of forces. Never
simple and direct, but, by the co-operation of so many causes,
made irregular, involved, and always rhythmical, the course of
social change cannot be judged of in its general direction by
inspecting any small portion of it. Each action will inevitably
be followed, after a while, by some direct or indirect reaction,
and this again by a re-reaction ; and until the successive effects
have shown themselves, no one can say how the total motion
will be modified. You must compare positions at great distances
from one another in time, before you can perceive rightly whither
things are tending. Even so simple a thing as a curve of single
curvature cannot have its nature determined unless there is a
considerable length of it. See here these four points close
together. The curve passing through them may be a circle, an
ellipse, a parabola, an hyperbola ; or it may be a catenarian, a
cycloid, a spiral. Let the points be further apart, and it becomes
possible to form some opinion of the nature of the curve—it is
obviously not a circle. Let them be more remote still, and it
may be seen that it is neither an ellipse nor a parabola. And
when the distances are relatively great, the mathematician can
say with certainty what curve alone will pass through them all.
Surely, then, in such complex and slowly-evolving movements as
those of a nation's life, all the smaller and greater rhythms of
which fall within certain general directions, it is impossible that
such general directions can be traced by looking at stages that
are close together—it is impossible that the effect wrought on
any general direction by some additional force, can be truly com-
puted from observations extending over but a few years, or but a
few generations.

For, in the case of these most-involved of all movements, there
is the difficulty, paralleled in no other movements (being only
approached in those of individual evolution), that each new
factor, besides modifying in an immediate way the course of a

movement, modifies it also in a remote way, by changing the amounts and directions of all other factors. A fresh influence brought into play on a society, not only affects its members directly in their acts, but also indirectly in their characters. Continuing to work on their characters generation after generation, and altering by inheritance the feelings which they bring into social life at large, this influence alters the intensities and bearings of all other influences throughout the society. By slowly initiating modifications of nature, it brings into play forces of many kinds, incalculable in their strengths and tendencies, that act without regard to the original influence, and may cause quite opposite effects.

Fully to exhibit this objective difficulty, and to show more clearly still how important it is to take as data for sociological conclusions, not the brief sequences, but the sequences that extend over centuries or are traceable throughout civilization, let us draw a lesson from a trait which all regulative agencies in all nations have displayed.

The original meaning of human sacrifices, otherwise tolerably clear, becomes quite clear on finding that where cannibalism is still rampant, and where the largest consumers of human flesh are the chiefs, these chiefs, undergoing apotheosis when they die, are believed thereafter to feed on the souls of the departed—the souls being regarded as duplicates equally material with the bodies they belong to. And should any doubt remain, it must be dissipated by the accounts we have of the ancient Mexicans, whose priests, when war had not lately furnished a victim, complained to the king that the god was hungry; and who, when a victim was sacrificed, offered his heart to the idol (bathing its lips with his blood, and even putting portions of the heart into his mouth), and then cooked and ate the rest of the body themselves. Here the fact to which attention is drawn, and which various civilizations show us, is that the sacrificing of prisoners or others, once a general usage among cannibal ancestry, continues as an ecclesiastical usage long after having died out in the ordinary life of a society. Two facts, closely allied with this fact, have like general implications. Cutting implements of stone remain in use for sacrificial purposes when implements of bronze, and even of iron, are used for all other purposes: the Hebrews are commanded in Deuteronomy to build altars of stone without using iron tools; the high priest of Jupiter at Rome was shaved with a bronze knife. Further, the primitive method of obtaining fire by the friction of pieces of wood, survives in religious ceremonies ages after its abandonment in the household ; and even now, among the Hindus, the flame for the altar is kindled by the " fire drill." These are striking instances of the pertinacity with which the oldest part of the regulative organization maintains its original traits in the teeth of influences that modify things around it.

The like holds in respect of the language, spoken and written, which it employs. Among the Egyptians the most ancient form of hieroglyphics was retained for sacred records, when more developed forms were adopted for other purposes. The continued use of Hebrew for religious services among the Jews, and the continued use of Latin for the Roman Catholic service, show us how strong this tendency is, apart from the particular creed. Among ourselves, too, a less dominant ecclesiasticism exhibits a kindred trait. The English of the Bible is of an older style than the English of the date at which the translation was made : and in the church service various words retain obsolete meanings, and others are pronounced in obsolete ways. Even the typography, with its illuminated letters of the rubric, shows traces of the same tendency ; while Puseyites and ritualists, aiming to reinforce ecclesiasticism, betray a decided leaning towards archaic print, as well as archaic ornaments. In the æsthetic direction, indeed, their movement has brought back the most primitive type of sculpture for monumental purposes ; as may be seen in Canterbury Cathedral, where, in two new monuments to ecclesiastics, one being Archbishop Sumner, the robed figures recline on their

6

backs, with hands joined, after the manner of the mailed knights on early tombs—presenting complete symmetry of attitude, which is a distinctive trait of barbaric art, as shown by every child's drawing of a man and every idol carved by a savage.

A conscious as well as an unconscious adhesion to the old in usage and doctrine is shown. Not only among Roman Catholics but among many Protestants, to ascertain what the Fathers said, is to ascertain what should be believed. In the pending controversy about the Athanasian Creed, we see how much authority attaches to an antique document. The antagonism between Convocation and the lay members of the Church —the one as a body wishing to retain the cursing clauses and the other to exclude them—further shows that official Protestantism adheres to antiquity much more than non-official Protestantism : a contrast equally displayed not long since between the opinions of the lay part and the clerical part of the Protestant Irish Church.

Throughout political organizations the like tendency, though less dominant, is very strong. The gradual establishment of law by the consolidation of custom, is the formation of something fixed in the midst of things that are changing ; and, regarded under its most general aspect as the agency which maintains a permanent order, it is in the very nature of a State-organization to be relatively rigid. The way in which primitive principles and practices, no longer fully in force among individuals ruled, survive in the actions of ruling agents, is curiously illustrated by the long retention between nobles of a right of feud after it had been disallowed between citizens. Chief vassals, too, retained this power to secure justice for themselves after smaller vassals lost it : not only was a right of war with one another recognized, but also a right of defence against the king. And we see that even now, in the dealings between Governments, armed force to remedy injuries is still employed, as it originally was between all individuals. As bearing in the same direction, it is significant that the right of trial by battle, which was a regulated form of the aboriginal system under which men administered justice in their own cases, survived among the ruling classes when no longer legal among inferior classes. Even on behalf of religious communities judicial duels were fought. Here the thing it concerns us to note is that the system of fighting in person and fighting by deputy, when no longer otherwise lawful, was retained, actually or formally, in various parts of the regulative organization. Up to the reign of George III., trial by battle could be claimed as an alternative of trial by jury. Duels continued till quite recently between members of the ruling classes, and especially between officers; and even now in Continental armies duelling is not only recognized as proper, but is, in some cases, imperative. And then, showing most strikingly how these oldest usages survive longest, in connexion with the oldest part of the governing organization, we have had in the coronation ceremony, up to modern times, a champion in armour uttering by herald a challenge to all comers on behalf of the monarch.

If, from the agencies by which law is enforced, we pass to legal forms, language, documents, &c., the like tendency is everywhere conspicuous. Parchment is retained for law-deeds though paper has replaced it for other purposes. The form of writing is an old form. Latin and Norman-French terms are still in use for legal purposes, though not otherwise in use ; and even old English words, such as "seize," retain in Law, meanings which they have lost in current speech. In the execution of documents, too, the same truth is illustrated ; for the seal, which was originally the signature, continues, though the written signature now practically replaces it—nay, we retain a symbol of the symbol, as may be seen in every share-transfer, where there is a paper-wafer to represent the seal. Even still more antique usages survive in legal transactions ; as in the form extant in Scotland of handing over a portion of rock when an estate is sold, which evidently answers to the ceremony among the ancient nations of sending earth and water as a sign of yielding territory.

From the working of State-departments, too, many kindred

illustrations might be given. Even under the peremptory requirements of national safety, the flint-lock for muskets was but tardily replaced by the percussion-lock; and the rifle had been commonly in use for sporting purposes generations before it came into more than sparing use for military purposes. Book-keeping by double entry had long been permanently established in the mercantile world before it superseded book-keeping by single entry in Government offices: its adoption dating back only to 1834, when a still more antique system of keeping accounts by notches cut on sticks, was put an end to by the conflagration that resulted from the burning of the Exchequer-tallies.

The like holds with apparel, in general and in detail. Cocked hats are yet to be seen on the heads of officers. An extinct form of dress still holds its ground as the Court-dress; and the sword once habitually worn by gentlemen has become the dress-sword worn only on State-occasions. Everywhere officialism has its established uniforms, which may be traced back to old fashions that have disappeared from ordinary life. Some of these antique articles of costume we see surmounting the heads of judges; others there are which still hang round the necks of the clergy; and others which linger on the legs of bishops.

Thus, from the use of a flint-knife by the Jews for the religious ceremony of circumcision, down to the pronunciation of the terminal syllable of the præterite in our Church-service, down to the *oyez* shouted in a law-court to secure attention, down to the retention of epaulets for officers, and down to the Norman-French words in which the royal assent is given, this persistence is everywhere traceable. And when we find this persistence displayed through all ages in all departments of the regulative organization,—when we see it to be the natural accompaniment of the function of that organization, which is essentially restraining—when we estimate the future action of the organization in any case, by observing the general sweep of its curve throughout long periods of the past; we shall see how misleading may be the conclusions drawn from recent facts taken by themselves.

Where the regulative organization is anywhere made to under-take additional functions, we shall not form sanguine anticipa-tions on the strength of immediate results of the desired kind; but we shall suspect that after the phase of early activity has passed by, the plasticity of the new structure will rapidly diminish, the characteristic tendency towards rigidity will show itself, and in place of expansive effect there will come a restric-tive effect.

The reader will now understand more clearly the meaning of the assertion that true conceptions of sociological changes are to be reached only by contemplating their slow genesis through centuries, and that basing inferences on results shown in short periods, is as illusory as would be judging of the Earth's curvature by observing whether we are walking up or down hill. After recognizing which truth he will perceive how great is another of the obstacles in the way of the Social Science.

"But does not all this prove too much? If it is so difficult to get sociological evidence that is not vitiated by the subjective states of the witnesses, by their prejudices, enthusiams, interests, &c.—if where there is impartial examination, the conditions to the inquiry are of themselves so apt to falsify the result—if there is so general a proneness to assert as facts observed what were really inferences from observations, and so great a tendency also to be blinded by exterior trivialities to interior essentials—if even where accurate data are accessible, their multitudinousness and diffusion in Space make it impracticable clearly to grasp them as wholes, while their unfolding in Time is so slow that ante-cedents and consequents cannot be mentally represented in their true relations; is it not manifestly impossible that a Social Science can be framed?"

It must be admitted that the array of objective difficulties thus brought together is formidable; and were it the aim of the Social Science to draw quite special and definite conclusions, which must depend for their truth upon exact data accurately co-ordinated, it would obviously have to be abandoned. But there are certain classes of general facts which remain after all errors in detail, however produced, have been allowed for. Whatever conflicts there may be among accounts of events that occurred during feudal ages, comparison of them brings out the incontestable truth that there was a Feudal System. By their implications, chronicles and laws indicate the traits of this system; and on putting side by side narratives and documents written, not to tell us about the Feudal System but for quite other purposes, we get tolerably clear ideas of these traits in their essentials—ideas made clearer still on collating the evidence furnished by different contemporary societies. Similarly throughout. By making due use not so much of that which past and present witnesses intend to tell us, as of that which they tell us by implication, it is possible to collect data for inductions respecting social structures and functions in their origin and development: the obstacles which arise in the disentangling of such data in the case of any particular society, being mostly surmountable by the help of the comparative method.

Nevertheless, the difficulties above enumerated must be ever present to us. Throughout, we have to depend on testimony; and in every case we have to beware of the many modes in which evidence may be vitiated—have to estimate its worth when it has been discounted in various ways; and have to take care that our conclusions do not depend on any particular class of facts gathered from any particular place or time.

CHAPTER VI.

SUBJECTIVE DIFFICULTIES—INTELLECTUAL.

If you watch the management of a child by a mother of small capacity, you may be struck by the inability she betrays to imagine the child's thoughts and feelings. Full of energy which he must expend in some way, and eager to see everything, her little boy is every moment provoking her by his restlessness. The occasion is perhaps a railway journey. Now he strives to look out of the window; and now, when forbidden to do that, climbs on the seats, or meddles with the small luggage. "Sit still," "Get down, I tell you," "Why can't you be quiet?" are the commands and expostulations she utters from minute to minute—partly, no doubt, to prevent the discomfort of fellow-passengers. But, as you will see at times when no such motive comes into play, she endeavours to repress these childish activities mainly out of regard for what she thinks propriety, and does it without any adequate recognition of the penalties she inflicts. Though she herself lived through this phase of extreme curiosity—this early time when almost every object passed has the charm of novelty, and when the overflowing energies generate a painful irritation if pent up; yet now she cannot believe how keen is the desire for seeing which she balks, and how difficult is the maintenance of that quietude on which she insists. Conceiving her child's consciousness in terms of her own consciousness, and feeling how easy it is to sit still and not look out of the window, she ascribes his behaviour to mere perversity.

I recall this and kindred cases to the reader's mind, for the purpose of exemplifying a necessity and a difficulty. The necessity is that in dealing with other beings and interpreting their actions, we must represent their thoughts and feelings in terms of our own. The difficulty is that in so representing them we can never be more than partially right, and are frequently very wrong. The conception which any one frames of another's mind, is inevitably more or less after the pattern of his own mind—is automorphic; and in proportion as the mind of which he has to frame a conception differs from his own, his automorphic interpretation is likely to be wide of the truth.

That measuring other person's actions by the standards our own thoughts and feelings furnish, often causes misconstruction, is a remark familiar even to the vulgar. But while among members of the same society, having natures nearly akin, it is seen that automorphic explanations are often erroneous, it is not seen with due clearness how much more erroneous such explanations commonly are, when the actions are those of men of another race, to whom the kinship in nature is comparatively remote. We do, indeed, perceive this, if the interpretations are not our own; and if both the interpreters and the interpreted are mentally alien to us. When, as in early English literature, we find Greek history conceived in terms of feudal institutions, and the heroes of antiquity spoken of as princes, knights, and squires, it becomes clear that the ideas concerning ancient civilization must have been utterly wrong. When we find Virgil named in religious stories of the middle ages as one among the prophets who visited the cradle of Christ—when an illustrated psalter gives scenes from the life of Christ in which there repeatedly figures a castle with a portcullis—when even the crucifixion is described by Langland in the language of chivalry, so that the man who pierced Christ's side with a spear is considered as a knight who disgraced his knighthood [1]—when we read of the Crusaders calling themselves "vassals of Christ;" we need no further proof that by carrying their own sentiments and ideas to the interpretation of social arrangements and transactions among the Jews, our ancestors were led into absurd misconceptions. But we do not recognize the fact that in virtue of the same tendency, we are ever framing conceptions which, if not so grotesquely untrue, are yet very wide of the truth. How difficult it is to imagine mental states remote from our own so correctly that we can understand how they issue in individual actions, and consequently in social actions, an instance will make manifest.

The feeling of vague wonder with which he received his first lessons in the Greek mythology, will most likely be dimly remembered by every reader. If not in words, still inarticulately, there passed through him the thought that faith in such stories was unaccountable. When, afterwards, he read in books of travels details of the amazing superstitions of savages, there was joined with a sense of the absurdity of these superstitions, much astonishment at their acceptance by any human beings, however ignorant or stupid. Such beliefs as that the people of a neighbouring tribe had descended from ducks, that rain fell when certain deities began to spit on the Earth, that the island lived upon had been pulled up from the bottom of the ocean by one of their gods, whose hook got fast when he was fishing— these, and countless beliefs equally laughable, seemed to imply an irrationality near to insanity. He interpreted them automorphically — carrying with him not simply his own faculties developed to a stage of complexity considerably beyond that reached by the faculties of the savage, but also the modes of thinking in which he was brought up, and the stock of information he had acquired. Probably it has never since occurred to him to do otherwise. Even if he now attempts to see things from the savage's point of view, he most likely fails entirely ; and if he succeeds at all, it is but partially. Yet only by seeing things as the savage sees them can his ideas be understood, his behaviour accounted for, and the resulting social phenomena explained. These apparently-strange superstitions are quite natural—quite rational, in a certain sense, in their respective times and places. The laws of intellectual action are the same for civilized and uncivilized. The difference between civilized and uncivilized is in complexity of faculty and in amount of knowledge accumulated and generalized. Given, reflective powers developed only to that lower degree in which they are possessed by the aboriginal man—given, his small stock of ideas, collected in a narrow area of space, and not added to by records extending through time—given, his impulsive nature incapable of patient inquiry ; and these seemingly-monstrous stories of his become in reality the most feasible explanations he can find of surrounding things. Yet even after concluding that this must be so, it is not easy to think from the savage's stand-point, clearly enough to follow the effects of his ideas on his acts, through all the relations of life, social and other.

A parallel difficulty stands in the way of rightly conceiving character remote from our own, so as to see how it issues in conduct. We may best recognize our inability in this respect, by observing the converse inability of other races to understand our characters, and the acts they prompt.

"Wonderful are the works of Allah ! Behold ! That Frank is trudging about when he can, if he pleases, sit still !"[2]

In like manner Captain Speke tells us,—

"If I walked up and down the same place to stretch my legs, they [Somali] formed councils of war on my motives, considering I must have some secret designs upon their country, or I would not do it, as no man in his senses could be guilty of working his legs unnecessarily."[3]

But while, by instances like these, we are shown that our characters are in a large measure incomprehensible by races remote in nature from us, the correlative fact that we cannot rightly conceive their sentiments and motives is one perpetually overlooked in our sociological interpretations. Feeling, for instance, how natural it is to take an easier course in place of a more laborious course, and to adopt new methods that are proved to be better methods, we are puzzled on finding the Chinese stick to their dim paper-lamps, though they admire our bright argand-lamps, which they do not use if given to them; or on finding that the Hindus prefer their rough primitive tools, after seeing how our improved tools do more work with less effort. And on descending to races yet more remote in civilization, we still oftener discover ourselves wrong when we suppose that under given conditions they will act as we should act.

Here, then, is a subjective difficulty of a serious kind. To understand any fact in social evolution, we have to see it as resulting from the joint actions of individuals having certain natures. We cannot so understand it without understanding their natures; and this, even by care and effort, we are able to do but very imperfectly. Our interpretations must be automorphic; and yet automorphism perpetually misleads us.

One would hardly suppose, à priori, that untruthfulness would habitually co-exist with credulity. Rather our inference might be that, because of the tendency above enlarged upon, people most given to making false statements must be people most inclined to suspect statements made by others. Yet, somewhat anomalously, as it seems, habitual veracity generally goes with inclination to doubt evidence; and extreme untrustworthiness of assertion often has for its concomitant, readiness to accept the greatest improbabilities on the slenderest testimony. If you compare savage with civilized, or compare the successive stages of civilization with one another, you find untruthfulness and credulity decreasing together; until you reach the modern man of science, who is at once exact in his statements and critical respecting evidence. The converse relation to that seen in the man of science, is even now startlingly presented in the East, where greediness in swallowing fictions goes along with superfluous telling of falsehoods. An Egyptian prides himself in a clever lie, uttered perhaps without motive ; and a dyer will even ascribe the failure in fixing one of his colours to the not having been successful in a deception. Yet so great is the readiness to believe improbabilities, that Mr. St. John, in his *Two Years' Residence in a Levantine Family*, narrates how, when the " Arabian Nights' Entertainments" was being read aloud, and when he hinted that the stories must not be accepted as true, there arose a strong protest against such scepticism : the question being asked,—" Why should a man sit down and write so many lies ? " [4]

I point out this union of seemingly-inconsistent traits, not because of the direct bearing it has on the argument, but because of its indirect bearing. For I have here to dwell on the mis- leading effects of certain mental states which similarly appear unlikely to co-exist, and which yet do habitually co-exist. I refer to the belief which, even while I write, I find repeated in the leading journal, that " the deeper a student of history goes, the more does he find man the same in all time ; " and to the opposite belief embodied in current politics, that human nature may be readily altered. These two beliefs, which ought to cancel one another but do not, originate two classes of errors in sociological speculation ; and nothing like correct conclusions in Sociology can be drawn until they have been rejected and re- placed by a belief which reconciles them—the belief that human nature is indefinitely modifiable, but that no modification of it can be brought about rapidly. We will glance at the errors to which each of these beliefs leads.

While it was held that the stars are fixed and that the hills are everlasting, there was a certain congruity in the notion that man continues unchanged from age to age; but now when we know that all stars are in motion, and that there are no such things as everlasting hills—now when we find all things through- out the Universe to be in a ceaseless flux, it is time for this crude conception of human nature to disappear out of our social con- ceptions ; or rather—it is time for its disappearance to be followed by that of the many narrow notions respecting the past and the future of society, which have grown out of it, and which linger notwithstanding the loss of their root. For, avowedly by some and tacitly by others, it continues to be thought that the human heart is as " desperately wicked " as it ever was, and that the state of society hereafter will be very much like the state of society now. If, when the evidence has been piled mass upon mass, there comes a reluctant admission that aboriginal man, of troglodyte or kindred habits, differed somewhat from man as he was during feudal times, and that the customs and sentiments and beliefs he had in feudal times, imply a character appreciably unlike that which he has now—if, joined with this, there is a recognition of the truth that along with these changes in man there have gone still more conspicuous changes in society; there is, nevertheless, an ignoring of the implication that here-after man and society will continue to change, until they have diverged as widely from their existing types as their existing types have diverged from those of the earliest recorded ages. It is true that among the more cultured the probability, or even the certainty, that such transformations will go on, may be granted ; but the granting is but nominal—the admission does not become a factor in the conclusions drawn. The first discussion on a political or social topic, reveals the tacit assumption that, in times to come, society will have a structure substantially like its existing structure. If, for instance, the question of domestic service is raised, it·mostly happens that its bearings are considered wholly in reference to those social arrangements which exist around us : only a few proceed on the supposition that these arrangements are probably but transitory. It is so throughout. Be the subject industrial organization, or class-relations, or rule by fashion, the thought which practically moulds the conclusions, if not the thought theoretically professed, is, that whatever changes they may undergo, our institutions will not cease to be recognizably the same. Even those who have, as they think, deliberately freed themselves from this per-

verting tendency—even M. Comte and his disciples, believing in
an entire transformation of society, nevertheless betray an incomplete emancipation; for the ideal society expected by them,
is one under regulation by a hierarchy essentially akin to
hierarchies such as mankind have known. So that everywhere
sociological thinking is more or less impeded by the difficulty of
bearing in mind that the social states towards which our race is
being carried, are probably as little conceivable by us as our present social state was conceivable by a Norse pirate and his
followers.

Note, now, the opposite difficulty, which appears to be surmountable by scarcely any of our parties, political or philanthropic,—the difficulty of understanding that human nature,
though indefinitely modifiable, can be modified but very slowly ;
and that all laws and institutions and appliances which count
on getting from it, within a short time, much better results than
present ones, will inevitably fail. If we glance over the pro-
grammes of societies, and sects, and schools of all kinds, from
Rousseau's disciples in the French Convention up to the
members of the United Kingdom Alliance, from the adherents
of the Ultramontane propaganda up to the enthusiastic advocates of an education exclusively secular, we find in them one
common trait. They are all pervaded by the conviction, now
definitely expressed and now taken as a self-evident truth, that
there needs but this kind of instruction or that kind of discipline, this mode of repression or that system of culture, to bring
society into a very much better state. Here we read that "it is
necessary completely to re-fashion the people whom one wishes
to make free": the implication being that a re-fashioning is
practicable. There it is taken as undeniable that when you
have taught children what they ought to do to be good citizens,
they will become good citizens. Elsewhere it is held to be a
truth beyond question, that if by law temptations to drink are
removed from men, they will not only cease to drink, but thereafter cease to commit crimes. And yet the delusiveness of all

such hopes is obvious enough to any one not blinded by a hypothesis, or carried away by an enthusiasm. The fact, often pointed
out to temperance-fanatics, that some of the soberest nations in
Europe yield a proportion of crime higher than our own, might
suffice to show them that England would not be suddenly
moralized if they carried their proposed restrictions into effect.
The superstition that good behaviour is to be forthwith produced by lessons learnt out of school-books, which was long ago
statistically disproved,[5] would, but for preconceptions, be utterly
dissipated by observing to what a slight extent knowledge
affects conduct—by observing that the dishonesty implied in
the adulterations of tradesmen and manufacturers, in fraudulent
bankruptcies, in bubble-companies, in "cooking" of railway
accounts and financial prospectuses, differs only in form, and not
in amount, from the dishonesty of the uneducated—by observing
how amazingly little the teachings given to medical students
affect their lives, and how even the most experienced medical
men have their prudence scarcely at all increased by their information. Similarly, the Utopian ideas which come out afresh
along with every new political scheme, from the "paper-consti-
tutions" of the Abbé Sieyès down to the lately-published programme of M. Louis Blanc, and from agitations for vote-by-
ballot up to those which have a Republic for their aim, might,
but for this tacit belief we are contemplating, be extinguished
by the facts perpetually and startlingly thrust on our attention.
Again and again for three generations has France been showing
to the world how impossible it is essentially to change the type
of a social structure by any re-arrangement wrought out through
a revolution. However great the transformation may for a time
seem, the original thing re-appears in disguise. Out of the no-
minally-free government set up a new despotism arises, differing
from the old by having a new shibboleth and new men to utter
it; but identical with the old in the determination to put down
opposition and in the means used to this end. Liberty, when obtained, is forthwith surrendered to an avowed autocrat; or,

as we have seen within this year, is allowed to lapse into the hands of one who claims the reality of autocracy without its title. Nay, the change is, in fact, even less; for the regulative organization which ramifies throughout French society, continues unaltered by these changes at the governmental centre. The bureaucratic system persists equally under Imperialist, Constitutional, and Republican arrangements. As the Duc d'Audiffret-Pasquier pointed out, "Empires fall, Ministries pass away, but Bureaux remain." The aggregate of forces and tendencies embodied, not only in the structural arrangements holding the nation together, but in the ideas and sentiments of its units, is so powerful, that the excision of a part, even though it be the government, is quickly followed by the substitution of a like part. It needs but to recall the truth exemplified some chapters back, that the properties of the aggregate are determined by the properties of its units, to see at once that so long as the characters of citizens remain substantially unchanged, there can be no substantial change in the political organization which has slowly been evolved by them.

This double difficulty of thought, with the double set of delusions fallen into by those who do not surmount it, is, indeed, naturally associated with the once-universal, and still-general, belief that societies arise by manufacture, instead of arising, as they do, by evolution. Recognize the truth that incorporated masses of men grow, and acquire their structural characters through modification upon modification, and there are excluded these antithetical errors that humanity remains the same and that humanity is readily alterable; and along with exclusion of these errors comes admission of the inference, that the changes which have brought social arrangements to a form so different from past forms, will in future carry them on to forms as different from those now existing. Once become habituated to the thought of a continuous unfolding of the whole and of each part, and these misleading ideas disappear. Take a word and observe how, while changing, it gives origin in course of time to a family of words, each changing member of which similarly has progeny; take a custom, as that of giving eggs at Easter, which has now developed in Paris into the fashion of making expensive presents of every imaginable kind inclosed in imitation-eggs, becoming at length large enough to contain a brougham, and which entails so great a tax that people go abroad to evade it; take a law, once quite simple and made to meet a special case, and see how it eventually, by successive additions and changes, grows up into a complex group of laws, as, out of two laws of William the Conqueror came our whole legal system regulating land-tenure;[6] take a social appliance, as the Press, and see how from the news-letter, originally private and written, and then assuming the shape of a printed fly-leaf to a written private letter, there has slowly evolved this vast assemblage of journals and periodicals, daily, weekly, general, and local, that have, individually and as an aggregate, grown in size while growing in heterogeneity;—do this, and do the like with all other established institutions, agencies, products, and there will come naturally the conviction that now, too, there are various germs of things which will in the future develop in ways no one imagines, and take shares in profound transformations of society and of its members: transformations that are hopeless as immediate results, but certain as ultimate results.

Try to fit a hand with five fingers into a glove with four. Your difficulty aptly parallels the difficulty of putting a complex conception into a mind not having a proportionately-complex faculty. As fast as the several terms and relations which make up a thought become many and varied, there must be brought into play many and varied parts of the intellectual structure, before the thought can be comprehended; and if some of these parts are wanting, only fragments of the thought can be taken in. Consider an instance.

What is meant by the ratio of A to B, may be explained to a

boy by drawing a short line A and a long line B, telling him that A is said to bear a small ratio to B; and then, after lengthening the line A, telling him that A is now said to bear a larger ratio to B. But suppose I have to explain what is meant by saying that the ratio of A to B, equals the ratio of C to D. Instead of two different quantities and one relation, there are now four different quantities and three relations. To understand the proposition, the boy has to think of A and B and their difference, and, without losing his intellectual grasp of these, he has to think of C and D and their difference, and, without losing his intellectual grasp of these, he has to think of the two differences as each having a like relation to its pair of quantities. Thus the number of terms and relations to be kept before the mind, is such as to imply the co-operation of many more agents of thought; any of which being absent, the proposition cannot be understood: the boy must be older before he will understand it, and, if uncultured, will probably never understand it at all. Let us pass on to a conception of still greater complexity—say that the ratio of A to B varies as the ratio of C to D. Far more numerous things have now to be represented in consciousness with approximate simultaneity. A and B have to be thought of as not constant in their lengths, but as one or both of them changing in their lengths; so that their difference is indefinitely variable. Similarly with C and D. And then the variability of the ratio in each case being duly conceived in terms of lines that lengthen and shorten, the thing to be understood is, that whatever difference any change brings about between A and B, the relation it bears to one or other of them, is always like that which the difference simultaneously arising between C and D bears to one or other of them. The greater multiplicity of ideas required for mentally framing this proposition, evidently puts it further beyond the reach of faculties not developed by appropriate culture, or not capable of being so developed. And as the type of proposition becomes still more involved, as it does when two such groups of dependent variables are compared and conclusions drawn, it begins to require a grasp that is easy only to the disciplined mathematician.

One who does not possess that complexity of faculty which, as we here see, is requisite for grasping a complex conception, may, in cases like these, become conscious of his incapacity; not from perceiving what he lacks, but from perceiving that another person achieves results which he cannot achieve. But where no such thing as the verifying of exact predictions comes in to prove to one of inferior faculty that his faculty is inferior, he is usually unaware of the inferiority. To imagine a higher mode of consciousness, is in some degree to have it; so that until he has it in some degree, he cannot really conceive of its existence. An illustration or two will make this clear.

Take a child on your knee, and, turning over with him some engravings of landscapes, note what he observes. "I see a man in a boat," says he, pointing. "Look at the cows coming down the hill." "And there is a little boy playing with a dog." These and other such remarks, mostly about the living objects in each scene, are all you get from him. Never by any chance does he utter a word respecting the scene as a whole. There is an absolute unconsciousness of anything to be pleased with in the combination of wood and water and mountain. And while the child is entirely without this complex æsthetic consciousness, you see that he has not the remotest idea that such a consciousness exists in others but is wanting in himself. Note now a case in which a kindred defect is betrayed by an adult. You have, perhaps, in the course of your life, had some musical culture; and can recall the stages through which you have passed. In early days a symphony was a mystery; and you were somewhat puzzled to find others applauding it. An unfolding of musical faculty, that went on slowly through succeeding years, brought some appreciation; and now these complex musical combinations which once gave you little or no pleasure, give you more pleasure than any others. Remembering all this, you suspect that your indifference to certain still more involved musical combinations may arise from incapacity in you, and not from faults in them. See, on the other hand, what happens with one who has undergone no such series of changes—say, an old naval officer, whose life at sea kept him out of the way of concerts and operas. You hear him occasionally confess, or rather boast, how much he enjoys the bagpipes. While the last cadences of a sonata which a young lady has just played, are still in your ears, he goes up to her and asks whether she can play "Polly, put the kettle on," or "Johnny comes marching home." And then, when concerts are talked about at table, he seizes the occasion for expressing his dislike of classical music, and scarcely conceals his contempt for those who go to hear it. On contemplating his mental state, you see that along with absence of the ability to grasp complex musical combinations, there goes no consciousness of the absence—there is no suspicion that such complex combinations exist, and that other persons have faculties for appreciating them.

And now for the application of this general truth to our subject. The conceptions with which sociological science is concerned, are complex beyond all others. In the absence of faculty having a corresponding complexity, they cannot be grasped. Here, however, as in other cases, the absence of an adequately-complex faculty is not accompanied by any consciousness of incapacity. Rather do we find that deficiency in the required kind of mental grasp, is accompanied by extreme confidence of judgment on sociological questions, and a ridicule of those who. after long discipline, begin to perceive what there is to be understood, and how difficult is the right understanding of it. A simple illustration of this will prepare the way for more-involved illustrations.

A few months ago the *Times* gave us an account of the last achievement in automatic printing—the "Walter-Press," by which its own immense edition is thrown off in a few hours every morning. Suppose a reader of the description, adequately

familiar with mechanical details, follows what he reads step by
step with full comprehension : perhaps making his ideas more
definite by going to see the apparatus at work and questioning
the attendants. Now he goes away thinking he understands all
about it. Possibly, under its aspect as a feat in mechanical
engineering, he does so. Possibly also, under its biographical
aspect, as implying in Mr. Walter and those who co-operated
with him certain traits, moral and intellectual, he does so. But
under its sociological aspect he probably has no notion of its
meaning; and does not even suspect that it has a sociological
aspect. Yet if he begins to look into the genesis of the thing, he
will find that he is but on the threshold of the full explana-
nation. On asking not what is its proximate but what is
its remote origin, he finds, in the first place, that this automatic
printing-machine is lineally descended from other automatic
printing-machines, which have undergone successive developments—each pre-supposing others that went before : without
cylinder printing-machines long previously used and improved,
there would have been no "Walter-Press." He inquires a step
further, and discovers that this last improvement became possible
only by the help of *papier-mâché* stereotyping, which, first employed for making flat plates, afforded the possibility of making
cyclindrical plates. And tracing this back, he finds that plaster-
of-paris stereotyping came before it, and that there was another
process before that. Again, he learns that this highest form of
automatic printing, like the many less-developed forms preceding
it, depended for its practicability on the introduction of rollers
for distributing ink, instead of the hand-implements used by
"printer's-devils" fifty years ago ; which rollers, again, could
never have been made fit for their present purposes, without the
discovery of that curious elastic compound out of which they are
cast. And then, on tracing the more remote antecedents, he
finds an ancestry of hand printing-presses, which, through generations, had been successively improved. Now, perhaps, he
thinks he understands the apparatus, considered as a sociological

fact. Far from it. Its multitudinous parts, which will work together only when highly finished and exactly adjusted, came from machine-shops; where there are varieties of complicated, highly-finished engines for turning cylinders, cutting out wheels, planing bars, and so forth; and on the pre-existence of these the existence of this printing-machine depended. If he inquires into the history of these complex automatic tools, he finds they have severally been, in the slow course of mechanical progress, brought to their present perfection by the help of preceding complex automatic tools of various kinds, that co-operated to make their component parts—each larger, or more accurate, lathe or planing-machine having been made possible by pre-existing lathes and planing-machines, inferior in size or exactness. And so if he traces back the whole contents of the machine-shop, with its many different instruments, he comes in course of time to the blacksmith's hammer and anvil; and even, eventually, to still ruder appliances.   The explanation is now completed, he thinks. Not at all. No such process as that which the "Walter-Press" shows us, was possible until there had been invented, and slowly perfected, a paper-machine capable of making miles of paper without break. Thus there is the genesis of the paper-machine involved, and that of the multitudinous appliances and devices which preceded it, and are at present implied by it.   Have we now got to the end of the matter? No; we have just glanced at one group of the antecedents. All this development of mechanical appliances—this growth of the iron-manufacture, this extensive use of machinery made from iron, this production of so many machines for making machines—has had for one of its causes the abundance of the raw materials, coal and iron; has had for another of its causes the insular position which has favoured peace and the increase of industrial activity. There have been moral causes at work too. Without that readiness to sacrifice present ease to future benefit, which is implied by enterprise, there would never have arisen the machine in question,— nay, there would never have arisen the multitudinous improved instruments and processes that have made it possible. And beyond the moral traits which enterprise pre-supposes, there are those pre-supposed by efficient co-operation. Without mechanical engineers who fulfilled their contracts tolerably well, by executing work accurately, neither this machine itself nor the machines that made it, could have been produced; and without artizans having considerable conscientiousness, no master could insure accurate work. Try to get such products out of an inferior race, and you will find defective character an insuperable obstacle. So, too, will you find defective intelligence an insuperable obstacle. The skilled artizan is not an accidental product, either morally or intellectually. The intelligence needed for making a new thing is not everywhere to be found; nor is there everywhere to be found the accuracy of perception and nicety of execution without which no complex machine can be so made that it will act. Exactness of finish in machines has developed *pari* *passu* with exactness of perception in artizans. Inspect some mechanical appliance made a century ago, and you may see that, even had all other requisite conditions been fulfilled, want of the requisite skill in workmen would have been a fatal obstacle to the production of an engine requiring so many delicate adjustments. So that there are implied in this mechanical achievement, not only our slowly-generated industrial state, with its innumerable products and processes, but also the slowly-moulded moral and intellectual natures of masters and workmen. Has nothing now been forgotten? Yes, we have left out a whole division of all-important social phenomena—those which we group as the progress of knowledge. Along with the many other developments that have been necessary antecedents to this machine, there has been the development of Science. The growing and improving arts of all kinds, have been helped up, step after step, by those generalized experiences, becoming ever wider, more complete, more exact, which make up what we call Mathematics, Physics, Chemistry, &c. Without a considerably-developed Geometry, there could never have been the machines for making machines; still less this machine that has proceeded from them. Without a developed Physics, there would have been no steam-engine to move these various automatic appliances, primary and secondary; nor would the many implied metallurgic processes have been brought to the needful perfection. And in the absence of a developed Chemistry, many other requirements, direct and indirect, could not have been adequately fulfilled. So that, in fact, this organization of knowledge which began with civilization, had to reach something like its present stage before such a machine could come into existence; supposing all other pre-requisites to be satisfied. Surely we have now got to the end of the history. Not quite : there yet remains an essential factor. No one goes on year after year spending thousands of pounds and much time, and persevering through disappointment and anxiety, without a strong motive : the " Walter-Press " was not a mere *tour de force*. Why, then, was it produced ? To meet an immense demand with great promptness—to print, with one machine, 16,000 copies per hour. Whence arises this demand? From an extensive reading public, brought in the course of generations to have a keen morning-appetite for news of all kinds—merchants who need to know the latest prices at home and the latest telegrams from abroad; politicians who must learn the result of last night's division, be informed of the new diplomatic move, and read the speeches at a meeting; sporting men who look for the odds and the result of yesterday's race ; ladies who want to see the births, marriages, and deaths. And on asking the origin of these many desires to be satisfied, they prove to be concomitants of our social state in general—its trading, political, philanthropic, and other activities ; for in societies where these are not dominant, the demand for news of various kinds rises to no such intensity. See, then, how enormously involved is the genesis of this machine, as a sociological phenomenon. A whole encyclopædia of mechanical inventions—some dating from the earliest times—go to the explanation of it. Thousands of years of discipline, by which the impulsive improvident nature of the savage has been evolved into a comparatively self-controlling nature, capable of sacrificing present ease to future good, are pre-supposed. There is pre-supposed the equally-long discipline by which the inventive faculty, almost wholly absent in the savage, has been evolved; and by which accuracy, not even conceived by the savage, has been cultivated. And there is further pre-supposed the slow political and social progress, at once cause and consequence of these other changes, that has brought us to a state in which such a machine finds a function to fulfil.

The complexity of a sociological fact, and the difficulty of adequately grasping it, will now perhaps be more apparent. For as in this case there has been a genesis, so has there been in every other case, be it of institution, arrangement, custom, belief, &c.; but while in this case the genesis is comparatively easy to trace, because of the comparatively-concrete character of process and product, it is in other cases difficult to trace, because the factors are mostly not of sensible kinds. And yet only when the genesis has been traced—only when the antecedents of all orders have been observed in their co-operation, generation after generation, through past social states—is there reached that interpretation of a fact which makes it a part of sociological science, properly understood. If, for instance, the true meaning of such phenomena as those presented by trade-combinations is to be seen, it is needful to go back to those remote Old-English periods when analogous causes produced analogous results. As Brentano points out—

"The workmen formed their Trade-Unions against the aggressions of the then rising manufacturing lords, as in earlier times the old freemen formed their Frith-Gilds against the tyranny of medieval magnates, and the free handicraftsmen their Craft-Gilds against the aggressions of the Old-burghers." [7]

Then, having studied the successive forms of such organizations in relation to the successive industrial states, there have to be observed the ways in which they are severally related to other

7

phenomena of their respective times—the political institutions, the class-distinctions, the family-arrangements, the modes of distribution and degrees of intercourse between localities, the amounts of knowledge, the religious beliefs, the morals, the sentiments, the customs, the ideas. Considered as parts of a nation, having structures that form parts of its structure, and actions that modify and are modified by its actions, these trade-societies can have their full meanings perceived, only when they are studied in their serial genesis through many centuries, and their changes considered in relation to simultaneous changes throughout the social organism. And even then there remains the deeper inquiry—How does it happen that in nations of certain types no analogous institutions exist, and that in nations of other types the analogous institutions have taken forms more or less different?

That phenomena so involved cannot be seen as they truly are, even by the highest intelligence at present existing, is tolerably manifest. And it is manifest also that a Science of Society is likely for a long time hence to be recognized by but few; since, not only is there in most cases an absence of faculty complex enough to grasp its complex phenomena, but there is mostly an absolute unconsciousness that there are any such complex phenomena to be grasped.

To the want of due complexity of conceptive faculty, has to be added, as a further difficulty, the want of due plasticity of conceptive faculty. The general ideas of nearly all men have been framed out of experiences gathered within comparatively-narrow areas; and general ideas so framed are far too rigid readily to admit the multitudinous and varied combinations of facts which Sociology presents. The child of Puritanic parents, brought up in the belief that Sabbath-breaking brings after it all kinds of transgressions, and having had pointed out, in the village or small town that formed his world, various instances of this connexion, is somewhat perplexed in after-years, when acquaintance with more of his countrymen has shown him exemplary lives joined with non-observance of the Sunday. When during continental travel he finds that the best people of foreign societies neglect injunctions which he once thought essential to right conduct, he still further widens his originally small and stiff conception. Now the process thus exemplified in the change of a single superficial belief, has to be gone through with numerous beliefs of deeper kinds, before there can be reached the flexibility of thought required for dealing properly with sociological phenomena. Not in one direction, but in most directions, we have to learn that those connexions of social facts which we commonly regard as natural and even necessary, are not necessary, and often have no particular naturalness. On contemplating past social states, we are continually reminded that many arrangements, and practices, and convictions, that seem matters of course, are very modern; and that others which we now regard as impossible were quite possible a few centuries ago. Still more on studying societies alien in race as well as in stage of civilization, we perpetually meet with things contrary to everything we should have thought probable, and even such as we should have scarcely hit upon in trying to conceive the most unlikely things.

Take in illustration the varieties of domestic relations. That monogamy is not the only kind of marriage, we are early taught by our Bible-lessons. But though the conception of polygamy is thus made somewhat familiar, it does not occur to us that polyandry is also a possible arrangement; and we are surprised on first learning that it exists, and was once extremely general. When we contemplate these marital institutions unlike our own, we cannot at first imagine that they are practised with a sense of propriety like that with which we practise ours. Yet Livingstone narrates that in a tribe bordering one of the Central African lakes, the women were quite disgusted on hearing that in England a man has only one wife. This is a feeling by no means peculiar to them.

" An intelligent Kandyan chief with whom Mr. Bailey visited these

Veddahs was 'perfectly scandalised at the utter barbarism of living with only one wife, and never parting until separated by death.' It was, he said, 'just like the wanderoos' (monkeys)." [8]

Again, one would suppose that, as a matter of course, monogamy, polygamy, and polyandry, in its several varieties, exhausted the possible forms of marriage. An utterly-unexpected form is furnished us by one of the African tribes. Marriage, among them, is for so many days in the week—commonly for four days in the week, which is said to be " the custom in the best families: " the wife during the off-days being regarded as an independent woman who may do what she pleases. We are a little surprised, too, on reading that by some of the Hill-tribes of India, unfaithfulness on the part of the husband is held to be a grave offence, but unfaithfulness on the part of the wife a trivial one. We assume, as self-evident, that good usage of a wife by a husband, implies, among other things, absence of violence ; and hence it seems scarcely imaginable that in some places the opposite criterion holds. Yet it does so among the Tartars.

" A nursemaid of mine left me to be married, and some short time after she went to the Natchalnick of the place to make a complaint against her husband. He inquired into the matter, when she coolly told him her husband did not love her. He asked how she knew he did not love her ; ' Because,' she replied, 'he never whipped her.'" [9]

A statement which might be rejected as incredible were it not for the analogous fact that, among the South-African races, a white master who does not thrash his men, is ridiculed and reproached by them as not worthy to be called a master. Among domestic customs, again, who, if he had been set to imagine all possible anomalies, would have hit upon that which is found among the Basques, and has existed among other races —the custom that on the birth of a child the husband goes to bed and receives the congratulations of friends, while his wife returns to her household work ? Or who, among the results of having a son born, would dream of that which occurs among some Polynesian races, where the father is forthwith dispossessed of his property, and becomes simply a guardian of it on behalf of the infant? The varieties of filial relations and of accompanying sentiments, continually show us things equally strange, and at first sight equally unaccountable. No one would imagine that it might anywhere be thought a duty on the part of children to bury their parents alive. Yet it is so thought among the Fijians; of whom we read also that the parents thus put out of the way, go to their graves with smiling faces. Scarcely less incredible does it seem that a man's affection should be regarded as more fitly shown towards the children of others than towards his own children. Yet the Hill-tribes of India supply an example.

Among the Nairs " every man looks upon his sister's children as his heirs, . . . and he would be considered as an unnatural monster were he to show such signs of grief at the death of a child which . . . he might suppose to be his own, as he did at the death of a child of his sister." [10]

" The philoprogenitiveness of philosophical Europe is a strange idea, as well as term, to the Nair of Malabar, who learns with his earliest mind that his uncle is a nearer relation to him than his father, and consequently loves his nephew much more than his son." [11]

When, in the domestic relations, we meet with such varieties of law, of custom, of sentiment, of belief, thus indicated by a few examples which might be indefinitely multiplied, it may be imagined how multitudinous are the seeming incongruities among the social relations at large. To be made conscious of these, however, it is not needful to study uncivilized tribes, or alien races partially civilized. If we look back to the earlier stages of European societies, we find abundant proofs that social phenomena do not necessarily hang together in ways such as our daily experiences show us. Religious conceptions may be taken in illustration.

The grossness of these among civilized nations as they at present exist, might, indeed, prepare us for their still greater grossness during old times. When, close to Boulogne, one passes a crucifix, at the foot of which lies a heap of mouldering crosses, each made of two bits of lath nailed together, deposited by passers-by in the expectation of Divine favour to be so gained, one cannot but have a sense of strangeness on glancing at the adjacent railway, and on calling to mind the achievements of the French in science. Still more may one marvel on finding, as in Spain, a bull-fight got up in the interests of the Church—the proceeds being devoted to a "Holy House of Mercy!" And yet great as seem the incongruities between religious beliefs and social states now displayed, more astonishing incongruities are disclosed on going far back. Consider the conceptions implied by sundry mystery-plays; and remember that they were outgrowths from a theory of the Divine government, which men were afterwards burnt for rejecting. Payments of wages to actors are entered thus:—

> " Imprimis, to God, ij[s.]
> Item,   to Cayphas, iij[s.] iiij[d.]
> . . . .
> Item,   to one of the knights, ij[s.]
> Item,   to the devyll and to Judas, xviij[d.]

" We have frequently such entries as : ' Item, payd for the spret (spirit) God's cote, ij[s.]' We learn from these entries that God's coat was of leather, painted and gilt, and that he had a wig of false hair, also gilt." [12]

" Even the Virgin's conception is made a subject of ribaldry ; and in the Coventry collection we have a mystery, or play, on the subject of her pretended trial. It opens with the appearance of the somnour, who reads a long list of offences that appear in his book ; then come two ' detractors ' who repeat certain scandalous stories relating to Joseph and Mary, upon the strength of which they are summoned to appear before the ecclesiastical court. They are accordingly put upon their trial, and we have a broad picture of the proceedings in such a case," &c.[13]

Again, on looking into the illuminated missals of old times, there is revealed a mode of conceiving Christian doctrine which it is difficult to imagine as current in a civilized, or even semi-civilized, society : instance the ideas implied by a highly-finished figure of Christ, from whose wounded side a stream of wafers spouts on to a salver held by a priest. Or take a devotional book of later date—a printed psalter profusely illustrated with woodcuts representing incidents in the life of Christ. Page after page exhibits ways in which his sacrifice is utilized after a perfectly-material manner. Here are shown vines growing out of his wounds, and the grapes these vines bear are being devoured by bishops and abbesses. Here the cross is fixed on a large barrel, into which his blood falls in torrents, and out of which there issue jets on to groups of ecclesiastics. And here, his body being represented in a horizontal position, there rise from the wounds in his hands and feet fountains of blood, which priests and nuns are collecting in buckets and jars. Nay, even more astonishing is the mental state implied by one of the woodcuts, which tries to aid the devotional reader in conceiving the Trinity, by representing three persons standing in one pair of boots![14] Quite in harmony with these astoundingly-gross conceptions are the conceptions implied by the popular literature. The theological ideas that grew up in times when Papal authority was supreme, and before the sale of indulgences had been protested against, may be judged from a story contained in the Folk-lore collected by the Brothers Grimm, called " The Tailor in Heaven." Here is an abridged translation that has been made for me :—

" God, having one day gone out with the saints and the apostles for a walk, left Peter at the door of heaven with strict orders to admit no one. Soon after a tailor came and pleaded to be let in. But Peter said that God had forbidden any one to be admitted ; besides, the tailor was a bad character, and ' cabbaged ' the cloth he used. The tailor said the pieces he had taken were small, and had fallen into his basket ; and he was willing to make himself useful—he would carry the babies, and wash or mend the clothes. Peter at last let him in, but made him sit down in a corner, behind the door. Taking advantage of Peter's going outside for a minute or two, the tailor left his seat and looked about him. He soon came to a place where there were many stools, and a chair of massive gold and a golden footstool, which were God's. Climbing up on the chair, he could see all that was happening on the earth ; and he saw an old woman, who was washing clothes in a stream, making away with some of the linen. In his anger, he took up the footstool and threw it at her. As he could not get it back, he thought it best to return to his place behind the door, where he sat down, putting on an air of innocence. God now re-entered, without observing the tailor. Finding his footstool gone, he asked Peter what had become of it—had he let anyone in ? The apostle at first evaded the question, but confessed that he had let in one—only, however, a poor limping tailor. The tailor was then called, and asked what he had done with the footstool. When he had told, God said to him :—'O you knave, if I judged like you, how long do you think *you* would have escaped ? For long ago I should not have had a chair or even a poker left in the place, but should have hurled everything at the sinners.' . . . . ." [15]

These examples, out of multitudes that might be given, show the wide limits of variation within which social phenomena range. When we bear in mind that, along with theological ideas that now seem little above those of savages, there went (in England) a political constitution having outlines like the present, an established body of laws, a regular taxation, an emancipated working-class, an industrial system of considerable complexity, with the general intelligence and mutual trust implied by social co-operations so extensive and involved, we see that there are possibilities of combination far more numerous than we are apt to suppose. There is proved to us the need for greatly enlarging those stock-notions which are so firmly established in us by daily observations of surrounding arrangements and occurrences.

We might, indeed, even if limited to the evidence which our own society at the present time supplies, greatly increase the plasticity of our conceptions, did we contemplate the facts as they really are. Could we nationally, as well as individually, " see ourselves as others see us," we might find at home seeming contradictions, sufficient to show us that what we think necessarily-connected traits are by no means necessarily connected. We might learn from our own institutions, and books, and journals, and debates, that while there are certain constant relations among social phenomena, they are not the relations commonly supposed to be constant; and that when, from some conspicuous characteristic we infer certain other characteristics, we may be quite wrong. To aid ourselves in perceiving this, let us, varying a somewhat trite mode of representation, consider what might be said of us by an independent observer living in the far future—supposing his statements translated into our cumbrous language.

" Though the diagrams used for teaching make every child aware that many thousands of years ago the Earth's orbit began to recede from its limit of greatest excentricity ; and though all are familiar with the consequent fact that the glacial epoch, which has so long made a large part of the northern hemisphere uninhabitable, has passed its climax ; yet it is not universally known that in some regions, the retreat of glaciers has lately made accessible, tracts long covered. Amid moraines and under vast accumulations of detritus, have been found here ruins, there semi-fossilized skeletons, and in some places even records, which, by a marvellous concurrence of favourable conditions, have been so preserved that parts of them remain legible. Just as fossil cephalopods, turned up by our automatic quarrying-engines, are sometimes so perfect that drawings of them are made with the sepia taken from their own ink-bags ; so here, by a happy chance, there have come down to us, from a long-extinct race of men, those actual secretions of their daily life, which furnish colouring matter for a picture of them. By great perseverance our explorers have discovered the key to their imperfectly-developed language ; and in course of years have been able to put together facts yielding us faint ideas of the strange peoples who lived in the northern hemisphere during the last pre-glacial period.

" A report just issued refers to a time called by these peoples the middle of the nineteenth century of their era ; and it concerns a nation of considerable interest to us—the English. Though until now no traces of this ancient nation were known to exist, yet there survived the names of certain great men it produced—one a poet whose range of imagination and depth of insight are said to have exceeded those of all who went before him; the other, a man of science, of whom, profound as we may suppose in many ways, we know definitely this, that to all nations then living, and that have since lived, he taught how the Universe is balanced. What kind of people the English were, and what kind of civilization they had, have thus always been questions exciting curiosity. The facts disclosed by this report, are scarcely like those anticipated. Search was first made for traces of these great men, who, it was supposed, would be conspicuously commemorated. Little was found, however. It did, indeed, appear that the last of them, who revealed to mankind the constitution of the heavens, had received a name of honour like that which they gave to a successful trader who presented an address to their monarch; and besides a tree planted in his memory, a small statue to their great poet had been put up in one of their temples, where, however, it was almost lost among the many and large monuments to their fighting chiefs. Not that commemorative structures of magnitude were never erected by the English. Our explorers discovered traces of a gigantic one, in which, apparently, persons of distinction and deputies from all nations were made to take part in honouring some being—man he can scarcely have been. For it is difficult to conceive that any man could have had a worth transcendent enough to draw from them such extreme homage, when they thought so little of those by whom their name as a race has been saved from oblivion. Their distribution of monumental honours was, indeed, in all respects remarkable. To a physician named Jenner, who, by a mode of mitigating the ravages of a horrible disease, was said to have rescued many thousands from death, they erected a memorial statue in one of their chief public places. After some years, however, repenting them of giving to this statue so conspicuous a position, they banished it to a far corner of one of their suburban gardens, frequented chiefly by children and nursemaids; and in its place, they erected a statue to a great leader of their fighters—one Napier, who had helped them to conquer and keep down certain weaker races. The reporter does not tell us whether this last had been instrumental in destroying as many lives as the first had saved; but he remarks—'I could not cease wondering at this strange substitution among a people who professed a religion of peace.'   This does not seem to have been an act out of harmony with their usual acts: quite the contrary. The records show that to keep up the remembrance of a great victory gained over a neighbouring nation, they held for many years an annual banquet, much in the spirit of the commemorative scalp-dances of still more barbarous peoples; and there was never wanting a priest to ask on the banquet, a blessing from one they named the God of love. In some respects, indeed, their code of conduct seems not to have advanced beyond, but to have gone back from, the code of a still more ancient people from whom their creed was derived. One of the laws of this ancient people was, 'an eye for an eye, and a tooth for a tooth;' but sundry laws of the English, especially those concerning acts that interfered with some so-called sports of their ruling classes, inflicted penalties which imply that their principle had become 'a leg for an eye, and an arm for a tooth.' The relations of their creed to the creed of this ancient people, are, indeed, difficult to understand. They had at one time cruelly persecuted this ancient people—Jews they were called—because that particular modification of the Jewish religion which they, the English, nominally adopted, was one which the Jews would not adopt. And yet, marvellous to relate, while they tortured the Jews for not agreeing with them, they substantially agreed with the Jews. Not only, as above instanced, in the law of retaliation did they outdo the Jews, instead of obeying the quite-opposite principle of the teacher they worshipped as divine, but they obeyed the Jewish law, and disobeyed this divine teacher, in other ways—as in the rigid observance of every seventh day, which he had deliberately discountenanced. Though they were angry with those who did not nominally believe in Christianity (which was the name of their religion), yet they ridiculed those who really believed in it; for some few people among them, nicknamed Quakers, who aimed to carry out Christian precepts instead of Jewish precepts, they made butts for their jokes. Nay, more; their substantial adhesion to the creed they professedly repudiated, was clearly demonstrated by this, that in each of their temples they fixed up in some conspicuous place, the ten commandments of the Jewish religion, while they rarely, if ever, fixed up the two Christian commandments given instead of them. 'And yet,' says the reporter, after dilating on these strange facts, 'though the English were greatly given to missionary enterprises of all kinds, and though I sought diligently among the records of these, I could find no trace of a society for converting the English people from Judaism to Christianity.' This mention of their missionary enterprises introduces other remarkable anomalies. Being anxious to get adherents to this creed which they adopted in name but not in fact, they sent out men to various parts of the world to propagate it—one part, among others, being that subjugated territory above named. There the English missionaries taught the gentle precepts of their faith; and there the officers employed by their government exemplified these precepts: one of the exemplifications being that, to put down a riotous sect, they took fifty out of sixty-six who had surrendered, and, without any trial, blew them from the guns, as they called it—tied them to the mouths of cannon and shattered their bodies to pieces. And then, curiously enough, having thus taught and thus exemplified their religion, they expressed great surprise at the fact that the only converts their missionaries could obtain among these people, were hypocrites and men of characters so bad that no one would employ them.

"Nevertheless, these semi-civilized English had their good points. Odd as must have been the delusion which made them send out missionaries to inferior races, who were always ill used by their sailors and settlers, and eventually extirpated, yet on finding that they spent annually a million of their money in missionary and allied enterprises, we cannot but see some generosity of motive in them. Their country was dotted over with hospitals and almshouses, and institutions for taking care of the diseased and indigent; and their towns were overrun with philanthropic societies, which, without saying anything about the wisdom of their policy, clearly implied good feeling. They expended in the legal relief of their poor as much as, and at one time more than, a tenth of the revenue raised for all national purposes. One of their remarkable deeds was, that to get rid of a barbarous institution of those times, called slavery, under which, in their colonies, certain men held complete possession of others, their goods, their bodies, and practically even their lives, they paid down twenty millions of their money. And a not less striking proof of sympathy was that, during a war between two neighbouring nations, they contributed large sums, and sent out many men and women, to help in taking care of the wounded and assisting the ruined.

" The facts brought to light by these explorations are thus extremely instructive. Now that, after tens of thousands of years of discipline, the lives of men in society have become harmonious—now that character and conditions have little by little grown into adjustment, we are apt to suppose that congruity of institutions, conduct, sentiments, and beliefs, is necessary. We think it almost impossible that, in the same society, there should be daily practised principles of quite opposite kinds ; and it seems to us scarcely credible that men should have, or profess to have, beliefs with which their acts are absolutely irreconcilable. Only that extremely-rare disorder, insanity, could explain the conduct of one who, knowing that fire burns, nevertheless thrusts his hand into the flame ; and to insanity also we should ascribe the behaviour of one who, professing to think a certain course morally right, pursued the opposite course. Yet the revelations yielded by these ancient remains, show us that societies could hold together notwithstanding what we should think a chaos of conduct and of opinion. Nay more, they show us that it was possible for men to profess one thing and do another, without betraying a consciousness of inconsistency. One piece of evidence is curiously to the point. Among their multitudinous agencies for beneficent purposes, the English had a 'Naval and Military Bible Society'—a society for distributing copies of their sacred book among their professional fighters on sea and land; and this society was subscribed to, and chiefly managed by, leaders among these fighters. It is, indeed, suggested by the reporter, that for these classes of men they had an expurgated edition of their sacred book, from which the injunctions to 'return good for evil,' and to 'turn the cheek to the smiter,' were omitted. It may have been so; but, even if so, we have a remarkable instance of the extent to which conviction and conduct may be diametrically opposed, without any apparent perception that they are opposed. We habitually assume that a distinctive trait of humanity is rationality, and that rationality involves consistency; yet here we find an extinct race (unquestionably human and regarding itself as rational) in which the inconsistency of conduct and professed belief was as great as can well be imagined. Thus we are warned against supposing that what now seems to us natural was always natural. We have our eyes opened to an error which has been getting confirmed among us for these thousands of years, that social phenomena and the phenomena of human nature necessarily hang together in the ways we see around us."

Before summing up what has been said under the title of "Subjective difficulties—Intellectual," I may remark that this group of difficulties is separated from the group of "Objective Difficulties," dealt with in the last chapter, rather for the sake of convenience than because the division can be strictly maintained. In contemplating obstacles to interpretation—phenomena being on the one side and intelligence on the other—we may, as we please, ascribe failure either to the inadequacy of the intelligence or to the involved nature of the phenomena. An obstacle is subjective or objective according to our point of view. But the obstacles above set forth arise in so direct a way from conspicuous defects of human intelligence, that they may, more appropriately than the preceding ones, be classed as subjective. So regarding them, then, we have to beware, in the first place, of this tendency to automorphic interpretation; or rather, having no alternative but to conceive the natures of other men in terms furnished by our own feelings and ideas, we have to beware of the mistakes likely hence to arise—discounting our conclusions as well as we can. Further, we must be on our guard against the two opposite prevailing errors respecting Man, and against the sociological errors flowing from them: we have to get rid of the two beliefs that human nature is unchangeable, and that it is easily changed; and we have, instead, to become familiar with the conception of a human nature that is changed in the slow succession of generations by social discipline. Another obstacle not to be completely surmounted by any, and to be partially surmounted by but few, is that resulting from the want of intellectual faculty complex enough to grasp the extremely-complex phenomena which Sociology deals with. There can be no complete conception of a sociological fact, considered as a component of Social Science, unless there are present to thought all its essential factors; and the power of keeping them in mind with due clearness, as well as in their proper proportions and combinations, has yet to be reached. Then beyond this difficulty, only to be in a measure overcome, there is the further difficulty, not however by any means so great, of enlarging the conceptive capacity; so that it may admit the widely-divergent and extremely-various combinations of social phenomena. That rigidity of conception produced in us by experiences of our own social life in our own time, has to be exchanged for a plasticity that can receive with ease, and accept as natural, the countless combinations of social phenomena utterly unlike, and sometimes exactly opposite to, those we are familiar with.

Without such a plasticity there can be no proper understanding of co-existing social states allied to our own, still less of past social states, or social states of alien civilized races and races in early stages of development.

CHAPTER VII.

SUBJECTIVE DIFFICULTIES—EMOTIONAL.

THAT passion perverts judgment, is an observation sufficiently trite; but the more general observation of which it should form part, that emotion of every kind and degree disturbs the intellectual balance, is not trite, and even where recognized, is not duly taken into account. Stated in full, the truth is that no propositions, save those which are absolutely indifferent to us, immediately and remotely, can be contemplated without likings and repugnances affecting the opinions we form about them. There are two modes in which our conclusions are thus falsified. Excited feelings make us wrongly estimate probability; and they also make us wrongly estimate importance. Some cases will show this.

All who are old enough, remember the murder committed by Müller on the North London Railway some years ago. Most persons, too, will remember that for some time afterwards there was universally displayed, a dislike to travelling by railway in company with a single other passenger—supposing him to be unknown. Though, up to the date of the murder in question, countless journeys had been made by two strangers together in the same compartment without evil being suffered by either—though, after the death of Mr. Briggs, the probabilities were immense against the occurrence of a similar fate to another person similarly placed; yet there was habitually aroused a fear that would have been appropriate only had the danger been considerable. The amount of feeling excited was quite incommensurate with the risk. While the chance was a million to one against evil, the anticipation of evil was as strong as though the chance had been a thousand to one or a hundred to one. The emotion of dread destroyed the balance of judgment, and a rational estimate of likelihood became impossible; or rather, a rational estimate of likelihood if formed was wholly inoperative on conduct.

Another instance was thrust on my attention during the small-pox epidemic, which a while since so unaccountably spread, after twenty years of compulsory vaccination. A lady living in London, sharing in the general trepidation, was expressing her fears to me. I asked her whether, if she lived in a town of twenty thousand inhabitants and heard of one person dying of small-pox in the course of a week, she would be much alarmed. Naturally she answered, no; and her fears were somewhat calmed when I pointed out that, taking the whole population of London, and the number of deaths per week from small-pox, this was about the rate of mortality at that time caused by it. Yet in other minds, as in her mind, panic had produced an entire incapacity for forming a rational estimate of the peril. Nay, indeed, so perturbing was the emotion, that an unusual amount of danger to life was imagined at a time when the danger to life was smaller than usual. For the returns showed that the mortality from all causes was rather below the average than above it. While the evidence proved that the risk of death was less than common, this wave of feeling which spread through society produced an irresistible conviction that it was uncommonly great.

These examples show in a clear way, what is less clearly shown of examples hourly occurring, that the associated ideas constituting a judgment, are much affected in their relations to one another by the co-existing emotion. Two ideas will cohere feebly or strongly, according as the correlative nervous states involve a feeble or a strong discharge along the lines of nervous connexion;

and hence a large wave of feeling, implying as it does a voluminous discharge in all directions, renders such two ideas more coherent. This is so even when the feeling is not relevant to the ideas, as is shown by the vivid recollections of trivialities seen on occasions of great excitement; and it is still more so when the feeling is relevant—that is, when the proposition formed by the ideas is itself the cause of excitement. Much of the emotion tends, in such case, to discharge itself through the channels connecting the elements of the proposition; and predicate follows subject with a persistence out of all proportion to that which is justified by experience.

We see this with emotions of all orders. How greatly maternal affection falsifies a mother's opinion of her child, every one observes. How those in love fancy superiorities where none are visible to unconcerned spectators, and remain blind to defects that are conspicuous to all others, is matter of common remark. Note, too, how, in the holder of a lottery-ticket, hope generates a belief utterly at variance with probability as numerically estimated; or how an excited inventor confidently expects a success which calm judges see to be impossible. That "the wish is father to the thought," here so obviously true, is true more or less in nearly all cases where there is a wish. And in other cases, as where horror is aroused by the fancy of something supernatural, we see that in the absence of wish to believe, there may yet arise belief if violent emotion goes along with the ideas that are joined together.

Though there is some recognition of the fact that men's judgments on social questions are distorted by their emotions, the recognition is extremely inadequate. Political passion, class-hatred, and feelings of great intensity, are alone admitted to be large factors in determining opinions. But, as above implied, we have to take account of emotions of many kinds and of all degrees, down to slight likes and dislikes. For, if we look closely into our own beliefs on public affairs, as well as into the beliefs of those around us, we find them to be caused much more by aggregates of feelings than by examinations of evidence. No one, even if he tries, succeeds in preventing the slow growth of sympathies with, or antipathies to, certain institutions, customs, ideas, &c.; and if he watches himself, he will perceive that unavoidably each new question coming before him, is considered in relation to the mass of convictions which have been gradually moulded into agreement with his sympathies and antipathies.

When the reader has admitted, as he must if he is candid with himself, that his opinion on any political act or proposal is commonly formed in advance of direct evidence, and that he rarely takes the trouble to inquire whether direct evidence justifies it; he will see how great are those difficulties in the way of sociological science, which arise from the various emotions excited by the matters it deals with. Let us note, first, the effects of some emotions of a general kind, which we are apt to overlook.

The state of mind called impatience is one of these. If a man swears at some inanimate thing which he cannot adjust as he wishes, or if, in wintry weather, slipping down and hurting himself, he vents his anger by damning gravitation; his folly is manifest enough to spectators, and to himself also when his irritation has died away. But in the political sphere it is otherwise. A man may here, in spirit if not in word, damn a law of nature without being himself aware, and without making others aware, of his absurdity.

. The state of feeling often betrayed towards Political Economy exemplifies this. An impatience accompanying the vague consciousness that certain cherished convictions or pet schemes are at variance with politico-economical truths, shows itself in contemptuous words applied to these truths. Knowing that his theory of government and plans for social reformation are discountenanced by it, Mr. Carlyle manifests his annoyance by calling Political Economy "the dismal science." And among others than his adherents, there are many belonging to all parties, retrograde and progressive, who display repugnance to this body of doctrine with which their favourite theories do not agree. Yet a little thought might show them that their feeling is much of the same kind as would be scorn vented by a perpetual-motion schemer against the principles of Mechanics.

To see that these generalizations which they think of as cold and hard, and acceptable only by the unsympathetic, are nothing but statements of certain modes of action arising out of human nature, which are no less beneficent than necessary, they need only suppose for a moment that human nature had opposite tendencies. Imagine that, instead of preferring to buy things at low prices, men habitually preferred to give high prices for them; and imagine that, conversely, sellers rejoiced in getting low prices instead of high ones. Is it not obvious that production and distribution and exchange, assuming them possible under such conditions, would go on in ways entirely different from their present ways? If men went for each commodity to a place where it was difficult of production, instead of going to a place where it could be produced easily; and if instead of transferring articles of consumption from one part of a kingdom to another along the shortest routes, they habitually chose round-about routes, so that the cost in labour and time might be the greatest; is it not clear that, could industrial and commercial arrangements of any kinds exist, they would be so unlike the present arrangements as to be inconceivable by us? And if this is undeniable, is it not equally undeniable that the processes of production, distribution, and exchange, as they now go on, are processes determined by certain fundamental traits in human nature; and that Political Economy is nothing more than a statement of the laws of these processes as inevitably resulting from such traits?

That the generalizations of political economists are not all true, and that some, which are true in the main, need qualification, is very likely. But to admit this, is not in the least to admit that there are no true generalizations of this order to be made. Those who see, or fancy they see, flaws in politico-economical conclusions, and thereupon sneer at Political Economy, remind me of the theologians who lately rejoiced so much over the discovery of an error in the estimation of the Sun's distance; and thought the occasion so admirable a one for ridiculing men of science. It is characteristic of theologians to find a solace in whatever shows human imperfection; and in this case they were elated because astronomers discovered that, while their delineation of the Solar System remained exactly right in all its proportions, the absolute dimensions assigned were too great by about one-thirtieth. In one respect, however, the comparison fails; for though the theologians taunted the astronomers, they did not venture to include Astronomy within the scope of their contempt—did not do as those to whom they are here compared, who show contempt, not for political economists only, but for Political Economy itself.

Were they calm, these opponents of the political economists would see that as, out of certain physical properties of things there inevitably arise certain modes [of action, which, as generalized, constitute physical science; so out of the properties of men, intellectual and emotional, there inevitably arise certain laws of social processes, including, among others, those through which mutual aid in satisfying wants is made possible. They would see that, but for these processes, the laws of which Political Economy seeks to generalize, men would have continued in the lowest stage of barbarism to the present hour. They would see that instead of jeering at the science and those who pursue it, their course should be to show in what respects the generalizations thus far made are untrue, and how they may be so expressed as to correspond to the truth more nearly.

I need not further exemplify the perturbing influence of impatience in sociological inquiry. Along with the irrational hope so conspicuously shown by every party having a new project for the furtherance of human welfare, there habitually goes this irrational irritation in presence of stern truths which negative sanguine anticipations. Be it some way of remedying the evils of competition, some scheme for rendering the pressure of population less severe, some method of organizing a government so as to secure complete equity, some plan for reforming men by teaching, by restriction, by punishment; anything like calm consideration of probabilities as estimated from experience, is excluded by this eagerness for an immediate result; and instead of submission to the necessities of things, there comes vexation, felt if not expressed, against them, or against those who point them out, or against both.

That feelings of love and hate make rational judgments impossible in public affairs, as in private affairs, we can clearly enough see in others, though not so clearly in ourselves. Especially can we see it when these others belong to an alien society. France, during and since the late war, has furnished us almost daily with illustrations. The fact that while the struggle was going on, any foreigner in Paris was liable to be seized as a Prussian, and that, if charged with being a Prussian, he was forthwith treated as one, sufficiently proves that hate makes rational estimation of evidence impossible. The marvellous distortions which this passion produces were abundantly exemplified during the reign of the Commune; and yet again after the Commune was subdued. The "preternatural suspicion," as Mr. Carlyle called it, which characterized conduct during the first revolution, characterized conduct during the late catastrophe And it is displayed still. The sayings and doings of French political parties, alike in the Assembly, in the press, and in private societies, show that mutual hate causes mutual misinterpretations, fosters false inferences, and utterly vitiates sociological ideas.

While, however, it is manifest to us that among our neighbours, strong sympathies and antipathies make men's views unreasonable, we do not perceive that among ourselves sym-

pathies and antipathies distort judgments in degrees, not perhaps
so extreme, but still in very great degrees. Instead of French
opinion on French affairs, let us take English opinion on French
affairs—not affairs of recent date, but affairs of the past. And
instead of a case showing how these feelings falsify the estimates
of evidence, let us take a case showing how they falsify the estimates of the relative gravities of evils, and the relative degrees
of blameworthiness of actions.

Feudalism had decayed: its benefits had died out and only
its evils had survived. While the dominant classes no longer
performed their functions, they continued their exactions and
maintained their privileges. Seignorial power was exercised
solely for private benefit, and at every step met the unprivileged
with vexatious claims and restrictions. The peasant was called
from his heavily-burdened bit of land to work gratis for a
neighbouring noble, who gave him no protection in return. He
had to bear uncomplainingly the devouring of his crops by this
man's game; to hand him a toll before he could cross the river;
to buy from him the liberty to sell at market—nay, such portion
of grain as he reserved for his own use he could eat only after
paying for the grinding of it at his seigneur's mill, and for
having it baked at his bakehouse. And then, added to the
seignorial exactions, came the exactions of the Church, still more
mercilessly enforced.   Town-life was shackled as much
as country-life. Manufacturers were hampered by almost incredible restrictions. Government decided on the persons to be
employed, the articles to be made, the materials to be used, the
processes to be followed, and the qualities of the products.
State-officers broke the looms and burnt the goods that were not
made according to law. Improvements were illegal and in-
ventors were fined.[1] "Taxation was imposed exclusively on the
industrious classes, and in such a manner as to be an actual
penalty on production."[2] The currency had been debased to
one seventy-third of its original value. "No redress was obtainable for any injury to property or person when inflicted by people

of rank or court influence."[3] And the ruling power was upheld by "spies, false-witnesses, and pretended plots."   Along with these local tyrannies and universal abuses and exasperating obstacles to living almost beyond belief, there had gone on at the governing centre maladministration, corruption, extravagance: treasures were spent in building vast palaces, and enormous armies were sacrificed in inexcusable wars. Profuse expenditure, demanding more than could be got from crippled industry, had caused a chronic deficit. New taxes on the poor workers brought in no money, but only clamour and discontent; and to tax the rich idlers proved to be impracticable: the proposal that the clergy and *noblesse* should no longer be exempt from burdens such as were borne by the people, brought from these classes " a shriek of indignation and astonishment." And then, to make more conspicuous the worthlessness of the governing agencies of all orders, there was the corrupt life led by the Court, from the King downwards—France lying " with a harlot's foot on its neck."   Passing over the various phases of the break-up which ended this intolerable state—phases throughout which the dominant classes, good-for-nothing and unrepentant, strove to recover their power, and, enlisting foreign rulers, brought upon France invading armies—we come presently to a time when, mad with anger and fear, the people revenged themselves on such of their past tormentors as remained among them. Leagued, as many of these were, with those of their order who were levying war against liberated France—leagued, as many others were supposed to be, with these enemies to the Republic at home and abroad—incorrigible as they proved themselves by their plottings and treacheries ; there at length came down on them the September massacres and the Reign of Terror, during which nearly ten thousand of those implicated, or supposed to be implicated, were killed or formally executed. The Nemesis was sufficiently fearful. Lamentable sufferings and death fell on innocent as well as guilty. Hate and despair combined to arouse an undistinguishing cruelty, and, in some of the

8

leading actors, a cold-blooded ferocity. Nevertheless, recognizing all this—recognizing also the truth that those who wreaked this vengeance were intrinsically no better than those on whom it was wreaked—we must admit that the bloodshed had its excuse. The panic of a people threatened with re-imposition of dreadful shackles, was not to be wondered at. That the expected return of a time like that in which gaunt figures and haggard faces about the towns and the country, indicated the social disorganiza-tion, should excite men to a blind fury, was not unnatural. If they became frantic at the thought that there was coming back a state under which there might again be a slaying of hundreds of thousands of men in battles fought to gratify the spite of a King's concubine, we need not be greatly astonished. And some of the horror expressed at the fate of the ten thousand victims, might fitly be reserved for the abominations which caused it.

From this partially-excusable bloodshed, over which men shudder excessively, let us turn now to the immeasurably-greater bloodshed, having no excuse, over which they do not shudder at all. Out of the sanguinary chaos of the Revolution, there pre-sently rose a soldier whose immense ability, joined with his absolute unscrupulousness, made him now general, now consul, now autocrat. He was untruthful in an extreme degree : lying in his despatches day by day, never writing a page without bad faith,[4] nay, even giving to others lessons in telling falsehoods.[5] He professed friendship while plotting to betray ; and quite early in his career made the wolf-and-lamb fable his guide. He got antagonists into his power by promises of clemency, and then executed them. To strike terror, he descended to barbarities like those of the bloodthirsty conquerors of old, of whom his career reminds us : as in Egypt, when, to avenge fifty of his soldiers, he beheaded 2,000 fellahs, throwing their headless corpses into the Nile ; or as at Jaffa, when 2,500 of the garrison who finally surrendered, were, at his order, deliberately mas-sacred. Even his own officers, not over-scrupulous, as we may

suppose, were shocked by his brutality—sometimes refusing to
execute his sanguinary decrees.   Indeed, the instincts of the
savage were scarcely at all qualified in him by what we call
moral sentiments; as we see in his proposal to burn "two or
three of the larger communes" in La Vendée; as we see in his
wish to introduce bull-fights into France, and to revive the combats of he Roman arena; as we see in the cold-blooded sacrifice
of his own soldiers, when he ordered a useless outpost attack
merely that his mistress might witness an engagement! That
such a man should have prompted the individual killing of leading antagonists, and set prices on their heads, as in the cases of
Mourad-Bey and Count Frotté, and that to remove the Duc
d'Enghien he should have committed a crime like in its character
to that of one who hires a bravo, but unlike by entailing on him
no danger, was quite natural.   It was natural, too, that in addition to countless treacheries and breaches of faith in his dealings
with foreign powers, such a man should play the traitor to his
own nation, by stamping out its newly-gained free institutions,
and substituting his own military despotism.   Such being
the nature of the man, and such being a few illustrations of his
cruelty and unscrupulousness, contemplate now his greater crimes
and their motives.   Year after year he went on sacrificing by
tens of thousands and hundreds of thousands the French people
and the people of Europe at large, to gratify his lust of power
and his hatred of opponents.   To feed his insatiable ambition,
and to crush those who resisted his efforts after universal domi-
nion, he went on seizing the young men of France, forming army
after army, that were destroyed in destroying like armies raised
by neighbouring nations.   In the Russian campaign alone, out
of 552,000 men in Napoleon's army left dead or prisoners, but
few returned home; while the Russian force of more than
200,000 was reduced to 30,000 or 40,000 : implying a total sacrifice of considerably more than half-a-million lives.   And when
the mortality on both sides by death in battle, by wounds, and
by disease, throughout the Napoleonic campaigns is summed up,

it exceeds at the lowest computation two millions.[6] And all this slaughter, all this suffering, all this devastation, was gone through because one man had a restless desire to be despot over all men.

What has been thought and felt in England about the two sets of events above contrasted, and about the actors in them? The bloodshed of the Revolution has been spoken of with words of horror; and for those who wrought it there has been unqualified hate. About the enormously-greater bloodshed which these wars of the Consulate and the Empire entailed, little or no horror is expressed; while the feeling towards the modern Attila who was guilty of this bloodshed, is shown by decorating rooms with portraits and busts of him. See the beliefs which these respective feelings imply :—

Over ten thousand deaths we may fitly shudder and lament.

Two million deaths call for no shuddering or lamentation.

As the ten thousand were slain because of the tyrannies, cruelties, and treacheries, committed by them or their class, their deaths are very pitiable.

As the two millions, innocent of offence, were taken by force from classes already oppressed and impoverished, the slaughter of them need excite no pity.

The sufferings of the ten thousand and of their relatives, who expiated their own misdeeds and the misdeeds of their class, may fitly form subjects for heart-rending stories and pathetic pictures.

There is nothing heart-rending in the sufferings of the two millions who died for no crimes of their own or their class; nor is there anything pathetic in the fates of the families throughout Europe, from which the two millions were taken.

That despair and the indignation of a betrayed people, brought about this slaughter of ten thousand, makes the atrocity without palliation.

That one vile man's lust of power was gratified through the deaths of the two millions, greatly palliates the sacrifice of them.

These are the antithetical propositions tacitly implied in the opinions that have been current in England about the French Revolution and the Napoleonic wars. Only by acceptance of such propositions can these opinions be defended. Such have been the emotions of men that, until quite recently, it has been the habit to speak with detestation of the one set of events, and to speak of the other set of events in words betraying admiration. Nay, even now these feelings are but partially qualified. While the names of the leading actors in the Reign of Terror are names of execration, we speak of Napoleon as "the Great," and Englishmen worship him by visiting his tomb and taking off their hats!

How, then, with such perverting emotions, is it possible to take rational views of sociological facts? Forming, as men do, such astoundingly-false conceptions of the relative amounts of evils and the relative characters of motives, how can they judge truly among institutions and actions, past or present? Clearly, minds thus swayed by disproportionate hates and admirations, cannot frame those balanced conclusions respecting social phenomena which alone constitute Social Science.

The sentiment which thus vents itself in horror at bad deeds for which there was much excuse, while to deeds incomparably more dreadful and without excuse, it gives applause very slightly qualified with blame, is a sentiment which, among other effects, marvellously perverts men's political conceptions. This awe of power, by the help of which social subordination has been, and still is, chiefly maintained—this feeling which delights to contemplate the imposing, be it in military successes, or be it in the grand pageantries, the sounding titles, and the sumptuous modes of living that imply supreme authority—this feeling which is offended by outbreaks of insubordination and acts or words of the kind called disloyal; is a feeling that inevitably generates delusions respecting governments, their capacities, their achievements. It transfigures them and all their belongings; as does every strong emotion the objects towards which it is drawn out.

Just as maternal love, idealizing offspring, sees perfections but not defects, and believes in the future good behaviour of a worth-less son, notwithstanding countless broken promises of amend-ment; so this power-worship idealizes the State, as embodied either in a despot, or in king, lords, and commons, or in a repub-lican assembly, and continually hopes in spite of continual dis-appointments.

How awe of power sways men's political beliefs, will be per-ceived on observing how it sways their religious beliefs. We shall best see this by taking an instance supplied by a people whose religious ideas are extremely crude. Here is an abstract of a description given by Captain Burton :—

"A pot of oil with a lighted wick was placed every night by the half-bred Portuguese Indians, before the painted doll, the patron saint of the boat in which we sailed from Goa. One evening, as the weather appeared likely to be squally, we observed that the usual compliment was not offered to the patron, and had the curiosity to inquire why. 'Why?' vociferated the tindal [captain], indignantly, ' if that chap can't keep the sky clear, he shall have neither oil nor wick from me, d—n him !' 'But I should have supposed that in the hour of danger you would have paid him more than usual attention ?' ' The fact is, Sahib, I have found out that the fellow is not worth his salt : the last time we had an infernal squall with him on board, and if he does not keep this one off, I'll just throw him overboard, and take to Santa Caterina ; hang me, if I don't—the brother-in-law !'" [brother-in-law, a common term of insult].[7]

By us it is scarcely imaginable that men should thus behave to their gods and demi-gods—should pray to them, should insult and sometimes whip them for not answering their prayers, and then should presently pray to them again. Let us pause before we laugh. Though in the sphere of religion our conduct does not betray such a contradiction, yet a contradiction essentially similar is betrayed by our conduct in the political sphere. Perpetual disappointment does not here cure us of perpetual expectation. Conceiving the State-agency as though it were something more than a cluster of men (a few clever, many ordinary, and some decidedly stupid), we ascribe to it marvellous powers of doing multitudinous things which men otherwise clustered are unable to do. We petition it to procure for us in some way which we do not doubt it can find, benefits of all orders; and pray it with unfaltering faith to secure us from every fresh evil. Time after time our hopes are balked. The good is not obtained, or something bad comes along with it; the evil is not cured, or some other evil as great or greater is produced. Our journals, daily and weekly, general and local, perpetually find failures to dilate upon: now blaming, and now ridiculing, first this department and then that. And yet, though the rectification of blunders, administrative and legislative, is a main part of public business—though the time of the Legislature is chiefly occupied in amending and again amending, until, after the many mischiefs implied by these needs for amendments, there often comes at last repeal; yet from day to day increasing numbers of wishes are expressed for legal repressions and State-management. This emotion which is excited by the forms of governmental power, and makes governmental power possible, is the root of a faith that springs up afresh however often cut down. To see how little the perennial confidence it generates is diminished by perennial disappointment, we need but remind ourselves of a few State-performances in the chief State-departments.

On the second page of the first chapter, by way of illustrating Admiralty-mismanagement, brief reference was made to three avoidable catastrophes which had happened to vessels of war within the twelvemonth. Their frequency is further shown by the fact that before the next chapter was published, two others had occurred : the *Lord Clyde* ran aground in the Mediterranean, and the *Royal Alfred* was seven hours on the Bahama reef. And then, more recently still, we have had the collision of the *Northumberland* and *Hercules* at Funchal, and the sinking of a vessel at Woolwich by letting a 35-ton gun fall from the slings on to her bottom. That the authorities of the Navy commit errors which the merchant service avoids, has been repeatedly shown of late, as in times past. It was shown by the disclosure respecting the corrosion of the *Glatton's* plates, which proved that the Admiralty had not adopted the efficient protective methods long used by private shipowners. It was shown when the loss of the *Ariadne's* sailors made us aware that a twenty-six gun frigate had not as many boats for saving life as are prescribed for a passenger-ship of 400 tons; and that for lowering her boats there was on board neither Kynaston's apparatus nor the much better apparatus of Clifford, which experience in the merchant service has thoroughly tested. It was shown by the non-adoption of Silver's governor for marine steam-engines; long used in private steam-ships to save machinery from breakage, but only now being introduced into the Navy after machinery has been broken.   On going back a little, this relative inefficiency of administration is still more strikingly shown :—instance the fact that during the Chinese expedition of 1841, a mortality at the rate of three or four per day in a crew of three hundred, arose from drinking muddy water from the paddy-fields, though, either by boiling it or by filtering it through charcoal, much of this mortality might have been prevented ; instance the fact that, within the memory of living officers (I have it from the mouth of one who had the experience), vessels of war leaving Deptford, filled their casks with Thames-water taken at ebb-tide, which water, during its subsequent period of putrefaction, had to be filtered through handkerchiefs before drinking, and then swallowed while holding the nose; or instance the accumulation of abominable abuses and malversations and tyrannies which produced the mutiny at Spithead.   But, perhaps, of all such illustrations, the most striking is that which the treatment of scurvy furnishes. It was in 1593 that sour juices were first recommended by Albertus ; and in the same year Sir R. Hawkins cured his crew of scurvy by lemon-juice. In 1600 Commodore Lancaster, who took out the first squadron of the East India Company's ships, kept the crew of his own ship in perfect health by lemon-juice, while the crews of the three accompanying ships were so disabled that he had to send his men on board to set their sails. In 1636 this remedy was again recommended in medical works on scurvy. Admiral Wagner, commanding our fleet in the Baltic in 1726, once more showed it to be a specific. In 1757 Dr. Lind, the physician to the naval hospital at Haslar, collected and published in an elaborate work, these and many other proofs of its efficacy. Nevertheless, scurvy continued to carry off thousands of our sailors. In 1780, 2,400 in the Channel Fleet were affected by it; and in 1795 the safety of the Channel Fleet was endangered by it. At length, in that year, the Admiralty ordered a regular supply of lemon-juice to the navy. Thus two centuries after the remedy was known, and forty years after a chief medical officer of the Government had given conclusive evidence of its worth, the Admiralty, forced thereto by an exacerbation of the evil, first moved in the matter. And what had been the effect of this amazing perversity of officialism? The mortality from scurvy during this long period had exceeded the mortality by battles, wrecks, and all casualties of sea-life put together![3]

How, through military administration there has all along run, and still runs, a kindred stupidity and obstructiveness, pages of examples might be accumulated to show. The debates pending the abolition of the purchase-system furnish many; the accounts of life at Aldershot and of autumn manœuvres furnish many; and many might be added in the shape of protests like those made against martinet riding-regulations, which entail ruptures on the soldiers, and against " our ridiculous drill-book," as independent officers are now agreeing to call it. Even limiting ourselves to sanitary administration in the army, the files of our journals and the reports of our commissions would yield multitudinous instances of scarcely-credible bungling—as in bad barrack-arrangements, of which we heard so much a few years ago; as in an absurd style of dress, such as that which led to the wholesale cutting-down of the Twelfth Cameronians when they arrived in China in 1841; as in the carelessness which lately caused the immense mortality by cholera among the 18th Hussars at Secunderabad, where, spite of medical protests repeated ever since 1818, soldiers have continued to be lodged in barracks that had "throughout India an infamous notoriety."[9] Or, not further to multiply instances, take the long-continued ignoring of ipecacuanha as a specific for dysentery, which causes so much mortality in our Indian Service:—

"It is a singular fact, that the introducers of the ipecacuanha into European practice, the Brazilian traveller Marcgrav, and the physician Piso (in 1648), explicitly stated that the powder is a specific cure for dysentery, in doses of a drachm and upwards ; but that this information appears never to have been acted upon till 1813, when Surgeon G. Playfair, of the East Indian Company's service, wrote testifying to its use in these doses. Again, in 1831, a number of reports of medical officers were published by the Madras Medical Board, showing its great effects in hourly doses of five grains, till frequently 100 grains were given in a short period ; testimony which, notwithstanding its weight, was doomed to be similarly overlooked, till quite recently, when it has been again brought directly under the notice of the Indian Government, which is making very vigorous efforts to introduce the culture of the plant into suitable districts of India."[10]

So that, notwithstanding the gravity of the evil, and the pressing need for this remedy from time to time thrust on the attention of the Indian authorities, nearly sixty years passed before the requisite steps were taken.[11]

That the State, which fails to secure the health of men, even in its own employ, should fail to secure the health of beasts, might perhaps be taken as self-evident; though possibly some, comparing the money laid out on stables with the money laid out on cottages, might doubt the corollary. Be this as it may, however, the recent history of cattle-diseases and of legislation to prevent cattle-diseases, yields the same lessons as are yielded above. Since 1848 there have been seven Acts of Parliament bearing the general titles of Contagious Diseases (Animals) Acts. Measures to "stamp out," as the phrase goes, this or that disease, have been called for as imperative. Measures have been passed, and then, expectation not having been fulfilled, amended measures have been passed, and then re-amended measures; so that of late no session has gone by without a bill to cure evils which previous bills tried to cure, but did not. Notwithstanding the keen interest felt by the ruling classes in the success of these measures, they have succeeded so ill, that the "foot-and-mouth disease" has not been "stamped out," has not even been kept in check, but during the past year has spread alarmingly in various parts of the kingdom. Continually the *Times* has had blaming letters, and reports of local meetings called to condemn the existing laws and to insist on better. From all quarters there have come accounts of ineffective regulations and incapable officials—of policemen who do the work of veterinary surgeons—of machinery described by Mr. Fleming, veterinary surgeon of the Royal Engineers, as "clumsy, disjointed, and inefficient."[12]

Is it alleged that the goodness of State-agency cannot be judged by measures so recent, the administration of which is at present imperfect? If so, let us look at that form of State-agency which is of most ancient date, and has had the longest time for perfecting its adjustments—let us take the Law in general, and its administration in general. Needs there do more than name these to remind the reader of the amazing inefficiency, confusion, doubtfulness, delay, which, proverbial from early times, continue still? Of penal statutes alone, which are assumed to be known by every citizen, 14,408 had been enacted from the time of Edward III. down to 1844. As was said by Lord Cranworth in the House of Peers, 16th February, 1853, the judges were supposed to be acquainted with all these laws, but, in fact, no human mind could master them, and ignorance had ceased to be a disgrace.[13] To this has to be added the accumulation of civil laws, similarly multitudinous, involved, unclassified, and to this again the enormous mass of "case law," filling over 1200 volumes and rapidly increasing, before there can be formed an idea of the chaos.　　Consider next, how there has come this chaos; out of which not even the highest

legal functionaries, much less the lower functionaries, much
less the ordinary citizens, can educe definite conclusions. Session after session the confusion has been worse confounded
by the passing of separate Acts, and successive amendments
of Acts, which are left unconnected with the multitudinous
kindred Acts and amendments that lie scattered through the
accumulated records of centuries. Suppose a trader should
make, day by day, separate memoranda of his transactions
with A, B, C, and the rest of his debtors and creditors. Suppose he should stick these on a file, one after another as
they were made, never even putting them in order, much less
entering them in his ledger. Suppose he should thus go on
throughout his life, and that, to learn the state of his account
with A, B, or C, his clerks had to search through this enormous
confused file of memoranda: being helped only by their memories and by certain private note-books which preceding clerks
had made for their own guidance, and left behind them. What
would be the state of the business? What chance would A, B,
and C have of being rightly dealt with? Yet this, which, as a
method of conducting private business, is almost too ludicrous
for fiction, is in public business nothing more than grave fact.
And the result of the method is exactly the one to be anticipated.
Counsel's opinions differing, authorities contradicting one another,
judges at issue, courts in collision. The conflict extends all
through the system from top to bottom. Every day's law-reports
remind us that each decision given is so uncertain that the probability of appeal depends chiefly on the courage or pecuniary
ability of the beaten litigant—not on the nature of the decision;
and if the appeal is made, a reversal of the decision is looked
for as by no means unlikely.   And then, on contemplating
the ultimate effect, we find it to be—the multiplication of
aggressions. Were the law clear, were verdicts certain to be in
conformity with it, and did asking for its protection entail no
chance of great loss or of ruin, very many of the causes that
come before our courts would never be heard of, for the reason

that the wrongs they disclose would not be committed; nor would there be committed those yet more numerous wrongs to which the bad are prompted by the belief that the persons wronged will not dare to seek redress. Here, where State-agency has had centuries upon centuries in which to develop its appliances and show its efficiency, it is so inefficient that citizens dread employing it, lest instead of getting succour in their distress they should bring on themselves new sufferings. And then—startling comment on the system, if we could but see it!— there spring up private voluntary combinations for doing the business which the State should do, but fails to do. Here in London there is now proposed a Tribunal of Commerce, for administering justice among traders, on the pattern of that which in Paris settles eighteen thousand cases a year, at an average cost of fifteen shillings each!

Even after finding the State perform so ill this vital function, one might have expected that it would perform well such a simple function as the keeping of documents. Yet, in the custody of the national records, there has been a carelessness such as "no merchant of ordinary prudence" would show in respect to his account-books. One portion of these records was for a long time kept in the White Tower, close to some tons of gunpowder; and another portion was placed near a steam-engine in daily use. Some records were deposited in a temporary shed at the end of Westminster Hall, and thence, in 1830, were removed to other sheds in the King's Mews, Charing Cross, where, in 1836, their state is thus described by the Report of a Select Committee:—

"In these sheds 4,136 cubic feet of national records were deposited in the most neglected condition. Besides the accumulated dust of centuries, all, when these operations commenced (the investigation into the state of the Records), were found to be very damp. Some were in a state of inseparable adhesion to the stone walls. There were numerous fragments which had only just escaped entire consumption by vermin, and many were in the last stage of putrefaction. Decay and damp had rendered a large quantity so fragile as hardly to admit of being touched; others, particularly those in the form of rolls, were so coagulated together that they could not be uncoiled. Six or seven perfect skeletons of rats were found imbedded, and bones of these vermin were generally distributed throughout the mass."

Thus if we array in order the facts which are daily brought to light, but unhappily drop out of men's memories as fast as others are added, we find a like history throughout. Now the complaint is of the crumbling walls of the Houses of Parliament, which, built of stone chosen by a commission, nevertheless begin to decay in parts first built before other parts are completed. Now the scandal is about a new fort at Seaford, based on the shingle so close to the sea that a storm washes a great part of it away. Now there comes the account of a million and a half spent in building the Alderney harbour, which, being found worse than useless, threatens to entail further cost for its destruction. And then there is an astounding disclosure about financial irregularities in the Post-office and Telegraph departments—a disclosure showing that, in 1870-1, two-thirds of a million having been spent by officials without authority, and the offence having been condoned by Parliament, there again occurs, in 1871-2, a like unwarranted expenditure of four-fifths of a million—a disclosure showing that while the Audit-department disputes a charge of sixpence for porterage in a small bill, it lets millions slip through its fingers without check.[14] Scarcely a journal can be taken up that has not some blunder referred to in a debate, or brought to light by a Report, or pointed out in a letter, or commented on in a leader. Do I need an illustration? I take up the *Times* of this morning (November 13) and read that the new bankruptcy law, substituted for the bankruptcy laws which failed miserably, is administered in rooms so crowded and noisy that due care and thought on the part of officials is scarcely possible, and, further, that as one part of the court sits in the City and another part in Lincoln's Inn, solicitors have often to be in both places at the same time. Do I need more illustrations? They come in abundance between the day on which the foregoing sentence was written and the day (November 20)

on which I revise it. Within this short time mismanagement
has been shown in a treatment of the police that has created a
mutiny among them; in a treatment of government copying-
clerks that causes them publicly to complain of broken promises;
in a treatment of postmen that calls from them disrespectful
behaviour towards their superiors : all at the same time that
there is going on the controversy about Park-rules, which have
been so issued as to evade constitutional principles, and so administered as to bring the law into contempt.   Yet as fast
as there come proofs of mal-administration there come demands
that administration shall be extended.   Here, in the very same
copy of the *Times*, are two authorities, Mr. Reed and Sir W.
Fairbairn, speaking at different meetings, both condemning the
enormous bungling and consequent loss of life that goes on
under the existing Government-supervision of vessels, and both
insisting on "legislation" and "proper inspection" as the remedies.[15]   Just as, in societies made restive by despotism, the
proposed remedy for the evils and dangers brought about is
always more despotism; just as, along with the failing power of
a decaying Papacy, there goes, as the only fit cure, a re-assertion
of Papal infallibility, with emphatic *obbligato* from a Council ; so,
to set right the misdoings of State-agency, the proposal always
is more State-agency.   When, after long continuance of coal-
mine inspection, coal-mine explosions keep recurring, the cry is
for more coal-mine inspection.   When railway accidents multiply, notwithstanding the oversight of officials appointed by law
to see that railways are safe, the unhesitating demand is for
more such officials.   Though, as Lord Salisbury lately remarked
of governing bodies deputed by the State, " they begin by being
enthusiastic and extravagant, and they are very apt to end in
being wooden "—though, through the press and by private conversation, men are perpetually reminded that when it has ceased
to wield the new broom, each deputy governing power tends to
become either a king-stork that does mischief, or a king-log that
does nothing ; yet more deputy governing powers are asked for

with unwavering faith.   While the unwisdom of officialism is
daily illustrated, the argument for each proposed new department sets out with the postulate that officials will act wisely.
After endless comments on the confusion and apathy and delay
of Government offices, other Government offices are advocated.
After ceaseless ridicule of red-tape, the petition is for more red-
tape.   Daily we castigate the political idol with a hundred pens,
and daily pray to it with a thousand tongues.

The emotion which thus destroys the balance of judgment, lies
deep in the natures of men as they have been and still are.   This
root out of which there grow hopes that are no sooner blighted
than kindred hopes grow up in their places, is a root reaching
down to the lowest stages in civilization.   The conquering chief,
feared, marvelled at, for his strength or sagacity—distinguished
from others by a quality thought of as supernatural (when the
antithesis of this with natural becomes thinkable), ever excites a
disproportionate faith and expectation.   Having done or seen
things beyond the power or insight of inferiors, there is no
knowing what other things he may not do or see.   After death
his deeds become magnified by tradition; and his successor,
inheriting his authority, executing his commands, and keeping
up secret communication with him, acquires either thus, or by
his own superiority, or by both, a like credit for powers that
transcend the ordinary human powers.   So there accumulates
an awe of the ruler, with its correlative faith.   On tracing the
genealogy of the governing agent, thus beginning as god, and
descendant of the gods, and having titles and a worship in
common with the gods, we see there clings to it, through all its
successive metamorphoses, more or less of this same ascribed
character, exciting this same sentiment.   "Divinely descended"
becomes presently "divinely appointed," "the Lord's anointed,"
"ruler by divine right," "king by the grace of God," &c.   And
then as fast as declining monarchical power brings with it
decreasing belief in the supernaturalness of the monarch (which,

however, long lingers in faint forms, as instance the supposed cure of king's evil), the growing powers of the bodies that assume his functions bring to them a share of the still-surviving sentiment. The "divinity that doth hedge a king" becomes, in considerable measure, the divinity that doth hedge a parliament. The superstitious reverence once felt towards the one, is transferred, in a modified form, to the other; taking with it a tacit belief in an ability to achieve any end that may be wished, and a tacit belief in an authority to which no limits may be set.

This sentiment, inherited and cultivated in men from childhood upwards, sways their convictions in spite of them. It generates an irrational confidence in all the paraphernalia and appliances and forms of State-action. In the very aspect of a law-deed, written in an archaic hand on dingy parchment, there is something which raises a conception of validity not raised by ordinary writing on paper. Around a Government-stamp there is a certain glamour which makes us feel as though the piece of paper bearing it was more than a mere mass of dry pulp with some indented marks. To any legal form of words there seems to attach an authority greater than that which would be felt were the language free from legal involutions and legal technicalities. And so is it with all the symbols of authority, from royal pageants downwards. That the judge's wig gives to his decisions a weight and sacredness they would not have were he bare-headed, is a fact familiar to every one. And when we descend to the lowest agents of the executive organization, we find the same thing. A man in blue coat and white-metal buttons, which carry with them the thought of State-authority, is habitually regarded by citizens as having a trustworthiness beyond that of a man who wears no such uniform; and this confidence survives all disproofs. Obviously, then, if men's judgments are thus ridiculously swayed, notwithstanding better knowledge, by the mere symbols of State-power, still more must they be so swayed by State-power itself, as exercised in ways that leave greater scope for the imagination. If awe and faith are irresistibly called out towards things which perception and reason tell us positively should not call them out, still more will awe and faith be called out towards those State-actions and influences on which perception and reason can less easily be brought to bear. If the beliefs prompted by this feeling of reverence survive even where they are flatly contradicted by common sense, still more will they survive where common sense cannot flatly contradict them.

How deeply rooted is this sentiment excited in men by embodied supremacy, will be seen on noting how it sways in common all orders of politicians, from the old-world Tory to the Red Republican. Contrasted as the extreme parties are in the types of Government they approve, and in the theories they hold respecting the source of governmental authority, they are alike in their unquestioning belief in governmental authority, and in showing almost unlimited faith in the ability of a Government to achieve any desired end. Though the form of the agency towards which the sentiment of loyalty is directed, is much changed, yet there is little change in the sentiment itself, or in the general conceptions it creates. The notion of the divine right of a person, has given place to the notion of the divine right of a representative assembly. While it is held to be a self-evident falsity that the single will of a despot can justly override the wills of a people, it is held to be a self-evident truth that the wills of one-half of a people *plus* some small fraction, may with perfect justice override the wills of the other half *minus* this small fraction—may override them in respect of any matter whatever. Unlimited authority of a majority has been substituted for unlimited authority of an individual. So unquestioning is the belief in this unlimited authority of a majority, that even the tacit suggestion of a doubt produces astonishment. True, if of one who holds that power deputed by the people is subject to no restrictions, you ask whether, if the majority decided that no person should be allowed to live beyond sixty, the decision might be legitimately executed, he would possibly hesitate. Or if you asked him whether the majority, being Catholic, might rightly require of the Protestant minority that they should either embrace Catholicism or leave the country, he would, influenced by the ideas of religious liberty in which he has been brought up, probably say no. But though his answers to sundry such questions disclose the fact that State-authority, even when uttering the national will, is not believed by him to be absolutely supreme ; his latent conviction that there are limits to it, lies so remote in the obscure background of his conscious-ness as to be practically non-existent. In all he says about what a Legislature should do, or forbid, or require, he tacitly assumes that any regulation may be enacted, and when enacted must be obeyed. And then, along with this authority not to be gainsaid, he believes in a capacity not to be doubted. Whatever the governing body decides to do, can be done, is the postulate which lies hidden in the schemes of the most revolutionary reformers. Analyze the programme of the Communalists, observe what is hoped for by the adherents of the Social and Democratic Re-public, or study the ideas of legislative action which our own Trades-Unionists entertain, and you find the implied belief to be that a Government, organized after an approved pattern, will be able to remedy all the evils complained of and to secure each proposed benefit.

Thus, the emotion excited by embodied power is one which sways, and indeed mainly determines, the beliefs, not only of those classed as the most subordinate, but even of those classed as the most insubordinate. It has a deeper origin than any political creed; and it more or less distorts the conceptions of all parties respecting governmental action.

This sentiment of loyalty, making it almost impossible to study the natures and actions of governing agencies with perfect calm-ness, greatly hinders sociological science, and must long continue to hinder it. For the sentiment is all-essential. Throughout the past, societies have been mainly held together by it. It is still an indispensable aid to social cohesion and the maintenance of order. And it will be long before social discipline has so far modified human character, that reverence for law, as rooted in the moral order of things, will serve in place of reverence for the power which enforces law.

Accounts of existing uncivilized races, as well as histories of the civilized races, show us à *posteriori*, what we might infer with certainty à *priori*, that in proportion as the members of a society are aggressive in their natures, they can be held together only by a proportionately-strong feeling of unreasoning reverence for a ruler. Some of the lowest types of men, who show but little of this feeling, show scarcely any social cohesion, and make no progress—instance the Australians. Where appreciable social development has taken place, we find subordination to chiefs; and, as the society enlarges, to a king. If we need an illustration that where there is great savageness, social union can be maintained only by great loyalty, we have it among those ferocious cannibals, the Fijians. Here, where the barbarism is so extreme that a late king registered by a row of many hundred stones the number of human victims he had devoured, the loyalty is so extreme that a man stands unbound to be knocked on the head if the king wills it: himself saying that the king's will must be done. And if, with this case in mind, we glance back over the past, and note the fealty that went along with brutality, in feudal ages; or if, at the present time, we observe how the least advanced European nations show a superstitious awe of the ruler which in the more advanced has become conventional respect; we shall perceive that decrease of the feeling goes on, and can normally go on, only as fast as the fitness of men for social co-operation increases. Manifestly, throughout all past time, assemblages of men in whom the aggressive selfishness of the predatory nature existed without this feeling which induces obedience to a controlling power, dissolved and disappeared: leaving the world to be peopled by men who had the required emotional balance. And it is manifest that even in a civilized society, if the sentiment of subordination becomes enfeebled without self-control gaining in strength proportionately, there arises a danger of social dissolution : a truth of which France supplies an illustration.

Hence, as above said, the conceptions of sociological phenomena, or, at least, of those all-important ones relating to governmental structures and actions, must now, and for a long time to come, be rendered more or less untrue by this perturbing emotion. Here, in the concrete, may be recognized the truth before stated in the abstract, that the individual citizen, imbedded in the social organism as one of its units, moulded by its influences, and aiding reciprocally to re-mould it, furthering its life while enabled by it to live, cannot so emancipate himself as to see things around him in their real relations.   Unless the mass of citizens have sentiments and beliefs in something like harmony with the social organization in which they are incorporated, this organization cannot continue.   The sentiments proper to each type of society inevitably sway the sociological conclusions of its units. And among other sentiments, this awe of embodied power takes a large share in doing this. ·

How large a share it takes, we shall see on contemplating the astonishingly-perverted estimates of rulers it has produced, and the resulting perversions of history.   Recall the titles of adoration given to emperors and kings ; the ascription to them of capacities, beauties, powers, virtues, transcending those of mankind in general ; the fulsome flatteries used when commending them to God in prayers professing to utter the truth.   Now, side by side with these, put records of their deeds throughout all past times in all nations ; notice how these records are blackened with crimes of all orders ; and then dwell awhile on the contrast.   Is it not manifest that the conceptions of State-actions that went along with these profoundly-untrue conceptions of rulers, must also have been profoundly untrue ?   Take, as a single example, King James, who, as described by Mr. Bisset in agreement with other historians, was "in every relation of life in which he is viewed . . . equally an object of aversion or contempt;" but to whom, nevertheless, the English translation of the Bible is dedicated in sentences beginning—"Great and manifold were the blessings, most dread sovereign, which Almighty God, the Father of all mercies, bestowed upon us the people of England, when first He sent Your Majesty's Royal Person to rule and reign over us," &c., &c. Think of such a dedication of such a book to such a man; and then ask if, along with a sentiment thus expressing itself, there could go anything like balanced judgments of political transactions.

Does there need an illustration of the extent to which balanced judgments of political transactions are made impossible by this sentiment during times when it is strong? We have one in the warped conceptions formed respecting Charles I. and Cromwell, and respecting the changes with which their names are identified. Now that many generations have gone by, and it begins to be seen that Charles was not worthy to be prayed for as a martyr, while Cromwell deserved treatment quite unlike that of ex- huming his body and insulting it; it begins to be seen also, how utterly wrong have been the interpretations of the events these two rulers took part in, and how entirely men's sentiments of loyalty have incapacitated them for understanding those events under their sociological aspects.

Naming this as an instance of the more special perverting effects of this sentiment, we have here chiefly to note its more general perverting effects. From the beginning it has tended ever to keep in the foreground of consciousness, the governing agent as causing social phenomena; and so has kept in the background of consciousness all other causes of social phenomena—or rather, the one has so completely occupied consciousness as to exclude the other. If we remember that history has been full of the doings of kings, but that only in quite recent times have the phenomena of industrial organization, conspicuous as they are, attracted any attention,—if we remember that while all eyes and all thoughts have been turned to the actions of rulers, no eyes and no thoughts have, until modern days, been turned to those vital processes of spontaneous co-operation by which national life, and growth, and progress, have been carried on ; we shall not fail to see how profound have been the resulting errors in men's conclusions about social affairs.   And seeing this, we shall infer that the emotion excited in men by embodied political power must now, and for a long time to come, be a great obstacle to the formation of true sociological conceptions : tending, as it must ever do, to exaggerate the importance of the political factor in comparison with other factors.

Under the title of " Subjective Difficulties—Emotional," I have here entered upon an extensive field, the greater part of which remains to be explored.   The effects of impatience, the effects of that all-glorifying admiration felt for military success, the effects of that sentiment which makes men submit to authority by keeping up a superstitious awe of the agent exercising it, are but a few among the effects which the emotions produce on sociological beliefs.   Various other effects have now to be described and illustrated.   I propose to deal with them in chapters on—the Educational Bias, the Bias of Patriotism, the Class-Bias, the Political Bias, and the Theological Bias.

CHAPTER VIII.

THE EDUCATIONAL BIAS.

It would clear up our ideas about many things, if we distinctly recognized the truth that we have two religions. Primitive humanity has but one. The humanity of the remote future will have but one. The two are opposed; and we who live midway in the course of civilization have to believe in both.

These two religions are adapted to two conflicting sets of social requirements. The one set is supreme at the beginning; the other set will be supreme at the end; and a compromise has to be maintained between them during the progress from beginning to end. On the one hand, there must be social self-preservation in face of external enemies. On the other hand, there must be co-operation among fellow-citizens, which can exist only in proportion as fair dealing of man with man creates mutual trust. Unless the one necessity is met, the society disappears by extinction, or by absorption into some conquering society. Unless the other necessity is met, there cannot be that division of labour, exchange of services, consequent industrial progress and increase of numbers, by which a society is made strong enough to survive. In adjustment to these two conflicting requirements, there grow up two conflicting codes of duty; which severally acquire supernatural sanctions. And thus we get the two coexisting religions —the religion of enmity and the religion of amity.

Of course, I do not mean that these are both called religions.

Here I am not speaking of names; I am speaking simply of things. Nowadays, men do not pay the same verbal homage to the code which enmity dictates that they do to the code which amity dictates—the last occupies the place of honour. But the real homage is paid in large measure, if not in the larger measure, to the code dictated by enmity. The religion of enmity nearly all men actually believe. The religion of amity most of them merely believe they believe. In some discussion, say, about international affairs, remind them of certain precepts contained in the creed they profess, and the most you get is a tepid assent. Now let the conversation turn on the " tunding " at Winchester, or on the treatment of Indian mutineers, or on the Jamaica business; and you find that while the precepts tepidly assented to were but nominally believed, quite opposite precepts are believed undoubtingly and defended with fervour.

Curiously enough, to maintain these antagonist religions, which in our transitional state are both requisite, we have adopted from two different races two different cults. From the books of the Jewish New Testament we take our religion of amity. Greek and Latin epics and histories serve as gospels for our religion of enmity. In the education of our youth we devote a small portion of time to the one, and a large portion of time to the other. And, as though to make the compromise effectual, these two cults are carried on in the same places by the same teachers. At our Public Schools, as also at many other schools, the same men are priests of both religions. The nobility of self-sacrifice, set forth in Scripture-lessons and dwelt on in sermons, is made conspicuous every seventh day; while during the other six days, the nobility of sacrificing others is exhibited in glowing words. The sacred duty of blood-revenge, which, as existing savages show us, constitutes the religion of enmity in its primitive form —which, as shown us in ancient literature, is enforced by divine sanction, or rather by divine command, as well as by the opinion of men—is the duty which, during the six days, is deeply stamped on natures quite ready to receive it; and then something is done

9

towards obliterating the stamp, when, on the seventh day, vengeance is interdicted.

A priori, it might be thought impossible that men should continue through life holding two doctrines which are mutually destructive. But their ability to compromise between conflicting beliefs is very remarkable—remarkable, at least, if we suppose them to put their conflicting beliefs side by side; not so remarkable if we recognize the fact that they do not put them side by side. A late distinguished physicist, whose science and religion seemed to his friends irreconcilable, retained both for the reason that he deliberately refused to compare the propositions of the one with those of the other. To speak in metaphor—when he entered his oratory he shut the door of his laboratory; and when he entered his laboratory he shut the door of his oratory. It is because they habitually do something similar, that men live so contentedly under this logically-indefensible compromise between their two creeds. As the intelligent child, propounding to his seniors puzzling theological questions, and meeting many rebuffs, eventually ceases to think about difficulties of which he can get no solutions; so, a little later, the contradictions between the things taught to him in school and in church, at first startling and inexplicable, become by-and-by familiar, and no longer attract his attention. Thus while growing up he acquires, in common with all around him, the habit of using first one and then the other of his creeds as the occasion demands; and at maturity the habit has become completely established. Now he enlarges on the need for maintaining the national honour, and thinks it mean to arbitrate about an aggression instead of avenging it by war; and now, calling his servants together, he reads a prayer in which he asks God that our trespasses may be forgiven as we forgive trespasses against us. That which he prays for as a virtue on Sunday, he scorns as a vice on Monday.

The religion of amity and the religion of enmity, with the emotions they respectively enlist, are important factors in sociological conclusions; and rational sociological conclusions can be produced only when both sets of factors come into play. We have to look at each cluster of social facts as a phase in a continuous metamorphosis. We have to look at the conflicting religious beliefs and feelings included in this cluster of facts as elements in this phase. We have to do more. We have to consider as transitional, also, the conflicting religious beliefs and feelings in which we are brought up, and which distort our views not only of passing phenomena in our own society, but also of phenomena in other societies and in other times; and the aberrations they cause in our inferences have to be sought for and rectified. Of these two religions taught us, we must constantly remember that during civilization the religion of enmity is slowly losing strength, while the religion of amity is slowly gaining strength: We must bear in mind that at each stage a certain ratio between them has to be maintained. We must infer that the existing ratio is only a temporary one; and that the resulting bias to this or that conviction respecting social affairs is temporary. And if we are to reach those unbiassed convictions which form parts of the Social Science, we can do it only by allowing for this temporary bias.

To see how greatly our opposite religions respectively pervert sociological beliefs, and how needful it is that the opposite perversions they cause should be corrected, we must here contemplate the extremes to which men are carried, now by the one and now by the other.

As from antagonist physical forces, as from antagonist emotions in each man, so from the antagonist social tendencies men's emotions create, there always results, not a medium state, but a rhythm between opposite states. The one force or tendency is not continuously counterbalanced by the other force or tendency; but now the one greatly predominates, and presently by reaction there comes a predominance of the other. That which we are shown by variations in the prices of stocks, shares, or commodities, occurring daily, weekly, and in longer intervals—that

which we see in the alternations of manias and panics, caused
by irrational hopes and absurd fears—that which diagrams of these
variations express by the ascents and descents of a line, now to a
great height and now to an equivalent depth, we discover in all
social phenomena, moral and religious included. It is exhibited
on a large scale and on a small scale—by rhythms extending over
centuries and by rhythms of short periods. And we see it not
only in waves of conflicting feelings and opinions that pass through
societies as wholes, but also in the opposite excesses gone to by
individuals and sects in the same society at the same time. There
is nowhere a balanced judgment and a balanced action, but
always a cancelling of one another by contrary errors : "men
pair off in insane parties," as Emerson puts it. Something like
rationality is finally obtained as a product of mutually-destructive
irrationalities. As for example, in the treatment of our criminals,
there alternate, or co-exist, an unreasoning severity and an un-
reasoning lenity. Now we punish in a spirit of vengeance ; now
we pamper with a maudlin sympathy. At no time is there a due
adjustment of penalty to transgression such as the course of nature
shows us—an inflicting of neither more nor less evil than the
reaction which the action causes.

In the conflict between our two religions we see this general
law on a great scale. The religion of unqualified altruism arose
to correct by an opposite excess the religion of unqualified
egoism. Against the doctrine of entire selfishness it set the
doctrine of entire self-sacrifice. In place of the aboriginal creed
not requiring you to love your fellow-man at all, but insisting
only that certain of your fellow-men you shall hate even to the
death, there came a creed directing that you shall in no case do
anything prompted by hate of your fellow-man, but shall love him
as yourself. Nineteen centuries have since wrought some compromise between these opposite creeds. It has never been rational,
however, but only empirical—mainly, indeed, unconscious compromise. There is not yet a distinct recognition of what truth
each extreme stands for, and a perception that the two truths

must be co-ordinated; but there is little more than a partial rectifying of excesses one way by excesses the other way. By these persons purely-egoistic lives are led. By those, altruism is carried to the extent of bringing on ill health and premature death. Even on comparing the acts of the same individual, we find, not an habitual balance between the two tendencies, but now an effort to inflict great evil on some foreign aggressor or some malefactor at home, and now a disproportioned sacrifice on behalf of one often quite unworthy of it. That altruism is right, but that egoism is also right, and that there requires a continual compromise between the two, is a conclusion which but few consciously formulate and still fewer avow.

Yet the untenability of the doctrine of self-sacrifice in its extreme form is conspicuous enough; and is tacitly admitted by all in their ordinary inferences and daily actions. Work, enterprise, invention, improvement, as they have gone on from the beginning and are going on now, arise out of the principle that among citizens severally having unsatisfied wants, each cares more to satisfy his own wants than to satisfy the wants of others. The fact that industrial activities grow from this root, being recognized, the inevitable implication is that unqualified altruism would dissolve all existing social organizations : leaving the onus of proof that absolutely-alien social organizations would act. That they would not act becomes clear on supposing the opposite principle in force. Were A to be careless of himself, and to care only for the welfare of B, C, and D, while each of these, paying no attention to his own needs, busied himself in supplying the needs of the others; this roundabout process, besides being troublesome, would very ill meet the requirements of each, unless each could have his neighbour's consciousness. After observing this, we must infer that a certain predominance of egoism over altruism is beneficial; and that in fact no other arrangement would answer. Do but ask what would happen if, of A, B, C, D, &c., each declined to have a gratification in his anxiety that some one else should have it, and that the someone else similarly persisted in refusing it out of sympathy with his fellows—do but contemplate the resulting confusion and cross-purposes and loss of gratification to all, and you will see that pure altruism would bring things to a deadlock just as much as pure egoism. In truth nobody ever dreams of acting out the altruistic theory in all the relations of life. The Quaker who proposes to accept literally, and to practise, the precepts of Christianity, carries on his business on egoistic principles just as much as his neighbours. Though, nominally, he holds that he is to take no thought for the morrow, his thought for the morrow betrays as distinct an egoism as that of men in general; and he is conscious that to take as much thought for the morrows of others, would be ruinous to him and eventually mischievous to all.

While, however, no one is entirely altruistic—while no one really believes an entirely altruistic life to be practicable, there continues the tacit assertion that conduct *ought* to be entirely altruistic. It does not seem to be suspected that pure altruism is actually wrong. Brought up, as each is, in the nominal acceptance of a creed which wholly subordinates egoism to altruism, and gives sundry precepts that are absolutely altruistic, each citizen, while ignoring these in his business, and tacitly denying them in various opinions he utters, daily gives to them lip-homage, and supposes that acceptance of them is required of him though he finds it impossible. Feeling that he cannot call them in question without calling in question his religion as a whole, he pretends to others and to himself that he believes them—believes things which in his innermost consciousness he knows he does not believe. He professes to think that entire self-sacrifice must be right, though dimly conscious that it would be fatal.

If he had the courage to think out clearly what he vaguely discerns, he would discover that self-sacrifice passing a certain limit entails evil on all—evil on those for whom sacrifice is made as well as on those who make it. While a continual giving-up of pleasures and continual submission to pains is physically injurious, so that its final outcome is debility, disease, and abridgment of life; the continual acceptance of benefits at the expense of a fellow-being is morally injurious. Just as much as unselfishness is cultivated by the one, selfishness is cultivated by the other. If to surrender a gratification to another is noble, readiness to accept the gratification so surrendered is ignoble; and if repetition of the one kind of act is elevating, repetition of the other kind of act is degrading. So that though up to a certain point altruistic action blesses giver and receiver, beyond that point it curses giver and receiver—physically deteriorates the one and morally deteriorates the other. Everyone can remember cases where greediness for pleasures, reluctance to take trouble, and utter disregard of those around, have been perpetually increased by unmeasured and ever-ready kindnesses; while the unwise benefactor has shown by languid movements and pale face the debility consequent on disregard of self: the outcome of the policy being destruction of the worthy in making worse the unworthy.

The absurdity of unqualified altruism becomes, indeed, glaring on remembering that it can be extensively practised only if in the same society there coexist one moiety altruistic and one moiety egoistic. Only those who are intensely selfish will allow their fellows habitually to behave to them with extreme unselfishness. If all are duly regardful of others, there are none to accept the sacrifices which others are ready to make. If a high degree of sympathy characterizes all, no one can be so unsympathetic as to let another receive positive or negative injury that he may benefit. So that pure altruism in a society implies a nature which makes pure altruism impossible, from the absence of those towards whom it may be exercised!

Equally untenable does the doctrine show itself when looked at from another point of view. If life and its gratifications are valuable in another, they are equally valuable in self. There is no total increase of happiness if only as much is gained by one as is lost by another; and if, as continally happens, the gain is not equal to the loss—if the recipient, already inferior, is further demoralized by habitual acceptance of sacrifices, and so made less capable of happiness (which he inevitably is), the total amount of happiness is diminished : benefactor and beneficiary are both losers.

The maintenance of the individuality is thus demonstrably a duty. The assertion of personal claims is essential; both as a means to self-happiness, which is a unit in the general happiness, and as a means to furthering the general happiness altruistically. Resistance to aggression is not simply justifiable but imperative. Non-resistance is at variance with altruism and egoism alike. The extreme Christian theory, which no one acts upon, which no one really believes, but which most tacitly profess and a few avowedly profess, is as logically indefensible as it is impracticable.

The religion of amity, then, taken by itself, is incomplete—it needs supplementing. The doctrines it inculcates and the sentiments it fosters, arising by reactions against opposite doctrines and sentiments, run into extremes the other way.

Let us now turn to these opposite doctrines and sentiments, inculcated and fostered by the religion of enmity, and note the excesses to which they run.

Worthy of highest admiration is the "Tasmanian devil," which, fighting to the last gasp, snarls with its dying breath. Admirable, too, though less admirable, is our own bull-dog—a creature said sometimes to retain its hold even when a limb is cut off. To be admired also for their "pluck," perhaps nearly in as great a degree, are some of the carnivora, as the lion and the tiger; since when driven to bay they fight against great odds. Nor should we forget the game-cock, supplying as it does a word of eulogy to the mob of roughs who witness the hanging of a murderer, and who half condone his crime if he "dies game." Below these animals come mankind ; some of whom, indeed, as the American Indians, bear tortures without groaning. And then, considerably lower, must be placed the civilized man; who, fighting up to a certain point, and bearing considerable injury, ordinarily yields when further fighting is useless.

Is the reader startled by this classification? Why should he be? It is but a literal application of that standard of worth tacitly assumed by most, and by some deliberately avowed. Obviously it is the standard of worth believed in by M. Gambetta, who, after bloodshed carried to the extent of prostrating France, lately reproached the French Assembly by saying— "You preferred peace to *honour*; you gave five milliards and two provinces." And there are not a few among ourselves who so thoroughly agree in M. Gambetta's feeling, that this utterance of his has gone far to redeem him in their estimation. If the reader needs encouragement to side with such, plenty more may be found for him. The Staffordshire collier, enjoying the fighting of dogs when the fighting of men is not to be witnessed, would doubtless take the same view. In the slums of Whitechapel and St. Giles's, among leaders of "the fancy," it is an unhesitating belief that pluck and endurance are the highest of attributes; and probably most readers of *Bell's Life in London* would concur in this belief. Moreover, if he wants further sympathy to support him, he may find entire races ready to give it; especially that noble race of cannibals, the Fijians, among whom bravery is so highly honoured that, on their return from battle, the triumphant warriors are met by the women, who place themselves at their unrestricted disposal. So that whoever inclines to adopt this measure of superiority will find many to side with him—that is, if he likes his company.

Seriously, is it not amazing that civilized men should especially pride themselves on a quality in which they are exceeded by inferior varieties of their own race, and still more exceeded by inferior animals? Instead of regarding a man as manly in proportion as he possesses moral attributes distinctively human, we regard him as manly in proportion as he shows an attribute possessed in greater degrees by beings from whom we derive our

words of contempt. It was lately remarked by Mr. Greg that
we take our point of honour from the prize-ring; but we do
worse,—we take our point of honour from beasts. Nay, we take
it from a beast inferior to those we are familiar with; for the
"Tasmanian devil," in structure and intelligence, stands on a
much lower level of brutality than our lions and bull-dogs.

That resistance to aggression is to be applauded, and that the
courage implied by resistance is to be valued and admired, may
be fully admitted while denying that courage is to be regarded as
the supreme virtue. A large endowment of it is essential to a
complete nature; but so are large endowments of other things
which we do not therefore make our measures of worth. A
good body, well grown, well proportioned, and of such quality in
its tissues as to be enduring, should bring, as it does bring, its
share of admiration. Admirable, too, in their ways, are good
stomach and lungs, as well as a vigorous vascular system; for
without these the power of self-preservation and the power of
preserving others will fall short. To be a fine animal is, indeed,
essential to many kinds of achievement; and courage, which is
a general index of an organization capable of satisfying the requirements, is rightly valued for what it implies. Courage is,
in fact, a feeling that grows by accumulated experiences of
successful dealings with difficulties and dangers; and these successful dealings are proofs of competence in strength, agility,
quickness, endurance, &c. No one will deny that perpetual
failures, resulting from incapacity of one kind or other, produce
discouragement; or that repeated triumphs, which are proofs of
capacity, so raise the courage that there comes a readiness to
encounter greater difficulties. The fact that a dose of brandy, by
stimulating the circulation, produces "Dutch courage," as it is
called, joined with the fact well known to medical men, that
heart-disease brings on timidity, are of themselves enough to
show that bravery is the natural correlative of ability to cope
with circumstances of peril. But while we are thus taught that,
in admiring courage, we are admiring physical superiorities and

those superiorities of mental faculty which give fitness for dealing with emergencies, we are also taught that unless we rank as supreme the bodily powers and those powers which directly conduce to self-preservation, we cannot say that courage is the highest attribute, and that the degree of it should be our standard of honour.

That an over-estimate of courage is appropriate to our phase of civilization may be very true. It is beyond doubt that during the struggle for existence among nations, it is needful that men should admire extremely the quality without which there can be no success in the struggle. While, among neighbouring nations, we have one in which all the males are trained for war—while the sentiment of this nation is such that students slash one another's faces in duels about trifles, and are admired for their scars, especially by women—while the military ascendancy it tolerates is such that, for ill-usage by soldiers, ordinary citizens have no adequate redress—while the government is such that though the monarch as head of the Church condemns duelling as irreligious, and as head of the Law forbids it as a crime, yet as head of the Army he insists on it to the extent of expelling officers who will not fight duels—while, I say, we have a neighbouring nation thus characterized, something of a kindred character in appliances, sentiments, and beliefs, has to be maintained among ourselves. When we find another neighbouring nation believing that no motive is so high as the love of glory, and no glory so great as that gained by successful war—when we perceive the military spirit so pervading this nation that it loves to clothe its children in *quasi*-military costume—when we find one of its historians writing that the French army is the great civilizer, and one of its generals lately saying that the army is the soul of France— when we see that the vital energies of this nation run mainly to teeth and claws, and that it quickly grows new sets of teeth and claws in place of those pulled out; it is needful that we, too, should keep our teeth and claws in order, and should maintain ideas and feelings adapted to the effectual use of them. There is no gainsaying the truth that while the predatory instincts continue prompting nations to rob one another, destructive agencies must be met by antagonist destructive agencies; and that this may be done, honour must be given to the men who act as destructive agents, and there must be an exaggerated estimate of the attributes which make them efficient.

It may be needful, therefore, that our boys should be accustomed to harsh treatment, giving and receiving brutal punishments without too nice a consideration of their justice. It may be that as the Spartans and as the North-American Indians, in preparation for warfare, subjected their young men to tortures, so should we; and thus, perhaps, the "education of a gentleman" may properly include giving and receiving "hacking" of the shins at foot-ball: boot-toes being purposely made heavy that they may inflict greater damage. So, too, it may be well that boys should all in turn be subject to the tender mercies of elder boys; with whose thrashings and kickings the masters decline to interfere, even though they are sometimes carried to the extent of maiming for life. Possibly, also, it is fit that each boy should be disciplined in submission to any tyrant who may be set over him, by finding that appeal brings additional evils. That each should be made callous, morally as well as physically, by the bearing of frequent wrongs, and should be made yet more callous when, coming into power, he inflicts punishments as whim or spite prompts, may also be desirable. Nor, perhaps, can we wholly regret that confusion of moral ideas which results when breaches of conventional rules bring penalties as severe as are brought by acts morally wrong. For war does not consist with keen sensitiveness, physical or moral. Reluctance to inflict injury, and reluctance to risk injury, would equally render it impossible. Scruples of conscience respecting the rectitude of their cause would paralyze officers and soldiers. So that a certain brutalization has to be maintained during our passing phase of civilization. It may be, indeed, that "the Public School spirit," which, as truly said, is carried into our public life, is not the most desirable for a free country. It may be that early subjection to despotism and early exercise of uncontrolled power, are not the best possible preparations for legislators. It may be that those who, on the magistrate's bench, have to maintain right against might, could be better trained than by submission to violence and subsequent exercise of violence. And it may be that some other discipline than that of the stick, would be desirable for men who officer the press and guide public opinion on questions of equity. But, doubtless, while national antagonisms continue strong and national defence a necessity, there is a fitness in this semi-military discipline, with pains and bruises to uphold it. And a duly-adapted code of honour has the like defence.

Here, however, if we are to free ourselves from transitory sentiments and ideas, so as to be capable of framing scientific conceptions, we must ask what warrant there is for this exaltation of the destructive activities and of the qualities implied by them? We must ask how it is possible for men rightly to pride themselves on attributes possessed in higher degrees by creatures so much lower? We must consider whether, in the absence of a religious justification, there is any ethical justification for the idea that the most noble traits are such as cannot be displayed without the infliction of pain and death. When we do this, we are obliged to admit that the religion of enmity in its unqualified form, is as indefensible as the religion of amity in its unqualified form. Each proves itself to be one of those insane extremes out of which there comes a sane mean by union with its opposite. The two religions stand respectively for the claims of self and the claims of others. The first religion holds it glorious to resist aggression, and, while risking death in doing this, to inflict death on enemies. The second religion teaches that the glory is in not resisting aggression, and in yielding to enemies while not asserting the claims of self. A civilized humanity will render either glory just as impossible of achievement as its opposite. A diminishing egoism and an increasing altruism, must make each of these diverse kinds of honour unattainable. For such an advance implies a cessation of those aggressions which make possible the nobility of resistance ; while it implies a refusal to accept those sacrifices without which there cannot be the nobility of self-sacrifice. The two extremes must cancel ; leaving a moral code and a standard of honour free from irrational excesses. Along with a latent self-assertion, there will go a readiness to yield to others, kept in check by the refusal of others to accept more than their due.

And now, having noted the perversions of thought and senti-ment fostered by the religion of amity and the religion of enmity, under which we are educated in so chaotic a fashion, let us go on to note the ways in which these affect sociological conceptions. Certain important truths apt to be shut out from the minds of the few who are unduly swayed by the religion of amity, may first be set down.

One of the facts difficult to reconcile with current theories of the Universe, is that high organizations throughout the animal kingdom habitually serve to aid destruction or to aid escape from destruction. If we hold to the ancient view, we must say that high organization has been deliberately devised for such purposes. If we accept the modern view, we must say that high organization has been evolved by the exercise of destruc-tive activities during immeasurable periods of the past. Here we choose the latter alternative. To the never-ceasing efforts to catch and eat, and the never-ceasing endeavours to avoid being caught and eaten, is to be ascribed the development of the various senses and the various motor organs directed by them. The bird of prey with the keenest vision, has, other things equal, survived when members of its species that did not see so far, died from want of food ; and by such survivals, keenness of vision has been made greater in course of generations. The fleetest members of a herbivorous herd, escaping when the slower fell victims to a carnivore, left posterity ; among which, again, those with the most perfectly-adapted limbs survived : the carnivores themselves being at the same time similarly disciplined and their speed increased. So, too, with intelligence. Sagacity that detected a danger which stupidity did not perceive, lived and propagated ; and the cunning which hit upon a new deception, and so secured prey not otherwise to be caught, left posterity where a smaller endowment of cunning failed. This mutual perfecting of pursuer and pursued, acting upon their entire organizations, has been going on throughout all time ; and human beings have been subject to it just as much as other beings. Warfare among men, like warfare among animals, has had a large share in raising their organizations to a higher stage. The following are some of the various ways in which it has worked.

In the first place, it has had the effect of continually extirpating races which, for some reason or other, were least fitted to cope with the conditions of existence they were subject to. The killing-off of relatively-feeble tribes, or tribes relatively wanting in endurance, or courage, or sagacity, or power of co-operation, must have tended ever to maintain, and occasionally to increase, the amounts of life-preserving powers possessed by men.

Beyond this average advance caused by destruction of the least-developed races and the least-developed individuals, there has been an average advance caused by inheritance of those further developments due to functional activity. Remember the skill of the Indian in following a trail, and remember that under kindred stimuli many of his perceptions and feelings and bodily powers have been habitually taxed to the uttermost, and it becomes clear that the struggle for existence between neighbouring tribes has had an important effect in cultivating faculties of various kinds. Just as, to take an illustration from among ourselves, the skill of the police cultivates cunning among burglars, which, again, leading to further precautions generates further devices to evade them ; so, by the unceasing antagonisms between human societies, small and large, there has been a mutual culture of an adapted intelligence, a mutual culture of certain traits of character not to be undervalued, and a mutual culture of bodily powers.

A large effect, too, has been produced upon the development of the arts. In responding to the imperative demands of war, industry made important advances and gained much of its skill. Indeed, it may be questioned whether, in the absence of that exercise of manipulative faculty which the making of weapons originally gave, there would ever have been produced the tools required for developed industry. If we go back to the Stone-Age, we see that implements of the chase and implements of war are those showing most labour and dexterity. If we take still-existing human races which were without metals when we found them, we see in their skilfully-wrought stone clubs, as well as in their large war-canoes, that the needs of defence and attack were the chief stimuli to the cultivation of arts afterwards available for productive purposes. Passing over intermediate stages, we may note in comparatively-recent stages the same relation. Observe a coat of mail, or one of the more highly-finished suits of armour—compare it with articles of iron and steel of the same date; and there is evidence that these desires to kill enemies and escape being killed, more extreme than any other, have had great effects on those arts of working in metal to which most other arts owe their progress. The like relation is shown us in the uses made of gunpowder. At first a destructive agent, it has become an agent of immense service in quarrying, mining, railway-making, &c.

A no less important benefit bequeathed by war, has been the formation of large societies. By force alone were small nomadic hordes welded into large tribes; by force alone were large tribes welded into small nations; by force alone have small nations been welded into large nations. While the fighting of societies usually maintains separateness, or by conquest produces only temporary unions, it produces, from time to time, permanent unions; and as fast as there are formed permanent unions of small into large, and then of large into still larger, industrial progress is furthered in three ways. Hostilities, instead of being perpetual, are broken by intervals of peace. When they occur, hostilities do not so profoundly derange the industrial activities. And there arises the possibility of carrying out the division of labour much more effectually. War, in short, in the slow course of things, brings about a social aggregation which furthers that industrial state at variance with war; and yet nothing but war could bring about this social aggregation. These truths, that without war large aggregates of men cannot be formed, and that without large aggregates of men there cannot be a developed industrial state, are illustrated in all places and times. Among existing uncivilized and semi-civilized races, we everywhere find that union of small societies by a conquering society is a step in civilization. The records of peoples now extinct show us this with equal clearness. On looking back into our own history, and into the histories of neighbouring nations, we similarly see that only by coercion were the smaller feudal governments so subordinated as to secure internal peace. And even lately, the long-desired consolidation of Germany, if not directly effected by "blood and iron," as Bismarck said it must be, has been indirectly effected by them. The furtherance of industrial development by aggregation is no less manifest. If we compare a small society with a large one, we get clear proof that those processes of co-operation by which social life is made possible, assume high forms only when the numbers of the co-operating citizens are great. Ask of what use a cloth-factory, supposing they could have one, would be to the members of a small tribe, and it becomes manifest that, producing as it would in a single day a year's supply of cloth, the vast cost of making it and keeping it in order could never be compensated by the advantage gained. Ask what would happen were a shop like Shoolbred's, supplying all textile products, set up in a village, and you see that the absence of a sufficiently-extensive distributing function would negative its continuance. Ask what sphere a bank would have had in the Old-English period, when nearly all people grew their own food and spun their own wool, and it is at once seen that the various appliances for facilitating exchange can grow up only when a community becomes so large that the amount of exchange to be facilitated is great. Hence, unquestionably, that integration of societies effected by war, has been a needful preliminary to industrial development, and consequently to developments of other kinds—Science, the Fine Arts, &c.

Industrial habits too, and habits of subordination to social requirements, are indirectly brought about by the same cause. The truth that the power of working continuously, wanting in the aboriginal man, could be established only by that persistent coercion to which conquered and enslaved tribes are subject, has become trite. An allied truth is, that only by a discipline of submission, first to an owner, then to a personal governor, presently to government less personal, then to the embodied law proceeding from government, could there eventually be reached submission to that code of moral law by which the civilized man is more and more restrained in his dealings with his fellows.

Such being some of the important truths usually ignored by men too exclusively influenced by the religion of amity, let us now glance at the no less important truths to which men are blinded by the religion of enmity

Though, during barbarism and the earlier stages of civilization, war has the effect of exterminating the weaker societies, and of weeding out the weaker members of the stronger societies, and thus in both ways furthering the development of those valuable powers, bodily and mental, which war brings into play; yet during the later stages of civilization, the second of these actions is reversed. So long as all adult males have to bear arms, the average result is that those of most strength and quickness survive, while the feebler and slower are slain; but when the industrial development has become such that only some of the adult males are drafted into the army, the tendency is to pick out and expose to slaughter the best-grown and healthiest: leaving behind the physically-inferior to propagate the race. The fact that among ourselves, though the number of soldiers raised is not relatively large, many recruits are rejected by the examining surgeons, shows that the process inevitably works towards deterioration. Where, as in France, conscriptions have gone on taking away the finest men, generation after generation, the needful lowering of the standard proves how disastrous is the effect on those animal qualities of a race which form a necessary basis for all higher qualities. If the depletion is indirect also—if there is such an overdraw on the energies of the industrial population that a large share of heavy labour is thrown on the women, whose systems are taxed simultaneously by hard work and child-bearing, a further cause of physical degeneracy comes into play: France again supplying an example. War, therefore, after a certain stage of progress, instead of furthering bodily development and the development of certain mental powers, becomes a cause of retrogression.

In like manner, though war, by bringing about social consolidations, indirectly favours industrial progress and all its civilizing consequences, yet the direct effect of war on industrial progress is repressive. It is repressive as necessitating the abstraction of men and materials that would otherwise go to industrial growth; it is repressive as deranging the complex inter-dependencies among the many productive and distributive agencies; it is repressive as drafting off much administrative and constructive ability, which would else have gone to improve the industrial arts and the industrial organization. And if we contrast the absolutely-military Spartans with the partially-military Athenians, in their respective attitudes towards culture of every kind, or call to mind the contempt shown for the pursuit of knowledge in purely-military times like those of feudalism; we cannot fail to see that persistent war is at variance not only with industrial development, but also with the higher intellectual developments that aid industry and are aided by it.

So, too, with the effects wrought on the moral nature. While war, by the discipline it gives soldiers, directly cultivates the habit of subordination, and does the like indirectly by establishing strong and permanent governments; and while in so far it cultivates attributes that are not only temporarily essential, but are steps towards attributes that are permanently essential; yet it does this at the cost of maintaining, and sometimes increasing, detrimental attributes—attributes intrinsically anti-social. The aggressions which selfishness prompts (aggressions which, in a society, have to be restrained by some power that is strong in proportion as the selfishness is intense) can diminish only as fast as selfishness is held in check by sympathy; and perpetual warlike activities repress sympathy: nay, they do worse—they cultivate aggressiveness to the extent of making it a pleasure to inflict injury. The citizen made callous by the killing and wounding of enemies, inevitably brings his callousness home with him. Fellow-feeling, habitually trampled down in military conflicts, cannot at the same time be active in the relations of civil life. In proportion as giving pain to others is made a habit during war, it will remain a habit during peace: inevitably producing in the behaviour of citizens to one another, antagonisms, crimes of violence, and multitudinous aggressions of minor kinds, tending towards a disorder that calls for coercive government. Nothing like a high type of social life is possible without a type of human character in which the promptings of egoism are duly restrained by regard for others. The necessities of war imply absolute self-regard, and absolute disregard of certain others. Inevitably, therefore, the civilizing discipline of social life is antagonized by the uncivilizing discipline of the life war involves. So that beyond the direct mortality and miseries entailed by war, it entails other mortality and miseries by maintaining anti-social sentiments in citizens.

Taking the most general view of the matter, we may say that only when the sacred duty of blood-revenge, constituting the religion of the savage, decreases in sacredness, does there come a possibility of emergence from the deepest barbarism. Only as fast as retaliation, which for a murder on one side inflicts a murder or murders on the other, becomes less imperative, is it possible for larger aggregates of men to hold together and civilization to commence. And so, too, out of lower stages of civilization higher ones can emerge, only as there diminishes this pursuit of international revenge and re-revenge, which the code we inherit from the savage insists upon. Such advantages, bodily and mental, as the race derives from the discipline of war, are exceeded by the disadvantages, bodily and mental, but especially mental, which result after a certain stage of progress is reached. Severe and bloody as the process is, the killing-off of inferior races and inferior individuals, leaves a balance of benefit to mankind during phases of progress in which the moral development is low, and there are no quick sympathies to be continually seared by the infliction of pain and death. But as there arise higher societies, implying individual characters fitted for closer co-operation, the destructive activities exercised by such higher societies have injurious re-active effects on the moral natures of their members—injurious effects which outweigh the benefits resulting from extirpation of inferior races. After this stage has been reached, the purifying process, continuing still an important one, remains to be carried on by industrial war—by a competition of societies during which the best, physically, emotionally, and intellectually, spread most, and leave the least capable to disappear gradually, from failing to leave a sufficiently-numerous posterity.

Those educated in the religion of enmity—those who during boyhood, when the instincts of the savage are dominant, have revelled in the congenial ideas and sentiments which classic poems and histories yield so abundantly, and have become confirmed in the belief that war is virtuous and peace ignoble, are naturally blind to truths of this kind. Rather should we say, perhaps, that they have never turned their eyes in search of such truths.

And their bias is so strong that nothing more than a nominal recognition of such truths is possible to them; if even this. What perverted conceptions of social phenomena this bias produces, may be seen in the following passage from Gibbon :—

"It was scarcely possible that the eyes of contemporaries should discover in the public felicity the causes of decay and corruption. *The long peace, and the uniform government of the Romans*, had introduced a slow and secret poison into the vitals of the empire."

In which sentences there is involved the general proposition that in proportion as men are long held together in that mutual dependence which social co-operation implies, they will become less fit for mutual dependence and co-operation—the society will tend towards dissolution. While in proportion as they are habituated to antagonism and to destructive activities, they will become better adapted to activities requiring union and agreement.

Thus the two opposite codes in which we are educated, and the sentiments enlisted on behalf of their respective precepts, inevitably produce misinterpretations of social phenomena. Instead of acting together, now this and now the other sways the beliefs; and instead of consistent, balanced conclusions, there results a jumble of contradictory conclusions.

It is time, not only with a view to right thinking in Social Science, but with a view to right acting in daily life, that this acceptance in their unqualified forms of two creeds which contradict one another completely, should come to an end. Is it not a folly to go on pretending to ourselves and others that we believe certain perpetually-repeated maxims of entire self-sacrifice, which we daily deny by our business activities, by the steps we take to protect our persons and property, by the approval we express of resistance against aggression? Is it not a dishonesty to repeat in tones of reverence, maxims which we not only refuse to act out but dimly see would be mischievous if acted out? Everyone must admit that the relation between parent and child is one in which altruism is pushed as far as is practicable. Yet even here there needs a predominant egoism. The mother can suckle her infant only on condition that she has habitually gratified her appetite in due degree. And there is a point beyond which sacrifice of herself is fatal to her infant. The bread-winner, too, on whom both depend—is it not undeniable that wife and child can be altruistically treated by their protector, only on condition that he is duly egoistic in his transactions with his fellow citizens? If the dictate—live for self, is wrong in one way, the opposite dictate—"live for others," is wrong in another way. The rational dictate is—live for self and others. And if we all do actually believe this, as our conduct conclusively proves, is it not better for us distinctly to say so, rather than continue enunciating principles which we do not and cannot practise: thus bringing moral teaching itself into discredit?

On the other hand, it is time that a ferocious egoism, which remains unaffected by this irrational altruism, professed but not believed, should be practically modified by a rational altruism. This sacred duty of blood-revenge, insisted on by the still-vigorous religion of enmity, needs qualifying actually and not verbally. Instead of senselessly reiterating in catechisms and church services the duty of doing good to those that hate us, while an undoubting belief in the duty of retaliation is implied by our parliamentary debates, the articles in our journals, and the conversations over our tables, it would be wiser and more manly to consider how far the first should go in mitigation of the last. Is it stupidity or is it moral cowardice which leads men to continue professing a creed that makes self-sacrifice a cardinal principle, while they urge the sacrificing of others, even to the death, when they trespass against us? Is it blindness, or is it an insane inconsistency, which makes them regard as most admirable the bearing of evil for the benefit of others, while they lavish admiration on those who, out of revenge, inflict great evils in return for small ones suffered? Surely our barbarian code of right needs revision, and our barbarian standard of honour should be somewhat changed. Let us deliberately recognize what good they represent and what mixture of bad there is with it. Courage is worthy of respect when displayed in the maintenance of legitimate claims and in the repelling of aggressions, bodily or other. Courage is worthy of yet higher respect when danger is faced in defence of claims common to self and others, as in resistance to invasion. Courage is worthy of the highest respect when risk to life or limb is dared in defence of others; and becomes grand when those others have no claims of relationship, and still more when they have no claims of race. But though a bravery which is altruistic in its motive is a trait we cannot too highly applaud, and though a bravery which is legitimately egoistic in its motive is praiseworthy, the bravery that is prompted by aggressive egoism is not praiseworthy. The admiration accorded to the "pluck" of one who fights in a base cause is a vicious admiration, demoralizing to those who feel it. Like the physical powers, courage, which is a concomitant of these, is to be regarded as a servant of the higher emotions—very valuable, indispensable even, in its place; and to be honoured when discharging its function in subordination to these higher emotions. But otherwise not more to be honoured than the like attribute as seen in brutes.

Quite enough has been said to show that there must be a compromise between the opposite standards of conduct on which the religions of amity and enmity respectively insist, before there can be scientific conceptions of social phenomena. Even on passing affairs, such as the proceedings of philanthropic bodies and the dealings of nation with nation, there cannot be rational judgments without a balance between the self-asserting emotions and the emotions which put a limit to self-assertion, with an adjustment of the corresponding beliefs. Still less can there be rational judgments of past social evolution, or of social evolution in the future, if the opposing actions which these opposing creeds sanction, are not both continuously recognized as essential. No mere impulsive recognition, now of the purely-egoistic doctrine and now of the purely-altruistic one, will suffice. The curve described by a planet cannot be understood by thinking at one moment of the centripetal force and at another moment of the tangential force ; but the two must be kept before consciousness as acting simultaneously. And similarly, to understand social progress in the vast sweep of its course, there must be ever present to the mind, the egoistic and the altruistic forces as co-operative factors equally indispensable, and neither of them to be ignored or reprobated.

The criticism likely to be passed on this chapter, that " The Educational Bias " is far too comprehensive a title for it, is quite justifiable. There are in truth few, if any, of the several kinds of bias, that are not largely, or in some measure, caused by education—using this word in an extended sense. As, however, all of them could not be dealt with in one chapter, it seemed best to select these two opposite forms of bias which are directly traceable to teachings of opposite dogmas, and fosterings of opposite sentiments, during early life. Merely recognizing the fact that education has much to do with the other kinds of bias, we may now most conveniently deal with these each under its specific title.

10

CHAPTER IX.

"Our country, right or wrong," is a sentiment not unfrequently expressed on the other side of the Atlantic; and, if I remember rightly, an equivalent sentiment was some years ago uttered in our own House of Commons, by one who rejoices, or at least who once rejoiced, in the title of philosophical Radical.

Whoever entertains such a sentiment has not that equilibrium of feeling required for dealing scientifically with social phenomena. To see how things stand, apart from personal and national interests, is essential before there can be reached those balanced judgments respecting the course of human affairs in general, which constitute Sociology. To be convinced of this, it needs but to take a case remote from our own. Ask how the members of an aboriginal tribe regard that tide of civilization which sweeps them away. Ask what the North-American Indians said about the spread of the white man over their territories, or what the ancient Britons thought of the invasions which dispossessed them of England; and it becomes clear that events which, looked at from an un-national point of view, were steps towards a higher life, seemed from a national point of view entirely evil. Admitting the truth so easily perceived in these cases, we must admit that only in proportion as we emancipate ourselves from the bias of patriotism, and consider our own society as one among many, having their histories and their futures, and some of them, perhaps, having better claims than we have to the inheritance of the Earth—only in proportion as we do this, shall we recognize those sociological truths which have nothing to do with particular nations or particular races.

So to emancipate ourselves is extremely difficult. It is with patriotism as we lately saw it to be with the sentiment causing political subordination: the very existence of a society implies predominance of it. The two sentiments join in producing that social cohesion without which there cannot be co-operation and organization. A nationality is made possible only by the feeling which the units have for the whole they form. Indeed, we may say that the feeling has been gradually increased by the continual destroying of types of men whose attachments to their societies were relatively small; and who were therefore incapable of making adequate sacrifices on behalf of their societies. Here, again, we are reminded that the citizen, by his incorporation in a body politic, is in a great degree coerced into such sentiments and beliefs as further its preservation: unless this is the average result the body politic will not be preserved. Hence another obstacle in the way of Social Science. We have to allow for the aberrations of judgment caused by the sentiment of patriotism.

Patriotism is nationally that which egoism is individually— has, in fact, the same root; and along with kindred benefits brings kindred evils. Estimation of one's society is a reflex of self-estimation; and assertion of one's society's claims is an indirect assertion of one's own claims as a part of it. The pride a citizen feels in a national achievement, is the pride in belonging to a nation capable of that achievement: the belonging to such a nation having the tacit implication that in himself there exists the superiority of nature displayed. And the anger aroused in him by an aggression on his nation, is an anger against something which threatens to injure him also, by injuring his nation.

As, lately, we saw that a duly-adjusted egoism is essential; so now, we may see that a duly-adjusted patriotism is essential. Self-regard in excess produces two classes of evils: by prompting undue assertion of personal claims it breeds aggression and antagonism; and by creating undue estimation of personal powers it excites futile efforts that end in catastrophes. Deficient self-regard produces two opposite classes of evils: by not asserting personal claims, it invites aggression, so fostering selfishness in others; and by not adequately valuing personal powers it causes a falling short of attainable benefits. Similarly with patriotism. From too much, there result national aggressiveness and national vanity. Along with too little, there goes an insufficient tendency to maintain national claims, leading to trespasses by other nations; and there goes an undervaluing of national capacities and institutions, which is discouraging to effort and progress.

The effects of patriotic feeling which here concern us, are those it works on belief rather than those it works on conduct. As disproportionate egoism, by distorting a man's conceptions of self and of others, vitiates his conclusions respecting human nature and human actions; so, disproportionate patriotism, by distorting his conceptions of his own society and of other societies, vitiates his conclusions respecting the natures and actions of societies. And from the opposite extremes there result opposite distortions: which, however, are comparatively infrequent and much less detrimental.

Here we come upon one of the many ways in which the corporate conscience proves itself less developed than the individual conscience. For while excess of egoism is everywhere regarded as a fault, excess of patriotism is nowhere regarded as a fault. A man who recognizes his own errors of conduct and his own deficiencies of faculty, shows a trait of character considered praiseworthy; but to admit that our doings towards other nations have been wrong is reprobated as unpatriotic. Defending the acts of another people with whom we have a difference, seems to most citizens something like treason; and they use offensive comparisons concerning birds and their nests, by way of condemning those who ascribe misconduct to our own people rather than to the people with whom we are at variance. Not only do they exhibit the unchecked sway of this reflex egoism which constitutes patriotism—not only are they unconscious that there is anything blameworthy in giving the rein to this feeling; but they think the blameworthiness is in those who restrain it, and try to see what may be said on both sides. Judge, then, how seriously the patriotic bias, thus perverting our judgments about international actions, necessarily perverts our judgments about the characters of other societies, and so vitiates sociological conclusions.

We have to guard ourselves against this bias. To this end let us take some examples of the errors attributable to it.

What mistaken estimates of other races may result from over-estimation of one's own race, will be most vividly shown by a case in which we are ourselves valued at a very low rate by a race we hold to be far inferior. Here is such a case supplied by a tribe of negroes :—

" They amused themselves by remarking on the sly, 'The white man is an old ape.' The African will say of the European, ' He looks like folks,' [men], and the answer will often be, 'No, he don't.   .   .   . Whilst the Caucasian doubts the humanity of the Hamite, the latter repays the compliment in kind." [1]

Does anyone think this instance so far out of the ordinary track of error as to have no instruction for us ? To see the contrary he has but to look at the caricatures of Frenchmen that were common a generation ago, or to remember the popular statement then current respecting the relative strengths of French and English. Such reminders will convince him that the reflex self-esteem we call patriotism, has had, among ourselves, perverting effects sufficiently striking. And even now there are kindred opinions which the facts, when examined, do not bear out: instance the opinion respecting personal beauty. That the bias thus causing misjudgments in cases where it is checked by direct perception, causes greater misjudgments where direct perception cannot check it, needs no proof. How great are the mistakes it generates, all histories of international struggles show us, both by the contradictory estimates the two sides form of their respective leaders and by the contradictory estimates the two sides form of their deeds. Take an example :—

" Of the character in which Wallace first became formidable, the accounts in literature are distractingly conflicting. With the chroniclers of his own country, who write after the War of Independence, he is raised to the highest pinnacle of magnanimity and heroism. To the English contemporary chroniclers he is a pestilent ruffian ; a disturber of the peace of society; an outrager of all laws and social duties; finally, a robber—the head of one of many bands of robbers and marauders then infesting Scotland." [2]

That, along with such opposite distortions of belief about conspicuous persons, there go opposite distortions of belief about the conduct of the peoples they belong to, the accounts of every war demonstrate. Like the one-sidedness shown within our own society by the remembrance among Protestants of Roman Catholic cruelties only, and by the remembrance among Roman Catholics of Protestant cruelties only, is the one-sidedness shown in the traditions preserved by each nation concerning the barbarities of nations it has fought with. As in old times the Normans, vindictive themselves, were shocked at the vindictiveness of the English when driven to bay ; so in recent times the French have enlarged on the atrocities committed by Spanish guerillas, and the Russians on the atrocities the Circassians perpetrated. In this conflict between the views of those who commit savage acts, and the views of those on whom they are committed, we clearly perceive the bias of patriotism where both sides are aliens ; but we fail to perceive it where we are ourselves concerned as actors. Every one old enough remembers the reprobation vented here when the French in Algiers dealt so cruelly with Arabs who refused to submit—lighting fires at the mouths of caves in which they had taken refuge; but we do not see a like barbarity in deeds of our own in India, such as the executing a group of rebel sepoys by fusillade, and then setting fire to the heap of them because they were not all dead,[3] or in the wholesale shootings and burnings of houses, after the suppression of the Jamaica insurrection. Listen to what is said about such deeds in our own colonies, and you find that habitually they are held to have been justified by the necessities of the case. Listen to what is said about such deeds when other nations are guilty of them, and you find the same persons indignantly declare that no alleged necessities could form a justification. Nay, the bias produces perversions of judgment even more extreme. Feelings and deeds we laud as virtuous when they are not in antagonism with our own interests and power, we think vicious feelings and deeds when our own interests and power are endangered by them. Equally in the mythical story of Tell and in any account not mythical, we read with glowing admiration of the successful rising of an oppressed race; but admiration is changed into indignation if the race is one held down by ourselves. We can see nothing save crime in the endeavour of the Hindus to throw off our yoke; and we recognize no excuse for the efforts of the Irish to establish their independent nationality. We entirely ignore the fact that the motives are in all such cases the same, and are to be judged apart from results.

A bias which thus vitiates even the perceptions of physical appearances, which immensely distorts the beliefs about conspicuous antagonists and their deeds, which leads us to reprobate when others commit them, severities and cruelties we applaud when committed by our own agents, and which makes us regard acts of intrinsically the same kind as wrong or right according as they are or are not directed against ourselves, is a bias which inevitably perverts our sociological ideas. The institutions of a despised people cannot be judged with fairness ; and if, as often happens, the contempt is unwarranted, or but partially warranted, such value as their institutions have will certainly be underestimated. When antagonism has bred hatred towards another nation, and has consequently bred a desire to justify the hatred by ascribing hateful characters to members of that nation, it inevitably happens that the political arrangements under which they live, the religion they profess, and the habits peculiar to them, become associated in thought with these hateful characters —become themselves hateful, and cannot therefore have their natures studied with the calmness required by science.

An example will make this clear. The reflex egoism we name patriotism, causing among other things a high valuation of the religious creed nationally professed, makes us overrate the effects this creed has produced, and makes us underrate the effects produced by other creeds and by influences of other orders. The notions respecting savage and civilized races, in which we are brought up, show this.

The word savage, originally meaning wild or uncultivated, has come to mean cruel and blood-thirsty, because of the representations habitually made that wild or uncultivated tribes of men are cruel and blood-thirsty. And ferocity being now always thought of as a constant attribute of uncivilized races, which are also distinguished by not having our religion, it is tacitly assumed that the absence of our religion is the cause of this ferocity. But if, struggling successfully against the bias of patriotism, we correct the evidence which that bias has garbled, we find ourselves obliged to modify this assumption.

When, for instance, we read Cook's account of the Tahitians, as first visited by him, we are surprised to meet with some traits among them, higher than those of their civilized visitors. Though pilfering was committed by them, it was not so serious as that of which the sailors were guilty in stealing the iron bolts out of their own ship to pay the native women. And when, after Cook had enacted a penalty for theft, the natives complained of one of his own crew—when this sailor, convicted of the offence he was charged with, was condemned to be whipped, the natives tried to get him off, and failing to do this, shed tears on seeing preparations for the punishment. If, again, we compare critically the accounts of Cook's death, we see clearly that the Sandwich

Islanders behaved amicably until they had been ill-used, and had reason to fear further ill-usage. The experiences of many other travellers similarly show us that friendly conduct on the part of uncivilized races when first visited, is very general; and that their subsequent unfriendly conduct, when it occurs, is nothing but retaliation for injuries received from the civilized. Such a fact as that the natives of Queen Charlotte's Island did not attack Captain Carteret's party till after they had received just cause of offence,[4] may be taken as typical of the histories of transactions between wild races and cultivated races. When we inquire into the case of the missionary Williams, "the Martyr of Erromanga," we discover that his murder, dilated upon as proving the wickedness of unreclaimed natures, was a revenge for injuries previously suffered from wicked Europeans. Read a few testimonies about the relative behaviours of civilized and uncivilized :—

"After we had killed a man at the Marquesas, grievously wounded one at Easter Island, hooked a third with a boat-hook at Tonga-tabu, wounded one at Namocka, another at Mallicollo, and killed another at Tanna ; the several inhabitants behaved in a civil and harmless manner to us, though they might have taken ample revenge by cutting off our straggling parties." [5]

"Excepting at Cafta, where I was for a time supposed to come with hostile intent, I was treated inhospitably by no one during all my travels, excepting by Europeans, who had nothing against me but my apparent poverty." [6]

"In February, 1812, the people of Winnebah [Gold Coast] seized their commandant, Mr. Meredith," and so maltreated him that he died. The town and fort were destroyed by the English. "For many years afterwards, English vessels passing Winnebah were in the habit of pouring a broadside into the town, to inspire the natives with an idea of the severe vengeance which would be exacted for the spilling of European blood." [7]

Or, instead of these separate testimonies, take the opinion of one who collected many testimonies. Referring to the kind treatment experienced by Enciso from the natives of Cartagena (on the coast of New Granada), who a few years before had been cruelly treated by the Spaniards, Washington Irving says:—

" When we recall the bloody and indiscriminate vengeance wreaked upon this people by Ojida and his followers for their justifiable resistance of invasion, and compare it with their placable and considerate spirit when an opportunity for revenge presented itself, we confess we feel a momentary doubt whether the arbitrary appellation of savage is always applied to the right party."[8]

The reasonableness of this doubt will scarcely be questioned, after reading of the diabolical cruelties committed by the invading Europeans in America; as, for instance, in St. Domingo, where the French made the natives kneel in rows along the edge of a deep trench and shot them batch after batch, until the trench was full, or, as an easier method, tied numbers of them together, took them out to sea, and tumbled them overboard; and where the Spaniards treated so horribly the enslaved natives, that these killed themselves wholesale: the various modes of suicide being shown in Spanish drawings.

Does the Englishman say that these, and hosts of like demoniacal misdeeds, are the misdeeds of other civilized races in other times; and that they are attributable to that corrupted religion which he repudiates? If so, he may be reminded that sundry of the above facts are facts against ourselves. He may be reminded, too, that the purer religion he professes has not prevented a kindred treatment of the North American Indians by our own race. And he may be put to the blush by accounts of barbarities going on in our own colonies at the present time. Without detailing these, however, it will suffice to recall the most recent notorious case—that of the kidnappings and murders in the South Seas. Here we find repeated the typical transactions:—betrayals of many natives and merciless sacrifices of their lives; eventual retaliation by the natives to a small extent; a consequent charge against the natives of atrocious murder; and finally, a massacre of them, innocent and guilty together.

See, then, how the bias of patriotism indirectly produces erroneous views of the effects of an institution. Blinded by national self-love to the badness of our conduct towards inferior races, while remembering what there is of good in our conduct; forgetting how well these inferior races have usually behaved to us, and remembering only their misbehaviour, which we refrain from tracing to its cause in our own transgressions; we overvalue our own natures as compared with theirs. And then, looking at the two as respectively Christian and Heathen, we over-rate the good done by Christian institutions (which has doubtless been great), and we under-rate the advance that has been made without them. We do this habitually in other cases. As, for instance, when we ignore evidence furnished by the history of Buddhism; respecting the founder of which Canon Liddon lately told his hearers that "it might be impossible for honest Christians to think over the career of this heathen Prince without some keen feelings of humiliation and shame." [9] And ignoring all such evidence, we get one-sided impressions. Thus our sociological conceptions are distorted—do not correspond with the facts; that is, are unscientific.

To illustrate some among the many effects wrought by the bias of patriotism in other nations, and to show how mischievous are the beliefs it fosters, I may here cite evidence furnished by France and by Germany.

Contemplate that undue self-estimation which the French have shown us. Observe what has resulted from that exceeding faith in French power which the writings of M. Thiers did so much to maintain and increase. When we remember how, by causing under-valuation of other nations, it led to a disregard of their ideas and an ignorance of their doings—when we remember how, in the late war, the French, confident of victory, had maps of German territory but not of their own, and suffered catastrophes from this and other kinds of unpreparedness; we see what fatal evils this reflex self-esteem may produce when in excess. So, too, on studying the way in which it has

influenced French thought in other directions.   On reading the
assertion, "La chimie est une science française," with which
Wurtz commences his *Histoire des Doctrines Chimiques*, one cannot
but see that the feeling which prompted such an assertion must
vitiate the comparisons made between things in France and things
elsewhere.   Looking at Crimean battle-pieces, in which French
soldiers are shown to have achieved everything—looking at a
picture like Ingres' "Crowning of Homer," and noting French
poets conspicuous in the foreground, while the figure of Shakspeare in one corner is half in and half out of the picture—
reading the names of great men of all nations inscribed on the
string-course running round the *Palais de l'Industrie*, and finding
many unfamiliar French names, while (strange oversight, as we
must suppose) the name of Newton is conspicuous by its absence; we see exemplified a national sentiment which, generating
the belief that things not French deserve little attention, acts
injuriously on French thought and French progress.   From Victor
Hugo's magniloquent description of France as the "Saviour
of Nations," down to the declamations of those who urged that
were Paris destroyed the light of civilization would be extinguished, we see throughout, the conviction that France is the
teacher, and by implication needs not to be a learner.   The
diffusion of French ideas is an essential thing for other nations;
while the absorption of ideas from other nations is not an essential thing for France: the truth being, rather, that French ideas,
more than most other ideas, stand in need of foreign influence
to qualify the undue definiteness and dogmatic character they
habitually display.   That such a tone of feeling, and the
mode of thinking appropriate to it, should vitiate sociological
speculation, is a matter of course.   If there needs proof, we have
a conspicuous one in the writings of M. Comte; where excessive
self-estimation under its direct form, and under that reflex form
constituting patriotism, has led to astounding sociological misconceptions.   If we contemplate that scheme of Positivist re-
organization and federation in which France was, of course, to

be the leader—if we note the fact that M. Comte expected tho transformation he so rigorously formulated to take place during the life of his own generation; and if, then, we remember what has since happened, and consider what are the probabilities of the future, we shall not fail to see that great perversions are produced by this bias in the conceptions of social phenomena.

How national self-esteem, exalted by success in war, warps opinions about public affairs, is again shown of late in Germany. As a German professor writes to me :—"there is, alas, no want of signs" that the "happy contrast to French self-sufficiency" which Germany heretofore displayed, is disappearing "since the glory of the late victories." The German liberals, he says, "overflow with talk of Germanism, German unity, the German nation, the German empire, the German army and the German navy, the German church, and German science. . . . . They ridicule Frenchmen, and what animates them is, after all, the French spirit translated into German." To illustrate the injurious reaction on German thought, and on the estimates of foreign nations and their doings, he describes a discussion with an esteemed German professor of philosophy, against whom he was contending that the psychical and ethical sciences would gain in progress and influence by international communion, like that among the physico-mathematical sciences. He "to my astonishment declared that even if such an union were possible, he did not think it desirable, as it would interfere too much with the peculiarity of German thought. . . . . Second to Germany," he said, "it was Italy, which, in the immediate future, was most likely to promote philosophy. . . . . It appeared that what made him prefer the Italians . . . . was nothing else than his having observed that in Italy they were acquainted with every philosophical treatise published in Germany, however unimportant." And thus, adds my correspondent, "the finest German characteristics are disappearing in an exaggerated Teutonomania." One more truth his comments on German feeling disclose. An indirect antagonism exists between the sentiment of nationality and the sentiment of individuality ; the result of which is that exaltation of the one involves depression of the other, and a decreased regard for the institutions it originates. Speaking of the "so-called National Liberals," he says :—"A friend of mine was lately present at a discussion, in the course of which a professor of philosophy, of the University of ——, was very eloquently, and with perfect seriousness, contending that only one thing is now wanted to complete our German institutions—a national costume. Other people, who, no doubt, are fully aware of the ridiculousness of such things, are nevertheless guilty of an equally absurd and even more-intolerable encroachment on individual liberty ; since, by proposing to establish a national church, they aim at constraining the adherents of the various religious bodies into a spiritual uniform. Indeed, I should hardly have thought it possible that a German government could encourage such monstrous propositions, if they had not been expounded to me at the Ministry of Public Worship."

Saying no more about patriotism and its perverting effects on sociological judgments, which are, indeed, so conspicuous all through history as scarcely to need pointing out, let me devote the remaining space to the perverting effects of the opposite feeling —anti-patriotism. Though the distortions of opinion hence resulting are less serious, still they have to be guarded against.

In England the bias of anti-patriotism does not diminish in a marked way the admiration we have for our political institutions; but only here and there prompts the wish for a strong government, to secure the envied benefits ascribed to strong governments abroad. Nor does it appreciably modify the general attachment to our religious institutions ; but only in a few who dislike independence, shows itself in advocacy of an authoritative ecclesiastical system, fitted to remedy what they lament as a chaos of religious beliefs. In other directions, however, it is displayed so frequently and conspicuously as to affect public opinion in an injurious way. In respect to the higher orders of intellectual achievement, under-valuation of ourselves has become a fashion; and the errors it fosters react detrimentally on the estimates we make of our social *régime*, and on our sociological beliefs in general.

What is the origin of this undue self-depreciation? In some cases no doubt it results from disgust at the jaunty self-satisfaction caused by the bias of patriotism when excessive. In other cases it grows out of affectation: to speak slightingly of what is English seems to imply a wide knowledge of what is foreign, and brings a reputation for culture. In the remaining cases it is due to ignorance. Passing over such of these self-depreciatory estimates of our powers and achievements as have partial justifications, I will limit myself to one which has no justification. Among the classes here indicated, it is the custom to speak disrespectfully of the part we play in discovery and invention. There is an assertion occasionally to be met with in public journals, that the French invent and we improve. Not long since it was confessed by the Attorney-General that the English are not a scientific nation. Recently the *Times*, commenting on a speech in which Mr. Gladstone had been disparaging our age and its men, said:—" There is truth, however, in the assertion that we are backward in appreciating and pursuing abstract knowledge." [10] Such statements exhibit the bias of anti-patriotism creating a belief that is wholly indefensible. As we shall presently see, they are flatly contradicted by facts; and they can be accounted for only by supposing that those who make them have had a culture exclusively literary.

A convenient way of dealing with this bias of anti-patriotism will be to take an individual example of it. More than any other, Mr. Matthew Arnold has of late made himself an exponent of the feeling. His motive cannot be too highly respected; and for much that he has said in rebuke of the vainglorious, entire approval may rightly be felt. Many grave defects in our social state, many absurdities in our modes of action, many errors in our estimates of ourselves, are to be pointed out and dwelt upon; and great good is done by a writer who efficiently executes the task of making us feel our short-comings. In his condemnation of the ascetic view of life which still prevails here, one may entirely agree. That undue valua-tion of material prosperity common with us, is a fault justly insisted on by him. And the overweening confidence so often shown in a divine favour gained by our greater national piety, is also an attitude of mind to be reprobated. But by reaction Mr. Arnold is, I think, carried too far in the direction of anti-patriotism; and weakens the effect of his criticism by generating a re-reaction. Let us glance at some of his views.

The mode of procedure generally followed by Mr. Arnold, is not that of judicially balancing the evidence, but that of meeting the expression of self-satisfied patriotism by some few facts cal-culated to cause dissatisfaction: not considering what is their quantitative value. To reprove a piece of national self-laudation uttered by Mr. Roebuck, he comments on the murder of an illegitimate child by its mother, reported in the same paper. Now this would be effective if infanticide were peculiar to Eng-land, or if he could show a larger proportion of infanticide here than elsewhere; but his criticism is at once cancelled on calling to mind the developed system of baby-farming round Paris, and the extensive getting-rid of infants to which it is instrumental. By following Mr. Arnold's method, it would be easy to dispose of his conclusions.   Suppose, for instance, that I were to set down the many murders committed in England by foreigners within our own memories, including those by Courvoisier, by Mrs. Manning, by Barthélemi near Fitzroy Square, by a Frenchman in Foley Place (about 1854-7), that by Müller, that by Kohl in the Essex marshes, that by Lani in a brothel near the Hay-market, that by Marguerite Diblanc, the tragedy of the two young Germans (Maï·and Nagel) at Chelsea, ending with the recent one in Great Coram Street—suppose I were to compare the ratio between this number of murderers and the number of foreigners in England, with the answering ratio among our own people ; and suppose I were to take this as a test of the Continental culture Mr. Arnold so much admires. Probably he would not think the test quite relevant ; and yet it would be quite as relevant as that he uses—perhaps somewhat more relevant. Suppose, again, that by way of criticism on German administration, I were to dwell on the catastrophe at Berlin, where, during the celebration of victory, fourteen sightseers were killed and some hundreds injured ; or suppose I were to judge it by the disclosures of the leading Berlin physician, Virchow, who shows that one out of every three children born in Berlin dies the first year, and whose statistics prove the general mortality to be increasing so rapidly that while "in 1854 the death-rate was 1000, in 1851—63 it rose to 1164, and in 1864—8 to 1817 " [11]—suppose, I say, that I took these facts as proof of failure in the social system Mr. Arnold would have us copy. Possibly he would not be much shaken ; though it seems to me that this evidence would be more to the point than a case of infanticide among ourselves. Further, suppose I were to test French administration by the statistics of mortality in the Crimea, as given at the late meeting of the French Association for the Advancement of Science, by M. Le Fort, who pointed out that—

" Dans ces six mois d'hiver 1855-1856, alors qu'il n'y a plus guère d'hostilités, alors que les Anglais ont seulement en six mois 165 blessés, et les Français 323, l'armée anglaise, grâce aux précautions prises, n'a que peu de malades et ne perd que 606 hommes ; l'armée française voit éclater au milieu d'elle le typhus, qu'on eût pu éviter, et perd par les maladies seules 21,190 hommes ; "

and who further, respecting the relative mortalities from operations, said that—

" En Crimée, les armées anglaise et française se trouvent exposées aux mêmes besoins, aux mêmes vicissitudes atmosphériques, et cependant quelle différence dans la mortalité des opérés. Les Anglais perdent 24 pour 100 de leurs amputés du bras, nous en perdons plus du double, 55 sur 100 ; il en est de même pour l'amputation de la jambe : 35 contre 71 pour 100."

—suppose, I say, that I were thus to deal with the notion that "they manage these things better in France." Mr. Arnold would, very likely, not abandon his belief. And yet this contrast would certainly be as damaging as the fact about the girl Wragg, to which he more than once refers so emphatically. Surely it is manifest enough that by selecting the evidence, any society may be relatively blackened and any other society relatively whitened.

From Mr. Arnold's method let us turn to some of his specific statements; taking first the statement that the English are deficient in ideas. He says:—"There is the world of ideas, and there is the world of practice; the French are often for suppressing the one, and the English the other." [12] Admitting the success of the English in action, Mr. Arnold thinks that it goes along with want of faith in speculative conclusions. But by putting ideas and practice in this antithesis, he implies his acceptance of the notion that effectual practice does not depend on superiority of ideas. This is an erroneous notion. Methods that answer are preceded by thoughts that are true. A successful enterprise presupposes an imagination of all the factors, and conditions, and results—an imagination which differs from one leading to an unsuccessful enterprise in this, that what will happen is clearly and completely foreseen, instead of being foreseen vaguely and incompletely: there is greater ideality. Every scheme is an idea; every scheme more or less new, implies an idea more or less original; every scheme proceeded with, implies an idea vivid enough to prompt action; and every scheme which succeeds, implies an idea so accurate and exhaustive that the results correspond with it. When an English company accommodates Amsterdam with water (an element the Dutch are very familiar with, and in the management of which they, centuries ago, gave us lessons) must we not say that by leaving us to supply their chief city they show a want of confidence in results ideally seen? Is it replied that the Dutch are not an imaginative people? Then take the Italians. How happens it that such a pressing need as the draining of Naples, has never suggested to Italian rulers or Italian people the taking of measures to achieve it; and how happens it that the idea of draining Naples, instead of emanating from French or Germans, supposed by Mr. Arnold to have more faith in ideas, emanates from a company of Englishmen, who are now proposing to do the work without cost to the municipality.[13] Or what shall we infer as to relative faith in ideas, on learning that even within their respective territories the French and Germans wait for us to undertake new things for them ? When we find that Toulouse and Bordeaux were lighted with gas by an English company, must we not infer lack of ideas in the people of those places? When we find that a body of Englishmen, the Rhone Hydraulic Company, seeing that at Bellegarde there are rapids having a fall of forty feet, made a tunnel carrying a fourth of the river, and so got 10,000 horse-power, which they are selling to manufacturers ; and when we ask why this source of wealth was not utilized by the French themselves ; must we not say that it was because the idea did not occur to them, or because it was not vivid and definite enough to prompt the enterprise ? And when, on going north, we discover that not only in Belgium and Holland are the chief towns, Brussels, Antwerp, Lille, Ghent, Rotterdam, Amsterdam, Haarlem, &c., lighted by our Continental Gas Association, but that this combination of Englishmen lights many towns in Germany also—Hanover, Aix-la-Chapelle, Stolberg, Cologne, Frankfort, Vienna, nay, that even the head-quarters of *geist*, Berlin itself, had to wait for light until this Company supplied it, must we not say that more faith in ideas was shown by English than by Germans ? Germans have plenty of energy, are not without desire to make money, and knew that gas was used in England ; and if neither they nor their Governments undertook the work, we must infer that the benefits and means were inadequately conceived. English enterprises have often been led by ideas that looked wholly unpractical : as when the first English steamer astonished the people of Coblentz, in 1817, by making its appear-

ance there, so initiating the Rhine steam-navigation; or as when
the first English steamer started across the Atlantic.   Instead
of our practice being unideal, the ideas which guide it sometimes
verge on the romantic.   Fishing up a cable from the bottom of
an ocean three miles deep, was an idea seemingly more fitted for
The Arabian Nights than for actual life; and yet success proved
how truly those who conducted the operation had put together
their ideas in correspondence with the facts—the true test of
vivid imagination.

To show the groundlessness of the notion that new ideas are
not evolved and appreciated as much in England as elsewhere, I
am tempted here to enumerate our modern inventions of all
orders; from those directly aiming at material results, such as
Trevethick's first locomotive, up to the calculating-machines of
Babbage and the logic-machine of Jevons, quite remote from
practice in their objects.   But merely asserting that those who
go through the list will find that neither in number nor in importance do they yield to those of any nation during the same
period, I refrain from details.   Partly I do this because the space
required for specifying them would be too great; and partly
because inventions, mostly having immediate bearings on practice,
would perhaps not be thought by Mr. Arnold to prove fertility of
idea: though, considering that each machine is a theory before
it becomes a working reality, this would be a position difficult to
defend.   To avoid all possible objection, I will limit myself to
scientific discovery, from which the element of practice is
excluded; and to meet the impression that scientific discovery in
recent days has not maintained its former pace, I will name only
our achievements since 1800.

Taking first the Abstract Sciences, let us ask what has been
done in Logic.   We have the brief but pregnant statement of
inductive methods by Sir John Herschel, leading to the definite
systematization of them by Mr. Mill; and we have, in the work
of .Professor Bain, elaborately-illustrated applications of logical
methods to science and to the business of life.   Deductive Logic,

too, has been developed by a further conception. The doctrine of the quantification of the predicate, set forth in 1827 by Mr. George Bentham, and again set forth under a numerical form by Professor De Morgan, is a doctrine supplementary to that of Aristotle ; and the recognition of it has made it easier than before to see that Deductive Logic is a science of the relations implied by the inclusions, exclusions, and overlappings of classes.[14] Even were this all, the instalment of progress would be large for a single generation. But it is by no means all. In the work by Professor Boole, *Investigation of the Laws of Thought*, the application to Logic of methods like those of Mathematics, constitutes another step far greater in originality and in importance than any taken since Aristotle. So that, strangely enough, the assertion quoted above, that "we are backward in appreciating and pursuing abstract knowledge," and this complaint of Mr. Arnold that our life is wanting in ideas, come at a time when we have lately done more to advance the most abstract and purely-ideal science, than has been done anywhere else, or during any past period !

In the other division of Abstract Science—Mathematics, a recent revival of activity has brought results sufficiently striking. Though, during a long period, the bias of patriotism and undue reverence for that form of the higher calculus which Newton initiated, greatly retarded us ; yet since the re-commencement of progress, some five-and-twenty years ago, Englishmen have again come to the front. Sir W. R. Hamilton's method of Quaternions is a new instrument of research ; and whether or not as valuable as some think, undoubtedly adds a large region to the world of known mathematical truth. And then, more important still, there are the achievements of Cayley and Sylvester in the creation and development of the higher algebra. From competent and unbiassed judges I learn that the Theory of Invariants, and the methods of investigation which have grown out of it, constitute a step in mathematical progress larger than any made since the Differential Calculus. Thus, without enumerating the minor achievements of others, there is ample proof that abstract science, of this order also, is flourishing among us in great vigour.

Nor, on passing to the Abstract-Concrete Sciences, do we find better ground for this belief entertained by Mr. Arnold and others. Though Huyghens conceived of light as constituted of undulations, yet he was wrong in conceiving the undulations as allied in form to those of sound ; and it remained for Dr. Young to establish the true theory. Respecting the principle of interference of the rays of light propounded by Young, Sir John Herschel says,—"regarded as a physical law [it] has hardly its equal for beauty, simplicity, and extent of application, in the whole circle of science ; " and of Young's all-important discovery that the luminiferous undulations are transverse not longitudinal, he says that it showed " a sagacity which would have done honour to Newton himself." Just naming the discovery of the law of expansion of gases by Dalton, the laws of radiation by Leslie, the theory of dew by Wells, the discrimination by Wollaston of quantity and intensity in electricity, and the disclosure of electrolysis by Nicholson and Carlisle (all of them cardinal discoveries) and passing over minor contributions to physical science, we come to the great contributions of Faraday—magneto-electricity, the quantitative law of electrolysis, the magnetization of light, and dia-magnetism : not mentioning others of much significance. Next there is the great truth which men still living have finally established—the correlation and equivalence of the physical forces. In the establishment of this truth Englishmen have had a large share—some think the larger share. Remembering that in England the conception of heat as a mode of motion dates from Bacon, by whom it was expressed with an insight that is marvellous considering the knowledge of his time —remembering, too, that " Locke stated a similar view with singular felicity ; " we come, among Englishmen of the present century, first to Davy, whose experiments and arguments so conclusively supported those of Rumford ; then to the view of Roget and the postulate on which Faraday habitually reasoned, that all force arises only as other force is expended; then to the essay of Grove, in which the origin of the various forms of force out of one another was abundantly exemplified; and finally to the investigations by which Joule established the quantitative relations between heat and motion. Without dwelling on the important deductions from this great truth made by Sir W. Thomson, Rankine, Tyndall, and others, I will merely draw attention to its highly-abstract nature as again showing the baselessness of the above-quoted notion.

Equally conclusive is the evidence when we pass to Chemistry. The cardinal value of the step made by Dalton in 1808, when the *aperçu* of Higgins was reduced by him to a scientific form, will be seen on glancing into Wurtz' *Introduction to Chemical Philosophy*, and observing how the atomic theory underlies all subsequent chemical discovery. Nor, in more recent days, has the development of this theory fallen unduly into foreign hands. Prof. Williamson, by reconciling the theory of radicals with the theory of types, and by introducing the hypothesis of condensed molecular types, has taken a leading part in founding the modern views of chemical combinations. We come next to the cardinal conception of atomicity. In 1851, Prof. Frankland initiated the classification of the elements by their atomicities: his important interpretation being now avowedly accepted in Germany by those who originally disputed it; as by Kolbe in his *Moden der Modernen Chemie*. On turning from the more general chemical truths to the more special chemical truths, a like history meets us. Davy's discovery of the metallic bases of the alkalies and earths, revolutionized chemists' ideas. Passing over many other achievements in special chemistry, I may single out for their significance, the discoveries of Andrews, Tait, and especially of Brodie, respecting the constitution of ozone as an allotropic form of oxygen; and may join with these Brodie's discoveries respecting the allotropic forms of carbon, as throwing so much light on allotropy at large: And then we come to the all-important discoveries, general and special, of the late Prof. Graham. The truths he established respecting the hydration of compounds, the transpiration and the diffusion of liquids, the transpiration and the diffusion of gases, the dialysis of liquids and the dialysis of gases, and the occlusion of gases by metals, are all of them cardinal truths. And even of still greater value is his luminous generalization respecting the crystalloid and colloid states of matter—a generalization which, besides throwing light on many other phenomena, has given us an insight into organic processes previously incomprehensible. These results, reached by his beautifully-coherent series of researches extending over forty years, constitute a new revelation of the properties of matter.

Neither is it true that in advancing the Concrete Sciences we have failed to do our share. Take the first in order—Astronomy. Though, for the long period during which our mathematicians were behind, Planetary Astronomy progressed but little in England, and the development of the Newtonian theory was left chiefly to other nations, yet of late there has been no want of activity. When I have named the inverse problem of perturbations and the discovery of Neptune, the honour of which we share with the French, I have called to mind an achievement sufficiently remarkable. To Sidereal Astronomy we have made great contributions. Though the conception of Wright, of Durham, respecting stellar distribution was here so little attended to that when afterwards enunciated by Kant (who knew Wright's views) and by Sir W. Herschel, it was credited to them; yet since Sir W. Herschel's time the researches in Sidereal Astronomy by Sir John Herschel and others, have done much to further this division of the science. Quite recently the discoveries made by Mr. Huggins respecting the velocities with which certain stars are approaching us and others receding, have opened a new field of inquiry; and the inferences reached by Mr. Proctor respecting groupings of stars and the "drifting" of star-groups, now found to harmonize with the results otherwise reached by Mr. Huggins, go far to help us in conceiving the constitution of our galaxy. Nor must we forget how much has been done towards explaining the physical constitutions of the heavenly bodies, as well as their motions : the natures of nebulæ, and the processes going on in Sun and stars, have been greatly elucidated by Huggins, Lockyer, and others.

In Geology, the progress made here, and especially the progress in geological theory, is certainly not less—good judges say much greater—than has been made elsewhere.   Just noting that English Geology goes back to Ray, whose notions were far more philosophical than those set forth long afterwards by Werner, we come to Hutton, with whom in fact rational Geology commences.   For the untenable Neptunist hypothesis, asserting a once-universal aqueous action unlike the present, Hutton substituted an aqueous action, marine and fluviatile, continuously operating as we now see it, antagonized by a periodic igneous action.   He recognized denudation as producing mountains and valleys ; he denied so-called primitive rocks ; he asserted metamorphism ; he taught the meaning of unconformity.   Since his day rapid advances in the same direction had been made. . William Smith, by establishing the order of superposition of strata throughout England, prepared the way for positive generalizations ; and by showing that contained fossils are safer tests of correspondence among strata than mineral characters, laid the basis for subsequent classifications.   The better data thus obtained, theory quickly turned to account.   In his *Principles of Geology*, Lyell elaborately worked out the uniformitarian doctrine—the doctrine that the Earth's crust has been brought to its present complex structure by the continuous operation of forces like those we see still at work.   More recently, Prof. Ramsay's theory of lake-formation by glaciers has helped in the interpretation ; and by him, as well as by Prof. Huxley, much has been done towards elucidating past distributions of continents and oceans.   Let me name, too, Mallet's *Theory of Earthquakes*—the only scientific explanation of them yet given.   And there must be added another fact of moment.   Criticism has done far more here than abroad, towards overthrowing the crude

11

hypothesis of universal "systems" of strata, which succeeded the still cruder hypothesis of universal strata, enunciated by Werner.

That our contributions to Biological science have in these later times not been unimportant, may, I think, be also maintained. Just noting that the "natural system" of Plant-classification, though French by development is English by origin, since Ray made its first great division and sketched out some of its sub-divisions; we come, among English botanists, to Brown. He made a series of investigations in the morphology, classification, and distribution of plants, which in number and importance have never been equalled: the *Prodromus Floræ Novæ-Hollandiæ* is the greatest achievement in classification since Jussieu's *Natural Orders.* Brown, too, it was who solved the mystery of plant-fertilization. Again, there is the conception that existing plant-distribution has been determined by past geological and physical changes—a conception we owe to Dr. Hooker, who has given us sundry wide interpretations in pursuance of it. In Animal-physiology there is Sir Charles Bell's discovery respecting the sensory and motor functions of the nerve-roots in the spinal cord; and this underlies multitudinous interpretations of organic phenomena. More recently we have had Mr. Darwin's great addition to biological science. Following in the steps of his grandfather, who had anticipated Lamarck in enunciating the general conception of the genesis of organic forms by adaptive modifications, but had not worked out the conception as Lamarck did, Mr. Darwin, perceiving that both of them were mistaken in attributing the modifications to causes which, though some of them true, were inadequate to account for all the effects, succeeded, by recognizing the further cause he called Natural Selection, in raising the hypothesis from a form but partially tenable to a quite tenable form. This view of his, so admirably worked out, has been adopted by the great majority of naturalists; and, by making the process of organic evolution more comprehensible, it is revolutionizing biological conceptions throughout the world. In the words of Professor Cohn, "no book of recent times has influenced the conceptions of modern science like the first edition of Charles Darwin's *Origin of Species*." [15] Nor should we overlook the various kindred minor discoveries, partly dependent, partly independent : Mr. Darwin's own respecting the dimorphism of flowers ; Mr. Bates's beautiful interpretation of mimicry in insects, which led the way to many allied interpretations ; Mr. Wallace's explanations of dimorphism and polymorphism in *Lepidoptera*. Finally, Professor Huxley, besides dissipating some serious biological errors of continental origin, has made important contributions to morphology and classification.

Nor does the balance turn against us on passing to the next-highest concrete science. After those earlier inquiries by which Englishmen so largely advanced the Science of Mind, and set up much of the speculation subsequently active in France and Germany, there came a lull in English thinking ; and during this arose the absurd notion that the English are not a philosophical people. But the lull, ending some forty years ago, gave place to an activity which has quickly made up for lost time. On this point I need not rest in assertion, but will quote foreign testimony. The first chapter of Prof. Ribot's work, *La Psychologie Anglaise Contemporaine* begins thus :—

" 'Le sceptre de la psychologie, dit M. Stuart Mill, est décidément revenu à l'Angleterre.' On pourrait soutenir qu'il n'en est jamais sorti. Sans doute, les études psychologiques y sont maintenant cultivées par des hommes de premier ordre qui, par la solidité de leur méthode, et ce qui est plus rare, par la précision de leurs résultats, ont fait entrer la science dans une période nouvelle ; mais c'est plutôt un redoublement qu'un renouvellement d'éclat."

Similarly, on turning to Ethics considered under its psychological aspect, we find foreign testimony that English thinkers have done most towards the elaboration of a scientific system. In the preface to his late work, *La Morale nella Filosofia Positiva* (meaning by "*Positiva*" simply scientific), Prof. Barzellotti, of Florence, states that for this reason he limits himself to an account of English speculation in this department.[16]

And then, if, instead of Psychology and Ethics, Philosophy at large comes in question, there is independent testimony of kindred nature to be cited. Thus, in the first number of *La Critique Philosophique* (8 Février, 1872), published under the direction of M. Rénouvier, the acting editor, M. Pillon, writes :—

" On travaille beaucoup dans le champ des idées en Angleterre. . . Non-seulement l'Angleterre surpasse la France par l'ardeur et le travail, ce qui est malheureusement bien peu dire, et par l'intérêt des investigations et des débats de ses penseurs, mais même elle laisse loin derrière elle l'Allemagne en ce dernier point."

And still more recently M. Martins, in the leading French periodical, has been referring to—

" les nouvelles idées nées dans la libre Angleterre et appelées à transformer un jour les sciences naturelles." [17]

So that while Mr. Arnold is lamenting the want of ideas in England, it is discovered abroad that the genesis of ideas in England is very active. While he thinks our conceptions are commonplace, our neighbours find them new, to the extent of being revolutionary. Oddly enough, at the very time when he is reproaching his countrymen with lack of *geist*, Frenchmen are asserting that there is more *geist* here than anywhere else! Nor is there wanting testimony of kindred nature from other nations. In the lecture above cited, Dr. Cohn, while claiming for Germany a superiority in the number of her earnest workers, says that "England especially has always been, and is particularly now, rich in men whose scientific works are remarkable for their astonishing laboriousness, clearness, profundity, and independence of thought"—a further recognition of the truth that instead of merely plodding along the old ruts, the English strike out new tracks: are unusually imaginative.

In his essay on the " Functions of Criticism at the Present Time," Mr. Arnold insists that the thing most needful for us now, in all branches of knowledge, is " to see the object as in itself it really is "; and in *Friendship's Garland*, his *alter ego*, Arminius, exhorts our Philistinism "to search and not rest till it sees things more as they really are." Above, I have done that which Mr. Arnold urges; not by picking-up stray facts, but by a systematic examination. Feeling sure that Mr. Arnold has himself taken the course he advises, and is therefore familiar with all this evidence, as well as with the large quantity which might be added, I am somewhat puzzled on finding him draw from it a conclusion so different from that which presents itself to me. Were any one, proceeding on the foregoing data, to assert that since the beginning of this century, more has been done in England to advance scientific knowledge than has ever been done in a like interval, at any time, in any country, I should think his inference less wide of the truth than that which, strange to say, Mr. Arnold draws from the same data.

. And now to consider that which more immediately concerns us—the effect produced by the bias of anti-patriotism on sociological speculation. Whether in Mr. Arnold, whom I have ventured to take as a type, the leaning towards national self-depreciation was primary and the over-valuing of foreign institutions secondary, or whether his admiration of foreign institutions was the cause and his tendency to depreciatory estimates of our social state the effect, is a question which may be left open. For present purposes it suffices to observe that the two go together. Mr. Arnold is impatient with the unregulated and, as he thinks, anarchic state of our society; and everywhere displays a longing for more administrative and controlling agencies. " Force till right is ready," is one of the sayings he emphatically repeats: apparently in the belief that there can be a sudden transition from a coercive system to a non-coercive one—ignoring the truth that there has to be a continually-changing compromise between force and right, during which force decreases step by step as right increases step by step, and during which every step brings some temporary evil along with its ultimate good.

Thinking more force needful for us, and lauding institutions which exercise it, Mr. Arnold holds that even in our literature we should benefit by being under authoritative direction. Though he is not of opinion that an Academy would succeed here, he casts longing glances at the French Academy, and wishes we could have had over us an influence like that to which he ascribes certain excellencies in French literature.

The French Academy was established, as he points out, "to work with all the care and all the diligence possible at giving sure rules to our [the French] language, and rendering it pure, eloquent, and capable of treating the arts and sciences." Let us consider whether it has fulfilled this intention, by removing the most conspicuous defects of the language.   Down to the present time, there is in daily use the expression *qu'est ce que c'est ?* and even *qu'est ce que c'est que cela ?* If in some remote corner of England is heard the analogous expression,—"what is that there here ?" it is held to imply entire absence of culture': the use of two superflous words proves a want of that close adjustment of language to thought which even partially-educated persons among us have reached. How is it, then, that though in this French phrase there are five superfluous words (or six, if we take *cela* as two), the purifying criticism of the French Academy has not removed it from French speech—not even from the speech of the educated ?   Or why, again, has the Academy not condemned, forbidden, and so expelled from the language, the double negative ? If among ourselves any one lets drop the sentence, "I didn't say nothing," the inevitable inference is that he has lived with the ill-taught ; and, further, that in his mind words and ideas answer to one another very loosely. Though in French the second negative is by derivation positive, yet in acquiring a negative meaning it became alike superfluous and illogical ; and its use should then have been interdicted, instead of being enforced.   Once more, why has not the French Academy systematized the genders ? No one who considers language as an instrument of thought, which is good in proportion as its special parts are definitely adjusted to special functions, can doubt that a meaningless use of genders is a defect. It is undeniable that to employ marks of gender in ways always suggesting attributes that are possessed, instead of usually suggesting attributes that are not possessed, is an improvement. Having an example of this improvement before them, why did not the Academy introduce it into French? And then—more significant question still—how, without the aid of any Academy, came the genders to be systematized in English? Mr. Arnold, and those who, in common with him, seem to believe only in agencies that have visible organizations, might, perhaps, in seeking the answer to this question, lose faith in artificial appliances and gain faith in natural processes. For as, on asking the origin of language in general, we are reminded that all its complex, marvellously-adjusted parts and arrangements have been evolved without the aid or oversight of any embodied power, Academic or other; so, on asking the origin of this particular improvement in language, we find that it, too, arose naturally. Nay, more, it was made possible by one of those anarchic states which Mr. Arnold so much dislikes. Out of the conflict of Old-English dialects, sufficiently allied to co-operate but sufficiently different to have contradictory marks of gender, there came a disuse of meaningless genders and a survival of the genders having meaning—a change which an Academy, had one existed here in those days, would doubtless have done its best to prevent; seeing that during the transition there must have been a disregard of rules and apparent corruption of speech, out of which no benefit could have been anticipated.

Another fact respecting the French Academy is by no means congruous with Mr. Arnold's conception of its value. The compiling of an authoritative dictionary was a fit undertaking for it. Just recalling the well-known contrast between its dilatory execution of this undertaking, and the active execution of a kindred one by Dr. Johnson, we have more especially to note the recent like contrast between the performances of the Academy and the

performances of M. Littré. The Academy has long had in hand
two dictionaries—the one a second edition of its original dictionary, the other an historical dictionary. The first is at letter
D ; and the initial number of the other, containing A—B, issued
fifteen years ago, has not yet had a successor. Meanwhile, M.
Littré, single-handed, has completed a dictionary which, besides
doing all that the two Academy-dictionaries propose to do, does
much more. With which marvellous contrast we have to join
the startling fact, that M. Littré was refused admission to the
Academy in 1863, and at length admitted in 1871 only after
violent opposition.

Even if we pass over these duties which, in pursuance of its
original purpose, the French Academy might have been expected
to perform, and limit ourselves to the duty Mr. Arnold especially
dwells upon—the duty of keeping " the fine quality of the French
spirit unimpaired," and exercising " the authority of a recognised
master in matters of tone and taste" (to quote his approving
paraphrase of M. Renan's definition)—it may still, I think, be
doubted whether there have been achieved by it the benefits Mr.
Arnold alleges, and whether there have not been caused great
evils. That its selection of members has tended to encourage
bad literature instead of good, seems not improbable when we
are reminded of its past acts, as we are in the well-known letter
of Paul-Louis Courier, in which there occurs this, among other
passages similarly damaging :—

" Un duc et pair honore l'Académie française, qui ne veut point de
Boileau, refuse la Bruyère . . . . mais reçoit tout d'abord Chape-
lain et Conrart. De même nous voyons à l'Académie grecque le vicomte
invité, Coraï repoussé, lorsque Jomard y entre comme dans un
moulin." [13]

Nor have its verdicts upon great works been such as to encourage
confidence : instance the fact that it condemned the *Cid* of Cor-
neille, now one of the glories of French literature. Its critical
doctrines, too, have not been beyond question. Upholding those
canons of dramatic art which so long excluded the romantic

drama, and maintained the feeling shown by calling Shakspeare an "intoxicated barbarian," may possibly have been more detrimental than beneficial. And when we look, not at such select samples of French literary taste as Mr. Arnold quotes, but at samples from the other extreme, we may question whether the total effect has been great. If, as Mr. Arnold thinks, France "is the country in Europe where the *people* is most alive," it clearly is not alive to the teachings of the Academy: witness the recent revival of the *Père Duchêne;* the contents of which are no less remarkable for their astounding obscenity than for their utter stupidity. Nay, when we look only where we are told to look—only where the Academy exercises its critical function on modern literature, we find reason for scepticism. Instance the late award of the Halphen Prize to the author of a series of poems called *L'Invasion*, of which M. Patin, a most favourable critic, says:—

"Their chief characteristic is a warmth of sentiment and a '*verve*,' which one would wish to see under more restraint, but against which one hesitates to set up, however just might be their application under other circumstances, the cold requirements of taste."

Thus we have the Academy pandering to the popular feeling. The ebullitions of a patriotic sentiment which it is the misfortune of France to possess in too great a degree, are not checked by the Academy but encouraged by it: even at the expense of good taste.

And then, lastly, observe that some of the most cultivated Frenchmen, not so well satisfied with institutions of the Academy-type as Mr. Arnold seems to be, have recently established, on an English model, a French Association for the Advancement of Science. Here are passages from their prospectus, published in *La Revue Scientifique*, 20 Janvier, 1872; commencing with an account of the founding of the Royal Institution:—

"Il y avait cinquante-huit membres présents à cette réunion. Chacun d'eux souscrivit, sans plus attendre, une action de cinquante guinées ; c'est à peu près treize cents francs de notre monnaie, qui en vaudraient aujourd'hui bien près de deux mille cinque.　Le lendemain, la *Société* [*Institution*] *royale de Londres* était constituée.

"On sait depuis ce qu'elle est devenue.

"Ce qu'ont fait les Anglais en 1799, d'illustres savants de notre pays veulent le renouveler aujourd'hui pour la France.

"Eux aussi, ils ont jugé, comme Rumfort au siècle dernier, que la vieille suprématie du nom français dans tous les ordres de sciences commençait à être sérieusement ébranlée, et risquait de s'écrouler un jour.

"A Dieu ne plaise qu'ils accusent l'Académie de cette décadence ! ils en font presque tous partie eux-mêmes.　Mais l'Académie, qui a conservé en Europe le prestige de son nom, s'enferme un peu plus dans la majesté de sa grandeur.　Elle ne possède ni des moyens d'action assez puissants, ni une énergie assez active pour les mettre en œuvre.　Le nerf de la guerre, l'argent, lui manque, et plus encore peut-être l'initiative intelligente et hardie.　Elle s'est endormie dans le respect de ses traditions séculaires."

A further testimony from a foreigner to the value of our methods of aiding intellectual progress, in comparison with continental methods, has been still more recently given by M. Alphonse de Candolle, in his *Histoire des Sciences et des Savants*.　His fear for us is that we may adopt the continental policy and abandon our own.　Respecting Science in England, he says:—

"Je ne vois qu'un seul indice de faiblesse pour l'avenir, c'est une disposition croissante des hommes de science à solliciter l'appui du gouvernement.　On dirait qu'ils ne se fient plus aux forces individuelles, dont le résultat pourtant a été si admirable dans leur pays." [19]

Thus, curiously enough, we find another contrast parallel to that noted already.　As with English ideas so with English systems—while depreciated at home they are eulogized abroad. While Mr. Arnold is lauding French institutions, Frenchmen, recognizing their shortcomings, are adopting English institutions. From which we may fairly infer that, great as is Mr. Arnold's desire "to see the object as in itself it really is," he has not in this case succeeded ; and that, endeavouring to escape the bias of patriotism, he has been carried too far the other way by the bias of anti-patriotism.[20]

One more illustration of the effect this bias has on Mr. Arnold calls for brief comment. Along with his over-valuation of foreign regulative institutions, there goes an under-valuation of institutions at home which do not exhibit the kind of regulation he thinks desirable, and stand in the way of authoritative control. I refer to those numerous Dissenting organizations characterizing this "anarchy" of ours, which Mr. Arnold curiously makes the antithesis to "culture."

Mr. Arnold thinks that as a nation we show undue faith in machinery.

"Faith in machinery is, I said, our besetting danger. . . . . What is freedom but machinery? what is population but machinery? what is coal but machinery? what are railroads but machinery? what is wealth but machinery? what are religious organizations but machinery?"[21]

And in pursuance of this conception he regards the desire to get Church-rates abolished and certain restrictions on marriage removed, as proving undue belief in machinery among Dissenters; while his own disbelief in machinery he considers proved by wishing for stronger governmental restraints,[22] by lauding the supervision of an Academy, and by upholding a Church-establishment. I must leave unconsidered the question whether an Academy, if we had one, would authorize this use of language; which makes it seem that voluntary religious agency is machinery and that compulsory religious agency is not machinery. I must pass over, too, Mr. Arnold's comparison of Ecclesiasticism and Nonconformity in respect of the men they have produced. Nor have I space to examine what he says about the mental attitudes of the two. It must suffice to say that were the occasion fit, it might be shown that his endeavour "to see the object as in itself it really is," has not succeeded much better in this case than in the cases above dealt with. Here I must limit myself to a single criticism.

The trait which in Mr. Arnold's view of Nonconformity seems to me most remarkable, is that in breadth it so little transcends the view of the Nonconformists themselves. The two views greatly differ in one respect—antipathy replaces sympathy; but the two views are not widely unlike in extension. Avoiding that provincialism of thought which he says characterizes Dissenters, I should have expected Mr. Arnold to estimate Dissent, not under its local and temporary aspect, but under its general aspect as a factor in all societies at all times. Though the Nonconformists themselves think of Nonconformity as a phase of Protestantism in England, Mr. Arnold's studies of other nations, other ages, and other creeds, would, I should have thought, have led him to regard Nonconformity as a universal power in societies, which has in our time and country its particular embodiment, but which is to be understood only when contemplated in all its other embodiments. The thing is one in spirit and tendency, whether shown among the Jews or the Greeks—whether in Catholic Europe or in Protestant England. Wherever there is disagreement with a current belief, no matter what its nature, there is Nonconformity. The open expression of difference and avowed opposition to that which is authoritatively established, constitutes Dissent, whether the religion be Pagan or Christian, Monotheistic or Polytheistic. The relative attitudes of the dissenter and of those in power, are essentially the same in all cases; and in all cases lead to persecution and vituperation. The Greeks who poisoned Socrates were moved by just the same sentiment as the Catholics who burnt Cranmer, or as the Protestant Churchmen who imprisoned Bunyan and pelted Wesley. And while the manifestations of feeling are essentially the same, while the accompanying evils are essentially the same, the resulting benefits are essentially the same. Is it not a truism that without divergence from that which exists, whether it be in politics, religion, manners, or anything else, there can be no progress? And is it not an obvious corollary that the temporary ills accompanying the divergence, are out-balanced by the eventual good? It is certain, as Mr. Arnold holds, that sub-ordination is essential; but it is also certain that insubordination is essential—essential, if there is to be any improvement. There are two extremes in the state of a social aggregate, as of every other aggregate, which are fatal to evolution—rigidity and in-coherence. A medium plasticity is the healthful condition. On the one hand, a force of established structures and habits and beliefs, such as offers considerable resistance to change; on the other hand, an originality, an independence, and an opposition to authority, energetic enough to overcome the resistance little by little. And while the political nonconformity we call Radicalism has the function of thus gradually modifying one set of institu-tions, the religious nonconformity we call Dissent has the function of thus gradually modifying another set.

That Mr. Arnold does not take this entirely-unprovincial view, which would lead him to look on Dissenters with less aversion, may in part, I think, be ascribed to that over-valuation of foreign restraints and under-valuation of home freedom, which his bias of anti-patriotism fosters ; and serves further to illustrate the dis-turbing effects of this bias on sociological speculation.

And now to sum up this somewhat-too-elaborate argument. The general truth that by incorporation in his society, the citizen is in a measure incapacitated for estimating rightly its characters and actions in relation to those of other societies, has been made abundantly manifest. And it has been made manifest, also, that when he strives to emancipate himself from these influences of race, and country, and locality, which warp his judgment, he is apt to have his judgment warped in the opposite way. From the perihelion of patriotism he is carried to the aphelion of anti-patriotism ; and is almost certain to form views that are more or less excentric, instead of circular, all-sided, balanced views.

Partial escape from this difficulty is promised by basing our sociological conclusions chiefly on comparisons made among other societies—excluding our own. But even then these perverting sentiments are sure to intrude more or less ; for we cannot contemplate the institutions of other nations without our sympathies or antipathies being in some degree aroused by consciousness of likeness or unlikeness to our own institutions. Discounting our conclusions as well as we may, to allow for the errors we are thus led into, we must leave the entire elimination of such errors to a future in which the decreasing antagonisms of societies will go along with decreasing intensities of these sentiments.

CHAPTER X.

MANY years ago a solicitor sitting by me at dinner, complained bitterly of the injury which the then lately-established
County Courts, were doing his profession. He enlarged on the
topic in a way implying that he expected me to agree with him
in therefore condemning them. So incapable was he of going
beyond the professional point of view, that what he regarded as
a grievance he thought I also ought to regard as a grievance:
oblivious of the fact that the more economical administration of
justice of which his lamentation gave me proof, was to me, not
being a lawyer, matter for rejoicing.

The bias thus exemplified is a bias by which nearly all have
their opinions warped. Naval officers disclose their unhesitating
belief that we are in imminent danger because the cry for more
fighting ships and more sailors has not been met to their satisfaction. The debates on the purchase-system proved how strong
was the conviction of military men that our national safety depended on the maintenance of an army-organization like that in
which they were brought up, and had attained their respective ranks. Clerical opposition to the Corn-Laws showed how
completely that view which Christian ministers might have been
expected to take, was shut out by a view more congruous with
their interests and alliances. In all classes and sub-classes it
is the same. Hear the murmurs uttered when, because of the
Queen's absence, there is less expenditure in entertainments and

the so-called gaieties of the season, and you perceive that London
traders think the nation suffers if the consumption of superfluities is checked.   Study the pending controversy about
co-operative stores *versus* retail shops, and you find the shop-
keeping mind possessed by the idea that Society commits a
wrong if it deserts shops and goes to stores—is quite unconscious that the present distributing system rightly exists only as
a means of economically and conveniently supplying consumers,
and must yield to another system if that should prove more
economical and convenient.   Similarly with other trading
bodies, general and special—similarly with the merchants who
opposed the repeal of the Navigation Laws ; similarly with the
Coventry-weavers, who like free-trade in all things save ribbons.

The class-bias, like the bias of patriotism, is a reflex egoism ;
and like it has its uses and abuses.   As the strong attachments citizens feel for their nation cause that enthusiastic co-
operation by which its integrity is maintained in presence of
other nations, severally tending to spread and subjugate their
neighbours ; so the *esprit de corps* more or less manifest in each
specialized part of the the body politic, prompts measures to
preserve the integrity of that part in opposition to other parts, all
somewhat antagonistic.   The egoism of individuals leads to an
egoism of the class they form ; and besides the separate efforts,
generates a joint effort to get an undue share of the aggregate
proceeds of social activity.   The aggressive tendency of each class,
thus produced, has to be balanced by like aggressive tendencies
of other classes.   The implied feelings do, in short, develop
one another ; and the respective organizations in which they embody themselves develop one another.   Large classes of the
community marked-off by rank, and sub-classes marked-off by
special occupations, severally combine, and severally set up
organs advocating their interests : the reason assigned being in
all cases the same—the need for self-defence.

Along with the good which a society derives from this self-asserting and self-preserving action, by which each division and sub-division keeps itself strong enough for its functions, there goes, among other evils, this which we are considering—the aptness to contemplate all social arrangements in their bearings on class-interests, and the resulting inability to estimate rightly their effects on Society as a whole. The habit of thought produced [perverts not merely the judgments on questions which directly touch class-welfare; but it perverts the judgments on questions which touch class-welfare very indirectly, if at all. It fosters an adapted theory of social relations of every kind, with sentiments to fit the theory; and a characteristic stamp is given to the beliefs on public matters in general. Take an instance.

Whatever its technical ownership may be, Hyde Park is open for the public benefit: no title to special benefit is producible by those who ride and drive. It happens, however, that those who ride and drive make large use of it daily; and extensive tracts of it have been laid out for their convenience: the tracts for equestrians having been from time to time increased. Of people without carriages and horses, a few, mostly of the kinds who lead easy lives, use Hyde Park frequently as a promenade. Meanwhile, by the great mass of Londoners, too busy to go so far, it is scarcely ever visited: their share of the general benefit is scarcely appreciable. And now what do the few who have a constant and almost exclusive use of it, think about the occasional use of it by the many? They are angry when, at long intervals, even a small portion of it, quite distant from their haunts, is occupied for a few hours in ways disagreeable to them—nay, even when such temporary occupation is on a day during which Rotten Row is nearly vacant and the drives not one-third filled. In this, anyone unconcerned may see the influence of the class-bias. But he will have an inadequate conception of its distorting power unless he turns to some letters from members of the ruling class published in the *Times* in November last, when the question of the Park-Rules was being agitated. One writer, signing himself "A Liberal M.P.," expressing his disgust at certain addresses he heard, proposed, if others would join him, to give the offensive speakers punishment by force of fists; and then, on a subsequent day, another legislator, similarly moved, writes :—

"If 'M.P.' is in earnest in his desire to get some honest men together to take the law into their own hands, I can promise him a pretty good backing from those who are not afraid to take all the consequences.

"I am, Sir, your obedient servant,

"AN EX-M.P."

And thus we find class-feeling extinguishing rational political thinking so completely that, wonderful to relate, two law-makers propose to support the law by breaking the law !

In larger ways we have of late seen the class-bias doing the same thing—causing contempt for those principles of constitutional government slowly and laboriously established, and prompting a return to barbaric principles of government. Read the debate about the payment of Governor Eyre's expenses, and study the division-lists, and you see that acts which, according to the Lord Chief Justice, "have brought reproach not only on those who were parties to them, but on the very name of England," can nevertheless find numerous defenders among men whose class-positions, military, naval, official, &c., make them love power and detest resistance. Nay more, by raising an Eyre-Testimonial Fund and in other ways, there was shown a deliberate approval of acts which needlessly suspended orderly government and substituted unrestrained despotism. There was shown a deliberate ignoring of the essential question raised, which was—whether an executive head might, at will, set aside all those forms of administration by which men's lives and liberties are guarded against tyranny.

More recently, this same class-bias has been shown by the protest made when Mr. Cowan was dismissed for executing the Kooka rioters who had surrendered. The Indian Government, having inquired into the particulars, found that this killing of many men without form of law and contrary to orders, could not be defended on the plea of pressing danger ; and finding this, it ceased to employ the officer who had committed so astounding a deed, and removed to another province the superior officer who had approved of the deed. Not excessive punishment, one would say. Some might contend that extreme mildness was shown in thus inflicting no greater evil than is inflicted on a labourer when he does not execute his work properly. But now mark what is thought by one who displays in words the bias of the governing classes, intensified by life in India. In a letter published in the *Times* of May 15, 1872, the late Sir Donald M'Leod writes concerning this dismissal and removal :—

" All the information that reaches me tends to prove that a severe blow has been given to all chance of vigorous or independent action in future, when emergencies may arise. The whole service appears to have been astonished and appalled by the mode in which the officers have been dealt with."

That we may see clearly what amazing perversions of sentiment and idea are caused by contemplating actions from class points of view, let us turn from this feeling of sympathy with Mr. Cowan, to the feeling of detestation shown by members of the same class in England towards a man who kills a fox that destroys his poultry. Here is a paragraph from a recent paper :—

" Five poisoned foxes have been found in the neighbourhood of Penzance, and there is consequently great indignation among the western sportsmen. A reward of 20*l*. has been offered for information that shall lead to the conviction of the poisoner."

So that wholesale homicide, condemned alike by religion, by equity, by law, is approved, and the mildest punishment of it blamed; while vulpicide, committed in defence of property, and condemned neither by religion, nor by equity, nor by any law save that of sportsmen, excites an anger that cries aloud for positive penalties !

I need not further illustrate the more special distortions of

sociological belief which result from the class-bias. They may
be detected in the conversations over every table, and in the
articles appearing in every party-journal or professional publication. The effects here most worthy of our attention are the
general effects—the effects produced on the minds of the upper
and lower classes. Let us observe how greatly the prejudices
generated by their respective social positions, pervert the conceptions of employers and employed. We will deal with the
employed first.

As before shown, mere associations of ideas, especially when
joined with emotions, affect our beliefs, not simply without
reason but in spite of reason—causing us, for instance, to think
there is something intrinsically repugnant in a place where many
painful experiences have been received, and something intrinsically charming in a scene connected with many past delights.
The liability to such perversions of judgment is greatest where
persons are the objects with which pleasures and pains are
habitually associated. One who has often been, even uninten-
tionally, a cause of gratification, is favourably judged; and an
unfavourable judgment is formed of one who, even involun-
tarily, has often inflicted sufferings. Hence, when there are
social antagonisms, arises the universal tendency to blame the·
individuals, and to hold them responsible for the *system.*

It is thus with the conceptions the working-classes frame of
those by whom they are immediately employed, and of those
who fill the higher social positions. Feeling keenly what they
have to bear, and tracing sundry real grievances to men who buy
their labour and men who are most influential in making the
laws, artizans and rustics conclude that, considered individually
and in combination, those above them are personally bad—
selfish, or tyrannical, in special degrees. It never occurs to them
that the evils they complain of result from the average human
nature of our age. And yet were it not for the class-bias, they
would see in their dealings with one another, plenty of proofs

that the injustices they suffer are certainly not greater, and possibly less, than they would be were the higher social functions discharged by individuals taken from among themselves. The simple fact, notorious enough, that working-men who save money and become masters, are not more considerate than usual towards those they employ, but often the contrary, might alone convince them of this. On all sides there is ample evidence having kindred meaning. Let them inquire about the life in every kitchen where there are several servants, and they will find quarrels about supremacy, tyrannies over juniors who are made to do more than their proper work, throwings of blame from one to another, and the many forms of misconduct caused by want of right feeling; and very often the evils growing up in one of these small groups exceed in intensity the evils pervading society at large. The doings in workshops, too, illustrate in various ways the ill-treatment of artizans by one another. Hiding the tools and spoiling the work of those who do not conform to their unreasonable customs, prove how little individual freedom is respected among them. And still more conspicuously is this proved by the internal governments of their trade-combinations. Not to dwell on the occasional killing of men among them who assert their rights to sell their labour as they please, or on the frequent acts of violence and intimidation committed by those on strike against those who undertake the work they have refused, it suffices to cite the despotism exercised by trades-union officers. The daily acts of these make it manifest that the ruling powers set up by working-men, inflict on them grievances as great as, if not greater than, those inflicted by the ruling powers, political and social, which they decry. When the heads of an association he has joined forbid a collier to work more than three days in the week—when he is limited to a certain " get " in that space of time—when he dares not accept from his employer an increasing bonus for every extra day he works—when, as a reason for declining, he says that he should be made miserable by his comrades, and that even his wife would not be spoken to ; it becomes clear that he and the rest have made for themselves a tyranny worse than the tyrannies complained of. Did he look at the facts apart from class-bias, the skilful artizan, who in a given time can do more than his fellows, but who dares not do it because he would be " sent to Coventry " by them, and who consequently cannot reap the benefit of his superior powers, would see that he is thus aggressed upon by his fellows more seriously than by Acts of Parliament or combinations of capitalists. And he would further see that the sentiment of justice in his own class is certainly not greater than in the classes he thinks so unjust.

The feeling which thus warps working-men's conceptions, at the same time prevents them from seeing that each of their unions is selfishly aiming to benefit at the expense of the industrial population at large. When an association of carpenters or of engineers makes rules limiting the number of apprentices admitted, with the view of maintaining the rate of wages paid to to its members—when it thus tacitly says to every applicant beyond the number allowed, " Go and apprentice yourself elsewhere ; " it is indirectly saying to all other bodies of artizans. " You may have your wages lowered by increasing your numbers, but we will not." And when the other bodies of artizans severally do the like, the general result is that the incorporated workers of all orders, say to the surplus sons of workers who want to find occupations, "We will none of us let our masters employ you." Thus each trade, in its eagerness for self-protection, is regardless of other trades, and sacrifices numbers among the rising generation of the artizan-class. Nor is it thus only that the interest of each class of artizans is pursued to the detriment of the artizan-class in general. I do not refer to the way in which when bricklayers strike they throw out of employment the labourers who attend them, or to the way in which the colliers now on strike have forced idleness on the ironworkers ; but I refer to the way in which the course taken by any one set of operatives to get higher wages, is taken regardless of the fact that an eventual rise in the price of the commodity produced, is a disadvantage to all other operatives. The class-bias, fostering the belief that the question in each case is entirely one between employer and employed, between capital and labour, shuts out the truth that the interests of all consumers are involved, and that the immense majority of consumers belong to the working-classes themselves. If the consumers are named, such of them only are remembered as belong to the wealthier classes, who, it is thought, can well afford to pay higher prices. Listen to a passage from Mr. George Potter's paper read at the late Leeds Congress:—

" The consumer, in fact, in so high a civilization, so arrogant a luxu-riousness, and so impatient an expectancy as characterize him in our land and age, is ever ready to take the alarm and to pour out the vials of his wrath upon those whom he merely suspects of taking a course which may keep a feather out of his bed, a spice out of his dish, or a coal out of his fire; and, unfortunately for the chances of fairness, the weight of his anger seldom falls upon the capitalists, but is most certain to come crushing down upon the lowly labourer, who has dared to stand upon his own right and independence."

From which it might be supposed that all skilled and unskilled artizans, all farm-labourers, all other workers, with all their wives and children, live upon air—need no food, no clothing, no furni-ture, no houses, and are therefore unaffected by enhanced prices of commodities. However fully prepared for the distorting effects of class-bias, one would hardly have expected effects so great. One would have thought it manifest even to an extreme partizan of trades-unions, that a strike which makes coals as dear again, affects in a relatively-small degree the thousands of rich consumers above described, and is very keenly felt by the millions of poor consumers, to whom in winter the outlay for coal is a serious item of expenditure. One would have thought that a truth so obvious in this case, would be recognized throughout— the truth that with nearly all products of industry, the evil caused by a rise of price falls more heavily on the vast numbers who work for wages than on the small numbers who have moderate incomes or large incomes.

Were not their judgments warped by the class-bias, working-men might be more pervious to the truth that better forms of industrial organization would grow up and extinguish the forms which they regard as oppressive, were such better forms practicable. And they might see that the impracticability of better forms results from the imperfections of existing human nature, moral and intellectual. If the workers in any business could so combine and govern themselves that the share of profit coming to them as workers was greater than now, while the interest on the capital employed was less than now; and if they could at the same time sell the articles produced at lower rates than like articles produced in businesses managed as at present; then, manifestly, businesses managed as at present would go to the wall. That they do not go to the wall—that such better industrial organizations do not replace them, implies that the natures of working-men themselves are not good enough; or, at least, that there are not many of them good enough. Happily, to some extent organizations of a superior type are becoming possible: here and there they have achieved encouraging successes. But, speaking generally, the masses are neither sufficiently provident, nor sufficiently conscientious, nor sufficiently intelligent. Consider the evidence.

That they are not provident enough they show both by wasting their higher wages when they get them, and by neglecting such opportunities as occur of entering into modified forms of co-operative industry. When the Gloucester Waggon Company was formed, it was decided to reserve a thousand of its shares, of £10 each, for the workmen employed; and to suit them, it was arranged that the calls of a pound each should be at intervals of three months. As many of the men earned £2 10s. per week, in a locality where living is not costly, it was considered that the taking-up of shares in this manner would be quite practicable. All the circumstances were at the outset such as to promise that prosperity which the company has since achieved. The chairman is no less remarkable for his skill in the conduct of large undertakings than for that sympathy with the working-classes which led him to adopt this course. The manager had been a working-man; and possessed the confidence of working-men in so high a degree, that many migrated with him from the Midland counties when the company was formed. Further, the manager entered heartily into the plan—telling me himself, that he had rejoiced over the founding of a concern in which those employed would have an interest. His hopes, however, and those of the chairman, were disappointed. After the lapse of a year not one of the thousand shares was taken up; and they were then distributed among the proprietors. Doubtless, there have been in other cases more encouraging results. But this case is one added to others which show that the proportion of working-men adequately provident, is not great enough to permit an extensive growth of better industrial organizations.[1]

Again, the success of industrial organizations higher in type, requires in the members a nicer sense of justice than is at present general. Closer co-operation implies greater mutual trust; and greater mutual trust is not possible without more respect for one another's claims. When we find that in sick-clubs it is not uncommon for members to continue receiving aid when they are able to work, so that spies have to be set to check them; while, on the other hand, those who administer the funds often cause insolvency by embezzling them; we cannot avoid the inference that want of conscientiousness prevents the effective union of workers under no regulation but their own. When, among skilled labourers, we find a certain rate per hour demanded, because less "did not suffice for their natural wants," though the unskilled labourers working under them were receiving little more than half the rate per hour, and were kept out of the skilled class by stringent rules, we do not discover a moral sense so much above that shown by employers as to promise success for industrial combinations superior to our present ones. While

12

workmen think themselves justified in combining to sell their labour only on certain terms, but think masters not justified in combining to buy it only on certain terms, they show a conception of equity not high enough to make practicable a form of co-operation requiring that each shall recognize the claims of others as fully as his own. One pervading misconception of justice betrayed by them would alone suffice to cause failure— the misconception, namely, that justice requires an equal sharing of benefits among producers, instead of requiring, as it does, equal freedom to make the best of their faculties. The general policy of trades-unionism, tending everywhere to restrain the superior from profiting by his superiority lest the inferior should be disadvantaged, is a policy which, acted out in any industrial combinations, must make them incapable of competing with combinations based on the principle that benefit gained shall be proportioned to faculty put forth.

Thus, as acting on the employed in general, the class-bias obscures the truth, otherwise not easy to see, that the existing type of industrial organization, like the existing type of political organization, is about as good as existing human nature allows. The evils there are in it are nothing but the evils brought round on men by their own imperfections. The relation of master and workman has to be tolerated, because, for the time being, no other will answer as well. Looked at apart from special interests, this organization of industry we now see around us, must be considered as one in which the cost of regulation, though not so great as it once was, is still excessive. In any industrial combination there must be a regulating agency. That regulating agency, whatever its nature, must be paid for—must involve a deduction from the total proceeds of the labour regulated. The present system is one under which the share of the total proceeds that goes to pay for regulation, is considerable ; and under better systems to be expected hereafter, there will doubtless be a decrease in the cost of regulation. But, for the present, our comparatively-costly system has the justification that it alone succeeds.

Regulation is costly because the men to be regulated are defective. With decrease of their defects will come economy of regulation, and consequently greater shares of profit to themselves.

Let me not be misunderstood. The foregoing criticism does not imply that operatives have no grievances to complain of; nor does it imply that trade-combinations and strikes are without adequate justifications. It is quite possible to hold that when, instead of devouring their captured enemies, men made slaves of them, the change was a step in advance; and to hold that this slavery, though absolutely bad, was relatively good—was the best thing practicable for the time being. It is quite possible also to hold that when slavery gave place to a serfdom under which certain personal rights were recognized, the new arrangement, though in the abstract an inequitable one, was more equitable than the old, and constituted as great an amelioration as men's natures then permitted. It is quite possible to hold that when, instead of serfs, there came freemen working for wages, but held as a class in extreme subordination, this modified relation of employers and employed, though bad, was as good a one as could then be established. And so it may be held that at the present time, though the form of industrial government entails serious evils, those evils, much less than the evils of past times, are as small as the average human nature allows—are not due to any special injustice of the employing class, and can be remedied only as fast as men in general advance. On the other hand, while contending that the policy of trades-unions and the actions of men on strike, manifest an injustice as great as that shown by the employing classes, it is quite consistent to admit, and even to assert, that the evil acts of trade-combinations are the unavoidable accompaniments of a needful self-defence. Selfishness on the one side resisting selfishness on the other, inevitably commits sins akin to those it complains of—cannot effectually check harsh dealings without itself using harsh measures. Further, it may be fully admitted that the evils of working-class combinations, great as they are, go along with certain benefits, and will hereafter be followed by greater benefits —are evils involved by the transition to better arrangements.

Here my purpose is neither to condemn nor to applaud the ideas and actions of the employed in their dealings with employers; but simply to point out how the class-bias warps working-men's judgments of social relations—makes it difficult for working-men to see that our existing industrial system is a product of existing human nature, and can be improved only as fast as human nature improves.

The ruling and employing classes display an equally-strong bias of the opposite kind. From their point of view, the behaviour of their poorer fellow-citizens throughout these struggles appears uniformly blamable. That they experience from a strike inconvenience more or less considerable, sufficiently proves to them that the strike must be wrong. They think there is something intolerable in this independence which leads to refusals to work except at higher wages or for shorter times. That the many should be so reckless of the welfare of the few, seems to the few a grievance not to be endured. Though Mr. George Potter, as shown above, wrongly speaks of the consumer as though he were always rich, instead of being, in nine cases out of ten, poor; yet he rightly describes the rich consumer as indignant when operatives dare to take a course which threatens to raise the prices of necessaries and make luxuries more costly. This feeling, often betrayed in private, exhibited itself in public on the occasion of the late strike among the gas-stokers; when there were uttered proposals that acts entailing so much annoyance should be put down with a strong hand. And the same spirit was shown in that straining of the law which brought on the men the punishment for conspiracy, instead of the punishment for breach of contract; which was well deserved, and would have been quite sufficient.

This mental attitude of the employing classes is daily shown by the criticisms passed on servants. Read *The Greatest Plague in Life*, or listen to the complaints of every housewife, and you see that the minds of masters and mistresses are so much occupied with their own interests as to leave little room for the interests of the men and maids in their service. The very title, *The Greatest Plague in Life*, implies that the only life worthy of notice is the life to which servants minister; and there is an entire unconsciousness that a book with the same title, written by a servant about masters and mistresses, might he filled with equally-severe criticisms and grievances far more serious. The increasing independence of servants is enlarged upon as a change greatly to be lamented. There is no recognition of the fact that this increasing independence implies an increasing prosperity of the classes from which servants come; and that this amelioration in the condition of the many is a good far greater than the evil entailed on the few. It is not perceived that if servants, being in great demand and easily able to get places, will no longer submit to restrictions, say about dress, like those of past times, the change is part of the progress towards a social state which, if apparently not so convenient for the small regulating classes, implies an elevation of the large regulated classes.

The feeling shown by the rich in their thoughts about, and dealings with, the poor, is, in truth, but a mitigated form of the feeling which owners of serfs and owners of slaves displayed. In early times bondsmen were treated as though they existed simply for the benefit of their owners; and down to the present time the belief pervading the select ranks (not indeeed expressed but clearly enough implied) is, that the convenience of the select is the first consideration, and the welfare of the masses a secondary consideration. Just as an Old-English thane would have been astonished if told that the only justification for his existence as an owner of thralls, was that the lives of his thralls were on the whole better preserved and more comfortable than they would be did he not own them; so, now, it will astonish the dominant classes to assert that their only legitimate *raison d'être* is that by their instrumentality as regulators, the lives of the people are, on the average, made more satisfactory than they would otherwise be. And yet, looked at apart from class-bias, this is surely an undeniable truth. Ethically considered, there has never been any warrant for the subjection of the many to the few, except that it has furthered the welfare of the many; and at the present time, furtherance of the welfare of the many is the only warrant for that degree of class-subordination which continues. The existing conception must be, in the end, entirely changed. Just as the old theory of political government has been so transformed that the ruling agent, instead of being owner of the nation, has come to be regarded as servant of the nation; so the old theory of industrial and social government has to undergo a transformation which will make the regulating classes feel, while duly pursuing their own interests, that their interests are secondary to the interests of the masses whose labours they direct.

While the bias of rulers and masters makes it difficult for them to conceive this, it also makes it difficult for them to conceive that a decline of class-power and a decrease of class-distinction may be accompanied by improvement not only in the lives of the regulated classes, but in the lives of the regulating classes. The sentiments and ideas proper to the existing social organization, prevent the rich from seeing that worry and weariness and disappointment result to them indirectly from this social system apparently so conducive to their welfare. Yet, would they contemplate the past, they might find strong reasons for suspecting as much. The baron of feudal days never imagined the possibility of social arrangements that would serve him far better than the arrangements he so strenuously upheld; nor did he see in the arrangements he upheld the causes of his many sufferings and discomforts. Had he been told that a noble might be much happier without a moated castle, having its keep and secret passages and dungeons for prisoners—that he might be more secure without drawbridge and portcullis, men-at-arms and sentinels—that he might be in less danger having no vassals or hired mercenaries—that he might be wealthier without possessing a single serf; he would have thought the statements absurd even to the extent of insanity. It would have been useless to argue that the *régime* seeming so advantageous to him, entailed hardships of many kinds—perpetual feuds with his neighbours, open attacks, surprises, betrayals, revenges by equals, treacheries by inferiors; the continual carrying of arms and wearing of armour: the perpetual quarrellings of servants and disputes among vassals; the coarse and unvaried food supplied by an unprosperous agriculture; a domestic discomfort such as no modern servant would tolerate; resulting in a wear and tear that brought life to a comparatively-early close, if it was not violently cut short in battle or by murder. Yet what the class-bias of that time made it impossible for him to see, has become to his modern representative conspicuous enough. The peer of our day knows that he is better off without defensive appliances and retainers and serfs than his predecessor was with them. His country-house is more secure than was an embattled tower; he is safer among his unarmed domestics than a feudal lord was when surrounded by armed guards; he is in less danger going about weaponless than was the mail-clad knight with lance and sword. Though he has no vassals to fight at his command, there is no suzerain who can call on him to sacrifice his life in a quarrel not his own; though he can compel no one to labour, the labours of freemen make him immensely more wealthy than was the ancient holder of bondsmen; and along with the loss of direct control over workers, there has grown up an industrial system which supplies him with multitudinous conveniences and luxuries undreamt of by him who had workers at his mercy.

May we not, then, infer that just as the dominant classes of ancient days were prevented by the feelings and ideas appropriate to the then-existing social state, from seeing how much evil it brought on them, and how much better for them might be a social state in which their power was much less; so the dominant classes of the present day are prevented from seeing how the existing forms of class-subordination redound to their own injury, and how much happier may be their future representatives having social positions less prominent? Occasionally recognizing, though they do, certain indirect evils attending their supremacy, they do not see that by accumulation these indirect evils constitute a penalty which supremacy brings on them. Though they repeat the trite reflection that riches fail to purchase content, they do not draw the inference that there must be something wrong in a system which thus deludes them. You hear it from time to time admitted that great wealth is a heavy burden: the life of a rich peer being described as made like the life of an attorney by the extent of his affairs. You observe among those whose large means and various estates enable them to multiply their appliances to gratification, that every new appliance becomes an additional something to be looked after, and adds to the possibilities of vexation. Further, if you put together the open confessions and the tacit admissions, you find that, apart from these anxieties and annoyances, the kind of life which riches and honours bring is not a satisfactory life—its inside differs immensely from its outside. In candid moments the "social treadmill" is complained of by those who nevertheless think themselves compelled to keep up its monotonous round. As everyone may see, fashionable life is passed, not in being happy, but in playing at being happy. And yet the manifest corollary is not drawn by those engaged in this life.

To an outsider it is obvious that the benefits obtained by the regulative classes of our day, through the existing form of social organization, are full of disguised evils; and that this undue wealth which makes possible the passing of idle lives brings dissatisfactions in place of the satisfactions expected. Just as in feudal times the appliances for safety were the accompaniments to a social state that brought a more than equivalent danger; so, now, the excess of aids to pleasure among the rich is the accompaniment of a social state that brings a counterbalancing displeasure. The gratifications reached by those who make the pursuit of gratifications a business, dwindle to a minimum; while the trouble, and weariness, and vexation, and jealousy, and disappointment, rise to a maximum. That this is an inevitable result any one may see who studies the psychology of the matter. The pleasure-hunting life fails for the reason that it leaves large parts of the nature unexercised: it neglects the satisfactions gained by successful activity, and there is missing from it the serene consciousness of services rendered to others. Egoistic enjoyments continuously pursued, pall because the appetites for them are satiated in times much shorter than our waking lives give us: leaving times that are either empty or spent in efforts to get enjoyment after desire has ceased. They pall also from the want of that broad contrast which arises when a moiety of life is actively occupied. These negative causes of dissatisfaction are joined with the positive cause indicated—the absence of that content gained by successful achievement. One of the most massive and enduring gratifications is the sense of personal worth, ever afresh demonstrating itself to consciousness by effectual action; and an idle life is balked of its hopes partly because it lacks this. Lastly, the implied neglect of altruistic activities, or of activities felt to be in some way serviceable to others, brings kindred evils—a deficiency of certain positive pleasures of a high order, not easily exhausted, and a further falling-back on egoistic pleasures, again tending towards satiety. And all this, with its resulting weariness and discontent, we may trace to a social organization under which there comes to the regulating classes a share of produce great enough to make possible large accumulations that support useless descendants.

The bias of the wealthy in favour of arrangements apparently so conducive to their comforts and pleasures, while it shuts out the perception of these indirect penalties brought round on them by their seeming advantages, also shuts out the perception that there is anything mean in being a useless consumer of things which others produce. Contrariwise, there still survives, though much weakened, the belief that it is honourable to do nothing but seek enjoyment, and relatively dishonourable to pass life in supplying others with the means to enjoyment. In this, as in other things, our temporary state brings a temporary standard of honour appropriate to it; and the accompanying sentiments and ideas exclude the conception of a state in which what is now thought admirable will be thought disgraceful.   Yet it needs only, as before, to aid imagination by studying other times and other societies, remote in nature from our own, to see at least the possibility of this. When we contrast the feeling of the Fijians, among whom a man has a restless ambition to be acknowledged as a murderer, with the feeling among civilized races, who shrink with horror from a murderer, we get undeniable proof that men in one social state pride themselves in characters and deeds elsewhere held in the greatest detestation. Seeing which, we may infer that just as the Fijians, believing in the honourableness of murder, are regarded by us with astonishment; so those of our own day who pride themselves in consuming much and producing nothing, and who care little for the well-being of their society so long as it supplies them good dinners, soft beds, and pleasant lounging-places, may be regarded with astonishment by men of times to come, living under higher social forms.   Nay, we may see not merely the possibility of such a change in sentiment, but the probability. Observe, first, the feeling still extant in China, where the honourableness of doing nothing, more strongly held than here, makes the wealthy wear their nails so long that they have to be tied back out of the way, and makes the ladies submit to prolonged tortures that their crushed feet may show their incapacity for work. Next, remember that in generations gone by, both here and on the Continent, the disgracefulness of trade was an article of faith among the upper classes, maintained very strenuously. Now mark how members of the landed class are going into business, and even sons of peers becoming professional men and merchants; and observe among the wealthy the feeling that men of their order have public duties to perform, and that the absolutely-idle among them are blameworthy. Clearly, then, we have grounds for inferring that, along with the progress to a regulative organization higher than the present, there will be a change of the kind indicated in the conception of honour. It will become a matter of wonder that there should ever have existed those who thought it admirable to enjoy without working, at the expense of others who worked without enjoying.

But the temporarily-adapted mental state of the ruling and employing classes, keeps out, more or less effectually, thoughts and feelings of these kinds. Habituated from childhood to the forms of subordination at present existing—regarding these as parts of a natural and permanent order—finding satisfaction in supremacy, and conveniences in the possession of authority; the regulators of all kinds remain unconscious that this system, made necessary as it is by the defects of existing human nature, brings round penalties on themselves as well as on those subordinate to them, and that its pervading theory of life is as mistaken as it is ignoble.

Enough has been said to show that from the class-bias arise further obstacles to right thinking in Sociology. As a part of some general division of his community, and again as a part of some special sub-division, the citizen acquires adapted feelings and ideas which inevitably influence his conclusions about public affairs. They affect alike his conceptions of the past, his interpretations of the present, his anticipations of the future.

Members of the regulated classes, kept in relations more or less antagonistic with the classes regulating them, are thereby hindered from seeing the need for, and the benefits of, this organization which seems the cause of their grievances; they are at the same time hindered from seeing the need for, and the benefits of, those harsher forms of industrial regulation that existed during past times; and they are also hindered from seeing that the improved industrial organizations of the future, can come only through improvements in their own natures. On the other hand, members of the regulating classes, while partially blinded to the facts that the defects of the working-classes are the defects of natures like their own placed under different conditions, and that the existing system is defensible, not for its convenience to themselves, but as being the best now practicable for the community at large; are also partially blinded to the vices of past social arrangements, and to the badness of those who in past social systems used class-power less mercifully than it is used now; while they have difficulty in seeing that the present social order, like past social orders, is but transitory, and that the regulating classes of the future may have, with diminished power, increased happiness.

Unfortunately for the Social Science, the class-bias, like the bias of patriotism, is, in a degree, needful for social preservation. It is like in this, too, that escape from its influence is often only effected by an effort that carries belief to an opposite extreme—changing approval into a disapproval that is entire instead of partial. Hence in the one case, as in the other, we must infer that the resulting obstacle to well-balanced conclusions, can become less only as social evolution becomes greater.

CHAPTER XI.

EVERY day brings events that show the politician what the events of the next day are likely to be, while they serve also as materials for the student of Social Science. Scarcely a journal can be read, that does not supply a fact which, beyond the proximate implication seized by the party-tactician, has an ultimate implication of value to the sociologist. Thus à propos of political bias, I am, while writing, furnished by an Irish paper with an extreme instance. Speaking of the late Ministerial defeat, the *Nation* says :—

" Mr. Gladstone and his administration are hurled from power, and the iniquitous attempt to sow broadcast the seed of irreligion and infidelity in Ireland has recoiled with the impact of a thunderbolt upon its authors. The men who so long beguiled the ear of Ireland with specious promises, who mocked us with sham reforms and insulted us with barren concessions, who traded on the grievances of this country only to aggravate them, and who, with smooth professions on their lips, trampled out the last traces of liberty in the land, are to-day a beaten and outcast party."

Which exhibition of feeling we may either consider specially, as showing how the " Nationalists " are likely to behave in the immediate future ; or may consider more generally, as giving us a trait of Irish nature tending to justify Mr. Froude's harsh verdict on Irish conduct in the past ; or may consider most generally, after the manner here appropriate, as a striking exámple of the distortions which the political bias works in men's judgments.

When we remember that all are thus affected more or less, in estimating antagonists, their acts, and their views, we are reminded what an immense obstacle political partizanship is in the way of Social Science. I do not mean simply that, as all know, it often determines opinions about pending questions; as shown by cases in which a measure reprobated by Conservatives when brought forward by Liberals, is approved when brought forward by their own party. I refer to the far wider effect it has on men's interpretations of the past and of the future; and therefore on their sociological conceptions in general. The political sympathies and antipathies fostered by the conflicts of parties, respectively upholding this or that kind of institution, become sympathies and antipathies drawn out towards allied institutions of other nations, extinct or surviving. These sympathies and antipathies inevitably cause tendencies to accept or reject favourable or unfavourable evidence respecting such institutions. The well-known contrast between the pictures which the Tory Mitford and the Radical Grote have given of the Athenian democracy, serves as an instance to which many parallels may be found. In proof of the perverting effects of the political bias, I cannot do better than quote some sentences from Mr. Froude's lecture on "The Scientific Method applied to History."

" Thucydides wrote to expose the vices of democracy ; Tacitus, the historian of the Cæsars, to exhibit the hatefulness of Imperialism." [1]

" Read Macaulay on the condition of the English poor before the last century or two, and you wonder how they lived at all. Read Cobbett, and I may even say Hallam, and you wonder how they endure the contrast between their past prosperity and their present misery." [2]

" An Irish Catholic prelate once told me that to his certain knowledge two millions of men, women, and children had died in the great famine of 1846. I asked him if he was not including those who had emigrated. He repeated that over and above the emigration two millions had actually died ; and added, ' we might assert that every one of these deaths lay at the door of the English Government.' I mentioned this to a distinguished lawyer in Dublin, a Protestant. His grey eyes lighted up. He replied : ' Did he say two millions now—did he ? Why there were not a thousand died—there were not five hundred.' The true number, so far as can be gathered from a comparison of the census of 1841 with the census of 1851, from the emigration returns, which were carefully made, and from an allowance for the natural rate of increase, was about two hundred thousand." [3]

Further insistance on this point is needless. That the verdicts which will be given by different party-journals upon each ministerial act may be predicted, and that the opposite opinions uttered by speakers and applauded by meetings concerning the same measure, may be foreseen if the political bias is known ; are facts from which anyone may infer that the party politician must have his feelings greatly moderated before he can interpret, with even approximate truth, the events of the past, and draw correct inferences respecting the future.

Here, instead of dilating on this truth, I will call attention to kindred truths that are less conspicuous. Beyond those kinds of political bias indicated by the names of political parties, there are certain kinds of political bias transcending party-limits. Already in the chapter on " Subjective Difficulties—Emotional," I have commented on the feeling which originates them—the feeling drawn out towards the governing agency. In addition to what was there said respecting the general effects of this feeling on sociological inquiry, something must be said about its special effects. And first, let us contemplate a common fallacy in men's opinions about human affairs, which pervades the several fallacies fostered by the political bias.

Results are proportionate to appliances—see here the tacit assumption underlying many errors in the conduct of life, private and public. In private life everyone discovers the untruth of this assumption, and yet continues to act as though he had not discovered its untruth. Reconsider a moment, under this fresh aspect, a familiar experience lately dwelt upon.

"How happy I shall be," thinks the child, "when I am as old as my big brother, and own all the many things he will not let me have." "How happy," the big brother thinks, "shall I be when, like my father, I have got a house of my own and can do as I like." "How happy I shall be," thinks the father, "when, achieving the success in prospect, I have got a large income, a country house, carriages, horses, and a higher social position." And yet at each stage the possession of the much-desired aids to satisfaction does not bring all the happiness expected, and brings many annoyances.

A good example of the fallacy that results are proportionate to appliances, is furnished by domestic service. It is an inference naturally drawn that if one servant does so much, two servants will do twice as much; and so on. But when this common-sense theory is tested by practice, the results are quite at variance with it. Not simply does the amount of service performed fail to increase in proportion to the number of servants, but frequently it decreases: fewer servants do more work and do it better.

Take, again, the relation of books to knowledge. The natural assumption is that one who has stores of information at hand will become well-informed. And yet, very generally, when a man begins to accumulate books he ceases to make much use of them. The filling of his shelves with volumes and the filling of his brain with facts, are processes apt to go on with inverse rapidities. It is a trite remark that those who have become distinguished for their learning, have often been those who had great difficulties in getting books. Here, too, the results are quite out of proportion to the appliances.

Similarly if we go a step further in the same direction—not thinking of books as aids to information, but thinking of information as an aid to guidance. Do we find that the quantity of acquirement measures the quantity of insight? Is the amount of cardinal truth reached to be inferred from the mass of collected facts that serve as appliances for reaching it? By no means. Wisdom and information do not vary together. Though there must be data before there can be generalization, yet ungeneralized data accumulated in excess, are impediments to generalization. When a man's knowledge is not in order, the more of it he has the greater will be his confusion of thought. When facts are not organized into faculty, the greater the mass of them the more will the mind stagger along under its burden, hampered instead of helped by its acquisitions. A student may become a very Daniel Lambert of learning, and remain utterly useless to himself and all others. Neither in this case, then, are results proportionate to appliances.

It is so, too, with discipline, and with the agencies established for discipline. Take, as an instance, the use of language. From his early days the boy whose father can afford to give him the fashionable education, is drilled in grammar, practised in parsing, tested in detecting errors of speech. After his public-school career, during which words, their meanings, and their right applications, almost exclusively occupy him, he passes through a University where a large, and often the larger, part of his attention is still given to literary culture—models of style in prose and poetry being daily before him. So much for the preparation; now for the performance. It is notorious that commentators on the classics are among the most slovenly writers of English. Readers of *Punch* will remember how, years ago, the Provost and Head-Master of Eton were made to furnish food for laughter by quotations from a letter they had published. Recently the Head-Master of Winchester has given us, in entire unconsciousness of its gross defects, a sample of the English which long study of language produces. If from these teachers, who are literally the select of the select, we turn to men otherwise selected, mostly out of the same highly-disciplined class—men who are distilled into the House of Commons, and then re-distilled into the Ministry, we are again disappointed. Just as in the last generation, Royal Speeches drawn up by those so laboriously trained in the right uses of words, furnished for an

English grammar examples of blunders to be avoided ; so in the present generation, a work on style might fitly take from these documents which our Government annually lays before all the world, warning instances of confusions, and illogicalities, and pleonasms. And then on looking at the performances of men not thus elaborately prepared, we are still more struck by the seeming anomaly. How great the anomaly is, we may best see by supposing some of our undisciplined authors to use expressions like those used by the disciplined. Imagine the self-made Cobbett deliberately saying, as is said in the last Royal Speech, that—

" I have kept in *view* the double *object* of an equitable *regard* to existing circumstances, and of securing a general provision more permanent in its character, and resting on *a reciprocal and equal basis,* for the commercial and maritime transactions of the two countries." [4]

Imagine the poet who had " little Latin and less Greek," giving the order that—

" No such address shall be delivered in any place where the assemblage of persons to hear the same *may cause obstruction to the use of* any road or walk by the public." [5]

—an order which occurs, along with half-a-dozen lax and superfluous phrases, in the eighteen lines announcing the ministerial retreat from the Hyde-Park contest. Imagine the ploughman Burns, like one of our scholars who has been chosen to direct the education of gentlemen's sons, expressing himself in print thus—

" I should not have troubled you with this detail (which was, indeed, needless in my former letter) if it was not that I may appear to have laid a stress upon the dates which the boy's accident has prevented me from being able to claim to do." [6]

Imagine Bunyan, the tinker, publishing such a sentence as this, written by one of our bishops :—

" If the 546 gentlemen who signed the protest on the subject of deaconesses had thought proper to object to my having formally licensed a deaconess in the parish of Dilton's Marsh, or to what they speak of when they say that ' recognition had been made ' (I presume on a report of which no part or portion was adopted by resolution of the Synod) 'as to sisters living together in a more conventual manner and under stricter rule,' I should not have thought it necessary to do more than receive with silent respect the expression of their opinion ;" &c., &c.[7]

Or, to cite for comparison modern self-educated writers, imagine such a sentence coming from Hugh Miller, or Alexander Smith, or Gerald Massey, or "the Norwich weaver-boy" (W. J. Fox), or "the Journeyman Engineer." Shall we then say that in the case of literary culture, results are proportionate to appliances ? or shall we not rather say that, as in other cases, the relation is by no means so simple a one.

Nowhere, then, do we find verified this assumption which we are so prone to make. Quantity of effect does not vary as quantity of means. From a mechanical apparatus up to an educational system or a social institution, the same truth holds. Take a rustic to see a new machine, and his admiration of it will be in proportion to the multiplicity of its parts. Listen to the criticism of a skilled engineer, and you find that from all this complication he infers probable failure. Not elaboration but simplification is his aim : knowing, as he does, that every additional wheel or lever implies inertia and friction to be over-come, and occasional derangement to be rectified. It is thus everywhere. Up to a certain point appliances are needful for results ; but beyond that point, results decrease as appliances increase.

This undue belief in appliances, joined with the general bias citizens inevitably have in favour of governmental agencies, prompts the multiplication of laws. It fosters the notion that a society will be the better the more its actions are everywhere regulated by artificial instrumentalities. And the effect produced on sociological speculation is, that the benefits achieved by laws are exaggerated, while the evils they entail are overlooked.

Brought to bear on so immensely-complicated an aggregate as a society, a law rarely, if ever, produces as much direct effect as was expected, and invariably produces indirect effects, many in their kinds and great in their sum, that were not expected. It is so even with fundamental changes: witness the two we have seen in the constitution of our House of Commons. Both advocates and opponents of the first Reform Bill anticipated that the middle classes would select as representatives many of their own body. But both were wrong. The class-quality of the House of Commons remained very much what it was before. While, however, the immediate and special result looked for did not appear, there were vast remote and general results foreseen by no one. So, too, with the recent change. We had eloquently-uttered warnings that delegates from the working-classes would swamp the House of Commons; and nearly everyone expected that, at any rate, a sprinkling of working-class members would be chosen. Again all were wrong. The conspicuous alteration looked for has not occurred; but, nevertheless, governmental actions have already been much modified by the raised sense of responsibility. It is thus always. No prophecy is safer than that the results anticipated from a law will be greatly exceeded in amount by results not anticipated. Even simple physical actions might suggest to us this conclusion. Let us contemplate one.

You see that this wrought-iron plate is not quite flat: it sticks up a little here towards the left—"cockles," as we say. How shall we flatten it? Obviously, you reply, by hitting down on the part that is prominent. Well, here is a hammer, and I give the plate a blow as you advise. Harder, you say. Still no effect. Another stroke? Well, there is one, and another, and another. The prominence remains, you see: the evil is as great as ever—greater, indeed. But this is not all. Look at the warp which the plate has got near the opposite edge. Where it was flat before it is now curved. A pretty bungle we have made of it. Instead of curing the original defect, we have produced a second.

Had we asked an artizan practised in "planishing," as it is called, he would have told us that no good was to be done, but only mischief, by hitting down on the projecting part. He would have taught us how to give variously-directed and specially-adjusted blows with a hammer elsewhere: so attacking the evil not by direct but by indirect actions. The required process is less simple than you thought. Even a sheet of metal is not to be successfully dealt with after those common-sense methods in which you have so much confidence. What, then, shall we say about a society? "Do you think I am easier to be played on than a pipe?" asks Hamlet. Is humanity more readily straightened than an iron plate?

Many, I doubt not, failing to recognize the truth that in proportion as an aggregate is complex, the effects wrought by an incident force become more multitudinous, confused, and incalculable, and that therefore a society is of all kinds of aggregates the kind most difficult to affect in an intended way and not in unintended ways—many such will ask evidence of the difficulty. Response would perhaps be easier were the evidence less abundant. It is so familiar as seemingly to have lost its significance; just as perpetually-repeated salutations and prayers have done. The preamble to nearly every Act of Parliament supplies it; in the report of every commission it is presented in various forms; and for anyone asking instances, the direction might be—Hansard *passim*. Here I will give but a single example which might teach certain rash enthusiasts of our day, were they teachable. I refer to measures for the suppression of drunkenness.

Not to dwell on the results of the Maine Law, which, as I know from one whose personal experience verified current statements, prevents the obtainment of stimulants by travellers in urgent need of them, but does not prevent secret drinking by residents —not to dwell, either, upon the rigorous measures taken in Scotland in 1617, "for the restraint of the vile and detestable vice of drunkenness daily increasing," but which evidently did

not produce the hoped-for effect; I will limit myself to the case
of the Licensing Act, 9 Geo. II., ch. 23, for arresting the sale of
spirituous liquors (chiefly gin) by prohibitory licences.

" Within a few months after it passed, Tindal tells us, the commissioners of excise themselves became sensible of the impossibility or
unadvisableness of carrying it rigorously into execution. * * *
Smollett, who has drawn so dark a picture of the state of things the act
was designed to put down, has painted in colours equally strong the
mischiefs which it produced :—' The populace,' he writes, ' soon broke
through all restraint. Though no licence was obtained and no duty
paid, the liquor continued to be sold in all corners of the streets; informers were intimidated by the threats of the people ; and the justices
of the peace, either from indolence or corruption, neglected to put the
law in execution.' In fact, in course of time, ' it appeared,' he adds,
' that the consumption of gin had considerably increased every year
since those heavy duties were imposed.' " [8]

When, in 1743, this Act was repealed, it was shown during the
debates that—

" The quantity of gin distilled in England, which, in 1684, when the
business was introduced into this country, had been 527,000 gallons, had
risen to 948,000 in 1694, to 1,375,000 in 1704, to 2,000,000 in 1714, to
3,520,000 in 1724, to 4,947,000 in 1734, and to not less than 7,160,000
in 1742. * * * ' Retailers were deterred from vending them [spirit-
uous liquors] by the utmost encouragement that could be given to informers. * * * The prospect of raising money by detecting their
[unlicensed retailers'] practices incited many to turn information into a
trade ; and the facility with which the crime was to be proved encouraged some to gratify their malice by perjury, and others their avarice ;
so that the multitude of informations became a public grievance, and
the magistrates themselves complained that the law was not to be executed. The perjuries of informers were now so flagrant and common,
that the people thought all informations malicious ; or, at least, thinking
themselves oppressed by the law, they looked upon every man that
promoted its execution as their enemy; and therefore now began to
declare war against informers, many of whom they treated with great
cruelty, and some they murdered in the streets.' " [9]

Here, then, with absence of the looked-for benefit there went production of unlooked-for evils, vast in amount. To recur to our figure, the original warp, instead of being made less by these direct blows, was made greater; while other distortions, serious in kind and degree, were created. And beyond the encouragement of fraud, lying, malice, cruelty, murder, contempt of law, and the other conspicuous crookednesses named, multitudinous minor twists of sentiment and thought were caused or augmented. An indirect demoralization was added to a direct increase of the vice aimed at.

Joining with the prevalent fallacy that results are proportionate to appliances, the general political bias has the further effect of fostering an undue faith in political forms. This tendency to ascribe everything to a visible proximate agency, and to forget the hidden forces without which the agency is worthless—this tendency which makes the child gazing at a steam-engine suppose that all is done by the combination of parts it sees, not recognizing the fact that the engine is powerless without the steam-generating boiler, and the boiler powerless without the water and the burning fuel, is a tendency which leads citizens to think that good government can be had by shaping public arrangements in this way or that way. Let us frame our state-machinery rightly, they urge, and all will be well.

Yet this belief in the innate virtues of constitutions is as baseless as was the belief in the natural superiorities of royal personages. Just, as of old, loyalty to ruling men kept alive a faith in their powers and virtues, notwithstanding perpetual disproofs; so, in these modern days, loyalty to constitutional forms keeps alive this faith in their intrinsic worth, spite of recurring demonstrations that their worth is entirely conditional. That those forms only are efficient which have grown naturally out of character, and that in the absence of fit character forms artificially obtained will be inoperative, is well shown by the governments of trading corporations. Let us contemplate a typical instance of this government.

The proprietors of a certain railway (I am here giving my personal experience as one of them) were summoned to a special meeting.   The notice calling them together stated that the directors had agreed to lease their line to another company; that everything had been settled; that the company taking the lease was then in possession; and that the proprietors were to be asked for their approval on the day named in the notice.   The meeting took place.   The chairman gave an account of the negotiation and of the agreement entered into.   A motion expressing approval of the agreement was proposed and to some extent discussed—no notice whatever being taken of the extraordinary conduct of the board.   Only when the motion was about to be put, did one proprietor protest against the astounding usurpation which the transaction implied.   He said that there had grown up a wrong conception of the relation between boards of directors and bodies of proprietors; that directors had come to look on themselves as supreme and proprietors as subordinate, whereas, in fact, directors were simply agents appointed to act in the absence of their principals, the proprietors, and remained subject to their principals; that if, in any private business, an absent proprietor received from his manager the news that he had leased the business, that the person taking it was then in possession, and that the proprietor's signature to the lease was wanted, his prompt return would be followed by a result quite different from that looked for—namely, a dismissal of the manager for having exceeded his duty in a very astonishing manner.   This protest against the deliberate trampling down of principles recognized by the constitutions of companies, met with no response whatever—not a solitary sympathizer joined in the protest, even in a qualified form.   Not only was the motion of approval carried, but it was carried without any definite knowledge of the agreement itself.   Nothing more than the chairman's verbal description was vouchsafed : no printed copies of it had been previously circulated, or were to be had at the meeting. And yet, wonderful to relate, this proprietary body had been already once betrayed by an agreement with this same leasing company!—had been led to undertake the making of the line on the strength of a seeming guarantee which proved to be no guarantee! See, then, the lesson. The constitution of this company, like that of companies in general, was purely democratic. The proprietors elected their directors, the directors their chairman; and there were special provisions for restraining directors and replacing them when needful. Yet these forms of free government had fallen into disuse. And it is thus in all cases. Save on occasions when some scandalous mismanagement, or corruption bringing great loss, has caused a revolutionary excitement among them, railway-proprietors do not exercise their powers. Retiring directors being re-elected as a matter of form, the board becomes practically a close body; usually some one member, often the chairman, acquires supremacy; and so the government lapses into something between oligarchy and monarchy. All this, observe, happening not exceptionally but as a rule, happens among bodies of men mostly well educated, and many highly educated—people of means, merchants, lawyers, clergymen, &c. Ample disproof, if there needed any, of the notion that men are to be fitted for the right exercise of power by teaching.

And now to return. Anyone who looks through these facts and facts akin to them for the truth they imply, may see that forms of government are valuable only where they are products of national *character*. No cunningly-devised political arrangements will of themselves do anything. No amount of knowledge respecting the uses of such arrangements will suffice. Nothing will suffice but the emotional nature to which such arrangements are adapted—a nature which, during social progress, has evolved the arrangements. And wherever there is want of congruity between the nature and the arrangements—wherever the arrangements, suddenly established by revolution or pushed too far by reforming change, are of a higher type than the national character demands, there is always a lapse propor-

13

tionate to the incongruity. In proof I might enumerate the illustrations that lie scattered through the modern histories of Greece, of South America, of Mexico. Or I might dwell on the lesson (before briefly referred to) presented us in France; where the political cycle shows us again and again that new Democracy is but old Despotism differently spelt—where now, as heretofore, we find *Liberté*, *Egalité*, *Fraternité*, conspicuous on the public buildings, and now, as heretofore, have for interpretations of these words the extremest party-hatreds, vituperations and actual assaults in the Assembly, wholesale arrests of men unfriendly to those in power, forbiddings of public meetings, and suppressions of journals; and where now, as heretofore, writers professing to be ardent advocates of political freedom, rejoice in these acts which shackle and gag their antagonists. But I will take, instead, a case more nearly allied to our own.

For less strikingly, and in other ways, but still with sufficient clearness, this same truth is displayed in the United States. I do not refer only to such extreme illustrations of it as were at one time furnished in California; where, along with that complete political freedom which some think the sole requisite for social welfare, most men lived in perpetual fear for their lives, while others prided themselves on the notches which marked, on the hilts of their pistols, the numbers of men they had killed. Nor will I dwell on the state of society existing under republican forms in the West, where a white woman is burned to death for marrying a negro, where secret gangs murder in the night men whose conduct they dislike, where mobs stop trains to lynch offending persons contained in them, where the carrying of a revolver is a matter of course, where judges are intimidated and the execution of justice often impracticable. I do but name these as extreme instances of the way in which, under institutions that nominally secure men from oppression, they may be intolerably oppressed—unable to utter their opinions and to conduct their private lives as they please. Without going so far, we may find in the Eastern states proof enough that the forms of liberty and the reality of liberty are not necessarily commensurate. A state of things under which men administer justice in their own cases, are applauded for so doing, and mostly acquitted if tried, is a state of things which has, in so far, retrograded towards a less civilized state; for one of the cardinal traits of political progress is the gradual disappearance of personal retaliation, and the increasing supremacy of a ruling power which settles the differences between individuals and punishes aggressors. And in proportion as this ruling power is enfeebled the security of individuals is lessened. How security, lessened in this general way, is lessened in more special ways, we see in the bribery of judges, in the financial frauds by which many are robbed without possibility of remedy, in the corruptness of New York administration, which, taxing so heavily, does so little. And, under another aspect, we see the like in the doings of legislative bodies—in the unfair advantages which some individuals gain over others by "lobbying," in Crédit-Mobilier briberies, and the like. While the outside form of free government remains, there has grown up within it a reality which makes government not free. The body of professional politicians, entering public life to get incomes, organizing their forces and developing their tactics, have, in fact, come to be a ruling class quite different from that which the constitution intended to secure; and a class having interests by no means identical with public interests. This worship of the appliances to liberty in place of liberty itself, needs continually exposing. There is no intrinsic virtue in votes. The possession of representatives is not itself a benefit. These are but means to an end; and the end is the maintenance of those conditions under which each citizen may carry on his life without further hindrances from other citizens than are involved by their equal claims—is the securing to each citizen all such beneficial results of his activities as his activities naturally bring. The worth of the means must be measured by the degree in which this end is achieved. A citizen nominally having complete means and but partially securing the end, is less free than another who uses incomplete means to more purpose.

But why go abroad for proofs of the truth that political forms are of worth only in proportion as they are vitalized by national character? We have proofs at home. I do not mean those furnished by past constitutional history—I do not merely refer to those many facts showing us that the nominal power of our representative body became an actual power only by degrees; and that the theoretically-independent House of Commons took centuries to escape from regal and aristocratic sway, and establish a practical independence. I refer to the present time, and to actions of our representative body in the plenitude of its power. This assembly of deputies chosen by large constituencies, and therefore so well fitted, as it would seem, for guarding the individual of whatever grade against trespasses upon his individuality, nevertheless itself authorizes new trespasses upon his individuality. A popular government has established, without the slightest hindrance, an official organization that treats with contempt the essential principles of constitutional rule; and since it has been made still more popular, has deliberately approved and maintained this organization. Here is a brief account of the steps leading to these results.

On the 20th June, 1864, just before 2 o'clock in the morning, there was read a first time an Act giving, in some localities, certain new powers to the police. On the 27th of that month, it was read a second time, entirely without comment—at what hour Hansard does not show. Just before 2 o'clock in the morning on June 30th, there was appointed, without remark, a Select Committee to consider this proposed Act. On the 15th July the Report of this Committee was received. On the 19th the Bill was re-committed, and the Report on it received—all in silence. On the 20th July it was considered—still in silence— as amended. And on the 21st July it was read a third time and passed—equally in silence. Taken next day to the House of Lords, it there, in silence no less profound, passed through all its stages in four days (? three). This Act not proving strong enough to meet the views of naval and military officers (who, according to the testimony of one of the Select Committee, were the promoters of it), was, in 1866, "amended." At 1 o'clock in the morning on March 16th of that year, the Act amending it was read a first time ; and it was read a second time on the 22nd, when the Secretary of the Admiralty, describing it as an Act to secure the better health of soldiers and sailors, said "it was intended to renew an Act passed in 1864, with additional powers." And now, for the first time, there came brief adverse remarks from two members. On April 9th there was appointed a Select Committee, consisting mainly of the same members as the previous one—predominantly state-officers of one class or other. On the 20th, the Report of the Committee was received. On the 26th, the Bill was re-committed just before 2 o'clock in the morning ; and on the Report there came some short comments, which were, however, protested against on the ground that the Bill was not to be publicly discussed. And here observe the reception given to the only direct opposition raised. When, to qualify a clause defining the powers of the police, it was proposed to add, "that the justices before whom such information shall be made, shall in all cases require corroborative testimony and support thereof, other than that of the members of the police force," this qualification was negatived without a word. Finally, this Act was approved and made more stringent by the present House of Commons in 1869.

And now what was this Act, passed the first time absolutely without comment, and passed in its so-called amended form with but the briefest comments, made under protest that comments were interdicted ? What was this measure, so conspicuously right that discussion of it was thought superfluous ? It was a measure by which, in certain localities, one-half of the people were brought under the summary jurisdiction of magistrates, in respect of certain acts charged against them. Further, those by whom they were to be charged, and by whose unsupported testimony charges were to be proved, were agents of the law, looking for promotion as the reward of vigilance—agents placed under a permanent temptation to make and substantiate charges. And yet more, the substantiation of charges was made comparatively easy, by requiring only a single local magistrate to be convinced, by the testimony on oath of one of these agents of the law, that a person charged was guilty of the alleged acts—acts which, held to be thus proved, were punished by periodic examinations of a repulsive kind and forced inclusion in a degraded class. A House of Commons elected by large constituencies, many of them chiefly composed of working-men, showed the greatest alacrity in making a law under which, in sundry districts, the liberty of a working-man's wife or daughter remains intact, only so long as a detective does not give evidence which leads a magistrate to believe her a prostitute! And this Bill which, even had there been some urgent need (which we have seen there was not) for dispensing with precautions against injustice, should, at any rate, have been passed only after full debate and anxious criticism, was passed with every effort to maintain secrecy, on the pretext that decency forbade discussion of it; while Mordaunt-cases and the like were being reported with a fulness proportionate to the amount of objectionable details they brought out! Nor is this all. Not only do the provisions of the Act make easy the establishment of charges by men who are placed under temptations to make them; but these men are guarded against penalties apt to be brought on them by abusing their power. A poor woman who proceeds against one of them for making a groundless accusation ruinous to her character, does so with this risk before her; that if she fails to get a verdict she has to pay the defendant's costs; whereas a verdict in her favour does not give her costs: only by a special order of the judge does she get costs! And this is the "even-handed justice" provided by a government freer in form than any we have ever had! [10]

Let it not be supposed that in arguing thus I am implying that forms of government are unimportant. While contending that they are of value only in so far as a national character gives life to them, it is consistent also to contend that they are essential as agencies through which that national character may work out its effects. A boy cannot wield to purpose an implement of size and weight fitted to the hand of a man. A man cannot do effective work with the boy's implement: he must have one adapted to his larger grasp and greater strength. To each the implement is essential; but the results which each achieves are not to be measured by the size or make of the implement alone, but by its adaptation to his powers. Similarly with political instrumentalities. It is possible to hold that a political instrumentality is of value only in proportion as there exists a strength of character needful for using it, and at the same time to hold that a fit political instrumentality is indispensable. Here, as before, results are not proportionate to appliances; but they are proportionate to the force for due operation of which certain appliances are necessary.

One other still more general and more subtle kind of political bias has to be guarded against. Beyond that excess of faith in laws, and in political forms, which is fostered by awe of regulative agencies, there is, even among those least swayed by this awe, a vague faith in the immediate possibility of something much better than now exists—a tacit assumption that, even with men as they are, public affairs might be much better managed. The mental attitude of such may be best displayed by an imaginary conversation between one of them and a member of the Legislature.

" Why do your agents, with no warrant but a guess, make this surcharge on my income-tax return ; leaving me to pay an amount that is not due and to establish a precedent for future like payments, or else to lose valuable time in proving their assessment excessive, and, while so doing, to expose my affairs ? You require me to choose between two losses, direct and indirect, for the sole reason that your assessor fancies, or professes to fancy, that

I have under-stated my income. Why do you allow this ? Why
in this case do you invert the principle which, in cases between
citizens, you hold to be an equitable one—the principle that a
claim must be proved by him who makes it, not disproved by
him against whom it is made ? Is it in pursuance of old political
usages that you do this ? Is it to harmonize with the practice of
making one whom you had falsely accused, pay the costs of his
defence, although in suits between citizens you require the loser
to bear all the expense ?—a practice you have but lately re-
linquished. Do you desire to keep up the spirit of the good old
rulers who impressed labourers and paid them what they pleased,
or the still older rulers who seized whatever they wanted ? Would
you maintain this tradition by laying hands on as much as
possible of my earnings and leaving me to get part back if I can :
expecting, indeed, that I shall submit to the loss rather than
undergo the worry, and hindrance, and injury, needful to recover
what you have wrongfully taken ? I was brought up to regard
the Government and its officers as my protectors ; and now I find
them aggressors against whom I have to defend myself."

"What would you have ? Our agents could not bring forward proof that an income-tax return was less than it should be.
Either the present method must be pursued, or the tax must be
abandoned."

"I have no concern with your alternative. I have merely to
point out that between man and man you recognize no such plea.
When a plaintiff makes a claim but cannot produce evidence, you
do not make the defendant submit if he fails to show that the
claim is groundless. You say that if no evidence can be given,
nothing can be done. Why do you ignore this principle when
your agent makes the claim ? Why from the fountain of equity
comes there this inequity ? Is it to maintain consistency with
that system of criminal jurisprudence under which, while professing to hold a man innocent till proved guilty, you treat him
before trial like a convict—as you did Dr. Hessel ? Are your
views really represented by these Middlesex magistrates you have

appointed, who see no hardship to a man of culture in the seclusion of a prison-cell, and the subjection to prison-rules, on the mere suspicion that he has committed a murder? "

" The magistrates held that the rules allowed them to make no distinctions. You would not introduce class-legislation into prison-discipline? "

" I remember that was one of the excuses; and I cheerfully give credit to this endeavour to treat all classes alike. I do so the more cheerfully because this application of the principle of equality differs much from those which you ordinarily make— as when, on discharging some of your well-paid officials who have held sinecures, you give them large pensions, for the reason, I suppose, that their expensive styles of living have disabled them from saving anything; while, when you discharge dock-yard labourers, you do not give them compensation, for the reason, I suppose, that out of weekly wages it is easy to accumulate a competence. This, however, by the way. I am here concerned with that action of your judicial system which makes it an aggressor on citizens, whether rich or poor, instead of a protector. The instances I have given are but trivial instances of its general operation. Law is still a name of dread, as it was in past times. My legal adviser, being my friend, strongly recommends me not to seek your aid in recovering property fraudulently taken from me; and I perceive, from their remarks, that my acquaintances would pity me as a lost man if I got into your Court of Equity. Whether active or passive, I am in danger. Your arrangements are such that I may be pecuniarily knocked on the head by some one who pretends I have injured his property. I have the alternative of letting my pocket be picked by the scamp who makes this baseless allegation in the hope of being paid to desist, or of meeting the allegation in Chancery, and there letting my pocket be picked, probably to a still greater extent, by your agencies. Nay, when you have, as you profess, done me justice by giving me a verdict and condemning the scamp to pay costs, I find I may still be ruined by having to pay my own costs if he has no

means. To make your system congruous throughout, it only
needs that, when I call him to save me from the foot-pad, your
policeman should deal me still heavier blows than the foot-pad
did, and empty my purse of what remains in it."

"Why so impatient? Are we not going to reform it all?
Was it not last session proposed to make a Court of Appellate
Jurisdiction by appointing four peers with salaries of £7000
each? And has there not been brought forward this session,
even quite early, a Government-measure for preventing the conflict of Law and Equity, and for facilitating appeals?"

"Thanks in advance for the improvement. When I have failed
to ruin myself by a first suit, it will be a consolation to think that
I can complete my ruin by a second with less delay than heretofore. Meanwhile, instead of facilitating appeals, which you seem
to think of primary importance, I should be obliged if you would
diminish the occasion for appeals, by making your laws such as
it is possible for me to know, or at any rate, such as it is possible
for your judges to know; and I should be further obliged if you
would give me easier remedies against aggressions, instead of
remedies so costly, so deceptive, so dangerous, that I prefer
suffering the aggressions in silence. Daily I experience the futility
of your system. I start on a journey expecting that in conformity
with the advertised times, I shall just be able to reach a certain
distant town before night; but the train being an hour late at one
of the junctions, I am defeated—am put to the cost of a night
spent on the way and lose half the next day. I paid for a first-
class seat that I might have space, comfort, and unobjectionable
fellow-travellers; but, stopping at a town where a fair is going
on, the guard, on the plea that the third-class carriages are full,
thrusts into the compartment more persons than there are places
for, who, both by behaviour and odour, are repulsive. Thus in
two ways I am defrauded. For part of the fraud I have no
remedy; and for the rest my remedy, doubtful at best, is
practically unavailable. Is the reply that against the alleged
breach of contract as to time, the company has guarded itself, or

professes to have guarded itself, by disclaiming responsibility ? The allowing such a disclaimer is one of your countless negligences. You do not allow me to plead irresponsibility if I give the company bad money, or if, having bought a ticket for the second class, I travel in the first. On my side you regard the contract as quite definite ; but on the other side you practically allow the contract to remain undefined. And now see the general effects of your carelessness. Scarcely any trains keep their times ; and the result of chronic unpunctuality is a multiplication of accidents with increased loss of life."

"How about *laissez-faire ?* I thought your notion was that the less Government meddled with these things the better ; and now you complain that the law does not secure your comfort in a railway-carriage and see that you are delivered at your journey's end in due time. I suppose you approved of the proposal made in the House last session, that companies should be compelled to give foot-warmers to second-class passengers."

·"Really you amaze me. I should have thought that not even ordinary intelligence, much less select legislative intelligence, would have fallen into such a confusion. I am not blaming you for failing to secure me comfort or punctuality. I am blaming you for failing to enforce contracts. Just as strongly as I protest against your neglect in letting a company take my money and then not give me all I paid for ; so strongly should I protest did you dictate how much convenience should be given me for so much money. Surely I need not remind you that your civil law in general proceeds on the principle that the goodness or badness of a bargain is the affair of those who make it, not your affair ; but that it is your duty to enforce the bargain when made. Only in proportion as this is done can men's lives in society be maintained. The condition to all life, human or other, is that effort put forth shall bring the means of repairing the parts wasted by effort—shall bring, too, more or less of surplus. A creature that continuously expends energy without return in nutriment dies ; and a creature is indirectly killed by anything which, after energies have been expended, habitually intercepts the return.   This holds of associated human beings as of all other beings.   In a society, most citizens do not obtain sustenance directly by the powers they exert, but do it indirectly : each gives the produce of his powers exerted in his special way, in exchange for the produce of other men's powers exerted in other ways. The condition under which only this obtaining of sustenance to replace the matter wasted by effort, can be carried on in society, is fulfilment of contract.   Non-fulfilment of contract is letting energy be expended in expectation of a return, and then with-holding the return.   Maintenance of contract, therefore, is maintenance of the fundamental principle of all life, under the form given to it by social arrangements.   I blame you because you do not maintain this fundamental principle; and, as a con-sequence, allow life to be impeded and sacrificed in countless indirect ways.   You are, I admit, solicitous about my life as endangered by my own acts.   Though you very inadequately guard me against injuries from others, you seem particularly anxious that I shall not injure myself.   Emulating Sir Peter Laurie, who made himself famous by threatening to 'put down suicide,' you do what you can to prevent me from risking my limbs.   Your great care of me is shown, for instance, by enforc-ing a bye-law which forbids me to leave a railway-train in motion ; and if I jump out, I find that whether I hurt myself or not, you decide to hurt me—by a fine.[11]   Not only do you thus punish me when I run the risk of punishing myself; but your amiable anxiety for my welfare shows itself in taking money out of my pocket to provide me with various conveniences—baths and wash-houses, for example, and free access to books.   Out of my pocket, did I say ?   Not always.   Sometimes out of the pockets of those least able to afford it; as when, from poor authors who lose by their works, you demand *gratis* copies for your public libraries, that I and others may read them for nothing—Dives robbing Lazarus that he may give alms to the well-clad !   But these many things you offer are things I do not ask; and you will not effectually provide the one thing I do ask. I do not want you to ascertain for me the nature of the Sun's corona, or to find a north-west passage, or to explore the bottom of the sea; but I do want you to insure me against aggression, by making the punishment of aggressors, civil as well as criminal, swift, certain, and not ruinous to complainants. Instead of doing this, you persist in doing other things. Instead of securing me the bread due to my efforts, you give me a stone —a sculptured block from Ephesus. I am quite content to enjoy only what I get by my own exertions, and to have only that information and those pleasures for which I pay. I am quite content to suffer the evils brought on me by my own defects— believing, indeed, that for me and for all there is no other whole-some discipline. But you fail to do what is needed. You are careless about guaranteeing me the unhindered enjoyment of the benefits my efforts have purchased; and you insist on giving me, at other people's expense, benefits my efforts have not purchased, and on saving me from penalties I deserve."

"You are unreasonable. We are doing our best with the enormous mass of business brought before us: sitting on committees, reading evidence and reports, debating till one or two in the morning. Session after session we work hard at all kinds of measures for the public welfare—devising plans for educating the people; enacting better arrangements for the health of towns; making inquiries into the impurity of rivers; deliberating on plans to diminish drunkenness; prescribing modes of building houses that they may not fall; deputing commissioners to facilitate emigration; and so on. You can go to no place that does not show signs of our activity. Here are public gardens formed by our local lieutenants, the municipal bodies; here are lighthouses we have put up to prevent shipwrecks. Everywhere we have appointed inspectors to see that salubrity is maintained; everywhere there are vaccinators to see that due precautions against small-pox are observed; and if, happening to be in a district where our arrangements are in force, your desires are not well controlled, we do our best to insure you a healthy "——

"Yes, I know what you would say. It is all of a piece with the rest of your policy. While you fail to protect me against others, you insist on protecting me against myself. And your failure to do the essential thing, results from the absorption of your time in doing non-essential things. Do you think that your beneficences make up for the injustices you let me bear? I do not want these sops and gratuities; but I do want security against trespasses, direct and indirect—security that is real and not nominal. See the predicament in which I am placed. You forbid me (quite rightly I admit) to administer justice on my own behalf; and you profess to administer it for me. I may not take summary measures to resist encroachment, to reclaim my own, or to seize that which I bargained to have for my services : you tell me that I must demand your aid to enforce my claim. But demanding your aid commonly brings such frightful evils that I prefer to bear the wrong done me. So that, practically, having forbidden me to defend myself, you fail to defend me. By this my life is vitiated, along with the lives of citizens in general. All transactions are impeded; time and labour are lost; the prices of commodities are raised. Honest men are defrauded, while rogues thrive. Debtors outwit their creditors; bankrupts make purses by their failures and recommence on larger scales; and financial frauds that ruin their thousands go unpunished."

Thus far our impatient friend. And now see how untenable is his position. He actually supposes that it is possible to get government conducted on rational principles! His tacit assumption is that out of a community morally imperfect and intellectually imperfect, there may in some way be had legislative regulation that is not proportionately imperfect! He is under a delusion. Not by any kind of government, established after any method, can the thing be done. A good and wise autocrat cannot be chosen or otherwise obtained by a people not good and wise.

Goodness and wisdom will not characterize the successive families of an oligarchy, arising out of a bad and foolish people, any more than they will characterize a line of kings. Nor will any system of representation, limited or universal, direct or indirect, do more than represent the average nature of citizens. To dissipate his notion that truly-rational government can be provided for themselves by a people not truly rational, he needs but to read election-speeches and observe how votes are gained by clap-trap appeals to senseless prejudices and by fostering hopes of impossible benefits, while votes are lost by candid statements of stern truths and endeavours to dissipate groundless expectations. Let him watch the process, and he will see that when the fermenting mass of political passions and beliefs is put into the electoral still, there distils over not the wisdom alone but the folly also—sometimes in the larger proportion. Nay, if he watches closely, he may suspect that not only is the corporate conscience lower than the average individual conscience, but the corporate intelligence too. The minority of the wise in a constituency is liable to be wholly submerged by the majority of the foolish : often foolishness alone gets represented. In the representative assembly, again, the many mediocrities practically rule the few superiorities : the superior are obliged to express those views only which the rest can understand, and must keep to themselves their best and farthest-reaching thoughts as thoughts that would have no weight. He needs but remember that abstract principles are pooh-poohed in the House of Commons, to see at once that while the unwisdom expresses itself abundantly, what of highest wisdom there may be has to keep silence. And if he asks an illustration of the way in which the intelligence of the body of members brings out a result lower than would the intelligence of the average member, he may see one in those muddlings of provisions and confusions of language in Acts of Parliament, which have lately been calling forth protests from the judges.

Thus the assumption that it is possible for a nation to get, in

. the shape of law, something like embodied reason, when it is not itself pervaded by a correlative reasonableness, is improbable *à priori* and disproved *à posteriori*. The belief that truly-good legislation and administration can go along with a humanity not truly good, is a chronic delusion. While our own form of government, giving means for expressing and enforcing claims, is the best form yet evolved for preventing aggressions of class upon class, and of individuals on one another; yet it is hopeless to expect from it, any more than from other forms of government, a capacity and a rectitude greater than that of the society out of which it grows. And criticisms like the foregoing, which imply that its shortcomings can be set right by expostulating with existing governing agents or by appointing others, imply that subtlest kind of political bias which is apt to remain when the stronger kinds have been got rid of.

Second only to the class-bias, we may say that the political bias most seriously distorts sociological conceptions. That this is so with the bias of political party, everyone sees in some measure, though not in full measure. It is manifest to the Radical that the prejudice of the Tory blinds him to a present evil or to a future good. It is manifest to the Tory that the Radical does not see the benefit there is in that which he wishes to destroy, and fails to recognize the mischiefs likely to be done by the institution he would establish. But neither imagines that the other is no less needful than himself. The Radical, with his impracticable ideal, is unaware that his enthusiasm will serve only to advance things a little, but not at all as he expects; and he will not admit that the obstructiveness of the Tory is a wholesome check. The Tory, doggedly resisting, cannot perceive that the established order is but relatively good, and that his defence of it is simply a means of preventing premature change; while he fails to recognize in the bitter antagonism and sanguine hopes of the Radical, the agencies without which there could be no progress. Thus neither fully understands his own function or the function of his opponent; and by as much as he falls short of understanding it, he is disabled from understanding social phenomena.

The more general kinds of political bias distort men's sociological conceptions in other ways, but quite as seriously. There is this perennial delusion, common to Radical and Tory, that legislation is omnipotent, and that things will get done because laws are passed to do them; there is this confidence in one or other form of government, due to the belief that a government once established will retain its form and work as was intended; there is this hope that by some means the collective wisdom can be separated from the collective folly, and set over it in such way as to guide things aright;—all of them implying that general political bias which inevitably coexists with subordination to political agencies. The effect on sociological speculation is to maintain the conception of a society as something manufactured by statesmen, and to turn the mind from the phenomena of social evolution. While the regulating agency occupies the thoughts, scarcely any attention is given to those astounding processes and results due to the energies regulated. The genesis of the vast producing, exchanging, and distributing agencies, which has gone on spontaneously, often hindered, and at best only restrained, by governments, is passed over with unobservant eyes. And thus, by continually contemplating the power which keeps in order, and contemplating rarely, if at all, the activities kept in order, there is produced an extremely one-sided theory of Society.

Clearly, it is with this kind of bias as it is with the kinds of bias previously considered—the degree of it bears a certain necessary relation to the temporary phase of progress. It can diminish only as fast as Society advances. A well-balanced social self-consciousness, like a well-balanced individual self-consciousness, is the accompaniment of a high evolution.

CHAPTER XII.

" WHAT a log for hell-fire ! " exclaimed a Wahhabee, on seeing a corpulent Hindu. This illustration, startling by its strength of expression, which Mr. Gifford Palgrave gives[1] of the belief possessing these Mahommedan fanatics, prepares us for their general mode of thinking about God and man. Here is a sample of it :—

"When 'Abd-el-Lateef, a Wahhabee, was preaching one day to the people of Riad, he recounted the tradition according to which Mahomet declared that his followers should divide into seventy-three sects, and that seventy-two were destined to hell-fire, and one only to Paradise. 'And what, O messenger of God, are the signs of that happy sect to which is ensured the exclusive possession of Paradise ?' Whereto Mahomet had replied, 'It is those who shall be in all conformable to myself and to my companions.' 'And that,' added 'Abd-el-Lateef, lowering his voice to the deep tone of conviction, ' that, by the mercy of God, are we, the people of Riad.'"[2]

For present purposes we are not so much concerned to observe the parallelism between this conception and the conceptions that have been, and are, current among sects of Christians, as to observe the effects produced by such conceptions on men's views of those who have alien beliefs, and on their views of alien societies. What extreme misinterpretations of social facts result from the theological bias, may be seen still better in a case even more remarkable.

By Turner, by Erskine, and by the members of the United States' Exploring Expedition, the characters of the Samoans are, as compared with the characters of the uncivilized generally, very favourably described. Though, in common with savages at large, they are said to be "indolent, covetous, fickle, and deceitful," yet they are also said to be "kind, good-humoured, . . . desirous of pleasing, and very hospitable. Both sexes show great regard and love for their children;" and age is much respected. "A man cannot bear to be called stingy or disobliging." The women "are remarkably domestic and virtuous." Infanticide after birth is unknown in Samoa. "The treatment of the sick was . . . invariably humane and all that could be expected."　　　Observe, now, what is said of their cannibal neighbours, the Fijians. They are indifferent to human life; they live in perpetual dread of one another; and, according to Jackson, treachery is considered by them an accomplishment. "Shedding of blood is to him [the Fijian] no crime but a glory." They kill the decrepit, maimed, and sick. While, on the one hand, infanticide covers nearer two-thirds than one-half of the births, on the other hand, "one of the first lessons taught the infant is to strike its mother:" anger and revenge are fostered. Inferiors are killed for neglecting proper salutes; slaves are buried alive with the posts on which a king's house stands; and ten or more men are slaughtered on the decks of a newly-launched canoe, to baptize it with their blood. A chief's wives, courtiers, and aides-de-camp, are strangled at his death—being thereby honoured. Cannibalism is so rampant that a chief, praising his deceased son, ended his eulogy by saying that he would "kill his own wives if they offended him, and eat them afterwards." Victims were sometimes roasted alive before being devoured; and Tanoa, one of their chiefs, cut off a cousin's arm, drank the blood, cooked the arm and ate it in presence of the owner, who was then cut to pieces. Their gods, described as having like characters, commit like acts. They live on the souls of those who are devoured by men, having first "roasted" them (the "souls" being simply material duplicates). They "are proud and revengeful, and make war, and kill and eat each other;" and among the names of honour given to them are "the adulterer," "the woman-stealer," "the brain-eater," "the murderer."   Such being the account of the Samoans, and such the account of the Fijians, let us ask what the Fijians think of the Samoans. "The Feegeeans looked upon the Samoans with horror, because they had no religion, no belief in any such deities [as the Feegeean], nor any of the sanguinary rites which prevailed in other islands;"—a statement quite in harmony with that made by Jackson, who, having behaved disrespectfully to one of their gods, was angrily called by them "the white infidel."

Any one may read while running the lesson conveyed; and, without stopping to consider much, may see its application to the beliefs and sentiments of civilized races. The ferocious Fijian doubtless thinks that to devour a human victim in the name of one of his cannibal gods, is a meritorious act; while he thinks that his Samoan neighbour, who makes no sacrifice to these cannibal gods, but is just and kind to his fellows, thereby shows that meanness goes along with his shocking irreligion. Construing the facts in this way, the Fijian can form no rational conception of Samoan society. With vices and virtues interchanged in conformity with his creed, the benefits of certain social arrangements, if he thinks about them at all, must seem evils and the evils benefits.

Speaking generally, then, each system of dogmatic theology, with the sentiments that gather round it, becomes an impediment in the way of Social Science. The sympathies drawn out towards one creed and the correlative antipathies aroused by other creeds, distort the interpretations of all the associated facts. On these institutions and their results the eyes are turned with a readiness to observe everything that is good, and on those with a readiness to observe everything that is bad. Let us glance at some of the consequent perversions of opinion.

Already we have seen, by implication, that the theological element of a creed, subordinating the ethical element completely in early stages of civilization and very considerably in later stages, maintains a standard of right and wrong, relatively good perhaps, but perhaps absolutely bad—good, that is, as measured by the requirements of the place and time, bad as measured by the requirements of an ideal society. And sanctifying, as an associated theology thus does, false conceptions of right and wrong, it falsifies the measures by which the effects of institutions are to be estimated. Obviously, the sociological conclusions must be vitiated if beneficial and detrimental effects are not respectively recognized as such. An illustration enforcing this is worth giving. Here is Mr. Palgrave's account of Wahhabee morality, as disclosed in answers to his questions:—

" ' The first of the great sins is the giving divine honours to a creature.'

" ' Of course,' I replied, ' the enormity of such a sin is beyond all doubt. But if this be the first, there must be a second ; what is it ? '

" ' Drinking the shameful,' in English, ' smoking tobacco,' was the unhesitating answer.

" 'And murder, and adultery, and false witness ? ' I suggested.

" ' God is merciful and forgiving,' rejoined my friend ; ' that is, these are merely little sins.'

" ' Hence two sins alone are great, polytheism and smoking,' I continued, though hardly able to keep countenance any longer. And 'Abd-el-Kareem, with the most serious asseveration, replied that such was really the case."[4]

Clearly a creed which makes smoking one of the blackest crimes, and has only mild reprobation for the worst acts committed by man against man, negatives anything like Social Science. Deeds and habits and laws not being judged by the degrees in which they conduce to temporal welfare, the ideas of better and worse, as applying to social arrangements, cannot exist; and such notions as progress and retrogression are excluded. But that which holds so conspicuously in this case holds more or less in all cases. At the present time as in past times, and in our own society as in other societies, public acts are judged by two tests—the test of supposed divine approbation, and the test of conduciveness to human happiness. Though, as civilization advances, there grows up the belief that the second test is equivalent to the first—though, consequently, conduciveness to human happiness comes to be more directly considered; yet the test of supposed divine approbation, as inferred from the particular creed held, continues to be very generally used. The wrongness of conduct is conceived as consisting in the implied disobedience to the supposed commands, and not as consisting in its intrinsic character as causing suffering to others or to self. Inevitably the effect on sociological thinking is, that institutions and actions are judged more by their apparent congruity or incongruity with the established cult, than by their tendencies to further or to hinder well-being.

This effect of the theological bias, manifest enough everywhere, has been forced on my attention by one whose mental attitude often supplies me with matter for speculation—an old gentleman who unites the religion of amity and the religion of enmity in startling contrast. On the one hand, getting up early to his devotions, going to church even at great risk to his feeble health, always staying for the sacrament when there is one, he displays what is ordinarily regarded as an exemplary piety. On the other hand, his thoughts ever tend in the direction of warfare : fights on sea and land furnish topics of undying interest to him; he revels in narratives of destruction; his talk is of cannon. To say that he divides his reading between the Bible and Alison, or some kindred book, is an exaggeration; but still it serves to convey an idea of his state of feeling. Now you may hear him waxing wroth over the dis-establishment of the Irish Church, which he looks upon as an act of sacrilege; and now, when the conversation turns on works of art, he names as engravings which above all others he admires, Cœur-de-Lion fighting Saladin, and Wellington at Waterloo. Or after manifesting some kindly feeling, which, to give him his due, he frequently does, he will shortly pass to some bloody encounter, the narration of which makes his voice tremulous with delight. Marvelling though I did at first over these incongruities of sentiment and belief, the explanation was reached on observing that the subordination-element of his creed was far more dominant in his consciousness than the moral element. Watching the movements of his mind made it clear that to his imagination, God was symbolized as a kind of transcendently-powerful sea-captain, and made it clear that he went to church from a feeling akin to that with which, as a middy, he went to muster. On perceiving that this, which is the sentiment common to all religions, whatever be the name or ascribed nature of the deity worshipped, was supreme in him, it ceased to be inexplicable that the sentiment to which the Christian religion specially appeals should be so readily over-ridden. It became easier to understand how, when the Hyde-Park riots took place, he could wish that we had Louis Napoleon over here to shoot down the mob, and how he could recall, with more or less of chuckling, the deeds of press-gangs in his early days.

That the theological bias, thus producing conformity to moral principles from motives of obedience only, and not habitually insisting on such principles because of their intrinsic value, obscures sociological truths, will now not be difficult to see. The tendency is to substitute formal recognitions of such principles for real recognitions. So long as they are not contravened directly enough to suggest disobedience, they may readily be contravened indirectly; for the reason that there has not been cultivated the habit of contemplating consequences as they work out in remote ways. Hence it happens that social arrangements essentially at variance with the ethics of the creed, give no offence to those who are profoundly offended by whatever seems at variance with its theology. Maintenance of the dogmas and forms of the religion becomes the primary, all-essential thing; and the secondary thing, often sacrificed, is the securing of those relations among men which the spirit of the religion requires. How conceptions of good and bad in social affairs are thus warped, the pending controversy about the Athanasian creed shows us. Here we have theologians who believe that our national welfare will be endangered, if there is not in all churches an enforced repetition of the dogmas that Father, Son, and Holy Ghost, are each of them almighty; that yet there are not three Almighties, but one Almighty; that one of the Almighties suffered on the cross and descended into hell to pacify another of them; and that whoever does not believe this, "without doubt shall perish everlastingly." They say that if the State makes its priests threaten with eternal torments all who question these doctrines, things will go well; but if those priests who, in this threat, perceive the devil-worship of the savage usurping the name of Christianity, are allowed to pass it by in silence, woe to the nation! Evidently the theological bias leading to such a conviction entirely excludes Sociology, considered as a science.

Under its special forms, as well as under its general form, the theological bias brings errors into the estimates men make of societies and institutions. Sectarian antipathies, growing out of differences of doctrine, disable the members of each religious community from fairly judging other religious communities. It is always difficult, and often impossible, for the zealot to conceive that his own religious system and his own zeal on its behalf may have but a relative truth and a relative value; or to conceive that there may be relative truths and relative values in alien beliefs and the fanaticisms which maintain them. Though the adherent of each creed daily has thrust on his attention the fact that adherents of other creeds are no less confident than he is—though he can scarcely fail sometimes to reflect that these adherents of other creeds have, in nearly all cases, simply ac-

cepted the dogmas current in the places and families they were
born in, and that he has done the like; yet the special theological
bias which his education and surroundings have given him,
makes it almost beyond imagination that these other creeds
may, some of them, have justifications as good as, if not better
than, his own, and that the rest, along with certain amounts of
absolute worth, may have their special fitnesses to the people
holding them.

We cannot doubt, for instance, that the feeling with which
Mr. Whalley or Mr. Newdegate regards Roman Catholicism,
must cause extreme reluctance to admit the services which
Roman Catholicism rendered to European civilization in the
past; and must make almost impossible a patient hearing of
anyone who thinks that it renders some services now. Whether
great benefit did not arise in early times from the tendency
towards unification produced within each congeries of small
societies by a common creed authoritatively imposed?—whether
papal power supposed to be divinely deputed, and therefore
tending to subordinate the political authorities during turbulent
feudal ages, did not serve to curb warfare and further civilization?—whether the strong tendency shown by early Christianity
to lapse into separate local paganisms, was not beneficially
checked by an ecclesiastical system having a single head supposed to be infallible?—whether morals were not improved,
manners softened, slavery ameliorated, and the condition of
women raised, by the influence of the Church, notwithstanding
all its superstitions and bigotries?—are questions to which Dr.
Cumming, or other vehement opponent of popery, could not
bring a mind open to conviction. Similarly, from the
Roman Catholic the meaning and worth of Protestantism are
hidden. To the Ultramontane, holding that the temporal welfare no less than the eternal salvation of men depends on submission to the Church, it is incredible that Church-authority has
but a transitory value, and that the denials of authority which
have come along with accumulation of knowledge and change of

14

sentiment, mark steps from a lower social *régime* to a higher. Naturally, the sincere Papist thinks schism a crime; and books that throw doubt on the established beliefs seem to him accursed. Nor need we wonder when from such a one there comes a saying like that of the Mayor of Bordeaux, so much applauded by the Comte de Chambord, that " the Devil was the first Protestant;" or when, along with this, there goes a vilification of Protestants too repulsive to be repeated. Clearly, with such a theological bias, fostering such ideas respecting Protestant morality, there must be extremely-false estimates of Protestant institutions, and of all the institutions associated with them.

In less striking ways, but still in ways sufficiently marked, the special theological bias warps the judgments of Conformists and Nonconformists among ourselves. A fair estimate of the advantages which our State-Church has yielded, is not to be expected from the zealous dissenter: he sees only the disadvantages. Whether voluntaryism could have done centuries ago all that it can do now?—whether a State-supported Protestantism was not once the best thing practicable?—are questions which he is unlikely to discuss without prejudice. Contrariwise, the churchman is reluctant to believe that the union of Church and State is beneficial only during a certain phase of progress. He knows that within the Establishment divisions are daily increasing, while voluntary agency is doing daily a larger share of the work originally undertaken by the State; but he does not like to think that there is a kinship between such facts and the fact that outside the Establishment the power of Dissent is growing. That these changes are parts of a general change by which the political and religious agencies, which have been differentiating from the beginning, are being separated and specialized, is not an acceptable idea. He is averse to the conception that just as Protestantism at large was a rebellion against an Ecclesiasticism which dominated over Europe, so Dissent among ourselves is a rebellion against an Ecclesiasticism which dominates over England; and that the two are but successive stages of the same beneficial development. That is to say, his bias prevents him from contemplating the facts in a way favourable to scientific interpretations of them.

Everywhere, indeed, the special theological bias accompanying a special set of doctrines, inevitably pre-judges many sociological questions. One who holds a creed as absolutely true, and who by implication holds the multitudinous other creeds to be absolutely false in so far as they differ from his own, cannot entertain the supposition that the value of a creed is relative. That a particular religious system is, in a general sense, a natural part of the particular society in which it is found, is an entirely-alien conception; and, indeed, a repugnant one. His system of dogmatic theology he thinks good for all places and all times. He does not doubt that when planted among a horde of savages, it will be duly understood by them, duly appreciated by them, and work on them results such as those he experiences from it. Thus prepossessed, he passes over the proofs found everywhere, that a people is no more capable of suddenly receiving a higher form of religion than it is capable of suddenly receiving a higher form of government; and that inevitably with such religion, as with such government, there will go on a degradation which presently reduces it to one differing but nominally from its predecessor. In other words, his special theological bias blinds him to an important class of sociological truths.

The effects of the theological bias need no further elucidation. We will turn our attention to the distortions of judgment caused by the anti-theological bias. Not only the actions of religious dogmas, but also the reactions against them, are disturbing influences we have to beware of. Let us glance first at an instance of that indignation against the established creed, which all display more or less when they emancipate themselves from it.

"A Nepaul king, Rum Bahadur, whose beautiful queen, finding that her lovely face had been disfigured by small-pox, poisoned herself, 'cursed his kingdom, her doctors, and the gods of Nepaul, vowing vengeance on all.' Having ordered the doctors to be flogged, and the right ear and nose of each to be cut off, 'he then wreaked his vengeance on the gods of Nepaul, and after abusing them in the most gross way, he accused them of having obtained from him twelve thousand goats, some hundred-weights of sweetmeats, two thousand gallons of milk, &c., under false pretences.' . . . He then ordered all the artillery, varying from three to twelve-pounders, to be brought in front of the palace. . . . All the guns were then loaded to the muzzle, and down he marched to the head-quarters of the Nepaul deities. . . . All the guns were drawn up in front of the several deities, honouring the most sacred with the heaviest metal. When the order to fire was given, many of the chiefs and soldiers ran away panic-stricken, and others hesitated to obey the sacrilegious order ; and not until several gunners had been cut down, were the guns opened. Down came the gods and goddesses from their hitherto sacred positions ; and after six hours' heavy cannonading not a vestige of the deities remained." [5]

This, which is one of the most remarkable pieces of iconoclasm on record, exhibits in an extreme form the reactive antagonism usually accompanying abandonment of an old belief—an antagonism that is high in proportion as the previous submission has been profound. By stabling their horses in cathedrals and treating the sacred places and symbols with intentional insult, the Puritans displayed this feeling in a marked manner; as again did the French revolutionists by pulling down sacristies and altar-tables, tearing mass-books into cartridge-papers, drinking brandy out of chalices, eating mackerel off patenas, making mock ecclesiastical processions, and holding drunken revels in churches. Though in our day the breaking of bonds less rigid, effected by struggles less violent, is followed by a less excessive opposition and hatred ; yet, habitually, the throwing-off of the old form involves a replacing of the previous sympathy by more or less of antipathy : perversion of judgment caused by the antipathy taking the place of that caused by the sympathy. What before was reverenced as wholly true is now scorned as wholly false ; and what was treasured as invaluable is now rejected as valueless.

In some, this state of sentiment and belief continues. In others, the reaction is in course of time followed by a re-reaction. To carry out the Carlylean figure, the old clothes which had been outgrown and were finally torn off and thrown aside with contempt, come presently to be looked back upon with more calmness, and with recognition of the fact that they did good service in their time—nay, perhaps with the doubt whether they were not thrown off too soon. This re-reaction may be feeble or may be strong; but only when it takes place in due amount is there a possibility of balanced judgments either on religious questions or on those questions of Social Science into which the religious element enters.

Here we have to glance at the sociological errors caused by the anti-theological bias among those in whom it does not become qualified. Thinking only of what is erroneous in the rejected creed, they ignore the truth for which it stands; contemplating only its mischiefs they overlook its benefits; and doing this, they think that nothing but good would result from its general abandonment. Let us observe the tacit assumptions made in drawing this conclusion.

It is assumed, in the first place, that adequate guidance for conduct in life, private and public, could be had; and that a moral code, rationally elaborated by men as they now are, would be duly operative upon them. Neither of these propositions commends itself when we examine the evidence. We have but to observe human action as it meets us at every turn, to see that the average intelligence, incapable of guiding conduct even in simple matters, where but a very moderate reach of reason would suffice, must fail in apprehending with due clearness the natural sanctions of ethical principles. The unthinking ineptitude with which even the routine of life is carried on by the mass of men, shows clearly that they have nothing like the insight required for self-guidance in the absence of an authoritative code of conduct. Take a day's experience, and observe the lack of thought indicated from hour to hour.

You rise in the morning, and, while dressing, take up a phial containing a tonic, of which a little has been prescribed for you; but after the first few drops have been counted, succeeding drops run down the side of the phial, for the reason that the lip is shaped without regard to the requirement. Yet millions of such phials are annually made by glass-makers, and sent out by thousands of druggists: so small being the amount of sense brought to bear on business. Now, turning to the looking-glass, you find that, if not of the best make, it fails to preserve the attitude in which you put it; or, if what is called a " box " looking-glass, you see that maintenance of its position is insured by an expensive appliance which would have been superfluous had a little reason been used. Were the adjustment such that the centre of gravity of the glass came in the line joining the points of support (which would be quite as easy an adjustment), the glass would remain steady in whatever attitude you gave it. Yet, year after year, tens of thousands of looking-glasses are made without regard to so simple a need. Presently you go down to breakfast, and taking some Harvey or other sauce with your fish, find the bottle has a defect like that which you found in the phial: it is sticky from the drops which trickle down, and occasionally stain the table-cloth. Here are other groups of traders similarly so economical of thought, that they do nothing to rectify this obvious inconvenience. Having breakfasted, you take up the paper, and, before sitting down, wish to put some coal on the fire. But the lump you seize with the tongs slips out of them, and, if large, you make several attempts before you succeed in lifting it: all because the ends of the tongs are smooth. Makers and vendors of fire-irons go on, generation after generation, without meeting this evil by simply giving to these smooth ends some projecting points, or even roughening them by a few burrs made with a chisel. Having at length grasped the lump and put it on the fire, you begin to read; but before getting through the first column you are reminded, by the changes of position which your sensations prompt, that men still fail to make easy-chairs.

And yet the guiding principle is simple enough.   Just that advantage secured by using a soft seat in place of a hard one—the advantage, namely, of spreading over a larger area the pressure of the weight to be borne, and so making the pressure less intense at any one point—is an advantage to be sought in the *form* of the chair.   Ease is to be gained by making the shapes and relative inclinations of seat and back, such as will evenly distribute the weight of the trunk and limbs over the widest-possible support-ing surface, and with the least straining of the parts out of their natural attitudes. And yet only now, after these thousands of years of civilization, are there being reached (and that not rationally but empirically) approximations to the structure required.

Such are the experiences of the first hour; and so they con-tinue all the day through.   If you watch and criticize, you may see that the immense majority bring to bear, even on those actions which it is the business of their lives to carry on effectually, an extremely-small amount of faculty.   Employ a workman to do something that is partly new, and not the clearest explanations and sketches will prevent him from blundering; and to any expression of surprise, he will reply that he was not brought up to such work : scarely ever betraying the slightest shame in con-fessing that he cannot do a thing he was not taught to do. Similarly throughout the higher grades of activity.   Remember how generally improvements in manufactures come from out-siders, and you are at once shown with what mere unintelligent routine manufactures are commonly carried on.   Examine into the management of mercantile concerns, and you perceive that those engaged in them mostly do nothing more than move in the ruts that have gradually been made for them by the process of trial and error during a long succession of generations.   Indeed, it almost seems as though most men made it their aim to get through life with the least possible expenditure of thought.

How, then, can there be looked for such power of self-guidance as, in the absence of inherited authoritative rules, would require them to understand why, in the nature of things, these modes of action are injurious and those modes beneficial—would require them to pass beyond proximate results, and see clearly the involved remote results, as worked out on self, on others, and on society ?

The incapacity need not, indeed, be inferred : it may be seen, if we do but take an action concerning which the sanctified code is silent. Listen to a conversation about gambling ; and, where reprobation is expressed, note the grounds of the reprobation. That it tends towards the ruin of the gambler ; that it risks the welfare of family and friends ; that it alienates from business, and leads into bad company—these, and such as these, are the reasons given for condemning the practice. Rarely is there any recognition of the fundamental reason. Rarely is gambling condemned because it is a kind of action by which pleasure is obtained at the cost of pain to another. The normal obtainment of gratification, or of the money which purchases gratification, implies, firstly, that there has been put forth equivalent effort of a kind which, in some way, furthers the general good ; and implies, secondly, that those from whom the money is received, get, directly or indirectly, equivalent satisfactions. But in gambling the opposite happens. Benefit received does not imply effort put forth ; and the happiness of the winner involves the misery of the loser. This kind of action is therefore essentially anti-social— sears the sympathies, cultivates a hard egoism, and so produces a general deterioration of character and conduct.

Clearly, then, a visionary hope misleads those who think that in an imagined age of reason, which might forthwith replace an age of beliefs but partly rational, conduct would be correctly guided by a code directly based on considerations of utility. A utilitarian system of ethics cannot at present be rightly thought out even by the select few, and is quite beyond the mental reach of the many. The value of the inherited and theologically-enforced code is that it formulates, with some approach to truth, the accumulated results of past human experience. It has not arisen rationally but empirically. During past times mankind have eventually gone right after trying all possible ways of going wrong. The wrong-goings have been habitually checked by disaster, and pain, and death; and the right-goings have been continued because not thus checked. There has been a growth of beliefs corresponding to these good and evil results. Hence the code of conduct, embodying discoveries slowly and almost unconsciously made through a long series of generations, has transcendent authority on its side.

Nor is this all. Were it possible forthwith to replace a traditionally-established system of rules, supposed to be supernaturally warranted, by a system of rules rationally elaborated, no such rationally-elaborated system of rules would be adequately operative. To think that it would, implies the thought that men's beliefs and actions are throughout determined by intellect; whereas they are in much larger degrees determined by feeling.

There is a wide difference between the formal assent given to a proposition that cannot be denied, and the efficient belief which produces active conformity to it. Often the most conclusive argument fails to produce a conviction capable of swaying conduct; and often mere assertion, with great emphasis and signs of confidence on the part of the utterer, will produce a fixed conviction where there is no evidence, and even in spite of adverse evidence. Especially is this so among those of little culture. Not only may we see that strength of affirmation and an authoritative manner create faith in them; but we may see that their faith sometimes actually decreases if explanation is given. The natural language of belief displayed by another, is that which generates their belief—not the logically-conclusive evidence. The dependencies of this they cannot clearly follow; and in trying to follow, they so far lose themselves that premises and conclusion, not perceived to stand in necessary relation, are rendered less coherent than by putting them in juxtaposition and strengthening their connexion by a wave of the emotion which emphatic affirmation raises.

Nay, it is even true that the most cultivated intelligences, capable of criticizing evidence and valuing arguments to a nicety, are not thereby made rational to the extent that they are guided by intellect apart from emotion. Continually men of the widest knowledge deliberately do things they know to be injurious; suffer the evils that transgression brings; are deterred awhile by the vivid remembrance of them; and, when the remembrance has become faint, transgress again. Often the emotional consciousness over-rides the intellectual consciousness absolutely, as hypochondriacal patients show us. A sufferer from depressed spirits may have the testimony of his physicians, verified by numerous past experiences of his own, showing that his gloomy anticipations are illusions caused by his bodily state; and yet the conclusive proofs that they are irrational do not enable him to get rid of them: he continues to feel sure that disasters are coming on him.

All which, and many kindred facts, make it certain that the operativeness of a moral code depends much more on the emotions called forth by its injunctions, than on the consciousness of the utility of obeying such injunctions. The feelings drawn out during early life towards moral principles, by witnessing the social sanction and the religious sanction they possess, influence conduct far more than the perception that conformity to such principles conduces to welfare. And in the absence of the feelings which manifestations of these sanctions arouse, the utilitarian belief is commonly inadequate to produce conformity.

It is true that the sentiments in the higher races, and especially in superior members of the higher races, are now in considerable degrees adjusted to these principles: the sympathies that have become organic in the most developed men, produce spontaneous conformity to altruistic precepts. Even for such, however, the social sanction, which is in part derived from the religious sanction, is important as strengthening the influence of these precepts. And for persons endowed with less of moral sentiment, the social and religious sanctions are still more important aids to guidance.

Thus the anti-theological bias leads to serious errors, both when it ignores the essential share hitherto taken by religious systems in giving force to certain principles of action, in part absolutely good and in part good relatively to the needs of the time, and again when it prompts the notion that these principles might now be so established on rational bases as to rule men effectually through their enlightened intellects.

These errors, however, which the anti-theological bias produces, are superficial compared with the error that remains. The antagonism to superstitious beliefs habitually leads to entire rejection of them. They are thrown aside with the assumption that along with so much that is wrong there is nothing right. Whereas the truth, recognizable only after antagonism has spent itself, is that the wrong beliefs rejected are superficial, and that a right belief hidden by them remains when they have been rejected. Those who defend, equally with those who assail, religious creeds, suppose that everything turns on the maintenance of the particular dogmas at issue ; whereas the dogmas are but temporary forms of that which is permanent.

The process of Evolution which has gradually modified and advanced men's conceptions of the Universe, will continue to modify and advance them during the future. The ideas of Cause and Origin, which have been slowly changing, will change still further. But no changes in them, even when pushed to the extreme, will expel them from consciousness; and hence there can never be an extinction of the correlative sentiments. No more in this than in other things, will Evolution alter its general direction : it will continue along the same lines as hitherto. And if we wish to see whither it tends, we have but to observe how there has been thus far a decreasing concreteness of the consciousness to which the religious sentiment is related, to infer that hereafter this concreteness will further diminish :

leaving behind a substance of consciousness for which there is
no adequate form, but which is none the less persistent and
powerful.

Without seeming so, the development of religious sentiment
has been continuous from the beginning; and its nature when a
germ was the same as is its nature when fully developed.   The
savage first shows it in the feeling excited by a display of
power in another exceeding his own power—some skill, some
sagacity, in his chief, leading to a result he does not understand
—something which has the element of mystery and arouses his
wonder.   To his unspeculative intellect there is nothing wonderful
in the ordinary course of things around.   The regular sequences,
the constant relations, do not present themselves to him as problems needing interpretation.   Only anomalies in that course of
causation which he knows most intimately, namely, human will
and power, excite his surprise and raise questions.   And only
when experiences of phenomena of other classes become multiplied enough for generalization, does the occurrence of anomalies
among these also, arouse the same idea of mystery and the same
sentiment of wonder: hence one kind of fetichism.   Passing
over intermediate stages, the truth to be noted is, that as fast
as explanation of the anomalies dissipates the wonder they excited, there grows up a wonder at the uniformities: there arises
the question—How come they to be uniformities?   As fast as
Science transfers more and more things from the category of
irregularities to the category of regularities, the mystery that
once attached to the superstitious explanations of them becomes
a mystery attaching to the scientific explanations of them: there
is a merging of many special mysteries in one general mystery.
The astronomer, having shown that the motions of the Solar
System imply a uniform and invariably-acting force he calls
gravitation, finds himself utterly incapable of conceiving this
force.   Though he helps himself to think of the Sun's action on
the Earth by assuming an intervening medium, and finds he *must*
do this if he thinks about it at all; yet the mystery re-appears

when he asks what is the constitution of this medium. While compelled to use units of ether as symbols, he sees that they can be but symbols. Similarly with the physicist and the chemist. The hypothesis of atoms and molecules enables them to work out multitudinous interpretations that are verified by experiment; but the ultimate unit of matter admits of no consistent conception. Instead of the particular mysteries presented by those actions of matter they have explained, there rises into prominence the mystery which matter universally presents, and which proves to be absolute. So that, beginning with the germinal idea of mystery which the savage gets from a display of power in another transcending his own, and the germinal sentiment of awe accompanying it, the progress is towards an ultimate recognition of a mystery behind every act and appearance, and a transfer of the awe from something special and occasional to something universal and unceasing.

No one need expect, then, that the religious consciousness will die away or will change the lines of its evolution. Its specialities of form, once strongly marked and becoming less distinct during past mental progress, will continue to fade; but the substance of the consciousness will persist. That the object-matter can be replaced by another object-matter, as supposed by those who think the "Religion of Humanity" will be the religion of the future, is a belief countenanced neither by induction nor by deduction. However dominant may become the moral sentiment enlisted on behalf of Humanity, it can never exclude the sentiment, alone properly called religious, awakened by that which is behind Humanity and behind all other things. The child by wrapping its head in the bed-clothes, may, for a moment, suppress the consciousness of surrounding darkness; but the consciousness, though rendered less vivid, survives, and imagination persists in occupying itself with that which lies beyond perception. No such thing as a "Religion of Humanity" can ever do more than temporarily shut out the thought of a Power of which Humanity is but a small and fugitive product—a Power

which was in course of ever-changing manifestations before
Humanity was, and will continue through other manifestations
when Humanity has ceased to be.

To recognitions of this order the anti-theological bias is a
hindrance.   Ignoring the truth for which religions stand, it
under-values religious institutions in the past, thinks they are
needless in the present, and expects they will leave no representatives in the future.   Hence mistakes in sociological reasonings.

To the various other forms of bias, then, against which we
must guard in studying the Social Science, has to be added the
bias, perhaps as powerful and perverting as any, which religious
beliefs and sentiments produce.   This, both generally under
the form of theological bigotry, and specially under the form
of sectarian bigotry, affects the judgments about public affairs;
and reaction against it gives the judgments an opposite warp.

The theological bias under its general form, tending to maintain a dominance of the subordination-element of religion over
its ethical element—tending, therefore, to measure actions by
their formal congruity with a creed rather than by their intrinsic
congruity with human welfare, is unfavourable to that estimation of worth in social arrangements which is made by tracing
out results.   And while the general theological bias brings into
Sociology an element of distortion, by using a kind of measure
foreign to the science properly so called, the special theological
bias brings in further distortions, arising from special measures
of this kind which it uses.   Institutions, old and new, home and
foreign, are considered as congruous or incongruous with
particular sets of dogmas, and are liked or disliked accordingly :
the obvious result being that, since the sets of dogmas differ in
all times and places, the sociological judgments affected by them
must inevitably be wrong in all cases but one, and probably in
all cases.

On the other hand, the reactive bias distorts conceptions of
social phenomena by under-valuing religious systems.   It

generates an unwillingness to see that a religious system is a normal and essential factor in every evolving society; that the specialities of it have certain fitnesses to the social conditions; and that while its form is temporary its substance is permanent. In so far as the anti-theological bias causes an ignoring of these truths, or an inadequate appreciation of them, it causes misinterpretations.

To maintain the required equilibrium amid the conflicting sympathies and antipathies which contemplation of religious beliefs inevitably generates, is difficult. In presence of the theological thaw going on so fast on all sides, there is on the part of many a fear, and on the part of some a hope, that nothing will remain. But the hopes and the fears are alike groundless; and must be dissipated before balanced judgments in Social Science can be formed. Like the transformations that have succeeded one another hitherto, the transformation now in progress is but an advance from a lower form, no longer fit, to a higher and fitter form; and neither will this transformation, nor kindred transformations to come hereafter, destroy that which is transformed, any more than past transformations have destroyed it.

CHAPTER XIII

DISCIPLINE.

In the foregoing eight chapters we have contemplated, under their several heads, those "Difficulties of the Social Science" which the chapter bearing that title indicated in a general way. After thus warning the student against the errors he is liable to fall into, partly because of the nature of the phenomena themselves and the conditions they are presented under, and partly because of his own nature as observer of them, which by both its original and its acquired characters causes twists of perception and judgment; it now remains to say something about the needful preliminary studies. I do not refer to studies furnishing the requisite data; but I refer to studies giving the requisite discipline. Right thinking in any matter depends very much on the *habit* of thought; and the habit of thought, partly natural, depends in part on the artificial influences to which the mind has been subjected.

As certainly as each person has peculiarities of bodily action that distinguish him from his fellows, so certainly has he peculiarities of mental action that give a character to his conceptions. There are tricks of thought as well as tricks of muscular movement. There are acquired mental aptitudes for seeing things under particular aspects, as there are acquired bodily aptitudes for going through evolutions after particular ways. And there are intellectual perversities produced by certain modes of treating the mind, as there are incurable awkwardnesses due to certain physical activities daily repeated.

Each kind of mental discipline, besides its direct effects on the faculties brought into play, has its indirect effects on the faculties left out of play; and when special benefit is gained by extreme special discipline, there is inevitably more or less general mischief entailed on the rest of the mind by the consequent want of discipline. That antagonism between body and brain which we see in those who, pushing brain-activity to an extreme, enfeeble their bodies, and those who, pushing bodily activity to an extreme, make their brains inert, is an antagonism which holds between the parts of the body itself and the parts of the brain itself. The greater bulk and strength of the right arm resulting from its greater use, and the greater aptitude of the right hand, are instances in point; and that the relative incapacity of the left hand, involved by cultivating the capacity of the right hand, would become still more marked were the right hand to undertake all manipulation, is obvious. The like holds among the mental faculties. The fundamental antagonism between feeling and cognition, running down through all actions of the mind, from the conflicts between emotion and reason to the conflicts between sensation and perception, is the largest illustration. We meet with a kindred antagonism among the actions of the intellect itself, between perceiving and reasoning. Men who have aptitudes for accumulating observations are rarely men given to generalizing; while men given to generalizing are commonly men who, mostly using the observations of others, observe for themselves less from love of particular facts than from desire to put such facts to use. We may trace the antagonism within even a narrower range, between general reasoning and special reasoning. One prone to far-reaching speculations rarely pursues to much purpose those investigations by which particular truths are reached; while the scientific specialist ordinarily has but little tendency to occupy himself with wide views.

No more is needed to make it clear that habits of thought result from particular kinds of mental activity; and that each man's habits of thought influence his judgment on any question brought before him. It will be obvious, too, that in proportion as the question is involved and many-sided, the habit of thought must be a more important factor in determining the conclusion arrived at. Where the subject-matter is simple, as a geometrical truth or a mechanical action, and has therefore not many different aspects, perversions of view consequent on intellectual attitude are comparatively few; but where the subject-matter is complex and heterogeneous, and admits of being mentally seen in countless different ways, the intellectual attitude affects very greatly the form of the conception.

A fit habit of thought, then, is all-important in the study of Sociology; and a fit habit of thought can be acquired only by study of the Sciences at large. For Sociology is a science in which the phenomena of all other sciences are included. It presents those necessities of relation with which the Abstract Sciences deal; it presents those connexions of cause and effect which the Abstract-Concrete Sciences familiarize the student with; and it presents that concurrence of many causes and production of contingent results, which the Concrete Sciences show us, but which we are shown especially by the organic sciences. Hence, to acquire the habit of thought conducive to right thinking in Sociology, the mind must be familiarized with the fundamental ideas which each class of sciences brings into view; and must not be possessed by those of any one class, or any two classes, of sciences.

That this may be better seen, let me briefly indicate the indispensable discipline which each class of sciences gives to the intellect; and also the wrong intellectual habits produced if that class of sciences is studied exclusively.

Entire absence of training in the Abstract Sciences, leaves the mind without due sense of *necessity of relation*. Watch the mental movements of the wholly-ignorant, before whom there have been brought not even those exact and fixed connexions which Arithmetic exhibits, and it will be seen that they have nothing like irresistible convictions that from given data there is an inevitable inference. That which to you has the aspect of a certainty, seems to them not free from doubt. Even men whose educations have made numerical processes and results tolerably familiar, will show in a case where the implication is logical only, that they have not absolute confidence in the dependence of conclusion on premisses.

Unshakeable beliefs in necessities of relation, are to be gained only by studying the Abstract Sciences, Logic and Mathematics. Dealing with necessities of relation of the simplest class, Logic is of some service to this end; though often of less service than it might be, for the reason that the symbols used are not translated into thoughts, and hence the connexions stated are not really represented. Only when, for a logical implication expressed in the abstract, there is substituted an example so far concrete that the inter-dependencies can be contemplated, is there an exercise of the mental power by which logical necessity is grasped. Of the discipline given by Mathematics, also, it is to be remarked that the habit of dealing with necessities of numerical relation, though in a degree useful for cultivating the consciousness of necessity, is not in a high degree useful; because, in the immense majority of cases, the mind, occupied with the symbols used, and not passing beyond them to the groups of units they stand for, does not really figure to itself the relations expressed—does not really discern their necessities; and has not therefore the conception of necessity perpetually repeated. It is the more special division of Mathematics, dealing with Space-relations, which above all other studies yields necessary ideas; and so makes strong and definite the consciousness of necessity in general. A geometrical demonstration time after time presents premises and conclusion in such wise that the relation alleged is seen in thought —cannot be passed over by mere symbolization. Each step exhibits some connexion of positions or quantities as one that could not be otherwise; and hence the habit of taking such steps makes the consciousness of such connexions familiar and vivid.

But while mathematical discipline, and especially discipline in Geometry, is extremely useful, if not indispensable, as a means of preparing the mind to recognize throughout Nature the absoluteness of uniformities; it is, if exclusively or too-habitually pursued, apt to produce perversions of general thought. Inevitably it establishes a special bent of mind; and inevitably this special bent affects all the intellectual actions—causes a tendency to look in a mathematical way at matters beyond the range of Mathematics. The mathematician is ever dealing with phenomena of which the elements are relatively few and definite. His most involved problem is immeasurably less involved than are the problems of the Concrete Sciences. But, when considering these, he cannot help thinking after his habitual way : in dealing with questions which the Concrete Sciences present, he recognizes some few only of the factors, tacitly ascribes to these a definiteness which they have not, and proceeds after the mathematical manner to draw positive conclusions from these data, as though they were specific and adequate.

Hence the truth, so often illustrated, that mathematicians are bad reasoners on contingent matters. To older illustrations may be added the recent one yielded by M. Michel Chasles, who proved himself incapable as a judge of evidence in the matter of the Newton-Pascal forgeries. Another was supplied by the late Professor De Morgan, who, bringing his mental eye to bear with microscopic power on some small part of a question, ignored its main features.

By cultivation of the Abstract-Concrete Sciences, there is produced a further habit of thought, not otherwise produced, which is essential to right thinking in general; and, by implication, to right thinking in Sociology. Familiarity with the various orders of physical and chemical phenomena, gives distinctness and strength to the consciousness of *cause and effect*.

Experiences of things around do, indeed, yield conceptions of special forces and of force in general. The uncultured get from these experiences, degrees of faith in causation such that where they see some striking effect they usually assume an adequate cause, and where a cause of given amount is manifest, a proportionate effect is looked for. Especially is this so where the actions are simple mechanical actions. Still, these impressions which daily life furnishes, if unaided by those derived from physical science, leave the mind with but vague ideas of causal relations. It needs but to remember the readiness with which people accept the alleged facts of the Spiritualists, many of which imply a direct negation of the mechanical axiom that action and reaction are equal and opposite, to see how much the ordinary thoughts of causation lack quantitativeness—lack the idea of proportion between amount of force expended and amount of change wrought. Very generally, too, the ordinary thoughts of causation are not even qualitatively valid: the most absurd notions as to what cause will produce what effect are frequently disclosed. Take, for instance, the popular belief that a goat kept in a stable will preserve the health of the horses; and note how this belief, accepted on the authority of grooms and coachmen, is repeated by their educated employers—as I lately heard it repeated by an American general, and agreed in by two retired English officials. Clearly, the readiness to admit, on such evidence, that such a cause can produce such an effect, implies a consciousness of causation which, even qualitatively considered, is of the crudest kind. And such a consciousness is, indeed, everywhere betrayed by the superstitions traceable among all classes.

Hence we must infer that the uncompared and unanalyzed observations men make in the course of their dealings with things around, do not suffice to give them wholly-rational ideas of the process of things. It requires that physical actions shall be critically examined, the factors and results measured, and different cases contrasted, before there can be reached clear ideas of necessary causal dependence. And thus to investigate physical actions is the business of the Abstract-Concrete Sciences. Every experiment which the physicist or the chemist makes, brings afresh before his consciousness the truth, given countless times in his previous experiences, that from certain antecedents of particular kinds there will inevitably follow a particular kind of consequent; and that from certain amounts of the antecedents, the amount of the consequent will be inevitably so much. The habit of thought generated by these hourly-repeated experiences, always the same, always exact, is one which makes it impossible to think of any effect as arising without a cause, or any cause as expended without an effect; and one which makes it impossible to think of an effect out of proportion to its cause, or a cause out of proportion to its effect.

While, however, study of the Abstract-Concrete Sciences carried on experimentally, gives clearness and strength to the consciousness of causation, taken alone it is inadequate as a discipline; and if pursued exclusively, it generates a habit of thought which betrays into erroneous conclusions when higher orders of phenomena are dealt with. The process of physical inquiry is essentially analytical; and the daily pursuit of this process generates two tendencies—the tendency to contemplate singly those factors which it is the aim to disentangle and identify and measure; and the tendency to rest in the results reached, as though they were the final results to be sought. The chemist, by saturating, neutralizing, decomposing, precipitating, and at last separating, is enabled to measure what quantity of this element had been held in combination by a given quantity of that; and when, by some alternative course of analysis, he has verified the result, his inquiry is in so far concluded: as are kindred inquiries respecting other affinities of the element, when these are qualitatively and quantitatively determined. His habit is to get rid of, or neglect as much as possible, the concomitant disturbing factors, that he may ascertain the nature and amount of some one, and then of some other   and his end is achieved when accounts have been given of all the factors, individually considered. So is it, too, with the physicist. Say the problem is the propagation of sound through air, and the interpretation of its velocity—say, that the velocity as calculated by Newton is found less by one-sixth than observation gives; and that Laplace sets himself to explain the anomaly. He recognizes the evolution of heat by the compression which each sound-wave produces in the air; finds the extra velocity consequent on this; adds this to the velocity previously calculated; finds the result answer to the observed fact; and then, having resolved the phenomenon into its components and measured them, considers his task concluded. So throughout: the habit is that of identifying, parting, and estimating factors; and stopping after having done this completely.

This habit, carried into the interpretation of things at large, affects it somewhat as the mathematical habit affects it. It tends towards the formation of unduly-simple and unduly-definite conceptions; and it encourages the natural propensity to be content with proximate results. The daily practice of dealing with single factors of phenomena, and with factors complicated by but few others, and with factors ideally separated from their combinations, inevitably gives to the thoughts about surrounding things an analytic rather than a synthetic character. It promotes the contemplation of simple causes apart from the entangled *plexus* of co-operating causes which all the higher natural phenomena show us; and begets a tendency to suppose that when the results of such simple causes have been exactly determined, nothing remains to be asked.

Physical science, then, though indispensable as a means of developing the consciousness of causation in its simple definite forms, and thus preparing the mind for dealing with complex causation, is not sufficient of itself to make complex causation truly comprehensible. In illustration of its inadequacy, I might name a distinguished mathematician and physicist whose achievements place him in the first rank, but who, nevertheless, when entering on questions of concrete science, where the data are no longer few and exact, has repeatedly shown defective judgment. Choosing premisses which, to say the least, were gratuitous and in some cases improbable, he has proceeded by exact methods to draw definite conclusions; and has then enunciated those conclusions as though they had a certainty proportionate to the exactness of his methods.

The kind of discipline which affords the needful corrective, is the discipline which the Concrete Sciences give. Study of the *forms* of phenomena, as in Logic and Mathematics, is needful but by no means sufficient. Study of the *factors* of phenomena, as in Mechanics, Physics, Chemistry, is also essential, but not enough by itself, or enough even joined with study of the forms. Study of the *products* themselves, in their totalities, is no less necessary. Exclusive attention to forms and factors not only fails to give right conceptions of products, but even tends to make the conceptions of products wrong. The analytical habit of mind has to be supplemented by the synthetical habit of mind. Seen in its proper place, analysis has for its chief function to prepare the way for synthesis; and to keep a due mental balance, there must be not only a recognition of the truth that synthesis is the end to which analysis is the means, but there must also be a practice of synthesis along with a practice of analysis.

All the Concrete Sciences familiarize the mind with certain cardinal conceptions which the Abstract and Abstract-Concrete Sciences do not yield—the conceptions of *continuity, complexity,* and *contingency.* The simplest of the Concrete Sciences, Astronomy and Geology, yield the idea of continuity with great distinctness. I do not mean continuity of existence merely; I mean continuity of causation: the unceasing production of effect —the never-ending work of every force. On the mind of the astronomer there is vividly impressed the idea that any one planet which has been drawn out of its course by another planet, or by a combination of others, will through all future time follow a route different from that it would have followed but for the perturbation; and he recognizes its reaction upon the perturbing planet or planets, as similarly having effects which, while ever being complicated and ever slowly diffused, will never be lost during the immeasurable periods to come. So, too, the geologist sees in each change wrought on the Earth's crust, by igneous or aqueous action, a new factor that goes on perpetually modifying all subsequent changes. An upheaved portion of seabottom alters the courses of ocean-currents, modifies the climates of adjacent lands, affects their rain-falls and prevailing winds, their denudations and the deposits round their coasts, their floras and faunas; and these effects severally become causes that act unceasingly in ever-multiplying ways. Always there is traceable the persistent working of each force, and the progressive complication of the results through succeeding geologic epochs.

These conceptions, not yielded at all by the Abstract and Abstract-Concrete Sciences, and yielded by the inorganic Concrete Sciences in ways which, though unquestionable, do not arrest attention, are yielded in clear and striking ways by the organic Concrete Sciences—the sciences that deal with living things. Every organism, if we read the lessons it gives, shows us continuity of causation and complexity of causation. The ordinary facts of inheritance illustrate continuity of causation—very conspicuously where varieties so distinct as negro and white are united, and where traces of the negro come out generation after generation; and still better among domestic animals, where traits of remote ancestry show the persistent working of causes which date far back. Organic phenomena make us familiar with complexity of causation, both by showing the co-operation of many antecedents to each consequent, and by showing the multiplicity of results which each influence works out. If we observe how a given weight of a given drug produces on no two persons exactly like effects, and produces even on the same person different effects in different constitutional states; we see at once how involved is the combination of factors by which

15

the changes in an organism are brought about, and how extremely contingent, therefore, is each particular change. And we need but watch what happens after an injury, say of the foot, to perceive how, if permanent, it alters the gait, alters the adjustment and bend of the body, alters the movements of the arms, alters the features into some contracted form accompanying pain or inconvenience. Indeed, through the re-adjustments, muscular, nervous, and visceral, which it entails, this local damage acts and re-acts on function and structure throughout the whole body: producing effects which, as they diffuse, complicate incalculably.

While, in multitudinous ways, the Science of Life thrusts on the attention of the student the cardinal notions of continuity, and complexity, and contingency, of causation, it introduces him to a further conception of moment, which the inorganic Concrete Sciences do not furnish—the conception of what we may call *fructifying* causation. For as it is a distinction between living and not-living bodies that the first propagate while the second do not; it is also a distinction between them that certain actions which go on in the first are cumulative, instead of being, as in the second, dissipative. Not only do organisms as wholes reproduce, and so from small beginnings reach, by multiplication, great results; but components of them, normal and morbid, do the like. Thus a minute portion of a virus introduced into an organism, does not work an effect proportionate to its amount, as would an inorganic agent on an inorganic mass; but by appropriating materials from the blood of the organism, and thus immensely increasing, it works effects altogether out of proportion to its amount as originally introduced—effects which may continue with accumulating power throughout the remaining life of the organism. It is so with internally-evolved agencies as well as with externally-invading agencies. A portion of germinal matter, itself microscopic, may convey from a parent some constitutional peculiarity that is infinitesimal in relation even to its minute bulk; and from this there may arise, fifty years afterwards, gout or insanity in the resulting man: after this great lapse of time, slowly increasing actions and products show themselves in large derangements of function and structure. And this is a trait characteristic of organic phenomena. While from the *destructive* changes going on throughout the tissues of living bodies, there is a continual production of effects which lose themselves by subdivision, as do the effects of inorganic forces; there arise from those *constructive* changes going on in them, by which living bodies are distinguished from not-living bodies, certain classes of effects which increase as they diffuse—go on augmenting in volume as well as in variety.

Thus, as a discipline, study of the Science of Life is essential; partly as familiarizing the mind with the cardinal ideas of continuity, complexity, and contingency, of causation, in clearer and more various ways than do the other Concrete Sciences, and partly as familiarizing the mind with the cardinal idea of fructifying causation, which the other Concrete Sciences do not present at all. Not that, pursued exclusively, the Organic Sciences will yield these conceptions in clear forms: there requires a familiarity with the Abstract-Concrete Sciences to give the requisite grasp of simple causation. Studied by themselves, the Organic Sciences tend rather to make the ideas of causation cloudy; for the reason that the entanglement of the factors and the contingency of the results is so great, that definite relations of antecedents and consequents cannot be established: the two are not presented in such connexions as to make the conception of causal action, qualitative and quantitative, sufficiently distinct. There requires, first, the discipline yielded by Physics and Chemistry, to make definite the ideas of forces and actions as necessarily related in their kinds and amounts; and then the study of organic phenomena may be carried on with a clear consciousness that while the processes of causation are so involved as often to be inexplicable, yet there *is* causation, no less necessary and no less exact than causation of simpler kinds.

And now to apply these considerations on mental discipline to our immediate topic. For the effectual study of Sociology there needs a habit of thought generated by the studies of all these sciences—not, of course, an exhaustive, or even a very extensive, study; but such a study as shall give a grasp of the cardinal ideas they severally yield. For, as already said, social phenomena involve phenomena of every order.

That there are necessities of relation such as those with which the Abstract Sciences deal, cannot be denied when it is seen that societies present facts of number and quantity. That the actions of men in society, in all their movements and productive processes, must conform to the laws of the physical forces, is also indisputable. And that everything thought and felt and done in the course of social life, is thought and felt and done in harmony with the laws of individual life, is also a truth—almost a truism, indeed; though one of which few seem conscious.

Scientific culture in general, then, is needful; and above all, culture of the Science of Life. This is more especially requisite, however, because the conceptions of continuity, complexity, and contingency of causation, as well as the conception of fructifying causation, are conceptions common to it and to the Science of Society. It affords a specially-fit discipline, for the reason that it alone among the sciences produces familiarity with these cardinal ideas—presents the data for them in forms easily grasped, and so prepares the mind to recognize the data for them in the Social Science, where they are less easily grasped, though no less constantly presented.

The supreme importance of this last kind of culture, however, is not to be adequately shown by this brief statement. For besides generating habits of thought appropriate to the study of the Social Science, it furnishes special conceptions which serve as keys to the Social Science. The Science of Life yields to the Science of Society, certain great generalizations without which there can be no Science of Society at all. Let us go on to observe the relations of the two.

CHAPTER XIV.

PREPARATION IN BIOLOGY.

THE parable of the sower has its application to the progress of Science. Time after time new ideas are sown and do not germinate, or, having germinated, die for lack of fit environments, before they are at last sown under such conditions as to take root and flourish. Among other instances of this, one is supplied by the history of the truth here to be dwelt on—the dependence of Sociology on Biology. Even limiting the search to our own society, we may trace back this idea nearly three centuries. In the first book of Hooker's *Ecclesiastical Polity*, it is enunciated as clearly as the state of knowledge in his age made possible—more clearly, indeed, than was to be expected in an age when science and scientific ways of thinking had advanced so little. Along with the general notion of natural law—along, too, with the admission that human actions, resulting as they do from desires guided by knowledge, also in a sense conform to law; there is a recognition of the fact that the formation of societies is determined by the attributes of individuals, and that the growth of a governmental organization follows from the natures of the men who have associated themselves the better to satisfy their needs. Entangled though this doctrine is with a theological doctrine, through the restraints of which it has to break, it is expressed with considerable clearness: there needs but better definition and further development to make it truly scientific.

Among re-appearances of this thought in subsequent English writers, I will here name only one, which I happen to have observed in *An Essay on the History of Civil Society*, published a century ago by Dr. Adam Ferguson. In it the first part treats "of the General Characteristics of Human Nature." Section I., pointing out the universality of the gregarious tendency, the dependence of this on certain affections and ·antagonisms, and the influences of memory, foresight, language, and communicativeness, alleges that "these facts must be admitted as the foundation of all our reasoning relative to man." Though the way in which social phenomena arise out of the phenomena of individual human nature, is seen in but a general and vague way, yet it is seen—there is a conception of causal relation.

Before this conception could assume a definite form, it was necessary both that scientific knowledge should become more comprehensive and precise, and that the scientific spirit should be strengthened. To M. Comte, living when these conditions were fulfilled, is due the credit of having set forth with comparative definiteness, the connexion between the Science of Life and the Science of Society. He saw clearly that the facts presented by masses of associated men, are facts of the same order as those presented by groups of gregarious creatures of inferior kinds; and that in the one case, as in the other, the individuals must be studied before the assemblages can be understood. He therefore placed Biology before Sociology in his classification of the sciences. Biological preparation for sociological study, he regarded as needful not only because the phenomena of corporate life, arising out of the phenomena of individual life, can be rightly co-ordinated only after the phenomena of individual life have been rightly co-ordinated ; but also because the methods of inquiry which Biology uses, are methods to be used by Sociology. In various ways, which it would take too much space here to specify, he exhibits this dependence very satisfactorily. It may, indeed, be contended that certain of his other beliefs prevented him from seeing all the implications of this dependence. When, for instance, he speaks of " the intellectual anarchy which is the main source of our moral anarchy "—when he thus discloses the faith, pervading his *Course of Positive Philosophy*, that true theory would bring right practice; it becomes clear that the relation between the attributes of citizens and the phenomena of societies is incorrectly seen by him : the relation is far too deep a one to be changed by mere change of ideas. Again, denying, as he did, the indefinite modifiability of species, he almost ignored one of the cardinal truths which Biology yields to Sociology—a truth without which sociological interpretations must go wrong. Though he admits a certain modifiability of Man, both emotional and intellectual, yet the dogma of the fixity of species, to which he adhered, kept his conceptions of individual and social change within limits much too specific. Hence arose, among other erroneous pre-conceptions, this serious one, that the different forms of society presented by savage and civilized races all over the globe, are but different stages in the evolution of one form : the truth being, rather, that social types, like types of individual organisms, do not form a series, but are classifiable only in divergent and re-divergent groups. Nor did he arrive at that conception of the Social Science which alone fully affiliates it upon the simpler sciences—the conception of it as an account of the most complex forms of that continuous redistribution of matter and motion which is going on universally. Only when it is seen that the transformations passed through during the growth, maturity, and decay of a society, conform to the same principles as do the transformations passed through by aggregates of all orders, inorganic and organic—only when it is seen that the process is in all cases similarly determined by forces, and is not scientifically interpreted until it is expressed in terms of those forces ;—only then is there reached the conception of Sociology as a science, in the complete meaning of the word.

Nevertheless, we must not overlook the greatness of the step made by M. Comte. His mode of contemplating the facts was truly philosophical. Containing, along with special views not to be admitted, many thoughts that are true as well as large and suggestive, the introductory chapters to his *Sociology* show a breadth and depth of conception beyond any previously reached. Apart from the tenability of his sociological doctrines, his way of conceiving social phenomena was much superior to all previous ways; and among other of its superiorities, was this recognition of the dependence of Sociology on Biology.

Here leaving the history of this idea, let us turn to the idea itself. There are two distinct and equally-important ways in which these sciences are connected. In the first place, all social actions being determined by the actions of individuals, and all actions of individuals being vital actions that conform to the laws of life at large, a rational interpretation of social actions implies knowledge of the laws of life. In the second place, a society as a whole, considered apart from its living units, presents phenomena of growth, structure, and function, like those of growth, structure, and function in an individual body; and these last are needful keys to the first. We will begin with this analogical connexion.

Figures of speech, which often mislead by conveying the notion of complete likeness where only slight similarity exists, occasionally mislead by making an actual correspondence seem a fancy. A metaphor, when used to express a real resemblance, raises a suspicion of mere imaginary resemblance; and so obscures the perception of intrinsic kinship. It is thus with the phrases "body politic," "political organization," and others, which tacitly liken a society to a living creature: they are assumed to be phrases having a certain convenience but expressing no fact—tending rather to foster a fiction. And yet metaphors are here more than metaphors in the ordinary sense. They are devices of speech hit upon to suggest a truth at first dimly perceived, but which grows clearer the more carefully the evidence is examined. That there is a real analogy between an individual organism and a social organism, becomes undeniable when certain necessities determining structure are seen to govern them in common.

Mutual dependence of parts is that which initiates and guides organization of every kind. So long as, in a mass of living matter, all parts are alike, and all parts similarly live and grow without aid from one another, there is no organization: the un-differentiated aggregate of protoplasm thus characterized, belongs to the lowest grade of living things. Without distinct faculties, and capable of but the feeblest movements, it cannot adjust itself to circumstances; and is at the mercy of environing destructive actions. The changes by which this structureless mass becomes a structured mass, having the characters and powers possessed by what we call an organism, are changes through which its parts lose their original likenesses; and do this while assuming the unlike kinds of activity for which their respective positions towards one another and surrounding things fit them. These differences of function, and consequent dif-ferences of structure, at first feebly marked, slight in degree, and few in kind, become, as organization progresses, definite and numerous; and in proportion as they do this the requirements are better met.   Now structural traits expressible in the same language, distinguish lower and higher types of societies from one another; and distinguish the earlier stages of each society from the later. Primitive tribes show no established contrasts of parts. At first all men carry on the same kinds of activities, with no dependence on one another, or but occasional dependence. There is not even a settled chieftainship; and only in times of war is there a spontaneous and temporary subordina-tion to those who show themselves the best leaders. From the small unformed social aggregates thus characterized, the progress is towards social aggregates of increased size, the parts of which acquire unlikenesses that become ever greater, more definite, and more multitudinous. The units of the society as it evolves, fall into different orders of activities, determined by differences in their local conditions or their individual powers; and there slowly result permanent social structures, of which the primary ones become decided while they are being complicated by secondary ones, growing in their turns decided, and so on.

Even were this all, the analogy would be suggestive; but it is not all. These two metamorphoses have a cause in common. Beginning with an animal composed of like parts, severally living by and for themselves, on what condition only can there be established a change, such that one part comes to perform one kind of function, and another part another kind? Evidently each part can abandon that original state in which it fulfilled for itself all vital needs, and can assume a state in which it fulfils in excess some single vital need, only if its other vital needs are fulfilled for it by other parts that have meanwhile undertaken other special activities. One portion of a living aggregate cannot devote itself exclusively to the respiratory function, and cease to get nutriment for itself, unless other portions that have become exclusively occupied in absorbing nutriment, give it a due supply. That is to say, there must be exchange of services. Organization in an individual creature is made possible only by dependence of each part on all, and of all on each.   Now this is obviously true also of social organization. A member of a primitive society cannot devote himself to an order of activity which satisfies one only of his personal wants, thus ceasing the activities required for satisfying his other personal wants, unless those for whose benefit he carries on his special activity in excess, give him in return the benefits of their special activities. If he makes weapons instead of continuing a hunter, he must be supplied with the produce of the chase on condition that the hunters are supplied with his weapons. If he becomes a cultivator of the soil, no longer defending himself, he must be defended by those who have become specialized defenders. That is to say, mutual dependence of parts is essential for the commencement and advance of social organization, as it is for the commencement and advance of individual organization.

Even were there no more to be pointed out, it would be clear enough that we are not here dealing with a figurative resemblance, but with a fundamental parallelism in principles of structure. We have but begun to explore the analogy, however. The further we inquire, the closer we find it to be. For what, let us ask, is implied by mutual dependence—by exchange of services? There is implied some mode of communication between mutually-dependent parts. Parts that perform functions for one another's benefit, must have appliances for conveying to one another the products of their respective functions, or for giving to one another the benefits (when these are not material products) which their respective functions achieve. And obviously, in proportion as the organization becomes high, the appliances for carrying on the intercourse must become involved. This we find to hold in both cases. In the lowest types of individual organisms, the exchange of services between the slightly-differentiated parts is effected in a slow, vague way, by an irregular diffusion of the nutrient matters jointly elaborated, and by an irregular propagation of feeble stimuli, causing a rude co-ordination in the actions of the parts. It is thus, also, with small and simple social aggregates. No definite arrangements for interchanging services exist; but only indefinite ones. Barter of products—food, skins, weapons, or what not—takes place irregularly between individual producers and consumers throughout the whole social body : there is no trading or distributing system, as, in the rudimentary animal, there is no vascular system. So, too, the social organism of low type, like the individual organism of low type, has no appliances for combining the actions of its remoter parts. When co-operation of them against an enemy is called for, there is nothing but the spread of an alarm from man to man throughout the scattered population; just as in an undeveloped kind of animal, there is merely a slow undirected diffusion of stimulus from one point to all others. In either case, the evolution of a larger, more complex, more active organism, implies an increasingly-efficient set of agencies for conveying from part to part the material products of the respective parts, and an increasingly-efficient set of agencies for making the parts co-operate, so that the times and amounts of their activities may be kept in fit relations. And this, the facts everywhere show us. In the individual organism as it advances to a high structure, no matter of what class, there arises an elaborate system of channels through which the common stock of nutritive matters (here added to by absorption, there changed by secretion, in this place purified by excretion, and in another modified by exchange of gases) is distributed throughout the body for the feeding of the various parts, severally occupied in their special actions; while in the social organism as it advances to a high structure, no matter of what political type, there develops an extensive and complicated trading organization for the distribution of commodities, which, sending its heterogeneous currents through the kingdom by channels that end in retailers' shops, brings within reach of each citizen the necessaries and luxuries that have been produced by others, while he has been producing his commodity or small part of a commodity, or performing some other function or small part of a function, beneficial to the rest. Similarly, development of the individual organism, be its class what it may, is always accompanied by development of a nervous system which renders the combined actions of the parts prompt and duly proportioned, so making possible the adjustments required for meeting the varying contingencies; while, along with development of the social organism, there always goes development of directive centres, general and local, with established arrangements for inter-changing information and instigation, serving to adjust the rates and kinds of activities going on in different parts.

Now if there exists this fundamental kinship, there can be no rational apprehension of the truths of Sociology until there has been reached a rational apprehension of the truths of Biology. The services of the two sciences are, indeed, reciprocal. We have but to glance back at its progress, to see that Biology owes the cardinal idea on which we have been dwelling, to Sociology; and that having derived from Sociology this explanation of development, it gives it back to Sociology greatly increased in definiteness, enriched by countless illustrations, and fit for extension in new directions. The luminous conception first set forth by one whom we may claim as our countryman by blood, though French by birth, M. Milne-Edwards—the conception of "the physiological division of labour," obviously originates from the generalization previously reached in Political Economy. Recognition of the advantages gained by a society when different groups of its members devote themselves to different industries, for which they acquire special aptitudes and surround themselves with special facilities, led to recognition of the advantages which an individual organism gains when parts of it, originally alike and having like activities, divide these activities among them; so that each taking a special kind of activity acquires a special fitness for it.   But when carried from Sociology to Biology, this conception was forthwith greatly expanded. Instead of being limited to the functions included in nutrition, it was found applicable to all functions whatever. It turned out that the arrangements of the entire organism, and not of the viscera alone, conform to this fundamental principle—even the differences arising among the limbs, originally alike, were seen to be interpretable by it. And then mark that the idea thus developed into an all-embracing truth in Biology, returns to Sociology ready to be for it, too, an all-embracing truth. For it now becomes manifest that not to industrial arrangements only does the principle of the division of labour apply, but to social arrangements in general. The progress of organization, from that first step by which there arose a controlling chief, partially distinguished by his actions from those controlled, has been everywhere the same. Be it in the growth of a regulative class more or less marked off from classes regulated—be it in the partings of this regulative class into political, ecclesiastical, etc.—be it in those distinctions of duties within each class which are signified by gradations of rank; we may trace everywhere that fundamental law shown us by industrial organization. And when we have once adequately grasped this truth which Biology borrows from Sociology and returns with vast interest, the aggregate of phenomena which a society at any moment presents, as well as the series of developmental changes through which it has risen to them, become suddenly illuminated, and the *rationale* comparatively clear.

After a recognition of this fundamental kinship there can be no difficulty in seeing how important, as an introduction to the study of social life, is a familiarization with the truths of individual life. For individual life, while showing us this division of labour, this exchange of services, in many and varied ways, shows it in ways easily traced; because the structures and functions are presented in directly-perceivable forms. And only when multitudinous biological examples have stamped on the mind the conception of a growing inter-dependence that goes along with a growing specialization, and have thus induced a habit of thought, will its sociological applications be duly appreciated.

Turn we now from the indirect influence which Biology exerts on Sociology, by supplying it with rational conceptions of social development and organization, to the direct influence it exerts by furnishing an adequate theory of the social unit—Man. For while Biology is mediately connected with Sociology by a certain parallelism between the groups of phenomena they deal with, it is immediately connected with Sociology by having within its limits this creature whose properties originate social evolution. The human being is at once the terminal problem of Biology and the initial factor of Sociology.

If Man were uniform and unchangeable, so that those attributes of him which lead to social phenomena could be learnt and dealt with as constant, it would not much concern the sociologist to make himself master of other biological truths than those cardinal ones above dwelt upon. But since, in common with every other creature, Man is modifiable—since his modifications, like those of every other creature, are ultimately determined by surrounding conditions—and since surrounding conditions are in part constituted by social arrangements; it becomes requisite that the sociologist should acquaint himself with the laws of modification to which organized beings in general conform. Unless he does this he must continually err, both in thought and deed. As thinker, he will fail to understand the increasing action and reaction of institutions and character, each slowly modifying the other through successive generations. As actor, his furtherance of this or that public policy, being unguided by a true theory of the effects wrought on citizens, will probably be mischievous rather than beneficial; since there are more ways of going wrong than of going right. How needful is enlightenment on this point, will be seen on remembering that scarcely anywhere is attention given to the modifications which a new agency, political or other, will produce in men's natures. Immediate influence on actions is alone contemplated; and the immeasurably more important influence on the bodies and minds of future generations, is wholly ignored.

Yet the biological truths which should check this random political speculation and rash political action, are conspicuous; and might, one would have thought, have been recognized by everyone, even without special preparation in Biology. That faculties and powers of all orders, while they grow by exercise, dwindle when not used; and that alterations of nature descend to posterity; are facts continually thrust on men's attention, and more or less admitted by each. Though the evidence of heredity, when looked at in detail, seems obscure, because of the multitudinous differences of parents and of ancestors, which all take their varying shares in each new product; yet, when looked at in the mass, the evidence is overwhelming. Not to dwell on the countless proofs furnished by domesticated animals of many kinds, as modified by breeders, the proofs furnished by the human races themselves are amply sufficient. That each variety of man goes on so reproducing itself that adjacent generations are nearly alike, however appreciable may sometimes be the divergence in a long series of generations, is undeniable. Chinese are recognizable as Chinese in whatever part of the globe we see them; every one assumes a black ancestry for any negro he meets; and no one doubts that the less-marked racial varieties have great degrees of persistence. On the other hand, it is unquestionable that the likenesses which the members of one human stock preserve, generation after generation, where the conditions of life remain constant, give place to unlikenesses that slowly increase in the course of centuries and thousands of years, if the members of that stock, spreading into different habitats, fall under different sets of conditions. If we assume the original unity of the human race, we have no alternative but to admit such divergences consequent on such causes; and even if we do not assume this original unity, we have still, among the races classed by the community of their languages as Aryan, abundant proofs that subjection to different modes of life, produces in course of ages permanent bodily and mental differences: the Hindu and the Englishman, the Greek and the Dutchman, have acquired undeniable contrasts of nature, physical and psychical, which can be ascribed to nothing but the continuous effects of circumstances, material, moral, social, on the activities and therefore on the constitution. So that, as above said, it might have been expected that biological training would scarcely be needed to impress men with these large facts, all-important as elements in sociological conclusions.

As it is, however, we see that a deliberate study of Biology cannot be dispensed with. It is requisite that these scattered evidences which but few citizens put together and think about, should be set before them in an orderly way; and that they should recognize in them the universal truths which living things exhibit. There requires a multiplicity of illustrations, various in their kinds, often repeated and dwelt upon. Only thus can there be produced an adequately-strong conviction that all organic beings are modifiable, that modifications are inheritable, and that therefore the remote issues of any new influence brought to bear on the members of a community must be serious.

To give a more definite and effective shape to this general inference, let me here comment on certain courses pursued by philanthropists and legislators eager for immediate good results, but pursued without regard to biological truths which, if borne in mind, would make them hesitate if not desist.

Every species of creature goes on multiplying till it reaches the limit at which its mortality from all causes balances its fertility. Diminish its mortality by removing or mitigating any one of these causes, and inevitably its numbers increase until mortality and fertility are again in equilibrium. However many injurious influences are taken away, the same thing holds; for the reason that the remaining injurious influences grow more intense. Either the pressure on the means of subsistence becomes greater; or some enemy of the species, multiplying in proportion to the abundance of its prey, becomes more destructive; or some disease, encouraged by greater proximity, becomes more prevalent. This general truth, everywhere exemplified among inferior races of beings, holds of the human race. True, it is in this case variously traversed and obscured. By emigration, the limits against which population continually presses are partially evaded; by improvements in production, they are continually removed further away; and along with increase of knowledge there comes an avoidance of detrimental agencies. Still, these are but qualifications of an inevitable action and reaction.

Let us here glance at the relation between this general truth and the legislative measures adopted to ward off certain causes of death. Every individual eventually dies from inability to withstand some environing action. It may be a mechanical force that cannot be resisted by the strengths of his bodily structures; it may be a deleterious gas which, absorbed into his blood, so deranges the processes throughout his body as finally to overthrow their balance; or it may be an absorption of his bodily heat by surrounding things, that is too great for his enfeebled functions to meet. In all cases, however, it is one, or some, of the many forces to which he is exposed, and in presence of which his vital activities have to be carried on. He may succumb early or late, according to the goodness of his structure and the incidents of his career. But in the natural working of things, those having imperfect structures succumb before they have offspring: leaving those with fitter structures to produce the next generation. And obviously, the working of this process is such that as many will continue to live and to reproduce as can do so under the conditions then existing: if the assemblage of influences becomes more difficult to withstand, a larger number of the feebler disappear early ; if the assemblage of influences is made more favourable by the removal of, or mitigation of, some unfavourable influence, there is an increase in the number of the feebler who survive and leave posterity. Hence two proximate results, conspiring to the same ultimate result. First, population increases at a greater rate than it would otherwise have done : so subjecting all persons to certain other destroying agencies in more-intense forms. Second, by intermarriage of the feebler who now survive, with the stronger who would otherwise have alone survived, the general constitution is brought down to the level of strength required to meet these more-favourable conditions. That is to say, there by-and-by arises a state of things under which a general decrease in the power of withstanding this mitigated destroying cause, and a general increase in the activity of other destroying causes, consequent on greater numbers, bring mortality and fertility into the same relation as before—there is a somewhat larger number of a somewhat weaker race.

There are further ways in which this process necessarily works a like general effect, however far it is carried. For as fast as more and more detrimental agencies are removed or mitigated, and as fast as there goes on an increasing survival and propagation of those having delicately-balanced constitutions, there arise new destructive agencies. Let the average vitality be diminished by more effectually guarding the weak against adverse conditions, and inevitably there come fresh diseases. A general constitution previously able to bear without derangement certain variations in atmospheric conditions and certain degrees of other unfavourable actions, if lowered in tone, will become subject to new kinds of perturbation and new causes of death. In illustration, I need but refer to the many diseases from which civilized races suffer, but which were not known to the uncivilized. Nor is it only by such new causes of death that the rate of mortality, when decreased in one direction increases in another. The very precautions against death are themselves in some measure new causes of death. Every further appliance for meeting an evil, every additional expenditure of effort, every extra tax to meet the cost of supervision, becomes a fresh obstacle to living. For always in a society where population is pressing on the means of subsistence, and where the efforts required to fulfil vital needs are so great that they here and there cause premature death, the powers of producers cannot be further strained by calling on them to support a new class of non-producers, without, in some cases, increasing the wear and tear to a fatal extent. And in proportion as this policy is carried further—in proportion as the enfeeblement of constitution is made greater, the required precautions multiplied, and the cost of maintaining these precautions augmented; it must happen that the increasing physiological expenditure thrown on these enfeebled constitutions, must make them succumb so much the earlier : the mortality evaded in one shape must come round in another.

' The clearest conception of the state brought about, will be gained by supposing the society thus produced to consist of old people. Age differs from maturity and youth in being less able to withstand influences that tend to derange the functions, as well as less able to bear the efforts needed to get the food, clothing, and shelter, by which resistance to these influences may be carried on ; and where no aid is received from the younger, this decreased strength and increased liability to derangement by ·incident forces, make the life of age difficult and wearisome. Those who, though young, have weak constitutions, are much in the same position : their liabilities to derangement are similarly multiplied, and where they have to support themselves, they are similarly over-taxed by the effort, relatively great to them and made greater by the maintaining of precautions. A society of enfeebled people, then, must lead a life like that led by a society of people who had outlived the vigour of maturity, and yet had none to help them; and their life must also be like in lacking that overflowing energy which, while it makes labours easy, makes enjoyments keen. In proportion as vigour declines, not only do the causes of pain multiply, while the tax on the energies becomes more trying, but the possibilities of pleasure decrease : many delights demanding, or accompanying, exertion are shut out; and others fail to raise the flagging spirits. So that, to sum up, lowering the average type of constitution to a level of strength *below that which meets without difficulty the ordinary strains and per-turbations and dangers,* while it fails eventually to diminish the rate of mortality, makes life more a burden and less a gratification.

I am aware that this reasoning may be met by the criticism that, carried out rigorously, it would negative social ameliorations in general. Some, perhaps, will say that even those measures by which order is maintained, might be opposed on the ground that there results from them a kind of men less capable of self-protec-tion than would otherwise exist. And there will doubtless be suggested the corollary that no influences detrimental to health ought to be removed. I am not concerned to meet such criti-cisms, because I do not mean the conclusions above indicated to be taken without qualification. Manifestly, up to a certain point, the removal of destructive causes leaves a balance of benefit. The simple fact that with a largely-augmented population, longevity is greater now than heretofore, goes far towards showing that up to the time lived through by those who die in our day, there had been a decrease of the causes of mortality in some directions, greater than their increase in other directions. Though a considerable drawback may be suspected —though, on observing how few thoroughly-strong people we meet, and how prevalent are chronic ailments notwithstanding the care taken of health, it may be inferred that bodily life now is lower in quality than it was, though greater in quantity; yet there has probably been gained a surplus of advantage. All I wish to show is, that there are limits to the good gained by such a policy. It is supposed in the Legislature, and by the public at large, that if, by measures taken, a certain number of deaths by disease have been prevented, so much pure benefit has been secured. But it is not so. In any case, there is a set-off from the benefit; and if such measures are greatly multiplied, the deductions may eat up the benefit entirely, and leave an injury in its place. Where such measures ought to stop, is a question that may be left open. Here my purpose is simply to point out the way in which a far-reaching biological truth underlies rational conclusions in Sociology; and also to point out that formidable evils may arise from ignoring it.

Other evils, no less serious, are entailed by legislative actions and by actions of individuals, single and combined, which overlook or disregard a kindred biological truth. Besides an habitual neglect of the fact that the quality of a society is physically lowered by the artificial preservation of its feeblest members, there is an habitual neglect of the fact that the quality of a society is lowered morally and intellectually, by the artificial preservation of those who are least able to take care of themselves.

If anyone denies that children bear likenesses to their progenitors in character and capacity—if he holds that men whose parents and grandparents were habitual criminals, have tendencies as good as those of men whose parents and grandparents were industrious and upright, he may consistently hold that it matters not from what families in a society the successive generations descend. He may think it just as well if the most active, and capable, and prudent, and conscientious people die without issue; while many children are left by the reckless and dishonest. But whoever does not espouse so insane a proposition,

must admit that social arrangements which retard the multiplication of the mentally-best, and facilitate the multiplication of
the mentally-worst, must be extremely injurious.

For if the unworthy are helped to increase, by shielding them
from that mortality which their unworthiness would naturally
entail, the effect is to produce, generation after generation, a
greater unworthiness. From diminished use of self-conserving
faculties already deficient, there must result, in posterity, still
smaller amounts of self-conserving faculties. The general law
which we traced above in its bodily applications, may be traced
here in its mental applications. Removal of certain difficulties
and dangers which have to be met by intelligence and activity,
is followed by a decreased ability to meet difficulties and dangers.
Among children born to the more capable who marry with the
less capable, thus artificially preserved, there is not simply a
lower average power of self-preservation than would else have
existed, but the incapacity reaches in some cases a greater
extreme. Smaller difficulties and dangers become fatal in
proportion as greater ones are warded off. Nor is this the whole
mischief. For such members of a population as do not take care
of themselves, but are taken care of by the rest, inevitably bring
on the rest extra exertion; either in supplying them with the
necessaries of life, or in maintaining over them the required
supervision, or in both. That is to say, in addition to self-con-
servation and the conservation of their own offspring, the best,
having to undertake the conservation of the worst, and of their
offspring, are subject to an overdraw upon their energies. In
some cases this stops them from marrying; in other cases it
diminishes the numbers of their children; in other cases it causes
inadequate feeding of their children; in other cases it brings
their children to orphanhood—in every way tending to arrest the
increase of the best, to deteriorate their constitutions, and to pull
them down towards the level of the worst.

Fostering the good-for-nothing at the expense of the good, is
an extreme cruelty. It is a deliberate storing-up of miseries for

future generations. There is no greater curse to posterity than that of bequeathing them an increasing population of imbeciles and idlers and criminals. ·To aid the bad in multiplying, is, in effect, the same as maliciously providing for our descendants a multitude of enemies. It may be doubted whether the maudlin philanthropy which, looking only at direct mitigations, persistently ignores indirect mischiefs, does not inflict a greater total of misery than the extremest selfishness inflicts. Refusing to consider the remote influences of his incontinent generosity, the thoughtless giver stands but a degree above the drunkard who thinks only of to-day's pleasure and ignores to-morrow's pain, or the spendthrift who seeks immediate delights at the cost of ultimate poverty. In one respect, indeed, he is worse ; since, while getting the present pleasure produced in giving pleasure, he leaves the future miseries to be borne by others—escaping them himself. And calling for still stronger reprobation is that scattering of money prompted by misinterpretation of the saying that "charity covers a multitude of sins." For in the many whom this misinterpretation leads to believe that by large donations they can compound for evil deeds, we may trace an ·element of positive baseness—an effort to get a good place in another world, no matter at what injury to fellow-creatures.

How far the mentally-superior may, with a balance of benefit to society, shield the mentally-inferior from the evil results of their inferiority, is a question too involved to be here discussed at length. Doubtless it is in the order of things that parental affection, the regard of relatives, and the spontaneous sympathy of friends and even of strangers, should mitigate the pains which incapacity has to bear, and the penalties which unfit impulses bring round. Doubtless, in many cases the reactive influence of this sympathetic care which the better take of the worse, is morally beneficial, and in a degree.compensates by good in one direction for evil in another. It may be fully admitted that individual altruism, left to itself, will work advantageously— wherever, at least, it does not go to the extent of helping the

unworthy to multiply.   But an unquestionable injury is done
by agencies which undertake in a wholesale way to foster
good-for-nothings : putting a stop to that natural process of
elimination by which society continually purifies itself.   For
not only by such agencies is this preservation of the worst
and destruction of the best carried further than it would else be,
but there is scarcely any of that compensating advantage which
individual altruism implies.   A mechanically-working State-
apparatus, distributing money drawn from grumbling ratepayers,
produces little or no moralizing effect on the capables to make
up for multiplication of the incapables.   Here, however, it is
needless to dwell on the perplexing questions hence arising.   My
purpose is simply to show that a rational policy must recognize
certain general truths of Biology ; and to insist that only when
study of these general truths, as illustrated throughout the living
world, has woven them into the conceptions of things, is there
gained a strong conviction that disregard of them must cause
enormous mischiefs.[1]

Biological truths and their corollaries, presented under these
special forms as bases for sociological conclusions, are introductory to a more general biological truth including them—a
general biological truth which underlies all rational legislation.
I refer to the truth that every species of organism, including the
human, is always adapting itself, both directly and indirectly, to
its conditions of existence.

The actions which have produced every variety of man,—the
actions which have established in the Negro and the Hindu, constitutions that thrive in climates fatal to Europeans, and in the
Fuegian a constitution enabling him to bear without clothing an
inclemency almost too great for other races well clothed—the
actions which have developed in the Tartar-races nomadic habits
that are almost insurmountable, while they have given to North
American Indians desires and aptitudes which, fitting them for a
hunting life, make a civilized life intolerable—the actions doing

this, are also ever at work moulding citizens into correspondence with their circumstances. While the bodily natures of citizens are being fitted to the physical influences and industrial activities of their locality, their mental natures are being fitted to the structure of the society they live in. Though, as we have seen, there is always an approximate fitness of the social unit to its social aggregate, yet the fitness can never be more than approximate, and re-adjustment is always going on. Could a society remain unchanged, something like a permanent equilibrium between the nature of the individual and the nature of the society would presently be reached. But the type of each society is continually being modified by two causes—by growth, and by the actions, warlike or other, of adjacent societies. Increase in the bulk of a society inevitably leads to change of structure ; as also does any alteration in the ratio of the predatory to the industrial activities. Hence continual social metamorphosis, involving continual alteration of the conditions under which the citizen lives, produces in him an adaptation of character which, tending towards completeness, is ever made incomplete by further social metamorphosis.

While, however, each society, and each successive phase of each society, presents conditions more or less special, to which the natures of citizens adapt themselves ; there are certain general conditions which, in every society, must be fulfilled to a considerable extent before it can hold together, and which must be fulfilled completely before social life can be complete. Each citizen has to carry on his activities in such ways as not to impede other citizens in the carrying-on of their activities more than he is impeded by them. That any citizen may so behave as not to deduct from the aggregate welfare, it is needful that he shall perform such function, or share of function, as is of value equivalent at least to what he consumes ; and it is further needful that, both in discharging his function and in pursuing his pleasure, he shall leave others similarly free to discharge their functions and to pursue their pleasures. Obviously a society formed of units who

16

cannot live without mutual hindrance, is one in which the happiness is of smaller amount than it is in a society formed of units who can live without mutual hindrance—numbers and physical conditions being supposed equal. And obviously the sum of happiness in such a society is still less than that in a society of which the units voluntarily aid one another.

Now, under one of its chief aspects, civilization is a process of developing in citizens a nature capable of fulfilling these all-essential conditions; and, neglecting their superfluities, laws and the appliances for enforcing them, are expressions and embodiments of these all-essential conditions. On the one hand, those severe systems of slavery, and serfdom, and punishment for vagabondage, which characterized the less-developed social types, stand for the necessity that the social unit shall be self-supporting. On the other hand, the punishments for murder, assault, theft, etc., and the penalties on breach of contract, stand for the necessity that, in the course of the activities by which he supports himself, the citizen shall neither directly injure other citizens, nor shall injure them indirectly, by taking or intercepting the returns their activities bring. And it needs no detail to show that a fundamental trait in social progress, is an increase of industrial energy, leading citizens to support themselves without being coerced in the harsh ways once general; that another fundamental trait is the gradual establishment of such a nature in citizens that, while pursuing their respective ends, they injure and impede one another in smaller degrees; and that a concomitant trait is the growth of governmental restraints which more effectually check the remaining aggressiveness. That is to say, while the course of civilization shows us a clearer recognition and better enforcement of these essential conditions, it also shows us a moulding of humanity into correspondence with them.

Along with the proofs thus furnished that the biological law of adaptation, holding of all other species, holds of the human species, and that the change of nature undergone by the human species since societies began to develop, has been an adaptation of it to the conditions implied by harmonious social life, we receive the lesson, that the one thing needful is a rigorous maintenance of these conditions. While all see that the immediate function of our chief social institutions is the securing of an orderly social life by making these conditions imperative, very few see that their further function, and in one sense more important function, is that of fitting men to fulfil these conditions spontaneously. The two functions are inseparable. From the biological laws we have been contemplating, it is, on the one hand, an inevitable corollary that if these conditions are maintained, human nature will slowly adapt itself to them; while, on the other hand, it is an inevitable corollary that by no other discipline than subjection to these conditions, can fitness to the social state be produced. Enforce these conditions, and adaptation to them will continue. Relax these conditions, and by so much there will be a cessation of the adaptive changes. Abolish these conditions, and, after the consequent social dissolution, there will commence (unless they are re-established) an adaptation to the conditions then resulting—those of savage life. These are conclusions from which there is no escape, if Man is subject to the laws of life in common with living things in general.

It may, indeed, be rightly contended that if those who are but little fitted to the social state are rigorously subjected to these conditions, evil will result: intolerable restraint, if it does not deform or destroy life, will be followed by violent reaction. We are taught by analogy, that greatly-changed circumstances from which there is no escape, fail to produce adaptation because they produce death. Men having constitutions fitted for one climate, cannot be fitted to an extremely-different climate by persistently living in it, because they do not survive, generation after generation. Such changes can be brought about only by slow spreadings of the race through intermediate regions having intermediate climates, to which successive generations are accustomed little by little. And doubtless the like holds mentally. The intellectual and emotional natures required for high civilization, are not to be obtained by thrusting on the completely-uncivilized, the needful activities and restraints in unqualified forms: gradual decay and death, rather than adaptation, would result. But so long as a society's institutions are indigenous, no danger is to be apprehended from a too-strict maintenance of the conditions to the ideally-best social life; since there can exist neither the required appreciation of them nor the required appliances for enforcing them. Only in those abnormal cases where a race of one type is subject to a race of much-superior type, is this qualification pertinent. In our own case, as in the cases of all societies having populations approximately homogeneous in character, and having institutions evolved by that character, there may rightly be aimed at the greatest rigour possible. The merciful policy, no less than the just policy, is that of insisting that these all-essential requirements of self-support and non-aggression, shall be conformed to ——the just policy, because failing to insist is failing to protect the better or more-adapted natures against the worse or less-adapted; the merciful policy, because the pains accompanying the process of adaptation to the social state *must* be gone through, and it is better that they should be gone through once than gone through twice, as they have to be when any relaxation of these conditions permits retrogression.

Thus, that which sundry precepts of the current religion embody—that which ethical systems, intuitive or utilitarian, equally urge, is also that which Biology, generalizing the laws of life at large, dictates. All further requirements are unimportant compared with this primary requirement, that each shall so live as neither to burden others nor to injure others. And all further appliances for influencing the actions and natures of men, are unimportant compared with those serving to maintain and increase the conformity to this primary requirement. But unhappily, legislators and philanthropists, busy with schemes which, instead of aiding adaptation, indirectly hinder it, give little attention to the enforcing and improving of those arrangements by which adaptation is effected.

And here, on behalf of the few who uphold this policy of natural discipline, let me emphatically repudiate the name of *laissez-faire* as applied to it, and emphatically condemn the counter-policy as involving a *laissez-faire* of the most vicious kind. While holding that, when the State leaves each citizen to get what good for himself he can, and to suffer what evil he brings on himself, such a let-alone policy is eventually beneficial; I contend that, when the State leaves him to bear the evils inflicted by other citizens, and can be induced to defend him only at a ruinous cost, such a let-alone policy is both immediately and remotely injurious. When a Legislature takes from the worthy the things they have laboured for, that it may give to the unworthy the things they have not earned—when cause and consequence, joined in the order of Nature, are thus divorced by law-makers; then may properly come the suggestion—"Cease your interference." But when, in any way, direct or indirect, the unworthy deprive the worthy of their dues, or impede them in the quiet pursuit of their ends, then may properly come the demand—"Interfere promptly; and be, in fact, the protectors you are in name." Our politicians and philanthropists, impatient with a salutary *laissez-faire*, tolerate and even defend a *laissez-faire* that is in the highest degree mischievous. Without hesitation, this regulative agency we call the Government takes from us some £100,000 a year to pay for Art-teaching and to establish Art-museums; while, in guarding us against robbers and murderers, it makes convictions difficult by demurring to the cost of necessary evidence: even the outlay for a plan, admitted by the taxing-master, being refused by the Treasury! Is not that a disastrous *laissez-faire?* While millions are voted without a murmur for an expedition to rescue a meddling consul from a half-savage king, our Executive resists the spending of a few extra thousands to pay more judges: the result being not simply vast arrears and long delays, but immense injustices of other kinds,—costs being run up in cases which lawyers know will never be heard, and which, when brought into court, the over-burdened judges get rid of by appointing junior counsel as referees: an arrangement under which the suitors have not simply to pay over again all their agents, at extra rates, but have also to pay their judges.[2] Is not that, too, a flagitious *laissez-faire?* Though, in our solicitude for Negroes, we have been spending £50,000 a year to stop the East-African slave-trade, and failing to do it, yet only now are we providing protection for our own sailors against unscrupulous shipowners—only now have sailors, betrayed into bad ships, got something more than the option of risking death by drowning or going to prison for breach of contract! Shall we not call that, also, a *laissez-faire* that is almost wicked in its indifference? At the same time that the imperativeness of teaching all children to write, and to spell, and to parse, and to know where Timbuctoo lies, is being agreed to with acclamation, and vast sums raised that these urgent needs may be met, it is not thought needful that citizens should be enabled to learn the laws they have to obey; and though these laws are so many commands which, on any rational theory, the Government issuing them ought to enforce, yet in a great mass of cases it does nothing when told that they have been broken, but leaves the injured to try and enforce them at their own risk, if they please. Is not that, again, a demoralizing *laissez-faire*—an encouragement to wrong-doing by a half-promise of impunity? Once more, what shall we say of the *laissez-faire* which cries out because the civil administration of justice costs us £800,000 a year—because to protect men's rights we annually spend half as much again as would build an ironclad!—because to prevent fraud and enforce contracts we lay out each year nearly as much as our largest distiller pays in spirit-duty!—what, I ask, shall we say of the *laissez-faire* which thus thinks it an extravagance that one-hundredth part of our national revenue should go in maintaining the vital condition to national well-being? Is not that a *laissez-faire* which we might be tempted to call insane, did not most sane people agree in it? And thus it is throughout. The policy of quiescence is adopted where active interference is all-essential ; while time, and energy, and money, are absorbed in interfering with things that should be left to themselves. Those who condemn the let-alone policy in respect to matters which, to say the least, are not of vital importance, advocate or tolerate the let-alone policy in respect to vitally-important matters. Contemplated from the biological point of view, their course is doubly mischievous. They impede adaptation of human nature to the social state, both by what they do and by what they leave undone.

Neither the limits of this chapter, nor its purpose, permit exposition of the various other truths which Biology yields as data for Sociology. Enough has been said in proof of that which was to be shown—the use of biological study as a preparation for grasping sociological truths.

The effect to be looked for from it, is that of giving strength and clearness to convictions otherwise feeble and vague. Sundry of the doctrines I have presented under their biological aspects, are doctrines admitted in considerable degrees. Such acquaintance with the laws of life as they have gathered incidentally, lead many to suspect that appliances for preserving the physically-feeble, bring results that are not wholly good. Others there are who occasionally get glimpses of evils caused by fostering the reckless and the stupid. But their suspicions and qualms fail to determine their conduct, because the *inevitableness* of the bad consequences has not been made adequately clear by the study of Biology at large. When countless illustrations have shown them that all strength, all faculty, all fitness, presented by every living thing, has arisen partly by a growth of each power consequent on exercise of it, and partly by the more frequent survival and greater multiplication of the better-endowed individuals, entailing gradual disappearance of the worse-endowed—when it is seen that all perfection, bodily and mental, has been achieved through this process, and that suspension of it must cause cessation of progress, while reversal of

it would bring universal decay—when it is seen that the mischiefs entailed by disregard of these truths, though they may
be slow, are certain; there comes a conviction that social
policy must be conformed to them, and that to ignore them is
madness.

Did not experience prepare one to find everywhere a degree of
irrationality remarkable in beings who distinguish themselves as
rational, one might have assumed that, before devising modes of
dealing with citizens in their corporate relations, special attention
would be given to the natures of these citizens individually considered, and by implication to the natures of living things at
large. Put a carpenter into a blacksmith's shop, and set him to
forge, to weld, to harden, to anneal, etc., and he will not need the
blacksmith's jeers to show him how foolish is the attempt to
make and mend tools before he has learnt the properties of iron.
Let the carpenter challenge the blacksmith, who knows little
about wood in general and nothing about particular kinds of
wood, to do his work, and unless the blacksmith declines to
make himself a laughing-stock, he is pretty certain to saw askew,
to choke up his plane, and presently to break his tools or cut his
fingers. But while everyone sees the folly of supposing that
wood or iron can be shaped and fitted, without an apprentice-
ship during which their ways of behaving are made familiar; no
one sees any folly in undertaking to devise institutions, and to
shape human nature in this way or that way, without a preliminary study of Man, and of Life in general as explaining Man's
life. For simple functions we insist on elaborate special preparations extending through years; while for the most complex
function, to be adequately discharged not even by the wisest, we
require no preparation!

How absurd are the prevailing conceptions about these
matters, we shall see still more clearly on turning to consider
that more special discipline which should precede the study of
Sociology; namely, the study of Mental Science.

CHAPTER XV.

PREPARATION IN PSYCHOLOGY.

PROBABLY astonishment would make the reporters drop their pencils, were any member of Parliament to enunciate a psychological principle as justifying his opposition to a proposed measure. That some law of association of ideas, or some trait in emotional development, should be deliberately set forth as a sufficient ground for saying "aye" or "no" to a motion for second reading, would doubtless be too much for the gravity of legislators. And along with laughter from many there would come from a few cries of "question:" the entire irrelevancy to the matter in hand being conspicuous. It is true that during debates the possible behaviour of citizens under the suggested arrangements is described. Evasions of this or that provision, difficulties in carrying it out, probabilities of resistance, connivance, corruption, &c., are urged; and these tacitly assert that the mind of man has certain characters, and under the conditions named is likely to act in certain ways. In other words, there is an implied recognition of the truth that the effects of a law will depend on the manner in which human intelligence and human feeling are influenced by it. Experiences of men's conduct which the legislator has gathered, and which lie partially sorted in his memory, furnish him with empirical notions that guide his judgment on each question raised; and he would think it folly to ignore all this unsystematized knowledge about people's characters and actions. But at the same time he regards as foolish the proposal to proceed, not on vaguely-generalized facts, but on facts accurately generalized; and, as still more foolish, the proposal to merge these minor definite generalizations in generalizations expressing the ultimate laws of Mind. Guidance by intuition seems to him much more rational.

Of course, I do not mean to say that his intuition is of small value. How should I say this, remembering the immense accumulation of experiences by which his thoughts have been moulded into harmony with things? We all know that when the successful man of business is urged by wife and daughters to get into Parliament, that they may attain a higher social standing, he always replies that his occupations through life have left him no leisure to prepare himself, by collecting and digesting the voluminous evidence respecting the effects of institutions and policies, and that he fears he might do mischief. If the heir to some large estate, or scion of a noble house powerful in the locality, receives a deputation asking him to stand for the county, we constantly read that he pleads inadequate knowledge as a reason for declining: perhaps hinting that after ten years spent in the needful studies, he may have courage to undertake the heavy responsibilities proposed to him. So, too, we have the familiar fact that when, at length, men who have gathered vast stores of political information, gain the confidence of voters who know how carefully they have thus fitted themselves, it still perpetually happens that after election they find they have entered on their work prematurely. It is true that beforehand they had sought anxiously through the records of the past, that they might avoid legislative errors of multitudinous kinds, like those committed in early times. Nevertheless when Acts are proposed referring to matters dealt with in past generations by Acts long since cancelled or obsolete, immense inquiries open before them. Even limiting themselves to the 1126 Acts repealed in 1823—9, and the further 770 repealed in 1861, they find that to learn what these aimed at, how they worked, why they failed, and whence arose the mischiefs they wrought, is an arduous task, which yet they feel bound to undertake lest they should re-inflict these mischiefs ; and hence the reason why so many break down under the effort, and retire with health destroyed. Nay, more—on those with constitutions vigorous enough to carry them through such inquiries, there continually presses the duty of making yet further inquiries. Besides tracing the results of abandoned laws in other societies, there is at home, year by year, more futile law-making to be investigated and lessons to be drawn from it ; as, for example, from the 134 Public Acts passed in 1856—7, of which all but 68 are wholly or partially repealed.[1] And thus it happens that, as every autumn shows us, even the strongest men, finding their lives during the recess over-taxed with the needful study, are obliged so to locate themselves that by an occasional day's hard riding after the hounds, or a long walk over the moors with gun in hand, they may be enabled to bear the excessive strain on their nervous systems. Of course, therefore, I am not so unreasonable as to deny that judgments, even empirical, which are guided by such carefully-amassed experiences must be of much worth.

But fully recognizing the vast amount of information which the legislator has laboriously gathered from the accounts of institutions and laws, past and present, here and elsewhere; and admitting that before thus instructing himself he would no more think of enforcing a new law than would a medical student think of plunging an operating-knife into the human body before learning where the arteries ran ; the remarkable anomaly here demanding our attention is, that he objects to anything like analysis of these phenomena he has so diligently collected, and has no faith in conclusions drawn from the *ensemble* of them. Not discriminating very correctly between the word " general " and the word " abstract," and regarding as *abstract* principles what are in nearly all cases *general* principles, he speaks contemptuously of these as belonging to the region of theory, and as not concerning the law-maker. Any wide truth that is insisted upon as being implied in many narrow truths, seems to him remote from reality and unimportant for guidance. The results of recent experiments in legislation he thinks worth attending to; and if any one reminds him of the experiments he has read so much about, that were made in other times and other places, he regards these also, separately taken, as deserving of consideration. But if, instead of studying special classes of legislative experiments, someone compares many classes together, generalizes the results, and proposes to be guided by the generalization, he shakes his head sceptically. And his scepticism passes into ridicule if it is proposed to affiliate such generalized results on the laws of Mind. To prescribe for society on the strength of countless unclassified observations, appears to him a sensible course; but to colligate and systematize the observations so as to educe tendencies of human behaviour displayed throughout cases of numerous kinds, to trace these tendencies to their sources in the mental natures of men, and thence to draw conclusions for guidance, appears to him a visionary course.

Let us look at some of the fundamental facts he ignores, and at the results of ignoring them.

Rational legislation, based as it can only be on a true theory of conduct, which is derivable only from a true theory of mind, must recognize as a datum the direct connexion of action with feeling. That feeling and action bear a constant ratio, is a statement needing qualification; for at the one extreme there are automatic actions which take place without feeling, and at the other extreme there are feelings so intense that, by deranging the vital functions, they impede or arrest action. But speaking of those activities which life in general presents, it is a law tacitly recognized by all, though not distinctly formulated, that action and feeling vary together in their amounts. Passivity and absence of facial expression, both implying rest of the muscles, are held to show that there is being experienced neither much sensation nor much emotion. While the degree of external demonstration, be it in movements that rise finally to spasms and contortions, or be it in sounds that end in laughter and shrieks and groans, is habitually accepted as a measure of the pleasure or pain, sensational or emotional. And so, too, where continued expenditure of energy is seen, be it in a violent struggle to escape or be it in the persevering pursuit of an object, the quantity of effort is held to show the quantity of feeling.

This truth, undeniable in its generality, whatever qualifications secondary truths make in it, must be joined with the truth that cognition does *not* produce action. If I tread on a pin, or unawares dip my hand into very hot water, I start: the strong sensation produces motion without any thought intervening. Conversely, the proposition that a pin pricks, or that hot water scalds, leaves me quite unmoved. True, if to one of these propositions is joined the idea that a pin is about to pierce my skin, or to the other the idea that some hot water will fall on it, there results a tendency, more or less decided, to shrink. But that which causes shrinking is the ideal pain. The statement that the pin will hurt or the water scald, produces no effect so long as there is nothing beyond a recognition of its meaning: it produces an effect only when the pain verbally asserted, becomes a pain actually conceived as impending—only when there rises in consciousness a representation of the pain, which is a faint form of the pain as before felt. That is to say, the cause of movement here, as in other cases, is a feeling and not a cognition.   What we see even in these simplest actions, runs through actions of all degrees of complexity. It is never the knowledge which is the moving agent in conduct; but it is always the feeling which goes along with that knowledge, or is excited by it. Though the drunkard knows that after to-day's debauch will come to-morrow's headache, yet he is not deterred by consciousness of this truth, unless the penalty is distinctly represented—unless there rises in his consciousness a vivid idea of the misery to be borne—unless there is excited in him an adequate amount of feeling antagonistic to his desire for drink. Similarly with im-

providence in general.   If coming evils are imagined with clearness and the threatened sufferings ideally felt, there is a due
check on the tendency to take immediate gratifications without
stint; but in the absence of that consciousness of future ills
which is constituted by the ideas of pains, distinct or vague,
the passing desire is not opposed effectually.   The truth that
recklessness brings distress, fully acknowledged though it may
be, remains inoperative.   The mere cognition does not affect
conduct—conduct is affected only when the cognition passes out
of that intellectual form in which the idea of distress is little more
than verbal, into a form in which this term of the proposition is
developed into a vivid imagination of distress—a mass of painful
feeling.   It is thus with conduct of every kind.   See this
group of persons clustered at the river side.   A boat has upset,
and some one is in danger of drowning.   The fact that in the
absence of aid the youth in the water will shortly die, is known
to them all.   That by swimming to his assistance his life may
be saved, is a proposition denied by none of them.   The duty
of helping fellow-creatures who are in difficulties, they have
been taught all their lives ; and they will severally admit that
running a risk to prevent a death is praiseworthy.   Nevertheless,
though sundry of them can swim, they do nothing beyond shout-
ing for assistance or giving advice.   But now here comes one
who, tearing off his coat, plunges in to the rescue.   In what does
he differ from the others ?   Not in knowledge.   Their cognitions
are equally clear with his.   They know as well as he does that
death is impending ; and know, too, how it may be prevented.   In
him, however, these cognitions arouse certain correlative emotions more strongly than they are aroused in the rest.   Groups
of feelings are excited in all ; but whereas in the others the
deterrent feelings of fear, &c., preponderate, in him there is a
surplus of the feelings excited by sympathy, joined, it may be,
with others not of so high a kind.   In each case, however, the
behaviour is not determined by knowledge, but by emotion.
Obviously, change in the actions of these passive spectators is

not to be effected by making their cognitions clearer, but by making their higher feelings stronger.

Have we not here, then, a cardinal psychological truth to which any rational system of human discipline must conform? Is it not manifest that a legislation which ignores it and tacitly assumes its opposite, will inevitably fail? Yet much of our legislation does this; and we are at present, legislature and nation together, eagerly pushing forward schemes which proceed on the postulate that conduct is determined not by feelings, but by cognitions.

For what else is the assumption underlying this anxious urging-on of organizations for teaching? What is the root-notion common to Secularists and Denominationalists, but the notion that spread of knowledge is the one thing needful for bettering behaviour? Having both swallowed certain statistical fallacies, there has grown up in them the belief that State-education will check ill-doing. In newspapers, they have often met with comparisons between the numbers of criminals who can read and write and the numbers who can not; and finding the numbers who can not greatly exceed the numbers who can, they accept the inference that ignorance is the cause of crime. It does not occur to them to ask whether other statistics, similarly drawn up, would not prove with like conclusiveness that crime is caused by absence of ablutions, or by lack of clean linen, or by bad ventilation, or by want of a separate bed-room. Go through any jail and ascertain how many prisoners had been in the habit of taking a morning bath, and you would find that criminality habitually went with dirtiness of skin. Count up those who had possessed a second suit of clothes, and a comparison of the figures would show you that but a small percentage of criminals were habitually able to change their garments. Inquire whether they had lived in main streets or down courts, and you would discover that nearly all urban crime comes from holes and corners. Similarly, a fanatical advocate of total abstinence or of sanitary improvement, could get equally-strong statistical justifications for his belief. But if, not accepting the random inference presented to you that ignorance and crime are cause and effect, you consider, as above, whether crime may not with equal reason be ascribed to various other causes, you are led to see that it is really connected with an inferior mode of life, itself usually consequent on original inferiority of nature; and you are led to see that ignorance is simply one of the concomitants, no more to be held the cause of crime than various other concomitants.

But this obvious criticism, and the obvious counter-conclusion it implies, are not simply overlooked, but, when insisted on, seem powerless to affect the belief which has taken possession of men. Disappointment alone will now affect it. A wave of opinion reaching a certain height, cannot be changed by any evidence or argument; but has to spend itself in the gradual course of things before a reaction of opinion can arise. Otherwise it would be incomprehensible that this confidence in the curative effects of teaching, which men have carelessly allowed to be generated in them by the re-iterations of *doctrinaire* politicians, should survive the direct disproofs yielded by daily experience. Is it not the trouble of every mother and every governess, that perpetual insisting on the right and denouncing the wrong do not suffice? Is it not the constant complaint that on many natures reasoning and explanation and the clear demonstration of consequences are scarcely at all operative; that where they are operative there is a more or less marked difference of emotional nature; and that where, having before failed, they begin to succeed, change of feeling rather than difference of apprehension is the cause? Do we not similarly hear from every housekeeper that servants usually pay but little attention to reproofs; that they go on perversely in old habits, regardless of clear evidence of their foolishness; and that their actions are to be altered not by explanations and reasonings, but by either the fear of penalties or the experience of penalties—that is, by the emotions awakened in them? When we turn from domestic life to the life of the outer world, do not like disproofs everywhere meet us? Are not fraudulent bankrupts educated people, and getters-up of bubble-companies, and makers of adulterated goods, and users of false trade-marks, and retailers who have light weights, and owners of unseaworthy ships, and those who cheat insurance-companies, and those who carry on turf-chicaneries, and the great majority of gamblers? Or, to take a more extreme form of turpitude,—is there not, among those who have committed murder by poison within our memories, a considerable number of the educated—a number bearing as large a ratio to the educated classes as does the total number of murderers to the total population?

This belief in the moralizing effects of intellectual culture, flatly contradicted by facts, is absurd *à priori*. What imaginable connexion is there between the learning that certain clusters of marks on paper stand for certain words, and the getting a higher sense of duty? What possible effect can acquirement of facility in making written signs of sounds, have in strengthening the desire to do right? How does knowledge of the multiplication-table, or quickness in adding and dividing, so increase the sympathies as to restrain the tendency to trespass against fellow-creatures? In what way can the attainment of accuracy in spelling and parsing, &c., make the sentiment of justice more powerful than it was; or why from stores of geographical information, perseveringly gained, is there likely to come increased regard for truth? The irrelation between such causes and such effects, is almost as great as that between exercise of the fingers and strengthening of the legs. One who should by lessons in Latin hope to give a knowledge of geometry, or one who should expect practice in drawing to be followed by expressive rendering of a sonata, would be thought fit for an asylum; and yet he would be scarcely more irrational than are those who by discipline of the intellectual faculties expect to produce better feelings.

This faith in lesson-books and readings is one of the superstitions of the age. Even as appliances to intellectual culture books are greatly over-estimated. Instead of second-hand knowledge being regarded as of less value than first-hand knowledge, and as a knowledge to be sought only where first-hand knowledge cannot be had, it is actually regarded as of greater value. Something gathered from printed pages is supposed to enter into a course of education; but if gathered by observation of Life and Nature, is supposed not thus to enter. Reading is seeing by proxy—is learning indirectly through another man's faculties instead of directly through one's own faculties; and such is the prevailing bias that the indirect learning is thought preferable to the direct learning, and usurps the name of cultivation! We smile when told that savages consider writing as a kind of magic; and we laugh at the story of the negro who hid a letter under a stone, that it might not inform against him when he devoured the fruit he was sent with. Yet the current notions about printed information betray a kindred delusion: a kind of magical efficacy is ascribed to ideas gained through artificial appliances, as compared with ideas otherwise gained. And this delusion, injurious in its effects even on intellectual culture, produces effects still more injurious on moral culture, by generating the assumption that this, too, can be got by reading and the repeating of lessons.

It will, I know, be said that not from intellectual teaching but from moral teaching, is improvement of conduct and diminution of crime looked for. While, unquestionably, many of those who urge on educational schemes believe in the moralizing effects of knowledge in general, it must be admitted that some hold general knowledge to be inadequate, and contend that rules of right conduct must be taught. Already, however, reasons have been given why the expectations even of these, are illusory; proceeding, as they do, on the assumption that the intellectual acceptance of moral precepts will produce conformity to them. Plenty more reasons are forthcoming. I will not dwell on the contradictions to this assumption furnished by the Chinese, to all of whom the high ethical maxims of Confucius are taught, and who yet fail to show us a conduct proportionately exemplary. Nor will I enlarge on the lesson to be derived from the United States, the school-system of which brings up the whole population under the daily influence of chapters which set forth principles of right conduct, and which nevertheless in its political life, and by many of its social occurrences, shows us that conformity to these principles is anything but complete. It will suffice if I limit myself to evidence supplied by our own society, past and present; which negatives, very decisively, these sanguine expectations. For what have we been doing all these many centuries by our religious agencies, but preaching right principles to old and young? What has been the aim of services in our ten thousand churches week after week, but to enforce a code of good conduct by promised rewards and threatened penalties?—the whole population having been for many generations compelled to listen. What have the multitudinous Dissenting chapels been used for, unless as places where pursuance of right and desistance from wrong have been unceasingly commended to all from childhood upwards? And if now it is held that something more must be done—if, notwithstanding perpetual explanations and denunciations and exhortations, the misconduct is so great that society is endangered, why, after all this insistance has failed, is it expected that more insistance will succeed? See here the proposals and the implied beliefs. Teaching by clergymen not having had the desired effect, let us try teaching by schoolmasters. Bible-reading from a pulpit, with the accompaniment of imposing architecture, painted windows, tombs, and "dim religious light," having proved inadequate, suppose we try bible-reading in rooms with bare walls, relieved only by maps and drawings of animals. Commands and interdicts uttered by a surpliced priest to minds prepared by chant and organ-peal, not having been obeyed, let us see whether they will be obeyed when mechanically repeated in schoolboy sing-song to a threadbare usher, amid the buzz of lesson-learning and clatter of slates.

Not very hopeful proposals, one would say; proceeding, as they do, upon one or other of the beliefs, that a moral precept will be effective in proportion as it is received without emotional accompaniment, and that its effectiveness will increase in proportion to the number of times it is repeated. Both these beliefs are directly at variance with the results of psychological analysis and of daily experience. Certainly, such influence as may be gained by addressing moral truths to the intellect, is made greater if the accompaniments arouse an appropriate emotional excitement, as a religious service does; while, conversely, there can be no more effectual way of divesting such moral truths of their impressiveness, than associating them with the prosaic and vulgarizing sounds and sights and smells coming from crowded children. And no less certain is it that precepts often heard and little regarded, lose by repetition the small influence they had. What do public-schools show us?—are the boys rendered merciful to one another by listening to religious injunctions every morning? What do Universities show us?—have perpetual chapels habitually made undergraduates behave better than the average of young men? What do Cathedral-towns show us?—is there in them a moral tone above that of other towns, or must we from the common saying, "the nearer the Church," &c., infer a pervading impression to the contrary? What do clergymen's sons show us?—has constant insistance on right conduct made them conspicuously superior, or do we not rather hear it whispered that something like an opposite effect seems produced. Or, to take one more case, what do religious newspapers show us?—is it that the precepts of Christianity, more familiar to their writers than to other writers, are more clearly to be traced in their articles, or has there not ever been displayed a want of charity in their dealings with opponents, and is it not still displayed?[2] Nowhere do we find that repetition of rules of right, already known but disregarded, produces regard for them; but we find that, contrariwise, it makes the regard for them less than before.[3]

The prevailing assumption is, indeed, as much disproved by analysis as it is contradicted by familiar facts. Already we have seen that the connexion is between action and feeling; and hence the corollary that only by a frequent passing of feeling into action, is the tendency to such action strengthened. Just as two ideas often repeated in a certain order, become coherent in that order; and just as muscular motions, at first difficult to combine properly with one another and with guiding perceptions, become by practice facile, and at length automatic; so the recurring production of any conduct by its prompting emotion, makes that conduct relatively easy. Not by precept, though heard daily; not by example, unless it is followed; but only by action, often caused by the related feeling, can a moral habit be formed. And yet this truth, which Mental Science clearly teaches, and which is in harmony with familiar sayings, is a truth wholly ignored in current educational fanaticisms.

There is ignored, too, the correlative truth; and ignoring it threatens results still more disastrous. While we see an expectation of benefits which the means used cannot achieve, we see no consciousness of injuries which will be entailed by these means. As usually happens with those absorbed in the eager pursuit of some good by governmental action, there is a blindness to the evil reaction on the natures of citizens. Already the natures of citizens have suffered from kindred reactions, due to actions set up centuries ago; and now the mischievous effects are to be increased by further such reactions.

The English people are complained of as improvident. Very few of them lay by in anticipation of times when work is slack; and the general testimony is that higher wages commonly result only in more extravagant living or in drinking to greater excess. As we saw a while since, they neglect opportunities of becoming shareholders in the Companies they are engaged under; and those who are most anxious for their welfare despair on finding how little they do to raise themselves when they have the means. This tendency to seize immediate gratification regardless of future penalty, is commented on as characteristic of the English people ; and contrasts between them and their Continental neighbours having been drawn, surprise is expressed that such contrasts should exist. Improvidence is spoken of as an inexplicable trait of the race—no regard being paid to the fact that races with which it is compared are allied in blood. The people of Norway are economical and extremely prudent. The Danes, too, are thrifty ; and Defoe, commenting on the extravagance of his countrymen, says that a Dutchman gets rich on wages out of which an Englishman but just lives. So, too, if we take the modern Germans. Alike by the complaints of the Americans, that the Germans are ousting them from their own businesses by working hard and living cheaply, and by the success here of German traders and the preference shown for German waiters, we are taught that in other divisions of the Teutonic race there is nothing like this lack of self-control. Nor can we ascribe to such portion of Norman blood as exists among us, this peculiar trait: descendants of the Normans in France are industrious and saving. Why, then, should the English people be improvident? If we seek explanation in their remote lineage, we find none ; but if we seek it in the social conditions to which they have been subject, we find a sufficient explanation. The English are improvident because they have been for ages disciplined in improvidence. Extravagance has been made habitual by shielding them from the sharp penalties extravagance brings. Carefulness has been discouraged by continually showing to the careful that those who were careless did as well as, or better than, themselves. Nay, there have been positive penalties on carefulness. Labourers working hard and paying their way, have constantly found themselves called on to help in supporting the idle around them ; have had their goods taken under distress-warrants, that paupers might be fed ; and eventually have found themselves and their children reduced also to pauperism.[4] Well-conducted poor women, supporting themselves without aid or encouragement, have seen the ill-conducted receiving parish-pay for their illegitimate children. Nay, to such extremes has the process gone, that women with many illegitimate children, getting from the rates a weekly sum for each, have been chosen as wives by men who wanted the sums thus derived! Generation after generation the honest and independent, not marrying till they had means, and striving to bring up their families without assistance, have been saddled with extra burdens, and hindered from leaving a desirable posterity; while the dissolute and the idle, especially when given to that lying and servility by which those in authority are deluded, have been helped to produce and to rear progeny, characterized, like themselves, by absence of the mental traits needed for good citizenship. And then, after centuries during which we have been breeding the race as much as possible from the improvident, and repressing the multiplication of the provident, we lift our hands and exclaim at the recklessness our people exhibit! If men who, for a score generations, had by preference bred from their worst-tempered horses and their least-sagacious dogs, were then to wonder because their horses were vicious and their dogs stupid, we should think the absurdity of their policy paralleled only by the absurdity of their astonishment; but human beings instead of inferior animals being in question, no absurdity is seen either in the policy or in the astonishment.

And now something more serious happens than the overlooking of these evils wrought on men's natures by centuries of demoralizing influences. We are deliberately establishing further such influences. Having, as much as we could, suspended the civilizing discipline of an industrial life so carried on as to achieve self-maintenance without injury to others, we now proceed to suspend that civilizing discipline in another direction. Having in successive generations done our best to diminish the sense of responsibility, by warding-off evils which disregard of responsibility brings, we now carry the policy further by relieving parents from certain other responsibilities which, in the

order of nature, fall on them. By way of checking recklessness, and discouraging improvident marriages, and raising the
conception of duty, we are diffusing the belief that it is not the
concern of parents to fit their children for the business of life;
but that the nation is bound to do this. Everywhere there is a
tacit enunciation of the marvellous doctrine that citizens are not
responsible individually for the bringing-up, each of his own
children, but that these same citizens incorporated into a society,
are each of them responsible for the bringing-up of everybody
else's children! The obligation does not fall upon A in his
capacity of father, to rear the minds as well as the bodies of
his offspring; but in his capacity of citizen, there does fall on
him the obligation of mentally rearing the offspring of B, C,
D, and the rest; who similarly have their direct parental obligations made secondary to their indirect obligations to children
not their own! Already it is estimated that, as matters are now
being arranged, parents will soon pay in school-fees for their own
children, only one-sixth of the amount which is paid by them
through taxes, rates, and voluntary contributions, for children at
large: in terms of money, the claims of children at large to their
care, will be taken as six times the claim of their own children!
And if, looking back forty years, we observe the growth of the
public claim *versus* the private claim, we may infer that the
private claim will presently be absorbed wholly. Already the
correlative theory is becoming so definite and positive that you
meet with the notion, uttered as though it were an unquestionable truth, that criminals are "society's failures." Presently it
will be seen that, since good bodily development, as well as good
mental development, is a pre-requisite to good citizenship, (for
without it the citizen cannot maintain himself, and so avoid
wrong-doing,) society is responsible also for the proper feeding
and clothing of children: indeed, in School-Board discussions,
there is already an occasional admission that no logically-
defensible halting-place can be found between the two. And so
we are progressing towards the wonderful notion, here and there

finding tacit expression, that people are to marry when they feel inclined, and other people are to take the consequences!

And this is thought to be the policy conducive to improvement of behaviour. Men who have been made improvident by being shielded from many of the evil results of improvidence, are now to be made more provident by further shielding them from the evil results of improvidence. Having had their self-control decreased by social arrangements which lessened the need for self-control, other social arrangements are devised which will make self-control still less needful ; and it is hoped so to make self-control greater. This expectation is absolutely at variance with the whole order of things. Life of every kind, human included, proceeds on an exactly-opposite principle. All lower types of beings show us that the rearing of offspring affords the highest discipline for the faculties. The parental instinct is everywhere that which calls out the energies most persistently, and in the greatest degree exercises the intelligence. The self-sacrifice and the sagacity which inferior creatures display in the care of their young, are often commented upon ; and everyone may see that parenthood produces a mental exaltation not otherwise producible. That it is so among mankind is daily proved. Continually we remark that men who were random grow steady when they have children to provide for ; and vain, thoughtless girls, becoming mothers, begin to show higher feelings, and capacities that were not before drawn out. In both there is a daily discipline in unselfishness, in industry, in foresight. The parental relation strengthens from hour to hour the habit of postponing immediate ease and egoistic pleasure to the altruistic pleasure obtained by furthering the welfare of offspring. There is a frequent subordination of the claims of self to the claims of fellow-beings ; and by no other agency can the practice of this subordination be so effectually secured. Not, then, by a decreased, but by an increased, sense of parental responsibility is self-control to be made greater and recklessness to be checked. And yet the policy now so earnestly

17

and undoubtingly pursued is one which will inevitably diminish the sense of parental responsibility. This all-important discipline of parents' emotions is to be weakened that children may get reading and grammar and geography more generally than they would otherwise do. A superficial intellectualization is to be secured at the cost of a deep-seated demoralization.

Few, I suppose, will deliberately assert that information is important and character relatively unimportant. Everyone observes from time to time how much more valuable to himself and others is the workman who, though unable to read, is diligent, sober, and honest, than is the well-taught workman who breaks his engagements, spends days in drinking, and neglects his family. And, comparing members of the upper classes, no one doubts that the spendthrift or the gambler, however good his intellectual training, is inferior as a social unit to the man who, not having passed through the approved *curriculum*, nevertheless prospers by performing well the work he undertakes, and provides for his children instead of leaving them in poverty to the care of relatives. That is to say, looking at the matter in the concrete, all see that for social welfare, good character is more important than much knowledge. And yet the manifest corollary is not drawn. What effect will be produced on character by artificial appliances for spreading knowledge, is not asked. Of the ends to be kept in view by the legislator, all are unimportant compared with the end of character-making; and yet character-making is an end wholly unrecognized.

Let it be seen that the future of a nation depends on the natures of its units; that their natures are inevitably modified in adaptation to the conditions in which they are placed; that the feelings called into play by these conditions will strengthen, while those which have diminished demands on them will dwindle; and it will be seen that the bettering of conduct can be effected, not by insisting on maxims of good conduct, still less by mere intellectual culture, but only by that daily exercise of the higher sentiments and repression of the lower, which results from keeping men subordinate to the requirements of orderly social life—letting them suffer the inevitable penalties of breaking these requirements and reap the benefits of conforming to them. This alone is national education.

One further instance of the need for psychological inquiries as guides to sociological conclusions, may be named—an instance of quite a different kind, but one no less relevant to questions of the time. I refer to the comparative psychology of the sexes. Women, as well as men, are units in a society; and tend by their natures to give that society certain traits of structure and action. Hence the question—Are the mental natures of men and women the same?—is an important one to the sociologist. If they are, an increase of feminine influence is not likely to affect the social type in a marked manner. If they are not, the social type will inevitably be changed by increase of feminine influence.

That men and women are mentally alike, is as untrue as that they are alike bodily. Just as certainly as they have physical differences which are related to the respective parts they play in the maintenance of the race, so certainly have they psychical differences, similarly related to their respective shares in the rearing and protection of offspring. To suppose that along with the unlikenesses between their parental activities there do not go unlikenesses of mental faculties, is to suppose that here alone in all Nature, there is no adjustment of special powers to special functions.[5]

Two classes of differences exist between the psychical, as between the physical, structures of men and women, which are both determined by this same fundamental need — adaptation to the paternal and maternal duties. The first set of differences is that which results from a somewhat-earlier arrest of individual evolution in women than in men; necessitated by the reservation of vital power to meet the cost of reproduction. Whereas, in man, individual evolution continues until the physiological cost of self-maintenance very nearly balances what nutrition supplies, in woman, an arrest of individual development takes place while there is yet a considerable margin of nutrition: otherwise there could be no offspring. Hence the fact that girls come earlier to maturity than boys. Hence, too, the chief contrasts in bodily form: the masculine figure being distinguished from the feminine by the greater relative sizes of the parts which carry on external actions and entail physiological cost—the limbs, and those thoracic viscera which their activity immediately taxes. And hence, too, the physiological truth that throughout their lives, but especially during the child-bearing age, women exhale smaller quantities of carbonic acid, relatively to their weights, than men do; showing that the evolution of energy is relatively less as well as absolutely less. This rather earlier cessation of individual evolution thus necessitated, showing itself in a rather smaller growth of the nervo-muscular system, so that both the limbs which act and the brain which makes them act are somewhat less, has two results on the mind. The mental manifestations have somewhat less of general power or massiveness; and beyond this there is a perceptible falling-short in those two faculties, intellectual and emotional, which are the latest products of human evolution—the power of abstract reasoning and that most abstract of the emotions, the sentiment of justice—the sentiment which regulates conduct irrespective of personal attachments and the likes or dislikes felt for individuals.[6]

After this quantitative mental distinction, which becomes incidentally qualitative by telling most upon the most recent and most complex faculties, there come the qualitative mental distinctions consequent on the relations of men and women to their children and to one another. Though the parental instinct, which, considered in its essential nature, is a love of the helpless, is common to the two; yet it is obviously not identical in the two. That the particular form of it which responds to infantine helplessness is more dominant in women than in men, cannot be questioned. In man the instinct is not so habitually excited by the very helpless, but has a more generalized relation to all the relatively-weak who are dependent upon him. Doubtless, along with this more specialized instinct in women, there go special aptitudes for dealing with infantine life—an adapted power of intuition and a fit adjustment of behaviour. That there is here a mental specialization, joined with the bodily specialization, is undeniable; and this mental specialization, though primarily related to the rearing of offspring, affects in some degree the conduct at large.

The remaining qualitative distinctions between the minds of men and women, are those which have grown out of their mutual relation as stronger and weaker. If we trace the genesis of human character, by considering the conditions of existence through which the human race passed in early barbaric times and during civilization, we shall see that the weaker sex has naturally acquired certain mental traits by its dealings with the stronger. In the course of the struggles for existence among wild tribes, those tribes survived in which the men were not only powerful and courageous, but aggressive, unscrupulous, intensely egoistic. Necessarily, then, the men of the conquering races which gave origin to the civilized races, were men in whom the brutal characteristics were dominant; and necessarily the women of such races, having to deal with brutal men, prospered in proportion as they possessed, or acquired, fit adjustments of nature. How were women, unable by strength to hold their own, otherwise enabled to hold their own? Several mental traits helped them to do this. We may set down, first, the ability to please, and the concomitant love of approbation. Clearly, other things equal, among women living at the mercy of men, those who succeeded most in pleasing would be the most likely to survive and leave posterity. And (recognizing the predominant descent of qualities on the same side) this, acting on successive generations, tended to establish, as a feminine trait, a special solicitude to be approved, and an aptitude of manner to this end. Similarly, the wives of merciless savages must,

other things equal, have prospered in proportion to their powers
of disguising their feelings. Women who betrayed the state of
antagonism produced in them by ill-treatment, would be less
likely to survive and leave offspring than those who concealed
their antagonism; and hence, by inheritance and selection, a
growth of this trait proportionate to the requirement. In
some cases, again, the arts of persuasion enabled women to protect themselves, and by implication their offspring, where, in
the absence of such arts, they would have disappeared early, or
would have reared fewer children. One further ability
may be named as likely to be cultivated and established—the
ability to distinguish quickly the passing feelings of those
around. In barbarous times a woman who could from a movement, tone of voice, or expression of face, instantly detect in her
savage husband the passion that was rising, would be likely to
escape dangers run into by a woman less skilled in interpreting
the natural language of feeling. Hence, from the perpetual
exercise of this power, and the survival of those having most
of it, we may infer its establishment as a feminine faculty.
Ordinarily, this feminine faculty, showing itself in an aptitude
for guessing the state of mind through the external signs,
ends simply in intuitions formed without assignable reasons;
but when, as happens in rare cases, there is joined with
it skill in psychological analysis, there results an extremely-
remarkable ability to interpret the mental states of others. Of
this ability we have a living example never hitherto paralleled
among women, and in but few, if any, cases exceeded among
men. Of course, it is not asserted that the specialities
of mind here described as having been developed in women by
the necessities of defence in their dealings with men, are peculiar
to them: in men also they have been developed as aids to defence
in their dealings with one another. But the difference is that
whereas, in their dealings with one another, men depended on
these aids only in some measure, women in their dealings with
men depended upon them almost wholly—within the domestic

circle as well as without it. Hence, in virtue of that partial limitation of heredity by sex, which many facts throughout Nature show us, they have come to be more marked in women than in men.[7]

One further distinctive mental trait in women, springs out of the relation of the sexes as adjusted to the welfare of the race. I refer to the effect which the manifestation of power of every kind in men, has in determining the attachments of women. That this is a trait inevitably produced, will be manifest on asking what would have happened if women had by preference attached themselves to the weaker men. If the weaker men had habitually left posterity when the stronger did not, a progressive deterioration of the race would have resulted. Clearly, therefore, it has happened (at least, since the cessation of marriage by capture or by purchase has allowed feminine choice to play an important part), that, among women unlike in their tastes, those who were fascinated by power, bodily or mental, and who married men able to protect them and their children, were more likely to survive in posterity than women to whom weaker men were pleasing, and whose children were both less efficiently guarded and less capable of self-preservation if they reached maturity. To this admiration for power, caused thus inevitably, is ascribable the fact sometimes commented upon as strange, that women will continue attached to men who use them ill, but whose brutality goes along with power, more than they will continue attached to weaker men who use them well. With this admiration of power, primarily having this function, there goes the admiration of power in general; which is more marked in women than in men, and shows itself both theologically and politically. That the emotion of awe aroused by contemplating whatever suggests transcendent force or capacity, which constitutes religious feeling, is strongest in women, is proved in many ways. We read that among the Greeks the women were more religiously excitable than the men. Sir Rutherford Alcock tells us of the Japanese that "in the temples it is very rare to see any congregation except women and children; the men, at any time, are very few, and those generally of the lower classes." Of the pilgrims to the temple of Juggernaut, it is stated that " at least five-sixths, and often nine-tenths, of them are females." And we are also told of the Sikhs, that the women believe in more gods than the men do. Which facts, coming from different races and times, sufficiently show us that the like fact, familiar to us in Roman Catholic countries and to some extent at home, is not, as many think, due to the education of women, but has a deeper cause in natural character. And to this same cause is in like manner to be ascribed the greater respect felt by women for all embodiments and symbols of authority, governmental and social.

Thus the à priori inference, that fitness for their respective parental functions implies mental differences between the sexes, as it implies bodily differences, is justified; as is also the kindred inference that secondary differences are necessitated by their relations to one another. Those unlikenesses of mind between men and women, which, under the conditions, were to be expected, are the unlikenesses we actually find. That they are fixed in degree, by no means follows: indeed, the contrary follows. Determined as we see they some of them are by adaptation of primitive women's natures to the natures of primitive men, it is inferable that as civilization re-adjusts men's natures to higher social requirements, there goes on a corresponding re-adjustment between the natures of men and women, tending · in sundry respects to diminish their differences. Especially may we anticipate that those mental peculiarities developed in women as aids to defence against men in barbarous times, will diminish. It is probable, too, that though all kinds of power will continue to be attractive to them, the attractiveness of physical strength and the mental attributes that commonly go along with it, will decline; while the attributes which conduce to social influence will become more attractive. Further, it is to be anticipated that the higher culture of women, carried on within such limits as shall not unduly tax the *physique* (and here, by higher culture, I do not mean mere language-learning and an extension of the detestable cramming-system at present in use), will in other ways reduce the contrast. . Slowly leading to the result everywhere seen throughout the organic world, of a self-preserving power inversely proportionate to the race-preserving power, it will entail a less-early arrest of individual evolution, and a diminution of those mental differences between men and women, which the early arrest produces.

Admitting such to be changes which the future will probably see wrought out, we have meanwhile to bear in mind these traits of intellect and feeling which distinguish women, and to take note of them as factors in social phenomena—much more important factors than we commonly suppose. Considering them in the above order, we may note, first, that the love of the helpless, which in her maternal capacity woman displays in a more special form than man, inevitably affects all her thoughts and sentiments; and this being joined in her with a less-developed sentiment of abstract justice, she responds more readily when appeals to pity are made, than when appeals are made to equity. In foregoing chapters we have seen how much our social policy disregards the claims of individuals to whatever their efforts purchase, so long as no obvious misery is brought on them by the disregard; but when individuals suffer in ways conspicuous enough to excite commiseration, they get aid, and often as much aid if their sufferings are caused by themselves as if they are caused by others—often greater aid, indeed. This social policy, to which men tend in an injurious degree, women tend to still more. The maternal instinct delights in yielding benefits apart from deserts; and being partially excited by whatever shows a feebleness that appeals for help (supposing antagonism has not been aroused), carries into social action this preference of generosity to justice, even more than men do. A further tendency having the same general direction, results from the aptitude which the feminine intellect has to dwell on the concrete and proximate rather than on the abstract and remote. The representative faculty in women deals quickly and clearly with the personal, the special, and the immediate; but less readily grasps the general and the impersonal. A vivid imagination of simple direct consequences mostly shuts out from her mind the imagination of consequences that are complex and indirect. The respective behaviours of mothers and fathers to children, sufficiently exemplify this difference : mothers thinking chiefly of present effects on the conduct of children, and regarding less the distant effects on their characters; while fathers often repress the promptings of their sympathies with a view to ultimate benefits. And this difference between their ways of estimating consequences, affecting their judgments on social affairs as on domestic affairs, makes women err still more than men do in seeking what seems an immediate public good without thought of distant public evils. Once more, we have in women the predominant awe of power and authority, swaying their ideas and sentiments about all institutions. This tends towards the strengthening of governments, political and ecclesiastical. Faith in whatever presents itself with imposing accompaniments, is, for the reason above assigned, especially strong in women. Doubt, or criticism, or calling-in-question of things that are established, is rare among them. Hence in public affairs their influence goes towards the maintenance of controlling agencies, and does not resist the extension of such agencies : rather, in pursuit of immediate promised benefits, it urges on that extension; since the concrete good in view excludes from their thoughts the remote evils of multiplied restraints. Reverencing power more than men do, women, by implication, respect freedom less—freedom, that is, not of the nominal kind, but of that real kind which consists in the ability of each to carry on his own life without hindrance from others, so long as he does not hinder them.

As factors in social phenomena, these distinctive mental traits of women have ever to be remembered. Women have in all times played a part, and, in modern days, a very notable part, in determining social arrangements. They act both directly and indirectly. Directly, they take a large, if not the larger, share in that ceremonial government which supplements the political and ecclesiastical governments; and as supporters of these other governments, especially the ecclesiastical, their direct aid is by no means unimportant. Indirectly, they act by modifying the opinions and sentiments of men—first, in education, when the expression of maternal thoughts and feelings affects the thoughts and feelings of boys, and afterwards in domestic and social intercourse, during which the feminine sentiments sway men's public acts, both consciously and unconsciously. Whether it is desirable that the share already taken by women in determining social arrangements and actions should be increased, is a question we will leave undiscussed. Here I am concerned merely to point out that, in the course of a psychological preparation for the study of Sociology, we must include the comparative psychology of the sexes; so that if any change is made, we may make it knowing what we are doing.

Assent to the general proposition set forth in this chapter, does not depend on assent to the particular propositions unfolded in illustrating it. Those who, while pressing forward education, are so certain they know what good education is, that, in an essentially-Papal spirit, they wish to force children through their existing school-courses, under penalty on parents who resist, will not have their views modified by what has been said. I do not look, either, for any appreciable effect on those who shut out from consideration the reactive influence on moral nature, entailed by the action of a system of intellectual culture which habituates parents to make the public responsible for their children's minds. Nor do I think it likely that many of those who wish to change fundamentally the political *status* of women, will be influenced by the considerations above set forth on the comparative psychology of the sexes. But without acceptance of these illustrative conclusions, there may be acceptance of the general conclusion, that psychological truths underlie sociological truths, and must therefore be sought by the sociologist. For whether discipline of the intellect does or does not change the emotions ; whether national character is or is not progressively adapted to social conditions ; whether the minds of men and women are or are not alike ; are obviously psychological questions ; and either answer to any one of them, implies a psychological conclusion. Hence, whoever on any of these questions has a conviction to which he would give legislative expression, is basing a sociological belief upon a psychological belief; and cannot deny that the one is true only if the other is true. Having admitted this, he must admit that without preparation in Mental Science there can be no Social Science. For, otherwise, he must assert that the randomly-made and carelessly-grouped observations on Mind, common to all people, are better as guides than observations cautiously collected, critically examined, and generalized in a systematic way.

No one, indeed, who is once led to dwell on the matter, can fail to see how absurd is the supposition that there can be a rational interpretation of men's combined actions, without a previous rational interpretation of those thoughts and feelings by which their individual actions are prompted. Nothing comes out of a society but what originates in the motive of an individual, or in the united similar motives of many individuals, or in the conflict of the united similar motives of some having certain interests, with the diverse motives of others whose interests are different. Always the power which initiates a change is feeling, separate or aggregated, guided to its ends by intellect; and not even an approach to an explanation of social phenomena can be made, without the thoughts and sentiments of citizens being recognized as factors. How, then, can there be a true account of social actions without a true account of these thoughts and sentiments ? Manifestly, those who ignore Psychology as a preparation for Sociology, can defend their position only by proving that

while other groups of phenomena require special study, the phenomena of Mind, in all their variety and intricacy, are best understood without special study; and that knowledge of human
nature gained haphazard, becomes obscure and misleading in
proportion as there is added to it knowledge deliberately sought
and carefully put together.

CHAPTER XVI.

CONCLUSION.

OF readers who have accompanied me thus far, probably some think that the contents of the work go beyond the limits implied by its title. Under the head, *Study of Sociology*, so many sociological questions have been incidentally discussed, that the science itself has been in a measure dealt with while dealing with the study of it. Admitting this criticism, my excuse must be that the fault, if it is one, has been scarcely avoidable. Nothing to much purpose can be said about the study of any science without saying a good deal about the general and special truths it includes, or what the expositor holds to be truths. To write an essay on the study of Astronomy in which there should be no direct or implied conviction respecting the Copernican theory of the Solar System, nor any such recognition of the Law of Gravitation as involved acceptance or rejection of it, would be a task difficult to execute, and, when executed, probably of little value. Similarly with Sociology—it is next to impossible for a writer who points out the way towards its truths, to exclude all tacit or avowed expressions of opinion about those truths; and, were it possible to exclude such expressions of opinion, it would be at the cost of those illustrations needed to make his exposition effective.

Such must be, in part, my defence for having set down many thoughts which the title of this work does not cover. Especially have I found myself obliged thus to transgress, by representing the study of Sociology as the study of Evolution in its most complex form. It is clear that to one who considers the facts societies exhibit as having had their origin in supernatural interpositions, or in the wills of individual ruling men, the study of these facts will have an aspect wholly unlike that which it has to one who contemplates them as generated by processes of growth and development continuing through centuries. Ignoring, as the first view tacitly does, that conformity to law, in the scientific sense of the word, which the second view tacitly asserts, there can be but little community between the methods of inquiry proper to them respectively. Continuous causation, which in the one case there is little or no tendency to trace, becomes, in the other case, the chief object of attention; whence it follows that there must be formed wholly-different ideas of the appropriate modes of investigation. A foregone conclusion respecting the nature of social phenomena, is thus inevitably implied in any suggestions for the study of them.

While, however, it must be admitted that throughout this work there runs the assumption that the facts, simultaneous and successive, which societies present, have a genesis no less natural than the genesis of facts of all other classes ; it is not admitted that this assumption was made unawares, or without warrant. At the outset, the grounds for it were examined. The notion, widely accepted in name though not consistently acted upon, that social phenomena differ from phenomena of most other kinds as being under special providence, we found to be entirely discredited by its expositors ; nor, when closely looked into, did the great-man-theory of social affairs prove to be more tenable. Besides finding that both these views, rooted as they are in the ways of thinking natural to primitive men, would not bear criticism; we found that even their defenders continually betrayed their beliefs in the production of social changes by natural causes— tacitly admitted that after certain antecedents certain consequents are to be expected—tacitly admitted, therefore, that some prevision is possible, and therefore some subject-matter for Science.

From these negative justifications for the belief that Sociology is a science, we turned to the positive justifications. We found that every aggregate of units of any order, has certain traits necessarily determined by the properties of its units. Hence it was inferable, *à priori*, that, given the natures of the men who are their units, and certain characters in the societies formed are pre-determined—other characters being determined by the co-operation of surrounding conditions. The current assertion that Sociology is not possible, implies a misconception of its nature. Using the analogy supplied by a human life, we saw that just as bodily development and structure and function, furnish subject-matter for biological science, though the events set forth by the biographer go beyond its range; so, social growth, and the rise of structures and functions accompanying it, furnish subject-matter for a Science of Society, though the facts with which historians fill their pages mostly yield no material for Science. Thus conceiving the scope of the science, we saw, on comparing rudimentary societies with one another and with societies in different stages of progress, that they *do* present certain common traits of structure and of function, as well as certain common traits of development. Further comparisons similarly made, opened large questions, such as that of the relation between social growth and organization, which form parts of this same science; —questions of transcendent importance compared with those occupying the minds of politicians and writers of history.

The difficulties of the Social Science next drew our attention. We saw that in this case, though in no other case, the facts to be observed and generalized by the student, are exhibited by an aggregate of which he forms a part. In his capacity of inquirer, he should have no inclination towards one or other conclusion respecting the phenomena to be generalized; but in his capacity of citizen, helped to live by the life of his society, imbedded in its structures, sharing in its activities, breathing its atmosphere of thought and sentiment, he is partially coerced into such views as favour harmonious co-operation with his fellow-citizens. Hence immense obstacles to the Social Science, unparalleled by those standing in the way of any other science.

From considering thus generally these causes of error, we turned to consider them specially. Under the head of objective difficulties, we glanced at those many ways in which evidence collected by the sociological inquirer is vitiated. That extreme untrustworthiness of witnesses which results from carelessness, or fanaticism, or self-interest, was illustrated; and we saw that, in addition to the perversions of statement hence arising, there are others which arise from the tendency there is for some kinds of evidence to draw attention, while evidence of opposite kinds, much larger in quantity, draws no attention. Further, it was shown that the nature of sociological facts, each of which is not observable in a single object or act, but is reached only through registration and comparison of many objects and acts, makes the perception of them harder than that of other facts. It was pointed out that the wide distribution of social phenomena in Space, greatly hinders true apprehensions of them; and it was also pointed out that another impediment, even still greater, is consequent on their distribution in Time—a distribution such that many of the facts to be dealt with, take centuries to unfold, and can be grasped only by combining in thought multitudinous changes that are slow, involved, and not easy to trace. Beyond these difficulties which we grouped as distinguishing the science itself, objectively considered, we saw that there are other difficulties, conveniently to be grouped as subjective, which are also great. For the interpretation of human conduct as socially displayed, every one is compelled to use, as a key, his own nature—ascribing to others thoughts and feelings like his own; and yet, while this automorphic interpretation is indispensable, it is necessarily more or less misleading. Very generally, too, a subjective difficulty arises from the lack of intellectual faculty complex enough to grasp these social phenomena, which are so extremely involved. And again, very few have by culture gained that plasticity of faculty requisite for conceiving and accepting those immensely-varied actualities which societies in different times and places display, and those multitudinous possibilities to be inferred from them. Nor, of subjective difficulties, did these exhaust the list. From the emotional, as well as from the intellectual, part of the nature, we saw that there arise obstacles. The ways in which beliefs about social affairs are perverted by intense fears and excited hopes, were pointed out. We noted the feeling of impatience, as another common cause of misjudgment. A contrast was drawn showing, too, what perverse estimates of public events men are led to make by their sympathies and antipathies—how, where their hate has been aroused, they utter unqualified condemnations of ill-deeds for which there was much excuse, while, if their admiration is excited by vast successes, they condone inexcusable ill-deeds immeasurably greater in amount. And we also saw that among the distortions of judgment caused by the emotions, have to be included those immense ones generated by the sentiment of loyalty to a personal ruler, or to a ruling power otherwise embodied.

These distortions of judgment caused by the emotions, thus indicated generally, we went on to consider specially—treating of them as different forms of bias. Though, during education, understood in a wide sense, many kinds of bias are commenced or given, there is one which our educational system makes especially strong—the double bias in favour of the religions of enmity and of amity. Needful as we found both of these to be, we perceived that among the beliefs about social affairs, prompted now by the one and now by the other, there are glaring incongruities; and that scientific conceptions can be formed only when there is a compromise between the dictates of pure egoism and the dictates of pure altruism, for which they respectively stand. We observed, next, the warping of opinion which the bias of patriotism causes. Recognizing the truth that the preservation of a society is made possible only by a due amount of patriotic feeling in citizens, we saw that this feeling inevitably disturbs the judgment when comparisons between societies are made, and that the data required for Social Science are thus vitiated; and we saw that the effort to escape this bias, leading as it does to an opposite bias, is apt to vitiate the data in another way. While finding the class-bias to be no less essential, we found that it no less inevitably causes one-sidedness in the conceptions of social affairs. Noting how the various sub-classes have their specialities of prejudice corresponding to their class-interests, we noted, at greater length, how the more general prejudices of the larger and more widely-distinguished classes, prevent them from forming balanced judgments. That in politics the bias of party interferes with those calm examinations by which alone the conclusions of Social Science can be reached, scarcely needed pointing out. We observed, however, that beyond the political bias under its party-form, there is a more general political bias— the bias towards an exclusively-political view of social affairs, and a corresponding faith in political instrumentalities. As affecting the study of Social Science, this bias was shown to be detrimental as directing the attention too much to the phenomena of social regulation, and excluding from thought the activities regulated, constituting an aggregate of phenomena far more important. Lastly, we came to the theological bias, which, under its general form and under its special forms, disturbs in various ways our judgments on social questions. Obedience to a supposed divine command, being its standard of rectitude, it does not ask concerning any social arrangement whether it conduces to social welfare, so much as whether it conforms to the creed locally established. Hence, in each place and time, those conceptions about public affairs which the theological bias fosters, tend to diverge from the truth in so far as the creed then and there accepted diverges from the truth. And besides the positive evil thus produced, there is a negative evil, due to discouragement of the habit of estimating actions by the results they eventually cause — a habit which the study of Social Science demands.

Having thus contemplated, in general and in detail, the difficulties of the Social Science, we turned our attention to the preliminary discipline required. Of the conclusions reached so recently, the reader scarcely needs reminding. Study of the sciences in general having been pointed out as the proper means of generating fit habits of thought, it was shown that the sciences especially to be attended to are those treating of Life and of Mind. There can be no understanding of social actions without some knowledge of human nature; there can be no deep knowledge of human nature without some knowledge of the laws of Mind; there can be no adequate knowledge of the laws of Mind without knowledge of the laws of Life. And that knowledge of the Laws of Life, as exhibited in Man, may be properly grasped, attention must be given to the laws of Life in general.

What is to be hoped from such a presentation of difficulties and such a programme of preparatory studies? Who, in drawing his conclusions about public policies, will be made to hesitate by remembering the many obstacles that stand in the way of right judgments? Who will think it needful to fit himself by inquiries so various and so extensive? Who, in short, will be led to doubt any of the inferences he has drawn, or be induced to pause before he draws others, by consciousness of these many liabilities to error arising from want of knowledge, want of discipline, and want of duly-balanced sentiments?

To these questions there can be but the obvious reply—a reply which the foregoing chapters themselves involve—that very little is to be expected. The implication throughout the argument has been that for every society, and for each stage in its evolution, there is an appropriate mode of feeling and thinking; and that no mode of feeling and thinking not adapted to its degree of evolution, and to its surroundings, can be permanently established. Though not exactly, still approximately, the average opinion in any age and country, is a function of the social structure in that age and country. There may be, as we see during times of revolution, a considerable incongruity between the ideas that become current and the social arrangements which exist, and are, in great measure, appropriate; though even then the incongruity does but mark the need for a re-adjustment of institutions to character. While, however, those successive compromises which, during social evolution, have to be made between the changed natures of citizens and the institutions evolved by ancestral citizens, imply disagreements, yet these are but partial and temporary—in those societies, at least, which are developing and not in course of dissolution. For a society to hold together, the institutions that are needed and the conceptions that are generally current, must be in tolerable harmony. Hence, it is not to be expected that modes of thinking on social affairs, are to be in any considerable degree changed by whatever may be said respecting the Social Science, its difficulties, and the required preparations for studying it.

The only reasonable hope is, that here and there one may be led, in calmer moments, to remember how largely his beliefs about public matters have been made for him by circumstances, and how probable it is that they are either untrue or but partially true. When he reflects on the doubtfulness of the evidence which he generalizes, collected hap-hazard from a narrow area—when he counts up the perverting sentiments fostered in him by education, country, class, party, creed—when, observing those around, he sees that from other evidence selected to gratify sentiments partially unlike his own, there result unlike views; he may occasionally recollect how largely mere accidents have determined his convictions. Recollecting this, he may be induced to hold these convictions not quite so strongly; may see the need for criticism of them with a view to revision; and, above all, may be somewhat less eager to act in pursuance of them.

While the few to whom a Social Science is conceivable, may in some degree be thus influenced by what is said concerning the study of it, there can, of course, be no effect on the many to whom such a science seems an absurdity, or an impiety, or both. The feeling usually excited by the proposal to deal scientifically with these most-complex phenomena, is like that which was excited in ancient times by the proposal to deal scientifically with phenomena of simpler kinds. As Mr. Grote writes of Socrates—

" Physics and astronomy, in his opinion, belonged to the divine class of phænomena, in which human research was insane, fruitless, and impious." [1]

And as he elsewhere writes respecting the attitude of the Greek mind in general :—

" In his [the early Greek's] view, the description of the sun, as given in a modern astronomical treatise, would have appeared not merely absurd, but repulsive and impious : even in later times, when the positive spirit of inquiry had made considerable progress, Anaxagoras and other astronomers incurred the charge of blasphemy for dispersonifying Hêlios, and trying to assign invariable laws to the solar phenomena." [2]

That a likeness exists between the feeling then displayed respecting phenomena of inorganic nature, and the feeling now displayed respecting phenomena of Life and Society, is manifest. The ascription of social actions and political events entirely to natural causes, thus leaving out Providence as a factor, seems to the religious mind of our day, as seemed to the mind of the pious Greek the dispersonification of Hêlios and the explanation of celestial motions otherwise than by immediate divine agency. As was said by Mr. Gladstone, in a speech made shortly after the first publication of the second chapter of this volume—

" I lately read a discussion on the manner in which the raising up of particular individuals occasionally occurs in great crises of human history, as if some sacred, invisible power had raised them up and placed them in particular positions for special purposes. The writer says that they are not uniform, but admits that they are common—so common and so remarkable that men would be liable to term them providential in a pre-scientific age. And this was said without the smallest notion apparently in the writer's mind that he was giving utterance to anything that could startle or alarm—it was said as a kind of commonplace. It would seem that in his view there was a time when mankind, lost in ignorance, might, without forfeiting entirely their title to the name of rational creatures, believe in a Providence, but that since that period another and greater power has arisen under the name of science, and this power has gone to war with Providence, and Providence is driven from the field—and we have now the happiness of living in the scientific age, when Providence is no longer to be treated as otherwise than an idle dream."[3]

Of the mental attitude, very general beyond the limits of the scientific world, which these utterances of Mr. Gladstone exemplify, he has since given further illustration; and, in his anxiety to check a movement he thinks mischievous, has so conspicuously made himself the exponent of the anti-scientific view, that we may fitly regard his thoughts on the matter as typical. In an address delivered by him at the Liverpool College, and since re-published with additions, he says :—

"Upon the ground of what is termed evolution, God is relieved of the labour of creation ; in the name of unchangeable laws, He is discharged from governing the world."

This passage proves the kinship between Mr. Gladstone's conception of things and that entertained by the Greeks, to be even closer than above alleged ; for its implication is, not simply that the scientific interpretation of vital and social phenomena as conforming to fixed laws, is repugnant to him, but that the like interpretation of inorganic phenomena is repugnant. In common with the ancient Greek, he regards as irreligious, any explanation of Nature which dispenses with immediate divine superintendence. He appears to overlook the fact that the doctrine of gravitation, with the entire science of physical Astronomy, is open to the same charge as this which he makes against the doctrine of evolution ; and he seems not to have remembered that throughout the past, each further step made by Science has been denounced for reasons like those which he assigns.[4]

It is instructive to observe, however, that in these prevailing conceptions expressed by Mr. Gladstone, which we have here to note as excluding the conception of a Social Science, there is to be traced a healthful process of compromise between old and new. For as in the current conceptions about the order of events in the lives of persons, there is a partnership, wholly illogical though temporarily convenient, between the ideas of natural causation and of providential interference ; so, in the current political conceptions, the belief in divine interpositions goes along with, and by no means excludes, the belief in a natural production of effects on society by natural agencies set to work. In relation to the occurrences of individual life, we displayed our national aptitude for thus entertaining mutually-destructive ideas, when an unpopular prince suddenly gained popularity by outliving certain abnormal changes in his blood, and when, on the occasion of his recovery, providential aid and natural causation were unitedly recognized by a thanksgiving to God and a baronetcy to the doctor. And similarly, we see that throughout all our public actions, the theory which Mr. Gladstone represents, that great men are providentially raised up to do things God has decided upon, and that the course of affairs is supernaturally ordered thus or thus, does not in the least interfere with the passing of measures calculated to achieve desired ends in ways classed as natural, and nowise modifies the discussion of such measures on their merits, as estimated in terms of cause and consequence. While the prayers with which each legislative sitting commences, show a nominal belief in an immediate divine guidance, the votes with which the sitting ends, given in pursuance of reasons which the speeches assign, show us a real belief that the effects will be determined by the agencies set to work.

Still, it is clear that the old conception, while it qualifies the new but little in the regulating of actions, qualifies it very much in the forming of theories. There can be no complete acceptance of Sociology as a science, so long as the belief in a social order not conforming to natural law, survives. Hence, as already said, considerations touching the study of Sociology, not very influential even over the few who recognize a Social Science, can have scarcely any effects on the great mass to whom a Social Science is an incredibility.

I do not mean that this prevailing imperviousness to scientific conceptions of social phenomena is to be regretted. As implied in a foregoing paragraph, it is part of the required adjustment between existing opinions and the forms of social life at present requisite. With a given phase of human character there must, to maintain equilibrium, go an adapted class of institutions, and a set of thoughts and sentiments in tolerable harmony with those institutions. Hence, it is not to be wished that with the average human nature we now have, there should be a wide acceptance of views natural only to a more-highly-developed social state, and to the improved type of citizen accompanying such a state. The desirable thing is, that a growth of ideas and feelings tending to produce modification, shall be joined with a continuance of ideas and feelings tending to preserve stability. And it is one of our satisfactory social traits, exhibited in a degree never before paralleled, that along with a mental progress which brings about considerable changes, there is a devotion of thought and energy to the maintenance of existing arrangements, and creeds, and sentiments—an energy sufficient even to re-invigorate some of the old forms and beliefs that were decaying. When, therefore, a distinguished statesman, anxious for human welfare as he ever shows himself to be, and holding that the defence of established beliefs must not be left exclusively to its " standing army " of " priests and ministers of religion," undertakes to combat opinions at variance with a creed he thinks essential; the occurrence may be taken as adding another to the many signs of a healthful condition of society. That in our day, one in Mr. Gladstone's position should think as he does, seems to me very desirable. That we should have for our working-king one in whom a purely-scientific conception of things had become dominant, and who was thus out of harmony with our present

18

social state, would probably be detrimental, and might be disastrous.

For it cannot be too emphatically asserted that this policy of compromise, alike in institutions, in actions, and in beliefs, which especially characterizes English life, is a policy essential to a society going through the transitions caused by continued growth and development. The illogicalities and the absurdities to be found so abundantly in current opinions and existing arrangements, are those which inevitably arise in the course of perpetual re-adjustments to circumstances perpetually changing. Ideas and institutions proper to a past social state, but incongruous with the new social state that has grown out of it, surviving into this new social state they have made possible, and disappearing only as this new social state establishes its own ideas and institutions, are necessarily, during their survival, in conflict with these new ideas and institutions—necessarily furnish elements of contradiction in men's thoughts and deeds. And yet as, for the carrying-on of social life, the old must continue so long as the new is not ready, this perpetual compromise is an indispensable accompaniment of a normal development. Its essentialness we may see on remembering that it equally holds throughout the evolution of an individual organism. The structural and functional arrangements during growth, are never quite right: always the old adjustment for a smaller size is made wrong by the larger size it has been instrumental in producing—always the transition-structure is a compromise between the requirements of past and future, fulfilling in an imperfect way the requirements of the present. And this, which is shown clearly enough where there is simple growth, is shown still more clearly where there are metamorphoses. A creature which leads at two periods of its existence two different kinds of life, and which, in adaptation to its second period, has to develop structures that were not fitted for its first, passes through a stage during which it possesses both partially—during which the old dwindles while the new grows: as happens, for instance, in creatures that continue to breathe water by external branchiæ during the time they are developing the lungs that enable them to breathe air. And thus it is with the alterations produced by growth in societies, as well as with those metamorphoses accompanying change in the mode of life—especially those accompanying change from the predatory life to the industrial life. Here, too, there must be transitional stages during which incongruous organizations co-exist: the first remaining indispensable until the second has grown up to its work. Just as injurious as it would be to an am-phibian to cut off its branchiæ before its lungs were well developed; so injurious must it be to a society to destroy its old institutions before the new have become well-organized enough to take their places.

Non-recognition of this truth characterizes too much the reformers, political, religious, and social, of our own time; as it has characterized those of past times. On the part of men eager to rectify wrongs and expel errors, there is still, as there ever has been, so absorbing a consciousness of the evils caused by old forms and old ideas, as to permit no consciousness of the benefits these old forms and old ideas have yielded. This partiality of view is, in a sense, necessary. There must be division of labour here as elsewhere: some who have the function of attacking, and who, that they may attack effectually, must feel strongly the viciousness of that which they attack; some who have the function of defending and who, that they may be good defenders, must over-value the things they defend. But while this one-sidedness has to be tolerated, as in great measure unavoidable, it is in some respects to be regretted. Though, with grievances less serious and animosities less intense than those which existed here in the past, and which exist still abroad, there go mitigated ten-dencies to a rash destructiveness on the one side, and an un-reasoning bigotry on the other; yet even in our country and age there are dangers from the want of a due both-sidedness. In the speeches and writings of those who advocate various political and social changes, there is so continuous a presentation of injustices, and abuses, and mischiefs, and corruptions, as to leave the impression that for securing a wholesome state of things, there needs nothing but to set aside present arrangements. The implication seems ever to be that all who occupy places of power, and form the regulative organization, are alone to blame for whatever is not as it should be; and that the classes regulated are blameless. "See the injuries which these institutions inflict on you," says the energetic reformer. "Consider how selfish must be the men who maintain them to their own advantage and your detriment," he adds. And then he leaves to be drawn the manifest inference, that were these selfish men got rid of, all would be well. Neither he nor his audience recognizes the facts that regulative arrangements are essential; that the arrangements in question, along with their many vices, have some virtues; that such vices as they have do not result from an egoism peculiar to those who uphold and work them, but result from a general egoism—an egoism no less decided in those who complain than in those complained of. Inequitable government can be upheld only by the aid of a people correspondingly inequitable, in its sentiments and acts. Injustice cannot reign if the community does not furnish a due supply of unjust agents. No tyrant can tyrannize over a people save on condition that the people is bad enough to supply him with soldiers who will fight for his tyranny and keep their brethren in slavery. Class-supremacy cannot be maintained by the corrupt buying of votes, unless there are multitudes of voters venal enough to sell their votes. It is thus everywhere and in all degrees—misconduct among those in power is the correlative of misconduct among those over whom they exercise power.

And while, in the men who urge on changes, there is an unconsciousness that the evils they denounce are rooted in the nature common to themselves and other men, there is also an unconsciousness that amid the things they would throw away there is much worth preserving. This holds of beliefs more especially. Along with the destructive tendency there goes but little constructive tendency. The criticisms made, imply that it is requisite only to dissipate errors, and that it is needless to insist on truths. It is forgotten that, along with forms which are bad, there is a large amount of substance which is good. And those to whom there are addressed condemnations of the forms, unaccompanied by the caution that there is a substance to be preserved in higher forms, are left, not only without any coherent system of guiding beliefs, but without any consciousness that one is requisite.

Hence the need, above admitted, for an active defence of that which exists, carried on by men convinced of its entire worth ; so that those who attack may not destroy the good along with the bad.

And here let me point out distinctly, the truth already implied, that studying Sociology scientifically, leads to fairer appreciations of different parties, political, religious, and other. The conception initiated and developed by Social Science, is at the same time Radical and Conservative—Radical to a degree beyond anything which current Radicalism conceives; Conservative to a degree beyond anything conceived by present Conservatism. When there has been adequately seized the truth that societies are products of evolution, assuming, in their various times and places, their various modifications of structure, and function ; there follows the conviction that what, relatively to our thoughts and sentiments, were arrangements of extreme badness, had fitnesses to conditions which made better arrangements impracticable: whence comes a tolerant interpretation of past tyrannies at which even the bitterest Tory of our own days would be indignant. On the other hand, after observing how the processes that have brought things to their present stage are still going on, not with a decreasing rapidity indicating approach to cessation, but with an increasing rapidity that implies long continuance and immense transformations; there follows the conviction that the remote future has in store, forms of social life

higher than any we have imagined : there comes a faith transcending that of the Radical, whose aim is some re-organization
admitting of comparison to organizations which exist. And
while this conception of societies as naturally evolved, beginning
with small and simple types which have their short existences
and disappear, advancing to higher types that are larger, more
complex, and longer-lived, coming to still-higher types like
our own, great in size, complexity, and duration, and promising
types transcending these in times after existing societies have
died away—while this conception of societies implies that in the
slow course of things changes almost immeasurable in amount
are possible, it also implies that but small amounts of such
changes are possible within short periods.

Thus, the theory of progress disclosed by the study of Sociology as science, is one which greatly moderates the hopes and the
fears of extreme parties. After clearly seeing that the structures
and actions throughout a society are determined by the properties
of its units, and that (external disturbances apart) the society
cannot be substantially and permanently changed without its
units being substantially and permanently changed, it becomes
easy to see that great alterations cannot suddenly be made to much
purpose. And when both the party of progress and the party of
resistance perceive that the institutions which at any time exist
are more deeply rooted than they supposed—when the one
party perceives that these institutions, imperfect as they are, have
a temporary fitness, while the other party perceives that the maintenance of them, in so far as it is desirable, is in great measure
guaranteed by the human nature they have grown out of ; there
must come a diminishing violence of attack on one side, and a
diminishing perversity of defence on the other. Evidently, so
far as a doctrine can influence general conduct (which it can do,
however, in but a comparatively-small degree), the Doctrine of
Evolution, in its social applications, is calculated to produce a
steadying effect, alike on thought and action.

If, as seems likely, some should propose to draw the seemingly-awkward corollary that it matters not what we believe or what we teach, since the process of social evolution will take its own course in spite of us; I reply that while this corollary is in one sense true, it is in another sense untrue. Doubtless, from all that has been said it follows that, supposing surrounding conditions continue the same, the evolution of a society cannot be in any essential way diverted from its general course; though it also follows (and here the corollary is at fault) that the thoughts and actions of individuals, being natural factors that arise in the course of the evolution itself, and aid in further advancing it, cannot be dispensed with, but must be severally valued as increments of the aggregate force producing change. But while the corollary is even here partially misleading, it is, in another direction, far more seriously misleading. For though the process of social evolution is in its general character so far pre-determined, that its successive stages cannot be ante-dated, and that hence no teaching or policy can advance it beyond a certain normal rate, which is limited by the rate of organic modification in human beings; yet it is quite possible to perturb, to retard, or to disorder the process. The analogy of individual development again serves us. The unfolding of an organism after its special type, has its approximately-uniform course taking its tolerably-definite time; and no treatment that may be devised will fundamentally change or greatly accelerate these: the best that can be done is to maintain the required favourable conditions. But it is quite easy to adopt a treatment which shall dwarf, or deform, or otherwise injure: the processes of growth and development may be, and very often are, hindered or deranged, though they cannot be artificially bettered. Similarly with the social organism. Though, by maintaining favourable conditions, there cannot be more good done than that of letting social progress go on unhindered; yet an immensity of mischief may be done in the way of disturbing and distorting and repressing, by policies carried out in pursuance of erroneous conceptions. And thus, notwithstanding first appearances to the contrary, there is a very important part to be played by a true theory of social phenomena.

A few words to those who think these general conclusions discouraging, may be added. Probably the more enthusiastic, hopeful of great ameliorations in the state of mankind, to be brought about rapidly by propagating this belief or initiating that reform, will feel that a doctrine negativing their sanguine anticipations takes away much of the stimulus to exertion. If large advances in human welfare can come only in the slow process of things, which will inevitably bring them; why should we trouble ourselves?

Doubtless it is true that on visionary hopes, rational criticisms have a depressing influence. It is better to recognize the truth, however. As between infancy and maturity there is no shortcut by which there may be avoided the tedious process of growth and development through insensible increments; so there is no way from the lower forms of social life to the higher, but one passing through small successive modifications. If we contemplate the order of nature, we see that everywhere vast results are brought about by accumulations of minute actions. The surface of the Earth has been sculptured by forces which in the course of a year produce alterations scarcely anywhere visible. Its multitudes of different organic forms have arisen by processes so slow, that, during the periods our observations extend over, the results are in most cases inappreciable. We must be content to recognize these truths and conform our hopes to them. Light, falling upon a crystal, is capable of altering its molecular arrangements, but it can do this only by a repetition of impulses almost innumerable: before a unit of ponderable matter can have its rhythmical movements so increased by successive etherial waves, as to be detached from its combination and arranged in another way, millions of such etherial waves must successively make infinitesimal additions to its motion. Similarly, before there arise in human nature and human institutions, changes having that permanence which makes them àn acquired inheritance for the human race, there must go innumerable recurrences of the thoughts, and feelings, and actions, conducive to such changes. The process cannot be abridged; and must be gone through with due patience.

Thus, admitting that for the fanatic some wild anticipation is needful as a stimulus, and recognizing the usefulness of his delusion as adapted to his particular nature and his particular function, the man of higher type must be content with greatly-moderated expectations, while he perseveres with undiminished efforts. He has to see how comparatively little can be done, and yet to find it worth while to do that little : so uniting philanthropic energy with philosophic calm.

NOTES.

NOTES TO CHAPTER I.

[1] Of various testimonies to this, one of the most striking was that given by Mr. Charles Mayo, M.B., of New College, Oxford, who, having had to examine the drainage of Windsor, found "that in a previous visitation of typhoid fever, the poorest and lowest part of the town had entirely escaped, while the epidemic had been very fatal in good houses. The difference was this, that while the better houses were all connected with the sewers, the poor part of the town had no drains, but made use of cesspools in the gardens. And this is by no means an isolated instance."

[2] Debates, *Times*, February 12, 1852.

[3] Letter in *Daily News*, Nov. 28, 1851.

[4] Recommendation of a Coroner's Jury, *Times*, March 26, 1850.

[5] *Revue des Deux Mondes*, February 15, 1872.

[6] *Journal of Mental Science*, January, 1872.

[7] Boyle's *Borneo*, p. 116.

NOTES TO CHAPTER II.

[1] Daily paper, January 22, 1849.

[2] *The Theocratic Philosophy of English History*, vol. i. p. 49.

[3] *Ibid.*, vol. i. p. 289.

[4] *Ibid.*, vol. ii. p. 681.

[5] *La Main de l'Homme et le Doigt de Dieu dans les malheurs de la France.* Par J. C., Ex-aumonier dans l'armée auxiliaire. Paris, Douniol & Cie., 1871.

[6] *The Roman and the Teuton*, pp. 339-40.

[7] *Short Studies on Great Subjects*, vol. i. p. 11.

[8] *Ibid.*, vol. i. p. 22

[9] *Ibid.*, vol. i. p. 24.

[10] *Ibid.*, vol. i. p. 15.

[11] *History of England*, vol. v. p. 70.

[12] *Ibid.*, vol. v. p. 108.

[13] *Ibid.*, vol. v. p. 109.

[14] *Short Studies on Great Subjects*, p. 59.

[15] *The Limits of Exact Science as applied to History*, p. 20.

[16] *Ibid.*, p. 22.

[17] *Alton Locke*, new edition, preface, p. xxi.

[18] *Ibid.*, pp. xxiii. xxiv.

[19] *Ibid.*, preface (1854), p. xxvii.

NOTES TO CHAPTER V.

[1] Thomson's *New Zealand*, vol. i. p. 80.

[2] Hallam's *Middle Ages*, ch. ix., part ii.

[3] *Principles of Surgery.* 5th ed. p. 434.

[4] *British and Foreign Medico-Chirurgical Review*, January, 1870, p. 103.

[5] *Ibid.* p. 106.

[6] *British Medical Journal*, August 20th, 1870. I took the precaution of calling on Mr. Hutchinson to verify the extract given, and to learn from him what he meant by "severe." I found that he meant simply *recognizable.* He described to me the mode in which he had made his estimate ; and it was clearly a mode which tended rather towards exaggeration of the evil than otherwise. I also learned from him that in the great mass of cases those who have recognizable syphilitic taint pass lives that are but little impaired by it.

[7] *A Treatise on Syphilis*, by Dr. E. Lancereaux. Vol. ii. p. 120. This testimony I quote from the work itself, and have similarly taken from the original sources the statements of Skey, Simon, Wyatt, Acton, as well as the *British and Foreign Medico-Chirurgical Review* and *British Medical Journal.* The rest, with various others, will be found in the pamphlet of Dr. C. B. Taylor on *The Contagious Diseases Acts.*

[8] Professor Sheldon Amos. See also his late important work, *A*

Systematic View of the Science of Jurisprudence, pp. 119, 303, 512, and 514.

[9] Quoted by Nasse, *The Agricultural Community of the Middle Ages*, &c., English translation, p. 94.

[10] In one case, " out of thirty married couples, there was not one man then living with his own wife, and some of them had exchanged wives two or three times since their entrance." This, along with various kindred illustrations, will be found in tracts on the Poor-Law, by a late uncle of mine, the Rev. Thomas Spencer, of Hinton Charterhouse, who was chairman of the Bath Union during its first six years.

NOTES TO CHAPTER VI.

[1] Warton's *History of English Poetry*, vol. ii., p. 57, *note*.

[2] Burton's *Scinde*, vol. ii., p. 13.

[3] Speke's *Journal of Discovery of Source of the Nile*, p. 85.

[4] See pp. 79 and 127.

[5] *Summary of the Moral Statistics of England and Wales.* By Joseph Fletcher, Esq., one of Her Majesty's Inspectors of Schools.

[6] Reeves's *History of English Law*, vol. i., pp. 34-36. Second edition.

[7] Brentano's Introduction to *English Gilds*, p. cxcv.

[8] Lubbock's *Prehistoric Times*, p. 344. First edition.

[9] Mrs. Atkinson's *Recollections of Tartar Steppes*, p. 220.

[10] Quoted in M'Lennan's *Primitive Marriage*, p. 187.

[11] Burton's *History of Sindh*, p. 244.

[12] Wright's *Essays on Archæology*, vol. ii., pp. 175-6.

[13] *Ibid.*, vol. ii., p. 184.

[14] Only four copies of this psalter are known to exist. The copy from which I make this description is contained in the splendid collection of Mr. Henry Huth.

[15] *Kinder- und Hausmärchen*, by William and James Grimm. Larger edition (1870), pp. 140-2.

NOTES TO CHAPTER VII.

[1] M. Dunoyer, quoted in Mill's *Political Economy*.

[2] Mill's *Political Economy*.

[3] Mill's *Political Economy.*

[4] Translation of Lanfrey's *History of Napoleon the First,* vol. ii., p. 25.

[5] *Ibid.,* vol. ii., p. 442.

[6] M. Lanfrey sets down the loss of the French alone, from 1802 onwards, at nearly two millions. This may be an over-estimate ; though, judging from the immense armies raised in France, such a total seems quite possible. The above computation of the losses to European nations in general, has been made for me by adding up the numbers of killed and wounded in the successive battles, as furnished by such statements as are accessible. The total is 1,500,000. This number has to be greatly increased by including losses not specified—the number of killed and wounded on one side only, being given in some cases. It has to be further increased by including losses in numerous minor engagements, the particulars of which are unknown. And it has to be again increased by allowance for under-statement of his losses, which was habitual with Napoleon. Though the total, raised by these various additions probably to something over two millions, includes killed and wounded, from which last class a large deduction has to be made for the number who recovered ; yet it takes no account of the loss by disease. This may be set down as greater in amount than that which battles caused. (Thus, according to Kolb, the British lost in Spain three times as many by disease as by the enemy ; and in the expedition to Walcheren, seventeen times as many.) So that the loss by killed and wounded and by disease, for all the European nations during the Napoleonic campaigns, is probably much understated at two millions.

[7] Burton's *Goa,* &c., p. 167.

[8] See Tweedie's *System of Practical Medicine,* vol. v. pp. 62—69.

[9] Dr. Maclean : see *Times,* Jan. 6, 1873.

[10] *Report on the Progress and Condition of the Royal Gardens at Kew,* 1870, p. 5.

[11] My attention was drawn to this case by one who has had experience in various government services ; and he ascribed this obstructiveness in the medical service to the putting of young surgeons under old. The remark is significant, and has far-reaching implications. Putting young officials under old is a rule of all services—civil, military, naval, or other ; and in all services, necessarily has the effect of placing the advanced ideas and wider knowledge of a new generation, under control by the ignorance and bigotry of a generation to which change has become repugnant. This, which is a seemingly-ineradicable vice of public

organizations, is a vice to which private organizations are far less liable ; since, in the life-and-death struggle of competition, merit, even if young, takes the place of demerit, even if old.

[12] Let me here add what seems to be a not-impossible cause, or at any rate part-cause, of the failure. The clue is given by a letter in the *Times*, signed "Landowner," dating Tollesbury, Essex, Aug. 2, 1872. He bought "ten fine young steers, perfectly free from any symptom of disease," and "passed sound by the inspector of foreign stock." They were attacked by foot and mouth disease after five days passed in fresh paddocks with the best food. On inquiry he found that foreign stock, however healthy, "'mostly all go down with it' after the passage." And then, in proposing a remedy, he gives us a fact of which he does not seem to recognize the meaning. He suggests, "that, instead of the present quarantine at Harwich, which consists in driving the stock from the steamer into pens for a limited number of hours," &c., &c. If this description of the quarantine is correct, the spread of the disease is accounted for. Every new drove of cattle is kept for hours in an infected pen. Unless the successive droves have been all healthy (which the very institution of the quarantine implies that they have not been) some of them have left in the pen diseased matter from their mouths and feet. Even if disinfectants are used after each occupation, the risk is great—the disinfection is almost certain to be inadequate. Nay, even if the pen is adequately disinfected every time, yet if there is not also a complete disinfection of the landing appliances, the landing-stage, and the track to the pen, the disease will be communicated. No wonder healthy cattle "'mostly go down with it' after the passage." The quarantine regulations, if they are such as here implied, might properly be called "regulations for the better diffusion of cattle-diseases."

[13] Fischel's *English Constitution*, translated by Shee, p. 487.

[14] See Report of the Committee on Public Accounts, nominated on 7 Feb., 1873.

[15] *Times*, April 3, 1873 (I add this during the re-revision of these pages for permanent publication, as also the reference to the telegraph-expenditure. Hence the incongruities of the dates).

NOTE TO CHAPTER VIII.

[1] "*Decline and Fall*," &c., chap. ii.

NOTES TO CHAPTER IX.

[1] Burton's *Abeokuta*, vol. i. pp. 43, 44.

[2] Burton's *History of Scotland*, vol. ii. pp. 281-2.

[3] I make this statement on the authority of a letter read to me at the time by an Indian officer, written by a brother officer in India.

[4] Hawkesworth's *Voyages*, vol. i. p. 573.

[5] Forster's *Observations*, &c., p. 406.

[6] Parkyns's *Abyssinia*, vol. ii. p. 431.

[7] Cruickshank, *Eighteen Years on the Gold Coast of Africa*, vol. i. p. 100.

[8] *Companions of Columbus*, p. 115.

[9] *Times*, Jan. 22, 1873.

[10] *Times*, Dec. 23, 1872.

[11] *Lancet*, Dec. 28, 1872.

[12] *Essays in Criticism*, p. 12.

[13] *Times*, Jan. 22, 1873.

[14] Most readers of logic will, I suppose, be surprised on missing from the above sentence the name of Sir W. Hamilton. They will not be more surprised than I was myself on recently learning that Mr. George Bentham's work, *Outline of a New System of Logic*, was published six years before the earliest of Sir W. Hamilton's logical writings, and that Sir W. Hamilton reviewed it. The case adds another to the multitudinous ones in which the world credits the wrong man; and persists in crediting him in defiance of evidence. [In the number of the *Contemporary Review* following that in which this note originally appeared, Professor Baynes, blaming me for my incaution in thus asserting Mr. Bentham's claim, contended for the claim of Sir W. Hamilton and denied the validity of Mr. Bentham's. The month after, the question was taken up by Professor Jevons, who, differing entirely from Professor Baynes, gave reasons for assigning the credit of the discovery to Mr. Bentham. Considering that Professor Baynes, both as pupil of Sir W. Hamilton and as expositor of his developed logical system, is obviously liable to be biassed in his favour, and that, contrariwise, Professor Jevons is not by his antecedents committed on behalf of either claimant, it may I think, be held that, leaving out other reasons, his opinion is the most trustworthy. Other reasons justify this estimate. The assumption that Sir W. Hamilton, when he reviewed Mr. Bentham's work, did not read as far as the page on which the discovery in question is indicated, though

admissible as a defence, cannot be regarded as a very satisfactory ground for a counter-claim. That in Mr. Bentham's work the doctrine is but briefly indicated, whereas by Sir W. Hamilton it was elaborately developed, is an objection sufficiently met by pointing out that Mr. Bentham's work is an "*Outline* of a New System of Logic ;" and that in it he has said enough to show that if, instead of being led into another career, he had become a professional logician, the outline would have been adequately filled in. While these notes are still standing in type, Prof. Baynes has published (in the *Contemporary Review* for July, 1873) a rejoinder to Prof. Jevons. One who reads it critically may, I think, find in it more evidence against, than in favour of, the conclusion drawn. Prof. Baynes' partiality will be clearly seen on comparing the way in which he interprets Sir W. Hamilton's acts, with the way in which he interprets Mr. Bentham's acts. He thinks it quite a proper supposition that Sir W. Hamilton did not read the part of Mr. Bentham's work containing the doctrine in question. Meanwhile, he dwells much on the fact that during Sir W. Hamilton's life Mr. Bentham never made any claim ; saying—" The indifference it displays is incredible had Mr. Bentham really felt himself entitled to the honour publicly given to another :" the implication being that Mr. Bentham was of necessity cognizant of the controversy. Thus it is reasonable to suppose that Sir W. Hamilton read only part of a work he reviewed on his own special topic; but "incredible" that Mr. Bentham should not have read certain letters in the *Athenæum !*—the fact being that, as I have learnt from Mr. Bentham, he knew nothing about the matter till his attention was called to it. Clearly, such a way of estimating probabilities is not conducive to a fair judgment. Prof. Baynes' unfairness of judgment is, I think, sufficiently shown by one of his own sentences, in which he says of Mr. Bentham that, " while he constantly practises the quantification of the predicate, he never appears to have realized it as a principle." To an unconcerned observer, it seems a strong assumption that one who not only " constantly practises " the method, but who even warns the student against errors caused by neglect of it, should have no consciousness of the " principle " involved. And I am not alone in thinking this a strong assumption : the remark was made to me by a distinguished mathematician who was reading Prof. Baynes' rejoinder. But the weakness of Prof. Baynes' rejoinder is best shown by its inconsistency. Prof. Baynes contends that Sir W. Hamilton " had been acquainted with the occasional use of a quantified predicate by writers on logic " earlier than Mr. Bentham ; and Prof. Baynes speaks of Mr. Bentham as having done no more than many before him. But he also says of Sir W. Hamilton that, "had he at the time, therefore, looked into Mr. Bentham's eighth and ninth chapters, the mere use of a quantified predicate would have been no novelty to him, although, as I have said, it might have helped to stimulate his speculations on the subject." So that though Mr. Bentham did not carry the doctrine further than previous logicians had done, yet what he wrote about it was calculated " to stimulate" "speculations on the subject" in a way that they had not been stimulated by the writings of previous logicians. That is, Prof. Baynes admits in one part of his argument what he denies in another. One further point only will I name. Prof. Baynes says :—" Professor De Morgan's emphatic rejection of Mr. Bentham's claim, after examining the relevant chapters of his 'Outline,' is in striking contrast to Mr. Herbert Spencer's easy-going acceptance of it." Now though, to many readers, this will seem a telling comparison, yet to those who know that Prof. De Morgan was one of the parties to the controversy, and had his own claims to establish, the comparison will not seem so telling. To me, however, and to many who have remarked the perversity of Prof. De Morgan's judgments, his verdict on the matter, even were he perfectly unconcerned, will go for but little. Whoever will take the trouble to refer to the *Athenæum* for November 5, 1864, p. 600, and after reading a sentence which he there quotes, will look at either the title of the chapter it is taken from or the sentence which succeeds it, will be amazed that such recklessness of misrepresentation could be shown by a conscientious man ; and will be thereafter but little inclined to abide by Prof. De Morgan's authority on matters like that here in question.]

[15] These words are translated for me from *Die Entwicklung der Naturwissenschaft in den letzen fünfundzwanzig Jahren*. By Professor Dr. Ferdinand Cohn. Breslau, 1872.

[16] I am told that his reasons for this valuation are more fully given at p. 143.

[17] *Revue des Deux Mondes*, 1 Février, 1873, p. 731.

[18] *Œuvres de P. L. Courier* (Paris, 1845), p. 304.

[19] *Histoire des Sciences et des Savants, &c.*

[20] Before leaving the question of Academies and their influences, let me call attention to a fact which makes me doubt whether as a judge of style, considered simply as correct or incorrect, an Academy is to

be trusted. Mr. Arnold, insisting on propriety of expression, and giving instances of bad taste among our writers, due, as he thinks, to absence of Academic control, tacitly asserts that an Academy, if we had one, would condemn the passages he quotes as deserving condemnation, and, by implication, would approve the passages he quotes as worthy of approval. Let us see to what Mr. Arnold awards his praise. He says :—

"To illustrate what I mean by an example. Addison, writing as a moralist on fixedness in religious faith, says :—

" ' Those who delight in reading books of controversy do very seldom arrive at a fixed and settled habit of faith. The doubt which was laid revives again, and shows itself in new difficulties ; and that generally for this reason,— because the mind, which is perpetually tossed in controversies and disputes, is apt to forget the reasons which had once set it at rest, and to be disquieted with any former perplexity when it appears in a new shape, or is started by a different hand.'

" It may be said, that is classical English, perfect in lucidity, measure, and propriety. I make no objection ; but in my turn, I say that the idea expressed is perfectly trite and barren," &c., &c.

In Mr. Arnold's estimate of Addison's thought I coincide entirely ; but I cannot join him in applauding the " classical English " conveying the thought. Indeed, I am not a little astonished that one whose taste in style is proved by his own writing to be so good, and who to his poems especially gives a sculpturesque finish, should have quoted, not simply without condemnation but with tacit eulogy, a passage full of faults. Let us examine it critically, part by part. How shall we interpret into thought the words " arrive at a . . . habit " ? A habit is *produced*. But " arrival " implies, not *production* of a thing, but coming up to a thing that pre-exists, as at the end of a journey. What, again, shall we say of the phrase, " a fixed and settled habit " ? Habit is a course of action characterized by constancy, as distinguished from courses of action that are inconstant. If the word " settled " were unobjectionable, we might define habit as *a settled course of action;* and on substituting for the word this equivalent, the phrase would read " a fixed and settled settled course of action." Obviously the word habit itself conveys the whole notion ; and if there needs a word to indicate degree, it should be a word suggesting *force*, not suggesting *rest*. The reader is to be impressed with the *strength of a tendency* in something active, not with the *firmness* of something passive, as by the words " fixed and settled." And then why "fixed *and* settled"? Making no objection to the words as having inapplicable meanings, there is the objection that one of them would suffice : surely whatever is fixed must be settled.　　　Passing to the next sentence, we are arrested by a conspicuous fault in its first clause—"The doubt which was laid *revives again*." To revive is to live again ; so that the literal meaning of the clause is "the doubt which was laid lives again again." In the following line there is nothing objectionable ; but at the end of it we come to another pleonasm. The words run :—"and that generally for this reason,—because the mind . . ." The idea is fully conveyed by the words, "and that generally because the mind." The words "for this reason" are equivalent to an additional "because." So that we have here another nonsensical duplication. Going a little further there rises the question—Why "controversies *and* disputes"? 'Dispute' is given in dictionaries as one of the synonyms of 'controversy'; and though it may be rightly held to have not quite the same meaning, any additional meaning it has does not aid, but rather hinders, the thought of the reader. Though, where special attention is to be drawn to a certain element of the thought, two almost synonymous words may fitly be used to make the reader dwell longer on that element, yet where his attention is to be drawn to another element of the thought (as here to the *effect* of controversy on the mind), there is no gain, but a loss, in stopping him to interpret a second word if the first suffices. One more fault remains. The mind is said "to be disquieted with any former perplexity when it appears in a new shape, or is started by a different hand." This portion of the sentence is doubly defective. The two metaphors are incongruous. Appearing in a shape, as a ghost might be supposed to do, conveys one kind of idea ; and started by a hand, as a horse or a hound might be, conveys a conflicting kind of idea. This defect, however, is less serious than the other ; namely, the unfitness of the second metaphor for giving a concrete form to the abstract idea. How is it possible to 'start' a perplexity? 'Perplexity,' by derivation and as commonly used, involves the thought of entanglement and arrest of motion ; while to 'start' a thing is to set it in motion. So that whereas the mind is to be represented as enmeshed, and thus impeded in its movements, the metaphor used to describe its state is one suggesting the freedom and rapid motion of that which enmeshes it.

Even were these hyper-criticisms, it might be said that they are rightly to be made on a passage which is considered a model of style. But they are not hyper-criticisms. To show that the defects indicated are grave,

it only needs to read one of the sentences without its tautologies, thus :—
" The doubt which was laid revives, and shows itself in new difficulties ;
and that generally because the mind which is perpetually tossed in controversies is apt to forget the reasons which had once set it at rest" &c. &c.
Omitting the six superfluous words unquestionably makes the sentence
clearer—adds to its force without taking from its meaning. Nor would
removal of the other excrescences, and substitution of appropriate words
for those which are unfit, fail similarly to improve the rest of the passage.

And now is it not strange that two sentences which Mr. Arnold admits
to be " classical English, perfect in lucidity, measure, and propriety,"
should contain so many defects : some of them, indeed, deserving a
stronger word of disapproval ? It is true that analysis discloses occasional
errors in the sentences of nearly all writers—some due to inadvertence,
some to confusion of thought. Doubtless, from my own books examples
could be taken ; and I should think it unfair to blame any one for now
and then tripping. But in a passage of which the diction seems " perfect" to one who would like to have style refined by authoritative
criticism, we may expect entire conformity to the laws of correct expression ; and may not unnaturally be surprised to find so many deviations from those laws.   Possibly, indeed, it will be alleged that the
faults are not in Addison's English, but that I lack the needful æsthetic
perception. Having, when young, effectually resisted that classical
culture which Mr. Arnold thinks needful, I may be blind to the
beauties he perceives ; and my undisciplined taste may lead me to condemn as defects what are, in fact, perfections. Knowing absolutely nothing
of the masterpieces of ancient literature in the original, and very little
in translation, I suppose I must infer that a familiarity with them equal
to Mr. Arnold's familiarity, would have given me a capacity for admiring
these traits of style which he admires. Perhaps redundance of epithets
would have afforded me pleasure ; perhaps I should have been delighted
by duplications of meaning ; perhaps from inconsistent metaphors I
might have received some now-unimaginable gratification. Being,
however, without any guidance save that yielded by Mental Science
—having been led by analysis of thought to conclude that in writing,
words must be so chosen and arranged as to convey ideas with the
greatest ease, precision, and vividness ; and having drawn the corollaries
that superfluous words should be struck out, that words which have
associations at variance with the propositions to be set forth should be
avoided, and that there should be used no misleading figures of speech ;

I have acquired a dislike to modes of expression like these Mr. Arnold regards as perfect in their propriety. Almost converted though I have been by his eloquent advocacy of Culture, as he understands it, I must confess that, now I see what he applauds, my growing faith receives a rude check. While recognizing my unregenerate state, and while admitting that I have only Psychology and Logic to help me, I am perverse enough to rejoice that we have not had an Academy; since, judging from the evidence Mr. Arnold affords, it would, among other mischievous acts, have further raised the estimate of a style which even now is unduly praised.

[21] *Culture and Anarchy*, p. 16.

[22] *Ibid.*, pp. 130—140.

NOTE TO CHAPTER X.

[1] Shortly after the first publication of this chapter, I met with a kindred instance. At a Co-operative Congress :—" Mr. Head (of the firm of Fox, Head, & Co., Middlesbrough) * * * remarked that he had thrown his whole soul during the last six years into the carrying out of the principle involved in the Industrial Partnership at Middlesbrough with which he was connected. In that Industrial Partnership there was at present no arrangement for the workmen to invest their savings. A clause to give that opportunity to the workmen was at first put into the articles of agreement, but, as there was only one instance during three years of a workman under the firm applying to invest his savings, that clause was withdrawn. The firm consequently came to the conclusion that this part of their scheme was far ahead of the time."—*Times*, April 15, 1873.

NOTES TO CHAPTER XI.

[1] Froude, *Short Studies on Great Subjects*, Second Series, 1871, p. 480.

[2] *Ibid.*, p. 483.

[3] *Ibid.*, pp. 483-4.

[4] Daily papers, Feb. 7, 1873.

[5] *Times* and *Post*, Feb. 11, 1873.

[6] *Times,* Nov. 25, 1872.

[7] *Ibid.,* Nov. 27, 1872.

[8] Craik, in *Pict. Hist.,* vol. iv., p. 853.

[9] *Ibid.,* vol. iv., p. 853.

[10] When, in dealing with the vitiation of evidence, I before referred to the legislation here named, I commented on the ready acceptance of those one-sided statements made to justify such legislation, in contrast with the contempt for those multitudinous proofs that gross abuses would inevitably result from the arrangements made. Since that passage was written, there has been a startling justification of it. A murder has been committed at Lille by a gang of sham-detectives (one being a government *employé*); and the trial has brought out the fact that for the last three years the people of Lille have been subject to an organized terrorism which has grown out of the system of prostitute-inspection. Though, during these three years, five hundred women are said by one of these criminals to have fallen into their clutches—though the men have been blackmailed and the women outraged to this immense extent, yet the practice went on for the reason (obvious enough, one would have have thought, to need no proof by illustration) that those aggrieved preferred to submit rather than endanger their characters by complaining; and the practice would doubtless have gone on still but for the murder of one of the victims. To some this case will carry conviction : probably not, however, to those who, in pursuance of what they are pleased to call " practical legislation," prefer an induction based on a Blue Book to an induction based on Universal History.

[11] See case in *Times,* Dec. 11, 1872.

NOTES TO CHAPTER XII.

[1] *Journey through Central and Eastern Arabia,* vol. ii. p. 370.

[2] *Ibid.,* vol. ii. p. 22.

[3] Lubbock's *Prehistoric Times.* Second edition, p. 442.

[4] *Journey through Central and Eastern Arabia,* vol. ii. p. 11.

[5] *Five Years' Residence at Nepaul.* By Capt. Thomas Smith. Vol. i. p. 168.

NOTE TO CHAPTER XIV.

[1] Probably most readers will conclude that in this, and in the preceding section, I am simply carrying out the views of Mr. Darwin in their applications to the human race. Under the circumstances, perhaps, I shall be excused for pointing out that the same beliefs, otherwise expressed, are contained in Chapters XXV. and XXVIII. of *Social Statics*, published in December, 1850 ; and that they are set forth still more definitely in the *Westminster Review* for April, 1852 (pp. 498—500). As Mr. Darwin himself points out, others before him have recognized the action of that process he has called "Natural Selection," but have failed to see its full significance and its various effects. Thus in the Review-article just named, I have contended that "this inevitable redundancy of numbers—this constant increase of people beyond the means of subsistence," necessitates the continual carrying-off of "those in whom the power of self-preservation is the least ;" that all being subject to the "increasing difficulty of getting a living which excess of fertility entails," there is an average advance under the pressure, since "only those who *do* advance under it eventually survive ;" and that these "must be the select of their generation." There is, however, in the essay from which I here quote, no recognition of what Mr. Darwin calls "spontaneous variation," nor of that *divergence of type* which this natural selective process is shown by him to produce.

[2] And even then there are often ruinous delays. A barrister tells me that in a case in which he was himself the referee, they had but six meetings in two years.

NOTES TO CHAPTER XV.

[1] "The Statistics of Legislation," read before the Statistical Society, May, 1873, by Frederick H. Janson, Esq., F.L.S., vice-president of the Incorporated Law Society.

[2] Among recent illustrations of the truth that frequent repetition of Christian doctrines does not conduce to growth of Christian feelings, here are two that seem worth preserving. The first I quote from *The Church Herald* for May 14, 1873.

" Mr. J. Stuart Mill, who has just gone to his account, would have been a remarkable writer of English, if his innate self-consciousness and abounding self-confidence had not made him a notorious literary prig. * * * * * His death is no loss to anybody, for he was a rank but amiable infidel, and a most dangerous person. The sooner those 'lights of thought,' who agree with him, go to the same place, the better it will be for both Church and State."

The second, which to an English manifestation of sentiment yields a parallel from America, I am permitted to publish by a friend to whom it was lately addressed :—

(From a Clergyman of 28 years' service.)

" U.S. America, March 10th, 1873.

" J. TYNDALL,—How it ought to 'heap coals of fire on your head,' that, in return for your *insults to their Religion*, in your various works, the American people treated you with distinguished consideration. You have repeatedly raised your puny arm against God and His Christ! You have endeavoured to deprive mankind of its only consolation in life, and its only hope in death (*vide* 'Fragments of Science,' &c.), *without offering anything instead*, but the 'dry-light' of your molecules and atoms. Shall we praise you for this ? We praise you not !

" ' Do not I hate them, O Lord, that hate Thee ?'

" Every *suicide* in our land (and they are of daily occurrence) is indirectly the effect of *the bestial* doctrines of yourself, Darwin, Spencer, Huxley, *et id omne genus.*

" ' The pit is digged up for you all ?'

" ' Woe unto you that laugh now, for ye shall mourn and lament.'

" With the supremest contempt, I remain,

"A. F. F——."

³ To show how little operative on conduct is mere teaching, let me add a striking fact that has fallen under my own observation. Some twelve years ago was commenced a serial publication, grave and uninteresting to most, and necessarily limited in its circulation to the well-educated. It was issued to subscribers, from each of whom a small sum was due for every four numbers. As was to be expected, the notification, periodically made, that another subscription was due, received from some prompt attention ; from others an attention more or less tardy ; and from others no attention at all. The defaulters, from time to time reminded by new notices, fell, many of them, two subscriptions

19

in arrear; but after receiving from the publishers letters intimating the fact, some of these rectified what was simply a result of forgetfulness: leaving, however, a number who still went on receiving the serial without paying for it. When these were three subscriptions in arrear, further letters from the publishers, drawing their attention to the facts, were sent to them, bringing from some the amounts due, but leaving a remainder who continued to disregard the claim. Eventually these received from the publishers intimations that their names would be struck off for non-payment; and such of them as continued insensible were at length omitted from the list. After a lapse of ten years, a digest was made of the original list, to ascertain the ratio between the number of defaulters and the total number; and to ascertain, also, the ratios borne by their numbers to the numbers of their respective classes. Those who had thus finally declined paying for what they had year after year received, constituted the following percentages :—

Subscribers of unknown *status*	27 per cent.
Physicians	29 ,,
Clergymen (mostly of the Established Church) .	31 ,,
Secularists	32 ,,
Journalists	82 ,,

Admitting that the high percentage among the journalists may have been due to the habit of receiving *gratis* copies of books, we have to note, first of all, the surprising fact that nearly one-third of these highly educated men were thus regardless of an equitable claim. Further, on comparing the subdivisions, we discover that the class undistinguished by titles of any kind, and therefore including, as we must suppose, those whose education, though good, was not the highest, furnished the smallest percentage of defaulters: so far as the evidence goes, it associates increase of intellectual culture with decrease of conscientiousness. And then one more thing to be noted is the absence of that beneficial effect expected from repetition of moral precepts: the Clergy and the Secularists are nearly on a level. So that, both in general and in detail, this evidence, like the evidence given in the text, is wholly at variance with the belief that addressing the intellect develops the higher sentiments.

⁴ Even after the reform of the Poor-Law, this punishment for good behaviour was continued. Illustrations will be found in the beforementioned Tracts on the Poor-Laws, by a late uncle of mine—illustra-

tions that came under his personal observation as clergyman and as guardian.

[5] The comparisons ordinarily made between the minds of men and women are faulty in many ways, of which these are the chief :—

Instead of comparing either the average of women with the average of men, or the *élite* of women with the *élite* of men, the common course is to compare the *élite* of women with the average of men. Much the same erroneous impression results as would result if the relative statures of men and women were judged by putting very tall women side by side with ordinary men.

Sundry manifestations of nature in men and women, are greatly perverted by existing social conventions upheld by both. There are feelings which, under our predatory *régime*, with its adapted standard of propriety, it is not considered manly to show; but which, contrariwise, are considered admirable in women. Hence repressed manifestations in the one case, and exaggerated manifestations in the other ; leading to mistaken estimates.

The sexual sentiment comes into play to modify the behaviour of men and women to one another. Respecting certain parts of their general characters, the only evidence which can be trusted is that furnished by the conduct of men to men, and of women to women, when placed in relations which exclude the personal affections.

In comparing the intellectual powers of men and women, no proper distinction is made between receptive faculty and originative faculty. The two are scarcely commensurable ; and the receptivity may, and frequently does, exist in high degree where there is but a low degree of originality, or entire absence of it.

Perhaps, however, the most serious error usually made in drawing these comparisons is that of overlooking the limit of normal mental power. Either sex under special stimulations is capable of manifesting powers ordinarily shown only by the other; but we are not to consider the deviations so caused as affording proper measures. Thus, to take an extreme case, the mammæ of men will, under special excitation, yield milk : there are various cases of gynæcomasty on record, and in famines infants whose mothers have died have been thus saved. But this ability to yield milk, which, when exercised, must be at the cost of masculine strength, we do not count among masculine attributes. Similarly, under special discipline, the feminine intellect will yield products higher than the intellects of most men can yield. But we are not to count this productivity as truly feminine if it entails decreased fulfilment of the maternal functions. Only that mental energy is normally feminine which can coexist with the production and nursing of the due number of healthy children. Obviously a power of mind which, if general among the women of a society, would entail disappearance of the society, is a power not to be included in an estimate of the feminine nature as a social factor.

[6] Of course it is to be understood that in this, and in the succeeding statements, reference is made to men and women of the same society, in the same age. If women of a more-evolved race are compared with men of a less-evolved race, the statement will not be true.

[7] As the validity of this group of inferences depends on the occurrence of that partial limitation of heredity of sex here assumed, it may be said that I should furnish proof of its occurrence. Were the place fit, this might be done. I might detail evidence that has been collected showing the much greater liability there is for a parent to bequeath malformations and diseases to children of the same sex, than to those of the opposite sex. I might cite the multitudinous instances of sexual distinctions, as of plumage in birds and colouring in insects, and especially those marvellous ones of dimorphism and polymorphism among females of certain species of Lepidoptera, as necessarily implying (to those who accept the Hypothesis of Evolution) the predominant transmission of traits to descendants of the same sex. It will suffice, however, to instance, as more especially relevant, the cases of sexual distinctions within the human race itself, which have arisen in some varieties and not in others. That in some varieties the men are bearded and in others not, may be taken as strong evidence of this partial limitation of heredity; and perhaps still stronger evidence is yielded by that peculiarity of feminine form found in some of the negro races, and especially the Hottentots, which does not distinguish to any such extent the women of other races from the men. There is also the fact, to which Agassiz draws attention, that among the South American Indians males and females differ less than they do among the negroes and the higher races; and this reminds us that among European and Eastern nations the men and women differ, both bodily and mentally, not quite in the same ways and to the same degrees, but in somewhat different ways and degrees—a fact which would be inexplicable were there no partial limitation of heredity by sex.

NOTES TO CHAPTER XVI.

[1] *History of Greece*, vol. i. p. 498.

[2] *Ibid.* vol. i. p. 466.

[3] *Morning Post*, May 15, 1872.

[4] In the appendix to his republished address, Mr. Gladstone, in illustration of the views he condemns, refers to that part of *First Principles* which, treating of the reconciliation of Science and Religion, contends that this consists in a united recognition of an Ultimate Cause which, though ever present to consciousness, transcends knowledge. Commenting on this view, he says :—" Still it vividly recalls to mind an old story of the man who, wishing to be rid of one who was in his house, said, ' Sir, there are two sides to my house, and we will divide them ; you shall take the outside.' " This seems to me by no means a happily-chosen simile ; since it admits of an interpretation exactly opposite to the one Mr. Gladstone intends. The doctrine he combats is that Science, unable to go beyond the outsides of things, is for ever debarred from reaching, and even from conceiving, the Power within them ; and this being so, the relative positions of Religion and Science may be well represented by inverting the application of his figure.

THE END.

THE INTERNATIONAL
SCIENTIFIC SERIES.

D. APPLETON & CO. have the pleasure of announcing that they have made arrangements to issue a comprehensive series of books, under the above title, from eminent men of different countries. Although not specially designed for the instruction of beginners, these works will be adapted to the non-scientific public, and will be, as far as possible, explanatory in character and free from technicalities. The character and scope of the works will be best illustrated by a reference to the names and subjects in the following list:

Professor JOHN TYNDALL, LL.D., F.R.S.,
THE FORMS OF WATER IN CLOUDS, RAIN, RIVERS, ICE, AND GLACIERS. (Recently published.)

WALTER BAGEHOT.
PHYSICS AND POLITICS. (Recently published.)

Dr. EDWARD SMITH, F.R.S.
FOOD AND DIETS. (Recently published.)

Professor ALEXANDER BAIN, LL.D.
RELATIONS OF MIND AND BODY (Recently published.)

HERBERT SPENCER, Esq.
THE STUDY OF SOCIOLOGY. (Recently published.)

Professor JOSIAH P. COOKE, Jr. (of Harvard University).
THE NEW CHEMISTRY.

Dr. J. B. PETTIGREW, M.D., F.R.S.
LOCOMOTION OF ANIMALS.

Professor BALFOUR STEWART, LL.D., F.R.S.
THE CONSERVATION OF ENERGY.

Dr. W. B. CARPENTER, LL.D., F.R.S.
THE PRINCIPLES OF MENTAL PHYSIOLOGY.

1

Professor E. J. MAREY.
THE ANIMAL MACHINE.

Professor SHELDON AMOS.
THE SCIENCE OF LAW.

Professor C. A. YOUNG (of Dartmouth College).
THE SUN.

Professor T. H. HUXLEY, LL.D., F.R.S.
BODILY MOTION AND CONSCIOUSNESS.

Sir JOHN LUBBOCK, Bart., F.R.S.
THE ANTIQUITY OF MAN.

Professor RUDOLPH VIRCHOW (of the University of Berlin).
MORBID PHYSIOLOGICAL ACTION.

Dr. H. CHARLTON BASTIAN, M.D., F.R.S.
THE BRAIN AS AN ORGAN OF MIND.

Professor W. THISELTON DYER, B.A., B.Sc.
FORM AND HABIT IN FLOWERING PLANTS.

Professor W. KINGDON CLIFFORD, M.A.
THE FIRST PRINCIPLES OF THE EXACT SCIENCES
EXPLAINED TO THE NON–MATHEMATICAL.

Mr. J. N. LOCKYER, F.R.S.
SPECTRUM ANALYSIS.

W. LAUDER LINDSAY, M.D., F.R.S.E.
MIND IN THE LOWER ANIMALS.

Professor A. C. RAMSAY, LL.D., F.R.S.
EARTH SCULPTURE : Hills, Valleys, Mountains, Plains, Rivers,
Lakes; how they were produced, and how they have been destroyed.

Dr. HENRY MAUDSLEY.
RESPONSIBILITY IN DISEASE.

Professor MICHAEL FOSTER, M.D.
PROTOPLASM AND THE CELL-THEORY.

Rev. M. J. BERKELY, M.A., F.L.S.
FUNGI: their Nature, Influences, and Uses.

Professor CLAUDE BERNARD (of the College of France).
PHYSICAL AND METAPHYSICAL PHENOMENA OF LIFE.

Professor A. QUETELET (of the Brussels Academy of Sciences).
SOCIAL PHYSICS.

Professor H. SAINTE-CLAIRE DEVILLE.
AN INTRODUCTION TO GENERAL CHEMISTRY.

Professor WURTZ.
ATOMS AND THE ATOMIC THEORY.

Professor D. QUATREFAGES.
THE NEGRO RACES.

Professor LACAZE-DUTHIERS.
ZOOLOGY SINCE CUVIER.

Professor BERTHELOT.
CHEMICAL SYNTHESIS.

Professor JAMES D. DANA, M.A., LL.D.
ON CEPHALIZATION; or, Head Domination in its Relation to Structure, Grade, and Development.

Professor S. W. JOHNSON, M.A.
ON THE NUTRITION OF PLANTS.

Professor AUSTIN FLINT, Jr., M.D.
THE NERVOUS SYSTEM AND ITS RELATION TO THE BODILY FUNCTIONS.

Professor W. D. WHITNEY.
MODERN LINGUISTIC SCIENCE.

Other eminent authors, as WALLACE, HELMHOLTZ, PARKS, MILNE-EDWARDS, ROSENTHAL, and HÆCKEL, have given strong encouragement that they will also take part in the enterprise.

D. APPLETON & CO., Publishers,
549 and 551 Broadway, N. Y.

III.

Foods.

By Dr. EDWARD SMITH.

1 vol., 12mo. Cloth. Illustrated. . . . . Price, $1.75.

In making up THE INTERNATIONAL SCIENTIFIC SERIES, Dr. Edward Smith was selected as the ablest man in England to treat the important subject of Foods. His services were secured for the undertaking, and the little treatise he has produced shows that the choice of a writer on this subject was most fortunate, as the book is unquestionably the clearest and best-digested compend of the Science of Foods that has appeared in our language.

"The book contains a series of diagrams, displaying the effects of sleep and meals on pulsation and respiration, and of various kinds of food on respiration, which, as the results of Dr. Smith's own experiments, possess a very high value. We have not far to go in this work for occasions of favorable criticism; they occur throughout, but are perhaps most apparent in those parts of the subject with which Dr. Smith's name is especially linked."—*London Examiner.*

"The union of scientific and popular treatment in the composition of this work will afford an attraction to many readers who would have been indifferent to purely theoretical details. . . . Still his work abounds in information, much of which is of great value, and a part of which could not easily be obtained from other sources. Its interest is decidedly enhanced for students who demand both clearness and exactness of statement, by the profusion of well-executed woodcuts, diagrams, and tables, which accompany the volume. . . . The suggestions of the author on the use of tea and coffee, and of the various forms of alcohol, although perhaps not strictly of a novel character, are highly instructive, and form an interesting portion of the volume."—*N. Y. Tribune.*

IV.

Body and Mind.

THE THEORIES OF THEIR RELATION.

By ALEXANDER BAIN, LL. D.

PROFESSOR BAIN is the author of two well-known standard works upon the Science of Mind—"The Senses and the Intellect," and "The Emotions and the Will." He is one of the highest living authorities in the school which holds that there can be no sound or valid psychology unless the mind and the body are studied, as they exist, together.

"It contains a forcible statement of the connection between mind and body, studying their subtle interworkings by the light of the most recent physiological investigations. The summary in Chapter V., of the investigations of Dr. Lionel Beale of the embodiment of the intellectual functions in the cerebral system, will be found the freshest and most interesting part of his book. Prof. Bain's own theory of the connection between the mental and the bodily part in man is stated by himself to be as follows: There is 'one substance, with two sets of properties, two sides, the physical and the mental—a *double-faced unity*.' While, in the strongest manner, asserting the union of mind with brain, he yet denies 'the association of union *in place*,' but asserts the union of close succession in time,' holding that 'the same being is, by alternate fits, under extended and under unextended consciousness.' '—*Christian Register.*

D. APPLETON & CO., Publishers, New York.

DESCRIPTIVE SOCIOLOGY.

Mr. Herbert Spencer has been for several years engaged, with the aid of three educated gentlemen in his employ, in collecting and organizing the facts concerning all orders of human societies, which must constitute the data of a true Social Science. He tabulates these facts so as conveniently to admit of extensive comparison, and gives the authorities separately. He divides the races of mankind into three great groups: the savage races, the existing civilizations, and the extinct civilizations, and to each he devotes a series of works. The first installment,

THE SOCIOLOGICAL HISTORY OF ENGLAND,

in seven continuous tables, folio, with seventy pages of verifying text, is now ready. This work will be a perfect Cyclopædia of the facts of Social Science, independent of all theories, and will be invaluable to all interested in social problems. Price, five dollars. This great work is spoken of as follows:

From the British Quarterly Review.

"No words are needed to indicate the immense labor here bestowed, or the great sociological benefit which such a mass of tabulated matter done under such competent direction will confer. The work will constitute an epoch in the science of comparative sociology."

From the Saturday Review.

"The plan of the 'Descriptive Sociology' is new, and the task is one eminently fitted to be dealt with by Mr. Herbert Spencer's faculty of scientific organizing. His object is to examine the natural laws which govern the development of societies, as he has examined in former parts of his system those which govern the development of individual life. Now, it is obvious that the development of societies can be studied only in their history, and that general conclusions which shall hold good beyond the limits of particular societies cannot be safely drawn except from a very wide range of facts. Mr. Spencer has therefore conceived the plan of making a preliminary collection, or perhaps we should rather say abstract, of materials which when complete will be a classified epitome of universal history."

From the London Examiner.

"Of the treatment, in the main, we cannot speak too highly; and we must accept it as a wonderfully successful first attempt to furnish the student of social science with data standing toward his conclusions in a relation like that in which accounts of the structures and functions of different types of animals stand to the conclusions of the biologist."

807015